THE HOLOCAUST,
THE FRENCH,
AND THE JEWS

ZONE ATTACHED TO GERMAN MILITARY COMMAND IN BRUSSELS
PAS-DE-CALAIS

Belgium

English Channel

SEINE-INFÉRRE
SOMME
NORD
Lux.
Germany
ZONE ANNEXED BY GERMANY

MANCHE
CALVADOS
EURE
SEINE-ET-OISE
Drancy
• Paris
Les Tourelles
SEINE ET MARNE
MARNE
ARDENNES
AISNE
Compiègne
MEUSE
MEURTHE-ET-MOSELLE
Ecrouves
BAS RHIN
HAUTE RHIN

CÔTES-DU-NORD
Rennes •
ILLE-ET-VILAINE
ORNE
EURE-ET-LOIR
AUBE
Clairvaux
HAUTE-MARNE
VOSGES
Vittel

FINISTÈRE
MORBIHAN
MAYENNE
SARTHE
LOIRET
Pithiviers
Beaune-la-Rolande
YONNE
CÔTE D'OR
HAUTE-SAÔNE
DOUBS

LOIRE-INFRE
Angers •
MAINE-ET-LOIRE
INDRE ET LOIRE
La Lande
La Motse
Beuvron
LINE OF DEMARCATION
CHER
NIÈVRE

VENDÉE
DEUX SÈVRES
Poitiers •
VIENNE
Douadic
INDRE
ALLIER
SAÔNE-ET-LOIRE
La Guiche
JURA
Switz.
Lake Geneva

CHARENTE INFÉRIEURE
CHARENTE
St. Sauveur
VIENNE
Limoges •
Nexon
CREUSE
Clermont-Ferrand
PUY-DE-DÔME
LOIRE
Vennissieux
Lyon •
AIN
HAUTE-SAVOIE
Seviery
Ruffieux
SAVOIE
Italy

Bay of Biscay

Bordeaux •
GIRONDE
DORDOGNE
Moussac
CORRÈZE
Egleton
Beaulieu
CANTAL
HAUTE-LOIRE
RHÔNE
ISÈRE

Merignac
Bacalpoi
LOT-ET-GARONNE
Tombelouc
Casseneuil
LOT
AVEYRON
Rieucros
LOZÈRE
ARDÈCHE
DRÔME
HAUTES-ALPES

LANDES
TARN-ET-GARONNE
Septfonds
St. Sulpice
Brens
St. Antoine
TARN
Langlade
GARD
VAUCLUSE
BOUCHES DU RHÔNE
Les Milles
BASSES-ALPES
ALPES MARITIMES

GERS
Toulouse •
HAUTE-GARONNE
HÉRAULT
Agde
Montpellier •
Aubais
VAR

BASSES PYRÉNÉES
Gurs
Noe
Recoebedou
HAUTES PYRÉNÉES
Le Vernet
ARIÈGE
AUDE
Brahs
Rivel
Rivesaltes
PYRÉNÉES ORIENTALES
Argeles
St. Cyprien
Barcares
Marseille •
Hotel Bompard
Hotel Terminus Nord
Hotel du Levant
Hotel Brebant

Spain

Mediterranean Sea

[legend boxes]
OCCUPIED ZONE   FREE ZONE (until 11/11/42)   ITALIAN ZONE (11/11/42–9/8/43)

France in 1940-44. The map shows the Line of
Demarcation and the location of some of the
principal internment camps.

Map reproduced courtesy of Serge Klarsfeld.
Used with permission.

THE HOLOCAUST, THE FRENCH, AND THE JEWS

SUSAN ZUCCOTTI

BasicBooks
A Division of HarperCollins*Publishers*

Library of Congress Cataloging-in-Publication Data
Zuccotti, Susan, 1940–
  The Holocaust, the French and the Jews / by Susan Zuccotti.
    p.   cm.
  Includes bibliographical references and index.
  ISBN 0–465–03034–3
  1. Jews—France—Persecutions.   2. Holocaust, Jewish (1939–1945)—
France.   3. France—Ethnic relations,   I. Title.
DS135.F83Z83   1993   92–54519
940.53'18'0944—dc20   CIP

Designed by Ellen Levine

93 94 95 96 ❖/HC 9 8 7 6 5 4 3 2 1

This book is dedicated to the more than 3,500 Jewish children under the age of fourteen who were arrested in Paris on July 16, 1942, and forcibly separated from their mothers at the French camps of Pithiviers and Beaune-la-Rolande two weeks later. Their mothers were deported. The children had to fend for themselves until they too were deported, bewildered, terrified, and alone, in sealed cattle cars without light or air, to be murdered upon arrival at Auschwitz.

CONTENTS

LIST OF ABBREVIATIONS

AADJF	Amicale des anciens déportés juifs de France
AIP	Association des israélites pratiquants
AJ	Armée juive
AN	Archives nationales, Paris
BBC	British Broadcasting Corporation
CAR	Comité d'assistance aux refugiés
CDJC	Centre de documentation juive contemporaine, Paris
CGQJ	Commissariat général aux questions juives
CGT	Confédération générale du travail
CIMADE	Comité inter-mouvements auprès des évacués (Protestant relief agency)
CNR	Conseil national de la résistance
COMAC	Comité d'action militaire
CPL	Comité parisien de libération
CTE	Compagnies de travailleurs étrangers (forced-labor companies of foreign workers)
DCA	Direction des centres d'accueil
EFI	Entraide française israélite
EIF	Éclaireurs israélites de France (Jewish Boy Scouts of France)

EMIGDIRECT	an agency promoting direct emigration of East European Jews from Germany
ET	Entraide temporaire
FFDJF	Fils et filles des déportés juifs de France
FFI	Forces françaises de l'interieur (unified internal military Resistance organization)
FFL	Forces françaises libres (Free French military forces)
FSJF	Fédération des sociétés juives de France
FTP	Francs-tireurs et partisans (Communist military Resistance organization)
FTP-MOI	Francs-tireurs et partisans—Main-d'oeuvre immigrée (immigrant Communist military Resistance units of the FTP)
GMR	Groupes mobiles de réserve
GTE	Groupements de travailleurs étrangers (forced-labor groups of foreign workers)
HIAS	Hebrew Immigrant Aid and Sheltering Society, an American group
HICEM	a Jewish emigration association, comprised of HIAS, JCA, and EMIGDIRECT
JCA	Jewish Colonialisation Association, a British group
JO	*Journal officiel de la république française* (later, *. . . de l'état français*)
JOC	Jeunesse ouvrière chrétienne
MBF	Militärbefehlshaber in Frankreich (German military occupation authority in France)
MJS	Mouvement de la jeunesse sioniste (Zionist youth movement)
MSR	Mouvement social révolutionnaire
MUR	Mouvements unis de résistance
OJC	Organisation juive de combat
ORT	Organisation pour la reconstruction et le travail (Jewish vocational training organization)
OSE	Oeuvre de secours aux enfants (children's relief organization)
PPF	Parti populaire français
PQJ	Police aux questions juives
PSF	Parti social français
RNP	Rassemblement national populaire
RSHA	Reichssicherheitshauptamt (Reich Central Security Office, Berlin)

SCAP	Service de contrôle des administrateurs provisoires
SD	Sicherheitsdienst (Security Service)
SEC	Section d'enquête et de contrôle
SSAE	Service social d'aide aux émigrants
SSE	Service social des étrangers
SSJ	Service social des jeunes (the Sixième)
STO	Service de travail obligatoire
UGIF	Union générale des Israélites de France
UJRE	Union des Juifs pour la résistance et l'entraide
YIVO	YIVO Institute for Jewish Research, New York
YMCA	Young Men's Christian Association

ACKNOWLEDGMENTS

IN THEIR BOOKS, AUTHORS ACKNOWLEDGE AND THANK THOSE WHO
have helped them with such predictable regularity that their words
tend to repeat themselves and their phrases lose meaning. Yet the aid
extended is often enormous, representing ample gifts of time and
thought to scholars whom the givers may scarcely know, at least initially. Such generosity is noteworthy and memorable in our busy and
impersonal world. I was a beneficiary of a large dose of it. I am at a
loss for words with which to thank those who showed me how
highly they value the preservation of historical memory.

Vidar Jacobsen, chief archivist at the *Centre de documentation
juive contemporaine* in Paris, was invariably kind, patient, friendly,
and accessible. He listened carefully to my questions, searched dili-
gently for helpful documents, permitted me to return time and again,
provided most of the fine photographs reproduced within these
pages, and even continued his assistance by trans-Atlantic correspondence. His professionalism, efficiency, and pleasure in his craft were
a joy to witness and a profound help to me. He is an honor to his
fine institution. I cannot thank him enough.

Sara Halperyn, chief librarian at the same documentation center,
patiently sifted through the lists of books I hoped to find and
searched thoroughly for them. Her regret when a very few of them
were not on her shelves was always genuine and touching. Serge

Klarsfeld, a lawyer, a historian of the Holocaust, and himself a survivor, answered technical questions on numerous occasions. In spite
of his own hectic schedule, he always showed me the special care, attention, and thoughtfulness which typify his exceptional character.
Similarly, historian Léon Poliakov and OSE director Vivette Samuel
answered far more questions and gave me far more of their time than
I had any right to expect. I am deeply grateful to them all.

Many works of twentieth-century history draw upon the accounts
of participants in the events described. Interviews with individuals
who experienced the Holocaust, however, both Jews and non-Jews,
may be particularly difficult for those who are asked to remember. In
my case, I, a foreigner and a totally unknown stranger, called upon
survivors and rescuers to relate often excruciatingly painful and most
intimate memories—a procedure which invariably involved several
hours for each individual, and often led to repeated visits. I asked
them, implicitly, to trust me to respect and record their memories ac-
curately for the future. The generosity of their responses is overwhelming. I eagerly seize this opportunity to thank the following
people: Nina Adam, Madeleine Barot, Denise Baumann, Renée Be-
darida, Father Marie Benoît, Aline Berlin, Annette Muller Bessmann
and Daniel Bessmann, Henry Bulawko, Gaby Cohen, Fania and Emmanuel Ewenczyk, Georgette and Oscar Ewenczyk, George Frybergh, Albert Haas, Serge Klarsfeld, Annette Monod Leiris, Gilbert
Lesage, Peter Lipman-Wolf, Adam Munz, Hermine Orsi, Léon Poliakov, Maurice Rajsfus, Paul and Albert Reichmann, Germaine
Ribière, Vivette Samuel, Alexander Schick, Maurice Shotland, and
Denise Caraco Siekierski.

Among the many scholars who helped me over the years, I would
like to thank especially my teacher Robert O. Paxton, Mellon Professor of the Social Sciences at Columbia University. Also kind and
encouraging in support of this specific project were Mordecai
Paldiel, Director of the Department of the Righteous at Yad
Vashem, Israel; Pierre Sauvage, President of the Friends of Le Chambon; and Eva Fogelman, Founding Director of the Jewish Foundation for Christian Rescuers of the Anti-Defamation League. In addition, assistants whose names I often never learned aided me at several institutions: in Paris, the Centre de documentation juive contemporaine, the Bibliothèque nationale, the Archives nationales, the
archives of OSE and EIF, and the Bibliothèque historique de la ville de
Paris; in London, the Weiner Library; and in New York City, the New
York Public Library, the YIVO Institute, the Leo Baeck Institute, and

the libraries of Columbia University. These librarians and archivists welcomed a total stranger and helped her with her work. I am deeply grateful.

The Milstein Foundation provided me with a generous grant to help fund research and travel. I want to thank the Milstein family sincerely for their faith in me and for their support of Holocaust studies. I also thank Sherry Koplin, who read the manuscript with great care and made me the beneficiary of her knowledge and judgment.

I am grateful to my children Gianna, Andrew, and Milena, who for years have put up with a mother who was often distracted, single-minded, or just plain *busy*. Finally, I thank my husband John Zuccotti for his encouragement, support, suggestions, and patience. This book could not have been written without him.

INTRODUCTION

In 1920, Henri Rosencher, age five, immigrated to France from Poland with his father Joseph, mother Rose, and older brother Louis. Henri recalls: "Most [Jewish immigrants from Poland] went to the United States, where their dogged hard work allowed them to hope for riches. My father was looking for justice and equity. He chose France, which had had the courage and the glory of rendering justice to Dreyfus."[1] Joseph Rosencher's interpretation of the Dreyfus Affair seems surprising to us today, but it was not at all unusual at the time. In most other European countries around the turn of the century, a similar conviction of a presumed Jewish traitor would never have been reversed. Indeed, a Jewish officer like Captain Alfred Dreyfus could rarely have risen to such heights in the first place. Joseph Rosencher was correct. Given the available choices, France *was* a good place for Jews in 1920.

Joseph loved his chosen country. He worked as a furrier in Paris, while Henri went to school. "It was at the *lycée*," Henri remembers, "that I was first treated as a Jew."[2] It was not, he hastens to explain, because he was the first or only Jew at the school, but because he was working-class and foreign. He fought back, and soon the other students were more respectful.

Henri Rosencher became a French citizen in 1936 and began medical school. After the fall of France and the German occupation of the northern zone in June 1940, he volunteered for medical service at a camp for 10,000 French prisoners of war at Cravan (Yonne). The Germans twice asked for a list of Jews in the camp, but the French officer in charge refused to supply it. In December 1940, Henri Rosencher crossed the demarcation line into unoccupied France and made his way to Algeria in the hope of reaching the Forces françaises libres (FFL), the army of the Free French. He ultimately succeeded and fought against the Germans until the end of the war.

Joseph Rosencher, who had sought justice in France, was arrested by French police in August 1941 because he was a Jew. Rose and thirty-year-old Louis, a deaf-mute, were seized by French police on July 16, 1942, in the massive two-day roundup of 12,884 foreign Jews in Paris. Detained with them were Louis's pregnant wife Madeleine-Hélène, also a deaf-mute, and their two-year-old daughter Claudine. Louis was deported on July 19, Rose on July 27, and Joseph on July 29. All went to Auschwitz, and none returned. Madeleine-Hélène and Claudine were taken to the Rothschild Hospital, where a second daughter, Michèle, was born on April 7, 1943. On November 20, 1943, all three were deported, also to Auschwitz, and also without return.

French men and women failed to honor Joseph Rosencher's trust. He and his family were seized because the French government ordered French police to arrest foreign Jews. Their tragic story is negative in every respect. We do not know if anyone tried to help them or even viewed their arrests with regret. But other stories, including those of foreign Jews as well as natives, provide a glimpse of another France. After the war, an Auschwitz survivor identified only as Moschkovitch testified that until May 1943 he and his family lived openly, under their own name, in the village of Thimory (Loiret), not far from Orléans. Mr. Moschkovitch, then twenty years old, remembers:

All the [350] people of Thimory knew that we were Jews, from the mayor and the school teacher to the last farmer, and including the sister of the priest, Miss Louise Ruell, whose brother had been killed during the French campaign. The *gendarmes* of the brigade based in [nearby] Lorris knew us and came sometimes for a drink at our house. We were never denounced although there were many people there, not to say a majority, who thought well of Pétain and his government.[3]

The Moschkovitch family was arrested on May 5, 1943. They were caught by chance because the father, who had fled from Russia in 1910 and still had a discernible accent, was visiting a Jewish man in hiding when the latter was arrested. The man in hiding had been denounced, presumably by a Frenchman. The Moschkovitches were arrested, the son explains, by French agents of the Gestapo in Orléans. But despite these obvious cases of French participation in persecution, the son emphasizes, "My long description of our relationship with the residents of Thimory is not a waste of time, because it shows that we cannot judge an entire people from the acts of a few." He continues:

> This case . . . is not unique. My future wife found refuge with her mother, sister, and maternal grandparents who did not speak one word of French, in another village of the Loiret: Neuvy-en-Sullyas. . . . The entire village knew they were hidden there. . . . These facts, which are far from being isolated, must be recalled simply and honestly, not to whitewash those who tried to disfigure France by their dishonorable actions, but to point out that basically the French people, when they were the heirs of a Republican tradition, did not stoop to that informing which the media encouraged every day.[4]

About 24 percent of the approximately 330,000 Jews in France at the end of 1940 perished in the Holocaust. Of the foreign Jewish community, which included the Rosencher and Moschkovitch families, and numbered about 135,000 people, the statistic was much higher, reaching between 41 and 45 percent.[5] "How was it possible?" an anguished Annette Monod Leiris asked me rhetorically during an interview in 1990. A French Protestant, she had served as a Red Cross social worker during the war and cared for Jewish children at internment camps at Pithiviers, Beaune-la-Rolande, and Drancy until the Germans ejected her for showing excessive sympathy. "How could French gendarmes have rounded up even Jewish children alone without their families? How could they have forced those children, abandoned by the world, into dark and crowded freight cars bound for Auschwitz?"[6]

Mrs. Leiris, now a gracious elderly woman, lives in Paris's thirteenth arrondissement, near the Cité universitaire. She cherishes her walks in the Parc Montsouris and hopes to live in Paris for the rest of her life. She dedicated her life to prisoners—political, racial, common. Today she is tormented with questions about the past.

I ask her if she knew at the time that "her" children would be murdered upon arrival at the mysterious place they called "Pitchipoi"? Indeed, had the gendarmes known? "We did not know about the gas chambers," she answers firmly. "We learned about them from the prisoners who returned in the spring of 1945. But we suspected something. They sent children alone, for 'family regrouping,' but the youngest ones did not even know their names. How would they ever find their parents?"

And the notorious French anti-Semitism? I do not have to ask. It appears quite naturally in her account. "Some in the French Red Cross were in no hurry to help foreign Jews in the internment camps because . . . well, because they were foreigners and Jews." And another time:

> I asked a supervisor at the Red Cross to come with me to Beaune-la-Rolande to see the state of the little ones there, whose mothers had been deported ahead of them. They were in a terrible condition. Their clothes were soiled with urine, and there was no one to wash and change them. They were covered with fleas and lice. They slept on straw, and their skin was scratched and torn. "You never told me," remarked my supervisor, "that your little Jews were not as pretty as other children."

More than 24 percent of the Jews in France perished in the Holocaust. How was it possible? But the terrible statistic has another side. Nearly 76 percent survived. I ask Mrs. Leiris the reverse question. "How was survival possible, since the national and municipal police were so implacable, the Vichy policy so vicious, and the French people unsympathetic?" "But not all were," she responds sharply, as quick to praise as to condemn. Like her references to anti-Semitism, the other side creeps naturally into her conversation. "I used to visit Jewish families in Paris in their homes after their 8:00 curfew. I called them 'my after-eight families.' Many told me that local shopkeepers often brought them to the head of the long lines, so that they could make their purchases more quickly, to comply with the mandatory Jewish shopping hours." And, I ask, did this sympathy include direct assistance for survival? She responds:

Rescue organizations existed, mostly Jewish but there were also CIMADE, Amitiés chrétiennes, and others. But those organizations were clandestine. Most people had never heard of their illegal activities. Survival was a very individual matter. You asked a neighbor, a friend, a priest, a pastor for help, for an idea or suggestion, for a reference. A non-Jewish family took in a Jewish child or two. Another family employed their mother. A Jewish organization perhaps supplied false identification cards. *On se debrouillait.* One managed. Those stories are mostly gone now. We know of the organizations, but much less of the individuals.

She concludes, "Those who survived did so because the prevailing climate was rather more sympathetic than hostile."

This book is by no means a complete and definitive treatment of all aspects of the immensely complicated Holocaust in France. It is above all an attempt to understand the complexity and diversity to which Henri Rosencher, Mr. Moschkovitch, Annette Monod Leiris, and so many others bear witness. It is, in other words, an effort to understand popular responses, both Jewish and non-Jewish, to the persecution imposed upon the Jews by the Nazis and the French collaborators. As such, it poses certain specific sets of questions. First, it asks about the position of Jews in France before the war. How did Jews see themselves in relation to their non-Jewish compatriots? How comfortable did they feel in the society? Answers to these questions reveal much, both about attitudes of non-Jews and about Jewish preparedness to perceive the mortal danger when it threatened after 1940.

Second, the book analyzes how the persecution unfolded. What was the impact of the racial laws and the internments of foreign Jews? How did arrests and deportations proceed? Who were the first victims? Who made the arrests? How did the dangers escalate? How were French and foreign Jews treated differently? Only by knowing this chronology of persecution can we understand how contemporaries responded.

Third, and above all, the book examines the popular responses themselves. When did Jews perceive the danger and act upon it? What did they do? What options did they have? And when did non-Jews shift from indifference or even approval of a persecution perceived as directed mainly toward unwanted foreigners to an attitude of vague sympathy for suffering human beings? Or did they? If so, to what degree did they act upon that sympathy? As they formulated their responses, as they decided what action to take, what did Jews and non-Jews know about the death camps?

And finally, how did survival actually occur? Or not occur? How can we explain the rates of destruction and survival? How can we, in the last analysis, understand how human beings responded to the overwhelming horror that was the Holocaust?

1

Jews in France before the War

At the time of the French Revolution, the 40,000 Jews of France constituted one of the smallest and most diverse Jewish communities in Europe. Jews had been expelled from the kingdom of France in 1394, one hundred years before the more famous expulsions from Spain. Since that time, only about 500 had managed to trickle back into Paris, and another few hundred resided in other major cities. About 25,000 poor and strictly observant Ashkenazic Jews lived in traditional communities in Alsace and part of Lorraine, French possessions since the seventeenth century. The remaining 15,000 Jews resided in Bayonne and Bordeaux in the southwest, or in the Comtat Venaissin, a territory centered in Avignon and controlled by the papacy until 1791. Sephardic and Comtadin Jews, respectively, they were generally prosperous, educated, and partially integrated into the broader society before 1789.[1]

The French Revolution electrified Europeans in a multitude of ways, but not least significant was the emancipation of the Jews in 1790 and 1791.[2] France became, with the United States, the first country in the world to grant Jews full political, legal, and social equality, eliminating all formal barriers to their participation in every aspect of life.[3] In the minds of "enlightened" legislators, emancipation was intimately linked to the assumption that Jews would promptly assimilate and become socially and culturally indistinguishable from other citizens.[4] Most Sephardic and Comtadin Jews endorsed that objective without hesitation. Jews from eastern France were somewhat slower to sacrifice their traditional language, customs, and dress, but they too usually succumbed to the lure of integration within a generation or two.[5] Despite the personal and family disorientation that such adaptations must have entailed, most Jews regarded the principles of the Revolution with profound veneration.

In his memoirs, the writer Julien Benda (1867–1956) eloquently described these attitudes among French Jews of his parents' generation. Benda's mother's family had been French since the reign of Napoleon I; his father had immigrated to Paris from Belgium in 1827, seeking economic opportunity. "I was raised in the spirit of the Republic," Benda recalled. "Democratic principles were ingrained in my bones. These principles, as my parents adopted them, were: civil equality, I mean the abolition of privilege, a secular State, individual liberty." Benda realized that these "revolutionary" concepts were often less appreciated by the non-Jewish French bourgeoisie, and he explained: "The attachment of my father to the Revolution was due in part to the gratitude he felt because it had emancipated his race, given civil and political liberties to the Jews. I often heard him say that it was scandalous that a Jew should oppose it, for without it he would still be in the ghetto."[6]

The French political philosopher Raymond Aron (1905–83) wrote in a similar vein about his family during the late nineteenth century:

> My grandparents, Jews from the East [of France, i.e., Lorraine], exhibited an uncompromising patriotism. I do not believe that they ever asked themselves the question, so fashionable today: Jews or Frenchmen first? Even my father, as far as I can remember, although he was more upset by the Dreyfus Affair than by any other historic event, did not budge from his positions: Freemason in his youth, without religious concerns, with no or almost no Jewish practice, he did not differ, at least superficially, from his university friends, Catholics or atheists, vaguely leftist.[7]

The "uncompromising patriotism" of French Jews was inextricably linked to their remarkable economic, social, and political achievements during the century following emancipation. In the years of the Bourbon Restoration (1815–30), recently emancipated individuals moved to cities, educated their children in secular state schools, and prepared to enter the mainstream. As an indication of

their determination, Jews in the 1820s and 1830s were already pro-
portionally more highly represented than non-Jews in university-
oriented *lycées* and in the prestigious École polytechnique.[8] Under
the Orleanist monarchy from 1830 to 1848, Jews began to excel in
business, finance, politics, and the professions—developments that
became even more dramatic in subsequent regimes.[9] Rothschild
Frères, founded in Paris in 1812, was joined within a few decades
by numerous other vastly successful Jewish family banks and businesses, including those of the Péreires, Bambergers, Reinachs, Goud-
chauxes, and Bischoffsheims. Jewish politicians such as Achille Fould
(1800–67), Michel Goudchaux (1797–1862), and Adolphe Crémieux
(1796–1880) attained positions of power and influence.[10] And in the
last decades of the century, there were hundreds of Jewish military
officers, including ten generals. They constituted, at times, 3 percent
of the regular army officer corps.[11]

In intellectual and artistic endeavors, the accomplishments of
French Jews were equally impressive. By 1895, according to one estimate, 7 of the 260 members of the Institut de France, which included
the Académie française and the Académie des beaux-arts, were Jewish.[12] They represented 2.7 percent of the membership, while Jews
overall represented about 0.2 percent of the population. One of the
first to be so honored, in 1836, was Fromental Halévy (1799–1862),
the composer of more than twenty operas, a teacher at the Paris
Conservatory, and a chorus master at the Paris Opera. His nephew
Ludovic Halévy (1834–1908) was a dramatist and novelist and, especially, the librettist, with Henri Meilhac, of Georges Bizet's *Car-
men* (1875) and of several of Jacques Offenbach's most beloved
works, including *La Belle Hélène* (1865), *La Vie parisienne* (1867),
and *La Grande Duchesse de Gerolstein* (1867). The operettas of Ludovic Halévy and Jacques Offenbach (1819–80), the son of a German cantor and an immigrant to France, came to epitomize the flamboyant, tolerant Second Empire in much the same way that the films
of American Jews, many of them also immigrants, set the tone of an
era many decades later.[13] Jews also played significant roles in French
theatrical circles. Two incomparable actresses of the Parisian stage—
Rachel, born Elisabeth Rachel Felix (1821–58), and Sarah Bern-
hardt, born Rosine Bernard (1844–1923)—were Jewish.[14]

Among French writers, philosophers, and social scientists, Jewish
names are also prominent. To cite only a few examples, Henri Bergson (1859–1941), the internationally recognized philosopher elected
to the Académie française in 1914 and awarded the Nobel Prize for

Literature in 1927, was the son of an assimilated and prosperous Parisian Jewish family. Émile Durkheim (1858–1917), generally regarded as the father of contemporary sociology, was the son of a rabbi from Alsace. Of these two, a historian has written, "One was to rank as *the* philosopher, the other as *the* sociologist, of early twentieth-century France"—a remarkable indication of the contribution of Jewish intellectuals to French culture.[15] Also highly esteemed were the philosopher Léon Brunschvicg (1869–1944), the philosopher and sociologist Lucien Lévy-Bruhl (1857–1939), and the author Marcel Proust (1871–1922), whose mother was Jewish. Other Jewish authors include Julien Benda, Jules Isaac (1877–1963), André Spire (1868–1966), André Suarès (1868–1948), Edmond Fleg (1874–1963), and the brothers Élie and Daniel Halévy (1870–1937 and 1872–1962, respectively), to mention only a few. And in education at the end of the nineteenth century and beginning of the twentieth, at a time when Jews in Great Britain and the United States could rarely expect academic careers, French Jewish professors held prestigious chairs at most universities, including the Sorbonne and the elite *grandes écoles.*

The career of yet another memorable member of the Halévy family, Lucien Prévost-Paradol (1829–70), perhaps reveals most strikingly the intimate identification of integrated French Jews with their country. Prévost-Paradol, a graduate of the *École normale supérieure,* was a brilliant liberal journalist, author, politician, and political theorist. In 1866, he was elected as the youngest member of the Académie française. Four years later, while serving as a French minister in Washington, D.C., he committed suicide after receiving news of the Franco-Prussian War.

The vast majority of the roughly 80,000 Jews in France at the end of the nineteenth century, of course, did not rise to lofty pinnacles within their professions, but nearly all seem to have felt comfortable in their country, free from formal restrictions and widespread hostility.[16] As the pediatrician Robert Debré (1882–1978) recalled of the years of his own childhood, "It did not seem then that the anti-Semitism to which people alluded, relating with horror its ravages in other times and places, could reach us and trouble our human relations. It was only later, at the time of the Dreyfus Affair, that we in France suffered from the unleashing of that passion."[17]

Similarly, Jules Isaac, grandson of a soldier who had volunteered to play the trumpet in Napoleon I's Grand Army in 1810 at the age of nineteen, and son of another volunteer who came up through the

ranks to become an officer in the Imperial Guard in 1870, wrote of
his own school days in the 1880s, "Our biblical name never bothered
me at all. I had good friends named Gheerbrant, Prébois, Saint-
Quentin." He also observed, "I do not recall that at that time the
foolish nastiness distilled by anti-Semitism had really reached and
wounded me." Nothing in Isaac's early experience prepared him for
the virulent anti-Semitism unleashed during the Dreyfus Affair. "I
had measured neither its force nor its extent," he confessed. "I did
not suspect its deep roots."[18]

Unnoticed by the young Debré and Isaac, anti-Semitism began to
flourish in France in the early 1880s. The phenomenon was unre-
lated to demography, for the Jewish community at the time was the
smallest in any major European country except Italy. Even in Paris,
the 50,000 resident Jews represented only 1.8 percent of the local
population. Most Jews were French; until 1880, only a few thousand
foreign Jews, most of them German, had immigrated. Roughly 7,000
to 8,000 impoverished and visibly different Russian, Romanian, and
Galician Jews arrived suddenly on the scene in 1881 and 1882, escaping vicious pogroms in southern Russia and the Ukraine.[19] That
wave soon ceased, however, and between 1882 and 1900, just a few
thousand more arrived, settled quietly into poor neighborhoods, and
began the process of becoming devoted French men and women.
    As would occur again in the 1930s and in 1940 but in different
chronological order, the resurgence of anti-Semitism in France in the
1880s was preceded by a catastrophic military defeat, a fundamental
constitutional change, and a European depression. The lightning
German victory in the Franco-Prussian War in 1870–71 severely
wounded French national pride and self-confidence. The consequent
loss of Alsace and Lorraine to the newly unified German state created a sense of rancor, an upsurge of exaggerated chauvinism, and a
thirst for revenge that festered for decades. The same war led to the
emergence of the Third Republic, with a governing majority that,
after initial uncertainties, became increasingly anticlerical. Catholics
felt threatened by government efforts to remove men and women of
the Church from teaching positions in the public schools, dissolve the
religious congregations, and expel the Jesuits.
    In addition, many average citizens were disenchanted by what the
historian Eugen Weber has called the "endless crisis" of the 1880s
and 1890s—the recurrent dangers of war with Germany or Britain;
threats of political or military coups; sordid financial scandals and

corruption; anarchist violence; and rapid industrialization and modernization accompanied by unemployment, strikes, and social disorientation.[20] Then to political, social, and religious insecurities was added the impact of the depression that began in the early 1880s and lasted until well into the 1890s.

Why did these multiple anxieties provoke popular anti-Semitism, which had remained dormant in France under the Second Empire?[21] Conservatives, Catholics, and extreme Socialists and anarchists who, since the French Revolution, had never accepted a republic or a popularly elected parliament now needed a scapegoat for their troubles. The French Revolution had granted Jewish emancipation. Since most grateful Jews were consequently fervent Republicans, they were in the enemy camp in the eyes of all who opposed the Third Republic. Also, a large proportion of Jews in France in the 1880s had Alsatian roots, spoke French with German accents or intonations, or, like the family of Alfred Dreyfus, actually spoke German itself in addition to French. Even worse, some other Jews had personal roots in Germany and Eastern Europe and spoke German or Yiddish instead of French. To increasing numbers of Germanophobic French chauvinists bent on revenge for the loss of Alsace and Lorraine, these "German" Jews appeared to be potential traitors—as Dreyfus seemed in 1895. And as many Frenchmen, insecure in the wake of their humiliating defeat, became ever more concerned with cultural homogeneity, they began to view Jews in general as internationalists or unassimilable foreigners of dubious loyalty.

Among Catholics, Jews had been the targets of prejudice and hostility for centuries. The Church had long condemned them for the killing of Jesus and their refusal to convert. In the 1880s, Catholics who equally despised the relentless individualism, materialism, industrialization, and modernization associated with liberalism blamed those conditions on Jews, who seemed to be endorsing and profiting from them. Catholics also noted and exaggerated a Jewish presence among enemy anticlericals.[22] Meanwhile, victims of the depression—small farmers, shopkeepers, artisans, the unemployed—looked for someone to blame. Those jealous of the spectacular and very visible financial successes of a few Jewish banking families, of the gains of Jewish business competitors, or of poor Jewish workers who took scarce jobs for low wages, pointed in that direction. Conservatives, chauvinists, religious anti-Semites, and some antiparliamentarian anarchists and Socialists reinforced the charges, and many humble French men and women listened.

Also as in 1940, French anti-Semitism around the turn of the century involved a hearty dose of political opportunism. At least one well-known Jew-baiter was honest enough to admit as much. "Everything seemed impossible, or frightfully difficult, without this providential anti-Semitism," wrote Charles Maurras in 1911. "Because of it, everything arranged itself, evened itself off, and was simplified. If one was not anti-Semitic from patriotic will, one became so from a simple sense of opportunism."[23] As in Germany and Austria during the same years, anti-Semitism in France during the last two decades of the nineteenth century became a convenient tool for demagogues on both the extreme Right and the extreme Left—a device intended to attract the disaffected masses and galvanize them against the common enemy, the liberal state.

Major landmarks in the sorry tale of nineteenth-century French anti-Semitism can only be mentioned briefly here. In 1882, a bank called the Union générale, which had attracted the investments of French monarchists and Catholics of all types, from aristocrats to thousands of humble country priests and their parishioners, failed. A judicial inquiry blamed the disaster on the wild speculations of the bank's founder and director, Eugène Bontoux, a fervent Catholic previously employed by the Rothschilds. Bontoux himself, however, accused Jewish banks of unfair competition, and the anti-Semitic press fanned the charges for years.[24]

Four years after the collapse, a two-volume book entitled *La France juive* appeared. In the course of its 1,200 pages, the author, Édouard Drumont, blamed all the ills of modern France on the Jews, taking occasional swipes at Protestants, Freemasons, and anticlericals. Drumont aimed at a mass readership and attempted to appeal to French men and women in all walks of life. Establishing a pattern that would persist among anti-Semites until the Second World War, he assured workers that Jews were agents of capitalist exploitation, while telling the lower middle classes that Jews were responsible for Marxism. As the historian Jean-Louis Bredin has observed, "Thus [Drumont] was able to reconcile in anti-Semitism counter-Revolutionary thought, the Catholic tradition, and a populist anticapitalism of socialistic tendency. Thanks to anti-Semitism, class conflicts were dissolved."[25] Similar forces would prevail in 1940.

After a slow start and a lively press campaign, 100,000 copies of *La France juive* were sold by the end of 1886.[26] Its success was followed by a burst of other anti-Semitic publications, of which the best known were *La Libre parole,* a daily newspaper founded by Drumont himself in April 1892, and the Assumptionist Fathers' *La Croix,* dating from the early 1880s. By 1894, the year the Dreyfus Affair began, more than two million copies of various *La Croix* publications were being printed throughout the country each week.[27] And yet, despite those figures, popular anti-Semitism declined in the early 1890s. The French National Anti-Semitic League dissolved ignominiously in 1890. At the same time, officially anti-Semitic candidates in Parisian municipal elections received a total of only 3,083 votes.[28] Tens of thousands of Parisians turned out for the funeral in 1892 of Captain Armand Mayer, killed in a duel provoked by articles in *La Libre parole* attacking the numbers and alleged privileges of Jewish army officers. Minister of War Charles de Freycinet declared that the army made no distinctions between Catholics, Protestants, and Jews. Deputies unanimously voted it a crime to sow division in the army.[29] And after a brief surge in early 1893 because of its provocative coverage of the Panama Canal scandal, the circulation figures of *La Libre parole* sank to a few thousand copies by the summer of 1894.

If racial intolerance was not pervasive in fin de siècle France, neither was it exclusively directed toward Jews. Italians, Belgians, Germans, Poles, North Africans, and even Bretons, Auvergnats, and French southerners in general were unpopular among those with whom they competed for jobs. Against Italians in particular, who numbered roughly 300,000 in the 1890s (25 percent of all the foreigners in France, and nearly four times the number of French and foreign Jews combined), violent and often fatal clashes occurred frequently throughout the 1880s and 1890s. As Eugen Weber points out, "The history of the fin de siècle, which records little physical violence against Jews, is one long litany of outbursts against Italians, rising at times to what could be described as pogroms."[30]

The comparison is instructive, but there was a difference. Anti-Italian sentiment and more general hostility to migrant labor were largely a spontaneous product of the working class facing hard times. Anti-Semitism was that, and much more. Anti-Semitism was articulated and endorsed by an intellectual and political elite, for its own purposes. Especially in a country like France, where intellectuals were regarded with respect and deference, anti-Semitism sanctioned from above acquired prestige, stature, and a permanent place in the culture that working-class anti-Italianism could never hope to achieve.

* * *

The arrest for espionage of the Alsatian Jew Captain Alfred Dreyfus (1859–1935), the court-martial and sentence to perpetual deportation for treason, and the humiliating military degradation ceremony on January 5, 1895, gave popular anti-Semitism in France a new lease on life. Nor was the initial focus on a Jewish officer an accident. "I should have suspected it!" exclaimed Colonel Jean Sandherr, head of the army general staff's intelligence bureau, when investigators suggested Dreyfus's guilt to him.[31] For despite their accessibility to Jews, the upper echelons of the French officer corps were permeated with anti-Semitism. Many officers (including Lieutenant-Colonel Marie-Georges Picquart [1854–1914], who uncovered the most conclusive evidence of Dreyfus's innocence) had been educated in Jesuit schools and reflected the prejudices rampant there. Many were displaced Alsatians who combined the traditional anti-Semitism of the region with personal grudges against perceived "Germans." Many, also, had served in North Africa, where anti-Semitism was more prevalent than in France itself.[32] Poor pay, slow advancement, and the diminishing social status of military service fostered personal frustrations and the search for scapegoats.[33]

If the army's initial focus of suspicion on Dreyfus was an anti-Semitic act, however, other factors helped determine his conviction. The handwriting on the celebrated memorandum discovered at the German embassy in Paris and revealing the existence of a French traitor bore an unfortunate resemblance to Dreyfus's. His haughty demeanor and uncongenial personality, his linguistic and economic ties to his Alsatian birthplace, his class origins in a newly enriched upper bourgeois family rather than in the genteel, often impoverished nobility that provided so many French officers, and above all, the army's pressing need, in the glare of relentless journalistic scrutiny, to find a culprit, all played a role in distracting Dreyfus's judges from the evidence of his innocence. Those same factors, combined with the army's conviction that an admission of error and fallibility would irreparably weaken both the nation and the military, continued to discourage revision for twelve years, in the face of ever more overwhelming evidence in its favor. To contemporaries willing and able to understand the immensely complex case, whether Dreyfusard or anti-Dreyfusard, the Dreyfus Affair was in the last analysis only partially about Jews at all. It was primarily about an individual sacrificed to the needs and priorities of the nation and the social order.[34]

To largely urban masses fanned by a scurrilous popular press, however, the Jewish question remained paramount, releasing an appallingly primitive, vulgar, and violent popular hatred. In the days and weeks following the publication of Émile Zola's famous article "J'Accuse" on the front page of *L'Aurore* on January 13, 1898, thousands of young people marched through the streets of scores of French cities, calling for the death of Jews, smashing Jewish storefronts, and attempting to break into homes and synagogues. Meanwhile, in French Algeria, a virtual pogrom lasted for days, and several people were killed. Anti-Semitic leagues flourished, and 25,000 people, including 1,000 army officers, contributed to a fund established by *La Libre parole* to help the widow of Major Hubert-Joseph Henry, who had committed suicide in prison after being arrested for lies and forgeries of documents implicating Dreyfus. Letters accompanying the contributions, many from humble workers and artisans, explained motivations in the most lurid fashion. "Death to the Jews" was a restrained expression when compared to pathological calls for roasting, hanging, gassing, vivisection, and massacre, accompanied by references to Jews as kikes, pimps, lice, plagues, cancers, and filthy beings.[35]

The year 1898 was the high point, or, more appropriately, the low point of the Dreyfus Affair, however, and when justice finally prevailed, it did so quietly. At least as difficult to understand as the Affair itself is its peaceful, uncontested resolution. After 1898, the anti-Dreyfusard public, as if purged and shamed by the exhibition of its basest instincts, seemed to have lost interest, and efforts by the popular press to stir up anti-Jewish sentiments in the last years before revision were largely ignored. Alfred Dreyfus, who would have been lynched in many French cities in 1898, was acquitted by the High Court of Appeal in 1906, reinstated as a captain in the army, and awarded the Cross of the Legion of Honor. He returned to active service during the First World War, without recorded incidents, and died in 1935. His tragedy and triumph discredited anti-Semitism in France for the next twenty years. It would not resurface as a popular force until the decade of his death.

While the years just before the First World War may have been a period of vague unease for much of the European bourgeoisie, they were for French Jews "a golden age of symbiosis."[36] With anti-Semitism distinctly out of favor, Jews could generally live with their image of themselves comfortably intact. They were French, different from the majority only in religion. As such, they rejected the term Jew (*Juif*), which implied a distinct culture, and called themselves *Isráelites*. Many were also highly successful. Although Jews now constituted just 0.25 percent of the national population, they pointed proudly to the three to six Jewish members of the Chamber of Deputies during these years, or 0.5 percent to 1 percent of the total.[37] When André Spire, Léon Blum, and Paul Grunebaum-Ballin were admitted to the Council of State and Henri Bergson to the Académie française (not without some anti-Semitic protests), Jews had risen to the highest levels in the civil service and in the world of letters. By 1939, they constituted approximately one-third of all Parisian bankers, at least 12 percent of the doctors, 9 percent of the dentists, 10 percent of the lawyers, and 12 percent of the journalists.[38]

In religious matters, most French Jews were only mildly observant. Pierre Abraham regarded his mother and grandmother as typical of bourgeois women of all faiths around the turn of the century. Their attitudes were

> the same as those of Catholic or Protestant women toward their Church. They went to the synagogue for the major holy days of the year, and for the anniversaries of family deaths. They contributed publicly to the charitable agencies of the *Consistoire*. At home, they gave charity to recognized beggars. . . . In these ways, they fulfilled their religious duties.

They did not, however, abide by all the traditional religious proscriptions. Forbidden by Jewish law to utilize mechanical transportation on the Sabbath, they descended from their coach fifty meters from the door of the synagogue. Abraham's grandmother read the Jewish prayer book daily in Hebrew but understood "no more [of it] than an elderly Catholic lady reading her rite in Latin."[39] Judaism was a meaningful part of the family tradition, but individual members defined it very much in their own way.

Was French anti-Semitism really as dead at the turn of the century as Jews so eagerly wanted to believe? Many remember some blemishes. Charles Lopata, born in France in 1903 to poor Lithuanian immigrants, roamed the streets of Paris freely as a child and often heard the epithet "*sale Juif*" ("dirty Jew"), but his friends, usually non-Jews, always defended him.[40] Pierre Abraham, whose family had been French for generations, remembered that his brother Marcel was often beaten by other boys at the Lycée Condorcet during the

Dreyfus Affair, but that by the time he entered the school in 1901, the mood was calmer. However, he wrote,

> throughout my years of study my comrades never let me forget for long my fundamental flaw. A good grade in composition, a kind word from a teacher, an exemption from gym class, a quarrel during recess, everything was a pretext for insults in the younger classes, for crueler insinuations in the older classes.

In 1902, Abraham was taunted by a teacher for being not truly French and therefore not expected to remember the date of Napoleon's victory over the Prussians at Jena, even though none of his classmates knew it either. He was convinced that his father's career with the French railroad suffered because of his Jewishness until 1918, when the fact that his three sons had fought for France overcame pettier concerns. Until the post–World War I period, Abraham concluded, the family's Judaism was "a weight difficult to forget in the most banal of daily events."[41]

While 1914 disrupted the peace of a golden age, it confirmed Jewish patriotism. On August 3, 1914, the Fédération des sociétés juives de France, an association of foreign Jewish organizations in France, issued an appeal in French and Yiddish. It stated that, "if we are not yet French by law, we are in heart and soul, and our most sacred duty is to put ourselves immediately at the disposition of this great and noble nation in order to participate in its defense."[42] Ten thousand foreign Jews are believed to have enlisted from a total immigrant Jewish population in France in 1914 of perhaps 40,000.[43] Some 46,000 native and foreign Jews were mobilized and 6,500 were killed, from a population in 1914 of about 120,000.[44] One victim, killed in action on April 13, 1915, was Robert Hertz, the son of a German immigrant and himself a graduate of the École normale supérieure and a professor of philosophy. In a letter to his wife from the front, Hertz had expressed the love of country so typical of native and foreign Jews alike:

> Yes, I am filled with gratitude toward the country which accepts and overwhelms me. Nothing is too much to repay that, so that my little son may always walk with his head high and not know, in a restored France, the torment which poisoned many hours in our childhood and youth. "Am I French? Do I deserve to be?" No, little fellow, you have a country and you will be able to make your

footsteps resound on the land while reassuring yourself: "My papa was there and he gave everything to France."[45]

For Jews in the war, the terms *union sacrée* and "fraternity of the trenches" were more than just pretty words. Thirty-seven rabbis served along with Catholic priests and Protestant ministers as army chaplains, and stories of mutual support abound.[46] The best known involves the grand rabbi of Lyon, Abraham Bloch (1859–1914), an army chaplain killed while bringing a crucifix to a wounded Catholic soldier. His story and that of Hertz and others favorably impressed the nationalist writer Maurice Barrès (1862–1923). In 1902, Barrès had written of French Jews, "For us, *la patrie* is our soil and our ancestors, the land of our dead. For them, it is the place where their self-interest is best pursued."[47] In 1917, Barrès admitted, "Many *Israélites,* settled among us for generations and centuries, are natural members of the national body."[48] For Barrès, it was a profound concession.

Barrès's concession, however, applied only to French Jews of long standing, an ever diminishing portion of the Jews in France in the first four decades of the twentieth century. From 1880 to 1939, the population of French Jews remained stable, while the total number of Jews in France nearly quadrupled. Immigrants made up the difference. Between 1906, when revolution and pogroms in Russia prompted a resurgence of Jewish emigration, and 1939, between 150,000 and 200,000 foreign Jews entered the country. In Paris itself, which had numbered about 40,000 Jews in 1880, there were at least 150,000 in the 1930s. About 110,000 Jewish immigrants arrived in Paris between 1880 and 1939—almost three times the number of native Parisian Jews. Of these newcomers, roughly 90,000, or about 82 percent, were from Eastern Europe, with 20,000 arriving before the First World War and about 70,000 after 1918.[49]

In the timeless pattern of immigrants everywhere, Jews new to France tended to settle in neighborhoods where friends and relatives had already preceded them. In Paris, where native Jews had long since moved to comfortable quarters in the western part of the city, the most orthodox newcomers often crowded into dark and moldering buildings in the Marais, in the third and fourth arrondissements. In an area informally labeled the Pletzl, near the Saint-Paul stop on the *métro,* in narrow streets such as the rue des Rosiers, the rue des

Écouffes, and the rue Pavée, thousands of religious East European Jews tried to re-create life as it had been back home.[50] Others, often less observant, settled in Belleville, in the twentieth arrondissement in eastern Paris; near the furniture workshops along the rue du Faubourg St. Antoine, bordering the eleventh and twelfth arrondissements; in Montmartre or Clignancourt in the eighteenth; or in the Gobelins area in the thirteenth.

Separated from the native French, Jewish and non-Jewish alike, by their language (Yiddish) and geography, immigrants tended to be segregated also by employment and by economic and social organizations. Most were artisans in the garment industry, working with clothing, textiles, furs, skins, and leather goods—the so-called Jewish trades.[51] Others made jewelry, watches, or furniture. Many labored at home with the help of their entire family, making goods on a piecework basis and further isolated by workplaces and suppliers alike.

Immigrants operated their own soup kitchens, health clinics, and shelters, as well as hundreds of Yiddish newspapers, libraries, theaters, lecture series, and schools, including the Université populaire juive. Many also belonged to separate mutual-aid societies, independent Jewish trade unions under the auspices of the *Bund,* or special Yiddish-speaking sections of established French trade unions, more or less affiliated with the national Confédération générale du travail (CGT). After the split in the French Left in 1920–1921, most Jewish workers connected with the reformist CGT shifted their loyalties to the Communist-oriented Confédération générale du travail unitaire (CGTU) and to the Communist party itself—a move that severed any remaining cultural ties to a Jewish community transcending class interests.

In addition to obvious linguistic, geographic, economic, and political barriers, equally impenetrable social, cultural, and religious differences separated French and foreign Jews. Most French Jews were, as seen, only mildly observant and were eager to modernize their religious rituals. They favored, among other innovations, sermons in French with choral and organ accompaniment. They supported a more secular education for rabbis, to immerse them in French culture. They encouraged pastoral duties for rabbis similar to those of priests, such as visits to hospitals and prisons, and attendance at public functions. They discouraged separate Jewish schools, newspapers, and libraries and urged immigrants to integrate as quickly as possible.

East European Jews, on the other hand, were often traditional in observance and suspicious of change. While not all were orthodox believers, most regarded Judaism as an all-encompassing culture, a way of life, and an intimate definition of self. Rejecting the large, impersonal, and modernized French temples, they preferred their own little synagogues (*shuls*) or informal storefront meeting places (*oratoires*), where they could worship daily in their own way with friends from the old country. Despite the disapproval of native Jews, there were hundreds of oratoires in Paris by the 1930s.

The mutual antipathy between French and immigrant Jews was longstanding. As early as 1890, the French Jewish writer and journalist Bernard Lazare (1865–1903), soon to become a staunch Dreyfusard, referred to East European immigrants as "these predatory Tatars, coarse and dirty, who come in huge numbers to graze in a country which is not theirs."[52] Similarly, Pierre Abraham recalled the attitudes of his mother and grandmother:

> They considered with vaguely pitying repugnance the unhappy immigrant Jews from Eastern Europe who, with a copious supply of *tfilinn* on their arms and foreheads, with a great display of *thaless* on their shoulders, prove to you in a provocative way that you are less a believer than they. [French Jews] flattered themselves on being several generations more advanced than those who were not yet assimilated.[53]

French Jews generally regarded immigrants as old-fashioned, if not positively anachronistic, and considered that their exclusiveness, tight community ties, and distrust of outsiders were all very well in the countries from which they had come but were entirely inappropriate in the country of the rights of man. With a few notable exceptions, such as Edmond Fleg and André Spire, most French Jews opposed the Zionism popular among immigrants and emphasized French, rather than Jewish, rights in the Holy Land. Above all, French Jews were afraid that the immigrants, so visibly and unabashedly different and so vocal in demanding their rights, would provoke anti-Semitism and obliterate the gains they had worked generations to achieve.

Disagreements based on profound differences were often articulated in petty ways. French Jews charged that easterners were too fervent, too loud and disorderly in their religious observance. They spoke Yiddish too loudly in public; they refused to alter their mode of dress; they were too left-wing. In the apt description of one historian, "Immigrants were accused, among other things, of drinking tea 'in a country where wine or beer is preferred,' of being late for appointments, of ignoring local mores and defying government authorities, and of organizing noisy demonstrations and making trouble in the streets."[54] They refused, in other words, to make themselves invisible.

Immigrant Jews, on the other hand, could not understand French or Frenchified Jews and were appalled by their religious attitudes. As J. Tchernoff, a Russian Jewish student who arrived in Paris at the age of nineteen in 1892, later remembered:

> When they crossed the threshold of a temple in Paris, the Jews of Eastern Europe felt out of place, surprised by the attitude of the faithful. The behavior of these men, with their top hats, so formal, so correct, who talked in low voices about their business affairs during the service which only a few of the most initiated understood—men for whom the observance of the rites was part of their worldly snobbism—astonished and shocked these persecuted Jews who, while gesticulating wildly and rocking their bodies, put into their prayer the mystical ardor which was devouring them.[55]

Immigrants were also startled by the eating habits of their French coreligionists. A. Honig, who was born into an orthodox family in Poland in 1907 and immigrated to France in 1934, remembered the shock of being invited to a Jewish friend's home for dinner and being served pork.[56] Others noted with horror that native Jews shared the national predeliction for frogs' legs, snails, and shellfish—all forbidden to observant Jews.

If relations between native and foreign Jews were often tense, however, those between Jews and non-Jews were generally more amicable throughout the prosperous 1920s than they had been before the war. Philippe Erlanger, born into an affluent and prominent French Jewish family in 1903, summed up the mood of the 1920s in his memoirs. Erlanger's father's family had migrated to Paris from Alsace during the Second Empire. His mother's family had lost three sons on the western front during the First World War. Erlanger recalled:

> As a child, they had naturally talked to me about anti-Semitism. I understood that in France it was a question of a plague, conquered like rabies. The Great War, the heroism and sacrifices equally

shared had put an end to it. The Dreyfus Affair belonged to a distant past. After Verdun we would never see that again.

Of his own experiences at elite schools just after the First World War, he wrote, "As for me, neither at [the Lycée] Janson nor at *Sciences Politiques* where we played childishly at snobbism, was I ever humiliated because of an origin which I never considered hiding."[57]

Three Jews served in the victory cabinet of Georges Clemenceau (1849–1929) right after the First World War.[58] In 1926, a sympathetic French court acquitted the immigrant poet Scholem Schwartzbard for the murder in Paris of Semyon Petliura, the Ukrainian nationalist responsible for the deaths of thousands of Jews in pogroms in 1919. During the trial, people wept publicly over descriptions of those pogroms.[59] Factories starved for manpower after the devastations of war recruited foreign workers, including Jews, during the 1920s and welcomed the thousands who responded. In 1927, in a gesture of goodwill toward all immigrants, the French government significantly liberalized the naturalization law.

Within the Church, too, a distinct improvement in Jewish relations began in the 1920s and continued throughout the far more difficult 1930s. Under the leadership of Pope Pius XI, a decree from the Holy Office in 1928 formally condemned hatred of the people chosen by God. The papal encyclical *Mit brennender Sorge,* a protest in 1937 against atheistic Nazi confrontations with the Church in Germany, further declared, "Whoever takes race, or the people, or the State, or the form of the State . . . and divinizes them reverses and falsifies the order of things created and ordered by God."[60] Then in September 1938, Pius XI addressed a group of Belgian pilgrims with the following words:

Each time I read these words: the sacrifice of our brother Abraham, I cannot prevent myself from being profoundly moved. Take note: we call Abraham our Patriarch, our Ancestor. Anti-Semitism is incompatible with this great thought, the noble reality which this prayer expresses. Anti-Semitism is inadmissable; spiritually, we are all Semites.[61]

Among the French clergy, an emphasis on the historical continuity between Christians and Jews gained ground during the interwar period, and populist and religious Jew-hatred fell distinctly out of favor. The Assumptionist Fathers who published *La Croix,* for example, abjured anti-Semitism in 1927 and did not return to it until the time of the Spanish Civil War. Many French Jesuits also abandoned anti-Semitism during the 1920s, and unlike the publishers of *La Croix,* most did not revert. Jesuits led efforts to prove that *Protocols of the Elders of Zion,* first published in France in 1920, was a forgery—an altered copy of an anti-Bonapartist tract of the 1860s. Their success helps explain why the *Protocols* never had a following in France similar to that received in Germany and Great Britain.[62] Meanwhile, increased communication between Jewish and Christian leaders in the form of seminars, conferences, or simple human contacts led to new bonds of friendship and respect. Those bonds became invaluable during the Vichy years.

The limits of Jewish-Catholic understanding among common people of goodwill, however, and the distance yet to be traveled are suggested by the historian Pierre Pierrard, who recalls his attitudes as a young Catholic in Lille in the interwar period:

> A hundred times, as a child, I passed in front of the high and black facade [of the local synagogue] which rose above the tablets of the Law; for me, as for many young pupils in the religious schools, the synagogue on the rue Auguste-Angellier was a strange and forbidden place that our imagination associated with the big [Freemason] lodge on the rue Thiers of which we knew that its heavy walls, perpetually closed, hid horrible mysteries where profaned hosts played an essential role.

Pierrard also remembers "the emotions set off, during the long rather droning succession of 'great prayers' on Good Friday ... by the prayer *Pro perfidis Judaeis*" and by the fact that there was no collective kneeling by the congregation after the prayer for the Jews, as there was after other prayers. That, he says, made a great impression on young Catholics.[63]

As elsewhere in Europe, the onset of the depression in the 1930s put an abrupt end to the French tolerance of the 1920s and ushered in an era of economic, political, and social unrest. By 1932 in France, production was down 27 percent, and 250,000 people were unemployed. By late 1934, the figure reached 400,000.[64] Under these conditions, foreign workers were not only no longer welcome but deeply resented. France contained, however, about 2,453,000 foreigners in 1936, or nearly 7 percent of the population.[65] Most of these foreigners were non-Jewish; indeed, in 1935, among the five largest national groups—850,000 Italians, 650,000 Spaniards, 500,000 Poles, 200,000

Belgians, and 125,000 Africans—Jews were significantly represented only among the Poles.[66] But Jewish immigrants were among the most visible, especially in Paris where they were concentrated in specific neighborhoods.

As in the 1880s, economic depression was accompanied by a myriad of other social and political ills. Ministries unable to cope with fiscal crises came and went with increasing rapidity and decreasing prestige. A series of political scandals nourished popular disillusionment with the Republic. In one of these, scores of politicians were implicated in the fraudulent sale of municipal bonds and a subsequent cover-up—schemes concocted in 1934 by an unsavory foreign Jew named Alexandre Stavisky. The Stavisky Affair provoked massive right-wing demonstrations that terminated in a march on the Chamber of Deputies on February 6. As the government again fell, national self-confidence plummeted and antiparliamentarianism flourished.

Again as in the 1880s and early 1890s, with economic depression, political ineptitude and scandal, a sense of widespread decadence, and a loss of national self-confidence, many French men and women needed a scapegoat. Demagogic politicians, leaders of radical right-wing leagues, and opportunistic journalists found it more expedient to blame foreigners, and especially Jewish foreigners, than French citizens.[67] The French themselves proved receptive to that message, and the moderate public became accustomed to phrases like "Jewish question," "Jewish problem," and "special regulations for foreigners." *Métèques,* a pejorative word for foreigners in general and Jews in particular, were seen as the cause of unemployment, scandal, decadence, left-wing radicalism, and every other social ill. Had not foreign workers inundated the country? Was not Stavisky a Jew? And Léon Blum? Anti-Semitic invective from the right rose to a bitter frenzy after the electoral victories of the Popular Front in April and May 1936 and Blum's investiture as prime minister. Now government ineptitude in general could be blamed on outsiders, and Jewish citizens increasingly fell into that category.

As the decade proceeded, the growing threat from Hitler's Germany further complicated the situation. Roughly 50,000 predominantly anti-Nazi and left-wing refugees from the Third Reich passed through France between 1933 and 1939, of whom more than half were Jewish. Despite the fact that only about 10,000 of the 50,000 actually remained in the country, the newcomers provoked suspicion among French citizens fearful of being dragged into another war.[68]

Concern grew as anti-Nazi foreigners (and thousands of French citizens) participated in public protests, boycotts, and demonstrations against Nazism and anti-Semitism.[69] Fear and resentment peaked in March 1938 with the *Anschluss,* which brought thousands of additional unwanted anti-Nazi refugees to France; the humiliating Munich concessions over the Sudetenland in September; and *Kristallnacht* throughout the Third Reich on the night of November 9. The last was a Nazi response to the assassination of a German diplomat in Paris by a young Polish Jewish immigrant named Herschel Grynszpan. French fears of an explosive incident were confirmed.

Growing antiforeign sentiments in 1938 and 1939 were reflected in new laws and decrees to regulate immigration and limit the number of foreigners who could participate in specific trades, open new businesses, join certain organizations, or publish newspapers. A law enacted on November 12, 1938, established criteria by which immigrants naturalized under the generous terms defined in 1927 could be denaturalized. It also confirmed the right of the minister of the interior to expel foreigners deemed *indésirables* or, if no country would take them, to intern them or place them in supervised residence.[70] Police raids and document searches intensified in cafés, restaurants, hotels, shops, factories, and apartment buildings frequented by foreigners.

Eve Dessarre, who as a child of twelve in 1938 came to Paris with her German Jewish mother, a physician, has bitter memories. Her mother had to renew her *permis de séjour,* or residence permit, every three months at one of the police headquarters sometimes called the *bureau des larmes* (office of tears). French civil servants took every opportunity to humiliate her, making her wait in interminable lines and subjecting her to rude and impertinent interrogations. Men insulted her by insinuation, for she was not then living with Eve's father, a respected historian and philologist. Women, Dessarre recalls, were even worse. Her mother grew increasingly impoverished and depressed until, upon learning in 1940 that as a German national she was to be interned, she committed suicide.[71]

Unlike Dr. Dessarre, many political refugees entered France illegally, with no permits at all. They lived at the mercy of informers, unscrupulous employers, and corrupt bureaucrats. "An atmosphere of terror presently reigns in the Jewish refugee *milieux* of Belleville," the immigrant A. Honig lamented on September 12, 1938. He speculated that because German Jews were educated and not visibly impoverished, they inspired none of the sympathy and charity directed

toward poorer and orthodox East European Jews a decade earlier.
Worst of all, he stressed, many refugees of the 1930s spoke German,
a language the French did not want to hear.[72] But while Honig was
most conscious of his coreligionists, non-Jewish refugees were suffering equally. The influx of more than 400,000 from Spain as the civil
war ended there in early 1939 pushed French antiforeign sentiment
to the breaking point. Thousands were interned in camps near the
Spanish frontier—camps that would soon be filled with foreign Jews
as well.

While antiforeign and anti-Semitic sentiments flourished in the
1930s, however, and while refugees often suffered increased harassment or worse, those who looked could find grounds for reassurance. The Daladier-Marchandeau decree of April 21, 1939, for example, prohibited attacks on individuals in the press based on race or
religion.[73] Several of the most anti-Semitic sections of Drieu la
Rochelle's *Gilles* were censored in October of that same year.[74] Cler-
gymen no longer fueled popular anti-Semitism as they had in the late
nineteenth century, and several French bishops and archbishops
firmly condemned racism throughout the turbulent decade.[75] And
most of the moderate French press, although convinced that foreigners posed a problem, nonetheless disapproved of Kristallnacht in November 1938.

Most revealing, however, are the positive memories of the period
recorded by most French—as opposed to foreign—Jews. These citizens seem to have worked, studied, traveled, and socialized with
non-Jews with complete ease, unaffected by politics, the vitriolic
press, and the xenophobic rhetoric of the nationalist leagues. The
great medieval historian Marc Bloch (1886–1944), for example, described his experiences and emotional ties to his country with elo-
quence in 1943, in a last testament written after he joined the Resistance:

> A stranger to all credal dogmas, as to all pretended community of
> life and spirit based on race, I have, through life, felt that I was
> above all, and quite simply, a Frenchman. A family tradition, al-
> ready of long date, has bound me firmly to my country. I have
> found nourishment in her spiritual heritage and in her history. I
> can, indeed, think of no other land whose air I could have breathed
> with such a sense of ease and freedom. I have loved her greatly,
> and served her with all my strength. I have never found that the
> fact of being a Jew has at all hindered these sentiments.[76]

Philippe Erlanger, by 1940 the brilliant young director of the Service of International Artistic Exchange at the Ministry of Education, remembered of the immediate prewar years, "God knows that, since the rise of Hitler, this problem [of anti-Semitism] worried me, but I didn't feel myself personally involved. Like car accidents, this type of calamity was always for others. In truth, I didn't really believe in it."[77] Georges Friedmann, a successful French Jewish university professor in the 1930s, adds:

Having been born in Paris into a family in which the traditional observances had been given up and "mixed marriage" was no problem, and being deeply identified with France, her culture and her way of life, and with a circle of friends and colleagues in which no one asked questions about my "racial" origins or religious beliefs, I had never suffered from anti-Semitism, though my name indicated that I was a Jew, and I had never felt discriminated against in French society, even at school.[78]

Similarly, Gaby Cohen, a young teenager in the late 1930s, recalls no tension or animosity in her native Alsatian village of 2,000 people, of whom about 100 families were Jewish. On the contrary, she says, "our non-Jewish friends and neighbors used to scold us if we didn't respect and observe the Jewish holidays."[79] And Ginette Hirtz, born in Amiens in 1922 of French Jewish parents, declares, "I do not remember having consciously suffered from anti-Semitism during my childhood, except for one time when I was ten."[80]

Nor were foreign Jews always badly received, especially when they were prominent personalities. Of his stay at Sanary (Var) on the coast in Provence and of the abrupt change that occurred for him only after war broke out, the noted German Jewish writer Lion Feuchtwanger (1884–1958) later recalled:

We had been celebrated on our arrival some years before. The newspapers had published editorials of cordial and appreciative welcome. Government officials had explained that it was an honour for France to receive us as her guests. The President of the Republic had given me an audience. Now [autumn 1939] they were locking us up![81]

Many foreign Jews experienced less generosity. Thus Jean-Marie Cardinal Lustiger, presently archbishop of Paris, born in 1926 to poor Polish Jewish immigrants and converted to Catholicism in

1940, remembers difficult childhood experiences at school, where he dressed differently from the other students: "At the gates of the Lycée Montaigne, I was punched in the head because I was a Jew. When I approached the boys who were discussing among themselves, they used to say to me, 'That doesn't concern you, you are a dirty Jew.'"[82] As seen, Henri Rosencher from Poland had similar experiences at his lycée, not, he believed, because he was the first or only Jewish student there, but because he was not "bourgeois."[83]

When prejudice was not based on class, as with Lustiger and Rosencher, it was often rooted in xenophobia rather than in general anti-Semitism. Thus, Jacqueline Wolf, whose Jewish parents emigrated from Poland in the 1920s and settled in Épinal (Vosges), writes of her childhood years: "In France at that time, it was worse to be a foreigner than to be [native] Jewish. The economy was in a slump, and unemployment was high; therefore, French citizens resented any foreigners who appeared to be taking jobs that otherwise would be theirs."[84] Similarly, George Frybergh, a handsome, blue-eyed Czechoslovakian student in a French language camp in Brittany in 1933, remembers nastiness directed toward him as a métèque from individuals who had no idea he was Jewish.[85]

Clearly it was worse to be both. A. Honig observed that the French did not speak badly of Jews, as they did at home in Poland, but rather of métèques. However, "when they speak of foreigners who 'are invading France,' one readily suspects that they mean Jews."[86] And Eve Dessarre recalls her experiences in a girls' secondary school. A student "with skin the color of coffee with very little milk," from Martinique, was tormented and ostracized. She herself was called a "dirty *Boche.*" When her classmates learned that she was Jewish, the taunting grew distinctly worse.[87]

Nevertheless, while most Jewish newcomers to France in the 1930s had unpleasant experiences, nearly all continued to regard France as a land of hope, opportunity, and freedom, better than the countries from which they had come and no more hostile to immigrants than the United States or Britain. Charles Lopata's father, for example, who immigrated from Lithuania in 1891, loved his adopted country dearly despite the fact that his economic achievements there were modest. He had traveled to the United States and Britain before selecting France as a place of residence, and, according to his son, he never regretted that choice. Mr. Lopata sent his two sons to fight for France in 1939, but after the Germans occupied Paris in 1940, his life savings were confiscated and he committed suicide.[88]

Similarly, Claudine Vegh's father, Mr. Rozengard, deliberately chose France as a place to live, giving up a promised chair in criminology at the University of Warsaw and ultimately bringing six siblings to Paris. He had suffered humiliations as a Jew in Poland, and throughout the 1930s he repeatedly asked his daughter, "How is it possible to live in Poland when one has lived in France?" Then he regularly reminded her, "You, who as a child can breathe in this country, never forget how lucky you are!"[89] Her father kept his faith, but in 1941 the government of the country he loved so much prohibited him from practicing as a lawyer because he was Jewish.

Maurice Rajsfus's father arrived in Paris in 1923 from Poland and found work selling clothing from stalls in public markets. France did not treat him well. Since the elder Rajsfus was not observant and was rarely known to be Jewish, Maurice later attributed his father's troubles more to antiforeign prejudice than to anti-Semitism. Mr. Rajsfus's two children, born in Paris in 1925 and 1928, were declared French citizens upon his formal request, under the terms of the 1927 naturalization law. His own requests for naturalization, however, were rejected twice, in 1935 and 1938, without explanation, despite the fact that he had two children who were citizens, honorable work, excellent health, and no criminal record.

Maurice Rajsfus remembers that his father sometimes considered moving to the United States. He, too, chose to remain in Paris, secure in the knowledge that his children were citizens and would receive education and opportunity in a free land. And life was far better than in Poland. As with Claudine Vegh's father, however, his faith was not rewarded. He and his wife were arrested as foreign Jews in Paris on July 16, 1942, by French police. They did not return from Auschwitz.[90]

2

War Begins, 1939–1940

AT 4:45 A.M. ON FRIDAY, SEPTEMBER 1, 1939, GERMAN STUKAS attacked Danzig in the Polish corridor. The French government declared war on Nazi Germany on September 3, and French men and
women prepared reluctantly for war. About five million young men
were immediately mobilized and sent to frontier posts or training
camps. They would endure eight dreary months of "phony war"
there until the German invasion of France in May 1940. Workers
were similarly mobilized in the factories, where they were soon la-
boring sixty or sixty-five hours a week, in two or three shifts, in an
attempt to compensate for the cut in French industrial manpower.
The minority of French citizens who were Communists were thrown
into profound confusion by the Russo-German nonaggression pact,
just signed on August 23, 1939, and withheld active support of the
French war effort until after the German invasion of the Soviet
Union on June 22, 1941.

Predictably, the French Jewish response to war did not differ significantly from that of French non-Jews. The reaction of most foreign Jews in France to the declaration of war, however, with the exception of the Communist minority, was far more enthusiastic. Of
about 100,000 foreigners who had volunteered or been drafted into
the French army by May 1, 1940, about 30,000, or 30 percent—a

number enormously in excess of their proportion of the immigrant population—were non-French Jews.[1] As early as August 27, 1939, the Polish Jewish immigrant A. Honig arrived at a Foreign Legion recruiting station to find a huge line of young men trying to enlist. Observing that most were Jews, he recorded in his diary, "The fighting spirit which prevails among those who have come here contrasts with the slight enthusiasm which the French in general show for the war."[2] Foreign Jews, he explained, were eager to show their devotion to France, their adopted country that had given them opportunities undreamed of in Central and Eastern Europe. Their own private struggles against Hitler had often begun long before, with personal experience of Nazi militarism, totalitarianism, and anti-Semitism. In addition, the French government promised enlisting immigrants and their families protection from expulsion or internment—a measure that the Vichy regime revoked a year later.

Even as their men were volunteering for military service, however, the situation deteriorated drastically for enemy aliens, Jewish and non-Jewish alike. Ironically, many of the hardest hit were political refugees from the Third Reich—men and women in France because of their political opposition to the very regime against which the French were now fighting. Gustav Regler (1898–1963), for example, a non-Jewish German author and winner of the Iron Cross for bravery in combat against the French in the First World War, fled to France from Nazi Germany when residents of his native Saar Basin voted for reunification with the Third Reich in 1935. Wounded while fighting with the International Brigades during the Spanish Civil War, he was recuperating at the home of Ernest Hemingway in Key West, Florida, when war broke out in September 1939. He immediately returned to France and tried to enlist. He was thanked politely and told to return in a few days. Fourteen hours later, six French police arrested him as an enemy alien and sent him to Le Vernet (Ariège), an internment camp in the Pyrenees about thirty miles from the Spanish frontier.[3]

Arthur Koestler (1905–83), the well-known Jewish Austro-Hungarian author and anti-Fascist, was arrested in Paris on October 2, 1939, and held with other refugees from the Third Reich in the crowded coal cellar of the *préfecture de police* for two nights, and in the open air at the Roland Garros tennis stadium at Auteuil for another week. He too was ultimately sent to Le Vernet.[4] By February 1940, there were slightly more than 2,000 prisoners at Le Vernet, including Spanish Republicans interned before the war, common criminals, German, Austrian, and Czechoslovakian refugees, and French political dissidents.[5] Between 700 and 900 of the 2,000 were Jewish.[6] Many of the 2,000 were well known, including the journalists Bruno Frei and François Bondy and the writers Friedrich Wolf and Rudolph Leonhard.[7]

Arrests of enemy aliens during the fall and winter of 1939 focused on political activists but were by no means limited to them. Peter Lipman-Wulf, then a thirty-four-year-old apolitical German sculptor, had immigrated to France in 1933 because, as a Jew, he had lost his teaching position at the State Academy of Fine Arts in Berlin. In the autumn of 1939, in the Provençal town of Saint Raphaël (Var), he dutifully responded to an order to report to the authorities. Lipman-Wulf's Jewishness was not an issue, for he had never declared it in France. He was interned at a camp called Les Milles (Bouches-du-Rhône), south of Aix-en-Provence and within easy sight of Mont Sainte-Victoire, so often painted by Paul Cézanne (1839–1906). With him at Les Milles were the authors Lion Feuchtwanger and Alfred Kantorowicz; the painters Max Ernst, Hans Bellmer, and Robert Liebknecht (son of the assassinated German Communist leader Karl Liebknecht); the Dusseldorf opera producer Friedrich Schramm; the music critic Heinrich Strobel; the journalists Heinz Bieber-Georgi, Hugo Bloch, and Otto Heller; two winners of the Nobel Prize in Medicine, Otto Meyerhof and Thadeus Reichstein; and roughly 1,000 other prominent and not-so-prominent immigrants.[8] In France as a whole, an estimated 15,000 immigrants from the Third Reich, mostly non-Jewish and Jewish men under the age of fifty but including some women, were arrested in the first days of the war. By the end of the year, at least 8,000 were still being held throughout the country in hundreds of internment camps, euphemistically called *centres d'hébergement,* or "lodging centers."[9]

The arrest of enemy aliens upon the outbreak of war was not unique to France. The British arrested Germans, Austrians, and Italians in 1939 and 1940, and the Americans interned Japanese-Americans after December 7, 1941. French internment camps, however, were particularly primitive. Lipman-Wulf recalls that at Les Milles, a former brick factory and one of the more bearable camps, internees washed in water from one long outside pipe pierced with twenty holes. The water was not potable and froze solid in winter. In good weather, the men ate in the open air near the latrines. The mistral blew toilet paper through the dining area, but the food was adequate and there was little disease. Men slept on the floor inside the factory, which was immensely dusty from its former service and filled with fleas and vermin. There was no forced labor, and the forty or so artists in the group could continue their work. French guards readily supplied them with paint, paper, and canvas but then stole their creations. A camp commander stole work from the already famous non-Jewish German painter Max Ernst (1891–1976) and sold it in Paris. The commander was furious when he learned that a piece which he had sold for 100,000 francs was worth twice that price![10]

Unlike Les Milles, Le Vernet was officially a repressive camp for suspected criminals and political activists, and conditions there barely supported life. Inmates slept in flimsy huts with no heat, light, or blankets. Koestler calculated that each man in a crowded bunk had a width of twenty-one inches for sleeping. The food, woefully inadequate, consisted of a daily bread ration of eleven ounces, plus a cup of black coffee in the morning and a pint of thin soup at midday and evening. During the winter of 1939–40, prisoners worked six hours a day. Koestler's first job was to remove heavy stones with a pick and spade, under the eyes of French guards who beat prisoners when they faltered. He later spent his days collecting and emptying steaming latrine bins, some of which weighed sixty to seventy pounds. Four times a day, between working hours, the prisoners stood outside in lengthy roll calls. More than 25 percent of the men on any given day were sick. Guards were cruel, and offenders were beaten and placed in solitary confinement with bread and water only.

Regarding the direct physical treatment of prisoners, Koestler saw Le Vernet as a slight improvement over German camps:

> In Vernet beating-up was a daily occurrence; in Dachau it was prolonged until death ensued. In Vernet people were killed for lack of medical attention; in Dachau they were killed on purpose. In Vernet half of the prisoners had to sleep without blankets in 20 degrees of frost; in Dachau they were put in irons and exposed to the frost.

In other respects, however, the comparison was actually unfavorable to the French:

> As regards food, accommodation and hygiene, Vernet was even below the level of Nazi concentration camps. We had some thirty men in Section C who had previously been interned in various German camps, including the worst reputed, Dachau, Oranienburg, and Wolfsbuttel, and they had an expert knowledge of these questions.[11]

It was a severe indictment of the Third Republic in its death throes—before, it must be emphasized, the devastating defeat of June 1940. The victims were men who had fled from tyranny to the land of freedom, and who had been convicted of no crimes. Their treatment by harassed, indifferent, and suspicious bureaucrats set a dangerous precedent, easing the way for subsequent cruelties directed specifically against foreign Jews.

Except at Le Vernet, where only about 50 of the 2,000 prisoners were freed before the fall of France, a majority of the Germans and Austrians arrested after September 1939 were released by May 1940. The specially constituted Commission de criblage, composed of representatives of the Ministry of the Interior, the Ministry of War, and the Foreign Ministry, studied and decided each case. Outright Nazis, Communists, and "suspicious" individuals were usually not freed. Many with connections, however, were released after special intervention on their behalf. Koestler and Feuchtwanger, for example, benefited from specific protests from the British; Regler, from the soon-to-be minister of the interior, Georges Mandel (1885–1944); and Max Ernst and the German Jewish philosopher and literary critic Walter Benjamin, from famous French literary figures. Gradually, many others over the age of forty were freed, including prisoners with French spouses or children, those in poor health, former Legionnaires, and recipients of the Cross of the Legion of Honor or the *médaille militaire*.

Except at Le Vernet, most remaining male inmates under forty and holding valid immigration papers were given a choice during the spring of 1940 of enlisting in the Foreign Legion or joining special labor battalions called compagnies de travailleurs étrangers (CTEs), in the service of the French army. In April 1940, Lipman-Wulf chose labor and was sent, in the uniform of a so-called *prestataire,* to a construction site in Normandy. When the Germans invaded a month later, he escaped to the south of France from where, after a series of adventures, he crossed into Switzerland and survived the war. As will be seen, many prestataires remaining under the custody of the Vichy regime were not so lucky.

Nor were many of the released prisoners particularly lucky. Thousands, including Feuchtwanger, Ernst, and Benjamin, were rearrested in May 1940 as the "phony war" ended and the German army began to overrun France. This time French government orders were to intern *all* male immigrants from the Third Reich between the ages of seventeen and fifty-five, and all unmarried and childless married women. Included were Jews and non-Jews, political and racial refugees, simple economic immigrants, and mere tourists visiting France at the wrong moment. Despite the specified minimum age, at least 5,000 foreign children were also interned. It was, again, an ominous precedent.

These enemy aliens, or *indésirables,* as they were called, were often arrested and temporarily interned in the north of France. As the invading German army rapidly approached Paris, however, they were shuttled southward, in part to protect the anti-Nazis among them from falling to the Germans, and in part to prevent supposed "enemy agents" from rejoining their countrymen. Families were divided when women and children were sent to one camp, usually Gurs (Basses–Pyrénées, now Pyrénées-Atlantiques), while men were interned elsewhere, often at Saint-Cyprien or Rivesaltes (both in Pyrénées-Orientales).[12] The most politically "suspect" women went to Rieucros (Lozère), and the men to Le Vernet. Les Milles, which had actually closed in April, reopened and by June held 3,400 men detained in southeastern France. Foreign women and children in the same area were often sent to the Bompard, Terminus, Atlantique, and Levant hotels in nearby Marseille. Rooms at the hotels were dilapidated and overcrowded, and food was insufficient. French gendarmes stood guard outside.[13]

While in transit to the camps, immigrants who had come to France seeking political asylum from the Nazis were often in danger from the French themselves. Lisa Fittko, an anti-Nazi activist in Berlin long before Hitler's rise to power, remembers that the bus that took her and other German women to the Gare d'Austerlitz in Paris in May 1940 had its windows blackened and carried a sign reading "Refugees from the War Zone," to protect passengers from being lynched as *Boches.* Her train was stoned in Tours. Then at the end of the journey, she and the other women were stoned and spat upon as they walked from the train station at Oloron-Sainte-Marie to the buses that would take them to Gurs.[14] Once inside the camp, internees were relatively safe from the surrounding storm, but with the last government of the Third Republic struggling for its very existence, conditions at Gurs and other internment centers deteriorated further.

In the confusion of the fall of France and the weeks following the armistice of June 22, many internees escaped or were released from camps by guards who were either indifferent or wanted to help keep them out of Nazi hands. Gurs was virtually abandoned by its guards for a brief period in June, and thousands of women simply walked out.[15] Others, destitute and with no place to go, or afraid of losing contact with their men interned elsewhere, chose to remain. At Les Milles, the German writer Walter Hasenclever, believing that he was about to be delivered to the Nazis, committed suicide on the night of June 21. The next morning, guards placed about 2,000 equally terrified prisoners on a train and wandered throughout southwestern France with them for five days. After passing through Sète, Tarbes, Lourdes, and Bayonne, the train finally stopped at the Château de Saint Nicholas, near Nîmes, not far from its departure point. From there, some prisoners, including Lion Feuchtwanger, Max Ernst, and the historian Golo Mann, the son of Thomas Mann, managed to escape. The others returned to Les Milles on August 20.[16]

Escapees were soon replaced by other foreign indésirables, mostly war refugees fleeing the advancing German army in the Low Countries. By the end of 1940, some 40,000 to 50,000 people were interned in the unoccupied zone. Of these, about 70 percent were Jewish.[17]

The "phony war" had ended abruptly on May 10, 1940, with the German invasion of Belgium, Luxembourg, and the Netherlands. Within days, well over a million refugees were pouring into France, their most precious possessions crammed into wheelbarrows, baby carriages, or automobiles that often ran out of gas or broke down. The refugees, including an estimated 40,000 foreign Jews, mostly without papers, clogged the roads, filled the hotels, depleted local resources, and annoyed and frightened French civilians.[18] Close on their heels and often overtaking them was the German army itself, which had pierced the Maginot Line and entered France by May 15.

By June 10, as the Italians belatedly declared war and invaded France in the south and the Germans crossed the Seine and approached Paris in the north, another exodus began. The French government fled first to Tours and then to Bordeaux. About four million French men, women, and children, including hundreds of thousands of Parisians and from 100,000 to 200,000 Jews, now joined the foreigners on the road.[19] Whole families slept in barns or fields and ate what little they could buy from local peasants.

Testimonies differ with regard to the reception refugees received. Nina Gourfinkel, a Russian Jewish immigrant in Paris since 1925 who fled to Moissac (Tarn-et-Garonne) in June 1940, remembered that the French in the south were unwelcoming to les gens du nord in general, and to foreigners in particular. "A multitude of tiny individual ditches compartmentalizes the French, separating them from one another," she observed, "and a great ditch separates them from the exterior world, from everything that is not France or, in a manner still more narrow, from life *à la française*." Consequently, foreigners, and not only Jews, "walked, talked, and especially ate in an unacceptable manner" and were regarded with distaste.[20] On the other hand, many refugees, like Paul Reichmann, who today is a Canadian businessman but then was an ten-year-old whose family had escaped to Paris from Vienna after the Anschluss, remember kindness and generosity. "I still recall," Mr. Reichmann says, "that the French peasants received us with enormous hospitality, and shared food and shelter with us without hesitation."[21]

The treatment of legal immigrants by local French men and women was one thing, however, while the official reception of frantic recently arrived war refugees without documents was quite another. Those who had fled from the Low Countries to escape the German army, including 40,000 Jews, met with little but trouble. If they were citizens carrying valid Belgian, Luxembourg, or Dutch passports, they were sometimes allowed to proceed with special passes in lieu of French entry visas. If they were former citizens of the Third Reich, however, who had emigrated to the Low Countries a few years previously and now found themselves on the road again, they were regarded and treated as illegal enemy aliens or, if their passports had been revoked, as *apatrides*—stateless persons. Many, including about 10,000 of the 40,000 Jews, were soon apprehended by harassed French officials who did not know what else to do with them. They were sent to join other enemy aliens already in the camps.

Fourteen-year-old Arno Mayer and his family, Luxembourg Jews, were among the more fortunate refugees in France in May 1940. As he recalled:

We barely stayed ahead of the fast-moving Wehrmacht and managed to avoid roads that were being strafed by the Luftwaffe. Near Verdun we experienced our first bombing raid and came within a hairsbreadth of having our flight cut short at a military control point. Except for the totally fortuitous intervention of an understanding general of the French army, we would have been interned as security risks because my seventy-four-year-old paternal grandfather was still carrying a German passport . . . despite his fifty years in Luxembourg.[22]

Issued a special *laissez-passer*, the Mayers were able to make their way eventually to Morocco, Portugal, and the United States.

Gret Arnoldsen, age twenty, and his father were less fortunate. After harrowing experiences in Vienna, including a period of imprisonment during Kristallnacht, Gret and his parents had escaped illegally from Austria to Brussels. In May 1940, as the Germans were overrunning Belgium, they attempted to reach France. Separated involuntarily from Gret's mother, the men were jammed into a refugee train and sent to France, where they were immediately interned. After days of meandering through France in a locked and guarded train, they were deposited in flimsy huts surrounded by barbed wire on the sandy beaches of Saint-Cyprien. They spent the winter starving and freezing at Gurs, and a somewhat more comfortable period at Noé (Haute-Garonne), from where Gret was sent to a hospital in December 1941 with the pulmonary lesion that saved his life. The Vichy regime sent Gret's father to the occupied zone in 1942, and he was deported to Auschwitz soon after. A refugee from the Nazis in Vienna, he had spent more than two years in France without a day of freedom.[23]

Claude Vigée, a Jewish student from a family that had been French for generations and was thus never perceived as foreign and only occasionally as Jewish, had very different experiences while traveling south during the exodus. At Mayenne, friendly people took in his family and let them sleep in their own beds, declining any payment. At Taussat outside Bordeaux, a kindly old Republican innkeeper accepted the Vigées at his hotel and wept with them during Marshal Pétain's radio announcement of a cessation of hostilities. At Bordeaux, however, a doctor who had rented Vigée's uncle an apartment a few weeks before now refused to rent to Jews and broke the contract. Then at Pau (Basses–Pyrénées, today Pyrénées-Atlantiques),

> the good folk . . . did not lose such a rare chance to exploit this new type of tourist invading their city. The defeat was good for something. I saw with my own eyes these honest citizens . . . sell bottles of clear water for ten francs a liter to thirsty and exhausted refugees, old people, women or children, who asked them for something to drink at the entrance of the city.[24]

Vigée's mixed experiences were shared by most French Jews who fled south. Some non-Jewish French men and women were tolerant and generous; others were highly anti-Semitic. Many were grasping and mean toward all refugees at a time of political and economic uncertainty. The majority were simply indifferent, preoccupied with their own troubles. The divisions would continue, in ever more exaggerated form, throughout the war.

The German army occupied Paris early in the morning of Friday, June 14, marching in orderly fashion down the almost deserted Champs Élysées. Three days later, shortly after noon on June 17, the newly appointed French prime minister, eighty-four-year-old Marshal Henri Philippe Pétain (1856–1951), announced by radio that France must cease hostilities. The speech was greeted with widespread approval and relief. Frédéric Hammel, a French Jewish chemistry professor and researcher from the University of Strasbourg who was mobilized in 1939, stationed at a military laboratory in Paris, and evacuated to Montpellier in June 1940, heard the speech in a restaurant during lunch. He recalled:

> Everyone is hoping for the end of this war. When Marshal Pétain says in his tired voice: "the time has come to stop fighting," the relief of everyone is visible. Not a word of anger. Not a word of regret. I feel an undescribable shame. It would seem that I am the only one to realize what that means, to foresee what is awaiting us.[25]

Hammel was not quite the only one, of course. Claude Vigée, as seen, encountered a grieving old innkeeper. The French Jewish musician and composer Darius Milhaud (1892–1974), lunching at a bistro at the old port in Marseille, recalled that the message "came to rend our hearts," and that "all around us people wept in despair."[26] General Charles de Gaulle (1890–1970) broadcast his first defiant speech from London the following evening, inviting French officers and soldiers, engineers and skilled workers, to join him in a continuation of the struggle against Germany. A few thousand young patriots crossed the English Channel to volunteer for what were to become the political and military forces of "Free France," headed by de Gaulle and defined by him as the only true and legitimate heir of the Third Republic. Then on June 21, twenty-nine deputies and one senator sailed for North Africa on the *Massilia,* in the vain hope that the Pétain government would continue the war from the colonies. In France itself in the few days that remained until the armistice, some brave officers and their men continued to resist the invader. Fifty scarcely trained cadets from the cavalry school at Saumur died defending four bridges over the Loire on June 20 and 21. Elsewhere, at least two officers were actually killed for their resistance by angry French civilians or by their own men.

Other individuals grieved silently for the fall of France. Among these last were the throngs of foreigners in the country. But as Nina Gourfinkel remarked, many French citizens, instead of seeing the foreigners' grief as a sign of goodwill, reacted indignantly, complaining that people without a country could not teach *them* patriotism.[27] *On nous a vendu*—"They have sold us out"—became the popular cry, and Frenchmen defined "they" according to their political convictions. For many, "they" were above all the foreigners, and the Jews in general, who had dragged France into a hopeless and unnecessary war for personal reasons.

Indeed, since the unpopular declaration of war in September, expressions of anti-Semitism had increased daily. In February 1940, several months before the invasion, A. Honig recorded in his diary that citizens were often heard muttering to themselves, "While the blood of our men is flowing, the *métèques* are earning money and living the good life," despite all evidence of high numbers of foreign enlistments for military service.[28] Most French Jews, however, managed to ignore anti-Semitism until the defeat, but then the impact was immediate and brutal. Claude Mauriac, son of the noted Catholic novelist François Mauriac (1885–1970) and himself also a novelist, recorded a typical incident in his journal on August 4. A Jewish café patron in Toulouse, a war veteran twice wounded and decorated for service to France, was insulted as a *sale youpin* (dirty foreign Jew) responsible for the nation's troubles. After being severely beaten up by four drinkers led by an air force captain, he was thrown out, to the cheers of all.[29] Meanwhile, the thoroughly French Philippe Erlanger, who had never previously experienced anti-Semitism, wrote with some astonishment of the reaction among his closest friends and colleagues at the Ministry of Education:

As the situation worsens I feel a clearly hostile atmosphere thickening around me. The word "Jew" is not pronounced, at least in a loud voice, but one feels it ready to explode like a bomb.

Of the approximately four hundred people who now constitute our strange group, only Huisman and I belong to this dangerous species. No doubt about it! The war and the defeat are our doing.[30]

* * *

On June 22, 1940, in the forest of Compiègne, in the same rail-road car where Marshal Ferdinand Foch had delivered terms to a de-feated Germany in November 1918, French delegates signed the armistice with the Third Reich. The document was accepted in the expectation that Britain would be defeated within a few weeks. The war would end and the French would sign a definitive peace treaty, emerging as an equal partner with Germany in the new European order. To the surprise and humiliation of many, however, Britain did not fall, and the provisional armistice remained to govern Franco-German relations until the Liberation.

After the armistice, France was divided into several parts. The three departments in Alsace and Lorraine which had been German between 1871 and 1918 (Moselle, Bas-Rhin, and Haut-Rhin) were annexed to the Third Reich and administered by two Nazi *Gauleiters* (district leaders). The departments of the Nord and the Pas-de-Calais in northeastern France were placed under the administration of a German military governor based in Belgium. The vast area of France that remained was divided into an occupied and an unoccupied zone, separated by a demarcation line that quickly became a formidable barrier, difficult to cross legally and dangerous to cross illegally. About three-fifths of the country north of the Loire River and ex-tending south in a narrow strip along the Atlantic coast to the Span-ish frontier constituted the occupied zone, administered by a German military governor, or *Militärbefehlshaber in Frankreich* (MBF). About forty departments south of the line were unoccupied.[31] This arrange-ment continued until November 11, 1942, when, after the Allied landings in North Africa, the German army forcibly occupied the en-tire southern zone except for eight southeastern departments or parts of departments east of the Rhône River that fell to the Italians. After the Italians signed an armistice with the Allies on September 8, 1943, and attempted to withdraw from the war, those departments also came under German control.

By the terms of the armistice, the French government was to have sovereignty over the entire country while acknowledging and respect-ing "the rights of the occupying power." A formula as difficult to in-terpret then as it is today, it became the source of continual discus-sion, friction, and maneuvering. In effect, policies of the Vichy regime were enacted in the unoccupied zone, while in the occupied zone they applied so long as they did not conflict with those of the Germans. The armistice also imposed several other limitations upon

French sovereignty. Among these, the army in metropolitan France was limited to 125,000 officers and men. According to article 18, the whole of France was required to pay occupation costs eventually set at an exorbitant 20 million marks, or 400 million francs, a day. And in article 19, the French agreed to hand over any refugees from the Third Reich requested by the German government, thus violating rights of asylum and sentencing hundreds to certain death.[32] Again, the measure eased the way toward later deportations.

The French government that signed the armistice was a legally constituted organ of the Third Republic. Eight days after the German invasion of the Low Countries, Prime Minister Paul Reynaud summoned Marshal Pétain, the renowned "victor of Verdun," ambassador to Spain, and admirer of General Francisco Franco (1892–1975), into his cabinet as vice-prime minister (*vice-président du conseil*). Then on the evening of June 16, besieged on all sides by officers and politicians insisting on an armistice and with the German army in Paris, Reynaud resigned and recommended that President Albert Lebrun ask Pétain to form a government.

The Marshal's first acts as prime minister were to call for a cessation of hostilities and arrange an armistice. His next steps were equally momentous. On July 9 and 10, 1940, the senators and deputies elected to the Popular Front Parliament in 1936, or what was left of them (some seventy Communists had been expelled by Prime Minister Édouard Daladier in January 1940, and thirty were still in North Africa after sailing on the *Massilia*), agreed by an overwhelming majority to revoke the Third Republic Constitution of 1875 and award Pétain full powers to promulgate a new one. Within the next few hours, the Marshal issued three constitutional acts. The first gave him the title of chief of the French state, the second declared that the chief of state had a "totality of government power" and was responsible for making and executing all laws, and the third adjourned the Senate and the Chamber of Deputies indefinitely.

The Third Republic was not killed by the Germans; it committed suicide. It died because its elected officials did not believe it worth saving. Under the Third Republic, France had been fatally weakened, it was said, by laxity, indiscipline, and institutionalized dissent. France had also, under the Third Republic, suffered an economic depression, elected a Popular Front government, and, finally, lost a war in thirty-eight days. The hard-won victories and social cohesion of the 1914–18 war were forgotten, and it seemed time for a fresh start. But however well the military defeat of 1940, the popularity of the armistice, and the personal prestige of Marshal Pétain may be explained, it remains difficult to grasp how responsible elected officials from the center and left could have assigned the task of constitution-making to a man known to be authoritarian and antiparliamentarian. In so doing, they utterly abandoned the Republic for which they had struggled for more than half a century, and they abandoned their constituents as well. The "National Revolution" that resulted, with its dedication to *travail, famille, patrie*—work, family, country— would be popular for a time, not for its form or content but because it brought peace. But form and content would prove crucial in the long run, and peace would prove elusive. Meanwhile, millions of men, women, and children in France would suffer under a repressive authoritarian regime.

Of the roughly four million French who had fled south at the time of the German invasion, most non-Jews and as many as 30,000 Jews returned to their homes and businesses in the occupied zone after the armistice and the establishment of the Vichy regime.[33] Many, of course, had never left. Most French Jews were particularly anxious to resume a semblance of normal life. Their personal stories bear witness to their love and faith in their country—in turn a reflection of their prewar acceptance in the society.

Philippe Erlanger stubbornly remained at his post in Paris despite numerous insults and incidents, remarking that "I am discovering abominable sentiments from some whom I believed to be my friends, and a miraculous devotion where I never would have suspected it."[34] He consulted his friend René Blum, the director of the Ballets de Monte-Carlo and brother of the former prime minister Léon Blum. René Blum, in the United States with the dance company when France fell, had believed it his duty as a Frenchman to return after the armistice.[35] Both men now considered escaping to London to join de Gaulle, but both decided against it. They agreed, as Erlanger put it, that "a Jew with any kind of public recognition, especially if he holds a position, must not under any pretext leave his country. He must *bear witness*."[36] Erlanger finally left Paris in April 1941 for the unoccupied zone, where he survived. René Blum remained in Paris. He was among the 743 French Jewish professional men arrested in their homes in Paris by the Germans on December 12, 1941, in an unusual early reprisal action against Jewish citizens. He was interned at Compiègne and later at Drancy. On September 23, 1942, he was deported to Auschwitz, where he died in the gas chamber at the age of sixty-four.[37]

Like his brother and Erlanger, Léon Blum (1872–1950) also considered joining de Gaulle but rejected that option for the same reasons. Still a deputy, Blum traveled to Vichy in July to vote against granting Pétain full powers to draft a new constitution. He then retired near Toulouse. Ignoring all warnings of danger, he lived openly until September, when Vichy officials arrested him, not as a Jew but as a political offender. He was imprisoned and tried with other leaders of the Third Republic at Riom in February 1942. Found guilty of criminal responsibility for France's material and moral unpreparedness for war in 1939, he spent two years as a hostage in special quarters at Buchenwald, where he survived.[38]

Thousands echoed the determination of Erlanger and the Blums. Some paid for their decisions with their lives. The more fortunate eventually emigrated or went into hiding. Raymond-Raoul Lambert, French for generations, the winner of the Cross of the Legion of Honor and the *croix de guerre* from the First World War and a captain in the army in 1940, was among the former. On October 19, 1940, just two weeks after the racial laws were enacted,[39] he wrote in his diary, "I will never leave the country for which I was almost killed [in the war]."[40] He remained to serve his people as director in the southern zone of the Union générale des Israélites de France (UGIF), the German-imposed Jewish welfare organization. Arrested in Marseille on August 21, 1943, he was deported to Auschwitz on December 7 with his wife Simone and their four children, ages fourteen, eleven, four, and eighteen months. The entire family was gassed upon arrival on December 10.[41]

The pediatrician and professor Robert Debré also remained at his post at the Hôpital des Enfants-Malades in Paris. Despite the newly promulgated racial laws banning Jews from teaching, he even obtained a promotion in the autumn of 1940, by a unanimous vote without abstentions from members of his medical faculty. Although he later wrote of that period, "I had resolved, with more determination than ever, to pay no attention to those restrictive laws and to act towards the French and German police as if I had nothing to worry about," he was obliged to apply for a special exemption from the racial laws in order to continue working.[42] He was one of only ten Jewish professors in the country to receive it. Then in September 1943, as both a Jew and a Resistant, he was forced into hiding.[43]

The anthropologist Claude Lévi-Strauss and the historian Marc Bloch, both demobilized in June 1940 and both residents of the unoccupied zone during the summer, tried to return to their teaching positions in Paris in the fall. Both were directed into positions in the unoccupied zone by sympathetic bureaucrats in the Ministry of Education who understood the danger better than they. Of his official, Lévi-Strauss later recalled, "He told me that considering the name I bore, he would refuse to send me to Paris."[44] Lévi-Strauss promptly lost his new post in the south because of the racial laws there. He emigrated to New York, where he accepted a position at the New School for Social Research.

Bloch, instead, received an exemption from the racial laws and continued teaching. In November 1940, he accepted an offer from the New School, but when he could not obtain American visas for his two oldest children and his eighty-year-old mother, he changed his mind. Perhaps he was never committed to leaving. In June 1942, he wrote to his close friend and colleague Lucien Febvre, "In any case, and whatever happens, I am happy to be here, rather than there where I almost went. These months to come which I foresee as being so hard, it is in my country that I want to live them."[45] When the Germans occupied southern France, Marc Bloch, age fifty-six, joined the Resistance. Arrested on March 8, 1944, he was shot by the Gestapo on June 16, with twenty-seven others, in a lonely meadow on the outskirts of Lyon.[46] He was murdered not as a Jew but as a Resistant.

The French Jewish journalist and author Emmanuel Berl (1892–1976) fled south from Paris in May 1940, "to avoid," as he later explained, "being taken by the Germans."[47] Berl was actually summoned to help edit several of Pétain's speeches in June 1940. He then lived more or less normally in Vichy and Cannes until he went into hiding in July 1941—a much earlier date than usual for French Jews.

The French-naturalized journalist and author Joseph Kessel (1898–1979) escaped to Lisbon in June 1940, also to avoid the Germans. Soon homesick, he refused to admit to dangers in the unoccupied zone and longed for France. In a letter to his brother, in August 1940 he wrote, "I am sure that I will be less unhappy being hungry and cold and even afraid and persecuted in France than comfortably installed in a flat in New York or a house in Hollywood." He added, "Since I have done nothing in my life other than love and serve France without playing a political role, I cannot believe that [my request to return] will not be heard." He returned in September. On February 10, 1941, he wrote his brother that, "despite everything, France is not finished, not Nazified, not anti-Semitic." Kessel fled abroad only in December 1942, after the Germans occupied the south.[48]

The Russian-born Jewish painter Marc Chagall (1887–1985) and his wife Bella, both naturalized in 1937 and living happily in Gordes (Vaucluse) in the unoccupied zone in May 1940, were also slow to sense danger. When the American vice-consul, Harry Bingham, and the director of the American Emergency Rescue Committee, Varian Fry, personally brought them an invitation from the Museum of Modern Art in New York City to emigrate to the United States, they politely declined.[49] But life began to appear more hazardous during the winter of 1940–41, when their daughter and son-in-law were de-naturalized and they themselves were rounded up for interrogation by French police in Marseille. On May 7, 1941, they crossed the Pyrenees legally by train to Canfranc, Spain. They sailed from Portugal to New York in June, arriving as the Germans were invading the land of their birth. Their daughter and son-in-law followed a few weeks later.[50]

If most prominent and not-so-prominent French and naturalized Jews elected to stay put in 1940, so too did most foreign Jews. The American Jewish author Gertrude Stein (1874–1946) and her companion, Alice B. Toklas (1877–1967), longtime residents in France, lived openly throughout the war in their rented country homes in Bilignin and later in Culoz (Ain), near Belley and northwest of Chambéry. They felt deceptively safe near the Swiss border, despite the rough, mountainous terrain that separated them from the frontier. Their friend Bernard Faÿ, a historian and the director of the Bibliothèque nationale, promised to try to protect them. The mayor of Culoz, whose wife befriended the two American women, kept their names off the local books. Especially during the last year of the war, German officers and soldiers appeared daily in Culoz. The villagers all knew about Gertrude and Alice, and kept silent.[51]

Of course, not all Jews chose to remain in France in 1940. Approximately 5,000 Jews prudently fled the country between June 10 and 25, passing through Spain and Portugal on the way to Britain, the United States, or South America. With help from the Portuguese consul general of Bordeaux, Aristides de Sousa Mendes, and some Spanish border guards, the number had grown to 20,000 by early September.[52] At a slower rate, thousands more would escape through

Spain, North Africa, and Switzerland in the months and years to come. Others, including 6,449 aided by the Jewish emigration association HICEM, would leave France legally before all such departures were prohibited toward the end of 1942.[53]

Many emigrés were recent arrivals in France, with no personal ties or loyalties there and with fewer illusions about the fate of Jews under a Nazi regime. Some were outspoken anti-Nazis who feared political rather than racial persecution and possible deportation to the Third Reich under the terms of article 19 of the armistice. Many had been interned as enemy aliens, an experience hardly conducive to further residence in France. Prominent foreign emigrés obliged to leave illegally in 1940 because they could not obtain French exit visas included Lion and Marta Feuchtwanger, who escaped from Les Milles and Gurs, respectively; the non-Jewish German author Heinrich Mann (1871–1950), brother of Thomas Mann, with his nephew Golo Mann; and the Austrian Jewish author Franz Werfel (1890-1945) and his non-Jewish wife Alma Mahler-Werfel. All of them crossed the Pyrenees on foot, in two separate groups, and sailed from Lisbon to New York in October.[54] Despite physical weakness, Walter Benjamin also crossed the Pyrenees illegally in an agonizing ten-hour ordeal on foot in September 1940, only to be told by Spanish border guards that his transit visa was invalid and he would be sent back. Benjamin committed suicide with morphine at Port-Bou on the Spanish frontier, and the major work that he had painfully carried over the mountains disappeared with him.[55]

Not all Jewish emigrés in 1940 were foreigners, however. Darius Milhaud, whose father traced his roots in the Comtat Venaissin back to the fifteenth century, crossed the Pyrenees legally and sailed for the United States with his wife and son in July 1940. He wrote later, "I realized clearly that the capitulation would prepare the soil for fascism and its abominable train of monstruous persecutions."[56] The philosopher Raymond Aron and future Nobel Peace Prize winner René Cassin (1887–1976), responding separately to de Gaulle's radio appeal of June 18, found themselves on the same Polish troop ship bound for London five days later. Like Milhaud, Aron later wrote that he realized that "conquered France, reconciled with the Third Reich or submitting to it, would no longer have a place for the Jews."[57]

Two other prominent French Jews, Minister of the Interior Georges Mandel and the future prime minister, deputy Pierre Mendes France (1907–82), tried to continue the struggle against the Germans from North Africa by joining other government officials sailing on the *Massilia* on June 21. Both men were immediately arrested—like Léon Blum, not as Jews but as political offenders. And like other leaders of the Third Republic, they were tried for treason by the new Vichy authorities. Mendes France ultimately escaped and succeeded in joining de Gaulle.[58] Mandel was less fortunate. Transferred to Buchenwald with Léon Blum and some others, he was returned to Paris in July 1944 and turned over to the French *Milice,* an elite paramilitary force of fanatic Fascist volunteers. On July 7, in the forests of Fontainebleau, he was murdered by machine-gun fire in the back.[59]

Also among those trying to escape the Germans at the end of June 1940 was the future wife of Isaiah Berlin, Aline Strauss (née de Gunzbourg), then a young widow with a three-year-old child, a mother from a well established and highly integrated French Jewish family, and a Russian-born naturalized Jewish father. The task was daunting, and she did not initially succeed. She remained peacefully in unoccupied France until October, when the racial laws were decreed. The laws convinced her and her parents that they had to leave France.

Hoping to leave legally, Aline Strauss wrestled with government bureaucracies for weeks. Her top priority was to obtain entry visas to the United States for herself and her family—a supremely difficult challenge, for few such visas were being issued at the time. She also needed to secure French passports for herself and her family, transit visas through Spain and Portugal, French exit visas, and proof of ship passage. The entire process was complicated by endless bureaucratic obstruction and by the intricate time frame involved. Visas were often valid for only a limited period, and by the time they were all in place, a ship might well have sailed. Miraculously enough, Aline Strauss finally succeeded. She left France with her son in January 1941; her parents, to avoid giving the impression of a family exodus, followed three months later.[60]

Legal emigration from France was immensely difficult and expensive in 1940 and 1941. Illegal emigration was dangerous and often physically impossible for the very young, the old, and the infirm. Still, it may seem surprising that more did not leave legally while it was still possible, or illegally while frontier patrols were less frequent and punishments less deadly. Foreign Jews, with fewer ties and illusions and in greater danger of immediate internment, tried more readily than French Jews but had more difficulties with documents and money. Many, without money, connections, or even the ability to speak French, could not even hope to try.

French Jews more often had a choice but did not try. On the contrary, Aline Strauss recalls that her mother's French Jewish relatives were highly critical of her decision to leave, viewing it as an unpatriotic abandoning of France. They insisted on staying in France and in their own homes, and several were subsequently deported.[61] Their decisions in 1940 and 1941, however, must be examined not with the knowledge of subsequent events but in the context in which they were made. Most French Jews, while disillusioned and greatly inconvenienced by the Vichy regime, at least trusted in its willingness to protect them. Most believed, with Marc Bloch and Joseph Kessel, that it was better to be uncomfortable in their own country than comfortable in a strange and alien land. Most surely agreed with Emmanuel Berl, who later recalled, "The anti-Semitic movement . . . did not surprise me. Of course, I did not think that it would go as far as it did. And besides, we didn't ask ourselves too many questions. One lived from day to day."[62] Until it was too late.

3

Racial Laws, 1940–1941

THE FIRST GERMAN TROOPS TO OCCUPY NORTHERN FRANCE BEHAVED with courtesy and restraint. Denise Baumann, a nineteen-year-old university student who would ultimately lose her entire family at Auschwitz, wrote of the German soldiers in her diary that first summer: "What difference is there between them and other lads when they play on the beach, when they go swimming?"[1] The historian Léon Poliakov, then a thirty-year-old Russian Jewish immigrant in France, agreed, recalling later about those early days, "Although sad, made ugly by the uniforms and the white posters of the occupier, life in Paris appeared normal. We didn't even worry about the Jews. The Germans had been 'correct'; there had been no massacres nor pogroms."[2] Lisa Fittko's elderly German Jewish parents, who remained for a year in their home in Paris, also assured their daughter in the unoccupied zone that the Germans were invariably polite. Fittko commented wryly, "One clung to this image, because it helped make life under the occupation bearable."[3]

Henry Bulawko, a Jewish immigrant, Resistance activist, and survivor of Auschwitz, was equally confident in the beginning.

The fear and panic of the first days soon changed into an uneasy quiet. The Germans were "correct," as the posters and collaborationist press told us at the time. Their anti-Semitism seemed purely verbal.

We regained courage. We even went so far as to hassle the sellers of the anti-Semitic newspaper *Le Pilori* in the Place de la Republique. . . . Twice we chased out the little urchins who came to sell it in the well-known Jewish quarter.[4]

With the renewal of confidence, many Jews came back to homes and businesses in the occupied zone until their return was prohibited by a German ordinance on September 27. Philippe Erlanger even observed that many returned to Paris because growing anti-Semitism in the unoccupied zone so disturbed them that they decided to take their chances with the Nazis and try to resume normal lives.[5] One who returned, twenty-two-year-old Emmanuel Ewenczyk, born in Poland but naturalized in 1938, later remarked, "The non-Jews saw the situation more clearly than the Jews, and were very surprised that the Jews came back."[6] His own friends insisted that he leave again, and by the end of 1940 he did. But many remained.

The Germans had indeed been "correct" that first summer, but signs of future behavior were there for those who wished to see. Anti-Semitic propaganda on Nazi-controlled radio networks in occupied France began immediately. In July, the Germans expelled into unoccupied France thousands of Jews from annexed departments in Alsace and Lorraine—remnants of the prewar community who had not already been evacuated in September 1939 or fled west in May 1940.[7] Irène B. later recalled that she and her family in Ingwiller (Bas-Rhin) were given forty-five minutes to prepare one suitcase per person, and were then driven in trucks through town for hours on Bastille Day, July 14, for all to see their humiliation. The next day they were driven to the demarcation line and dumped on the other side.[8] In a similar action on August 8, German police drove another 1,400 German Jewish refugees across the demarcation line from Bordeaux into the unoccupied zone, where the French immediately interned them at Saint-Cyprien.

The casual observer, however, probably first noticed anti-Semitism as it occurred, apparently spontaneously, among the French themselves. A. Honig recorded in his diary on July 30, 1940, that newspapers like the *Paris-Presse* and *L'Oeuvre,* which had castigated Germany for atrocities in Poland, including those against Jews, were now blaming Jews for France's troubles. Also in July, blue-shirted French Fascist militants began to picket Jewish shops in Paris and

put up anti-Semitic posters. By August, they and others were breaking windows. Honig noted that many Parisians were mouthing anti-
Semitic slogans in cafés, in restaurants, and in the streets. He believed that this was counter to the taste of most, but decided that
many ignored it out of naïveté or indifference.[9]

Although overt anti-Semitic acts were less visible in the unoccupied zone, the government at Vichy was not slow in making its antiforeign position known. On July 17, less than a week after it was
formed, it issued a law limiting employment in the public sector to
individuals born of French fathers.[10] The law was applicable, as
were all Vichy decrees, in both zones. Laws on August 16 and September 10 similarly regulated the practice of medicine and law, respectively.[11] On July 22, another measure authorized Minister of Justice Raphaël Alibert to establish a commission to review all grants of
French citizenship awarded under the liberalized law of August 10,
1927.[12] Within the next three years, the commission reviewed,
among others, the cases of 13,839 Jews, revoking the citizenship of
7,055.[13] On August 27, Alibert annulled the Daladier-Marchandeau
decree of April 21, 1939, which had prohibited attacks on individuals in the press based on race or religion. An anti-Semitic press, often
with covert Nazi funding, soon proliferated. Subsequent laws, on
September 3 and 27, gave prefects the power to intern individuals
considered dangerous to the national security, in the first case, and
all male immigrants between the ages of eighteen and fifty-five
who were judged to be "superfluous in the national economy" in the
second.[14]

Except for the revocation of the Daladier-Marchandeau decree,
these first government measures were aimed at foreigners in general,
including foreign Jews, rather than at Jews in particular. In addition
to anti-Semitism, the new laws reflected the national search for a
scapegoat for defeat and, as military demobilization returned thousands of former soldiers to the job market, popular concerns about
unemployment. Among the laws' victims, however, foreign Jews
were increasingly disproportionately represented as the months
passed.

Despite initial appearances of benevolence, the Germans in the occupied zone took the first official measures directed specifically
against Jews. An ordinance on September 27 began by defining who
was to be considered Jewish. It included anyone adhering or once adhering to the Jewish religion, or anyone with more than two Jewish
grandparents, as also determined by religious affiliation. In addition,

the ordinance prohibited Jews who had fled to the unoccupied zone from returning, called for a census of Jews in the occupied zone, demanded that the word *Juif* be stamped on identity cards, and required that Jewish shopkeepers place a yellow sign in two languages in their windows reading "*Enterprise juive*" and "*Judisches Geschäft*"—"Jewish Business." Honig noted in his diary on October 25 that the last measure had been obeyed, and he added sadly that other signs declaring "*Maison 100% française*" had also appeared, but freely, without duress.[15]

The German-decreed census was conducted in the occupied zone between October 3 and 19. In the Paris region, 149,734 Jews of all ages, including 85,664 citizens and 64,070 foreigners, officially registered their names, addresses, professions, and places of birth at local police headquarters and received the requisite stamp, "*Juif*."[16] An estimated 10 percent ignored the census. The reasons for this overwhelming response are elusive. Obviously, many Jews had no choice. Observant members of a particular synagogue, well-known public figures (like Philippe Erlanger or Henri Bergson), individuals with recognizable Jewish names such as Blum, Bloch, Weill, Cohen, Rothschild, or Lévy, and visibly orthodox, Yiddish-speaking immigrants could not escape registration. But in a country where religion had not been recorded in census data since 1872, many nonobservers had not been regarded as Jews for generations. They could easily have hidden their identities.

David Lemberger, age fifty in 1940, had immigrated to Paris in 1936. At the time of the Jewish census, he went promptly to register his entire family. Probably he had no choice. He undoubtedly spoke French with an accent, and he had perhaps recorded his Jewishness in earlier official documents. As he waited in line to register, he overheard the exchange between the census taker and the man in front of him—a dignified elderly French man wearing the rosette of the Legion of Honor. The man declared that his name was "Dubois Pierre" and added that he was Jewish. The census worker paused and finally asked, "But, with a name like that . . . do you really want to declare yourself as a Jew?" Without hesitation, the old man replied, "It is the law, *Monsieur le Commissaire.*"[17]

Even those with foreign-sounding names often had a real alternative. As Léon Poliakov later remembered, "My family name ended in 'ov,' my birth certificate was in Leningrad and I had no enemies. Therefore, impossible for the Germans to verify my racial affiliation."[18] According to Maurice Rajsfus, his Polish Jewish parents in

suburban Vincennes, who had never attended religious observances
and had a typically Polish name, could also have ignored the census.[19] And so could the parents of Denise Baumann in Paris, French
refugees from the war in eastern France, unknown in their new community, non-observant, and with no revealing name.[20] Yet Dubois,
Poliakov, the Rajsfuses, and the Baumanns registered, as did thousands of others like them. Why?

Erlanger, who admitted that he was too well known as a Jew to ignore the law, recorded that "many others for whom it would have
been easy to camouflage themselves did not think of it." He went on
to ponder "the submission of the majority of the Jews, their fatalism
in the face of their eternal unhappiness."[21] Poliakov explained his
own obedience not as fatalism but as "a characteristic mixture of op-
posing motivations: the refusal to deny my origins on the one hand,
the habit of obeying the law on the other."[22] His explanation applied
to many. The refusal to deny origins was linked to a widespread re-
vival of pride in the Jewish heritage during a period of persecution.
The habit of obeying the law was an equally understandable characteristic among educated and patriotic middle-class people who had
always taken pride in their good citizenship. It was an especially
strong habit among Jews in France who had discovered that the law
offered reliable protection.

Foreign Jews who had acquired a suspicion of authority and of
non-Jews in general in their countries of origin were more ready to
disobey the law than their French coreligionists. In this, they often
shared the prevailing mentality of their former non-Jewish countrymen. A Russian friend of Poliakov reminded him that, "in my village, when the statistical services tried to take a census, the peasants,
knowing that nothing good could come of it, hid in the woods. I beg
of you, follow their example."[23] Such thinking was alien to French
Jews, and to Jews who would be French.

Linked to the desire to obey the law, of course, was a real fear of
the consequences of disobedience. Coming so early in the occupation, at a time when the Germans still seemed benevolent, the census
could appear benign. The possibility of denunciation and punishment for disobedience was more frightening, and no Jewish leaders,
including Communists, advised their people to ignore the census.
Such attitudes necessarily altered with time, but even as late as the
summer of 1942, most Jews persisted in believing that as long as they
obeyed every regulation, their law-abiding society would spare them.

With regard to the census, they were wrong. Census data formed the basis of the lists used during all future roundups for deportation. Census data provided addresses, since subsequent moves or travel became illegal without special permission and registration. Census data recorded national origins, essential when police were composing lists of specific nationalities for a particular roundup. The Rajsfuses, the Baumanns, and thousands like them were arrested two or three years later at the addresses they had given the French police in 1940, and deported to their deaths at Auschwitz.

Individuals and families who might have lived out the war undetected as Jews became permanent targets as soon as they registered. They could not subsequently escape persecution without giving up everything and going underground. Half-measures to elude detection became hazardous. False documents and unregistered residences became essential for survival. Most Jews eventually entered the shady world of illegality, but they did so with great personal reluctance and fear. Those who did not rarely survived.

On October 3, 1940, less than three months after the establishment of the new Vichy regime and just six days after the first German anti-Jewish ordinance in the occupied zone, Pétain's government decreed its first *Statut des Juifs.* The timing suggests that the statute had been in preparation well before the publication of the German decrees. The surprising priority awarded the "Jewish question" cannot be explained as a result of direct German pressure. Even Henri du Moulin de Labarthète, Pétain's private secretary at the time, later admitted, "Germany was not at the origin of the anti-Jewish legislation of Vichy. This legislation was, if I dare say it, spontaneous, native."[24] It seems to have come from the government's desire to present a demoralized public with a visible scapegoat for defeat, from a wish to preempt German regulation of the issue, and from the prejudices of Pétain himself. In his journal entry for October 1, 1940, Foreign Minister Paul Baudouin wrote of the Council of Ministers meeting that day at which the statute was discussed: "It was the Marshal who was the most severe. He insisted particularly that the Justice and Education [Ministries] should contain no Jews."[25]

The law of October 3 actually broadened the German definition of who was Jewish, as it applied in the occupied zone, to include anyone with just two grandparents "of Jewish race" who was also married to a Jew.[26] In addition to the definition, the law specifically excluded Jews from public service, the officer corps of the armed forces, teaching, journalism, the theater, radio, and cinema. Exemptions for some positions might be granted, on special application, to Jewish war veterans and individuals of outstanding merit. Just how outstanding the merit had to be is demonstrated by the fact that of 125 Jewish university professors (of a total of about 4,000 in the country) who applied for exemptions based on their academic and/or military records, only 10 had been exempted by January 1941.[27] Just a few more received exemptions later.

The day following the first Statut des Juifs, a second law specifically authorized prefects to intern, assign to supervised residence, or enroll in forced labor any foreign Jews in their departments, as they saw fit.[28] Another on October 7 deprived the roughly 115,000 Jews of Algeria of the citizenship granted them by the Crémieux decree in 1870.[29] That measure prompted an anguished Raymond-Raoul Lambert to record in his diary on October 9, "The Marshal has been dishonored. What shame and what infamy! A father in Algeria who has lost his son in the war is, because he is Jewish, no longer a French citizen."[30] Then on October 25, the minister of war, among the first to enforce the statute of October 3, removed from the army not only Jewish officers, as required, but enlisted men as well.

It is difficult to exaggerate the devastating impact of the racial laws, particularly on French Jews who had considered themselves so profoundly French. Raymond-Raoul Lambert confided in his diary on October 19, "I wept last night like a man who has been suddenly abandoned by the woman who has been the only love of his life, the only guide of his thoughts, the only inspiration of his actions."[31] Nineteen-year-old Claude Vigée read of the new laws at a newspaper kiosk in Toulouse that same day and later remembered: "It seemed to me that I had been struck by a blow straight to my heart. I have never forgotten, I will never forget that moment. It managed to divide my life into two irreconcilable parts: that of confidence, and that of doubt and abandonment."[32]

Georges Friedmann, who, as seen, had not suffered from anti-Semitism before the war, despite his name, and who had never attended a synagogue service or met a rabbi, spoke for hundreds of others when he recalled the shock of receiving the official notification of dismissal as a university professor in Paris:

I was thrown out of my profession as if I were unworthy to exercise it and condemned to unemployment with other similarly placed members of the French community to whom I had not felt myself bound by any particular tie. Both intellectually and emotionally this was a shattering blow. For some weeks, in spite of the support of my friends, I was shaken to the core; the very foundations of my being trembled.[33]

Similarly, Frédéric Hammel, by then a university chemistry professor at Clermont-Ferrand, remembered receiving a dismissal notice, "without a personal word." He went on to describe the reaction of his colleagues:

> My professor of General Physics expresses his sadness in the most neutral manner and with the courtesy which is characteristic of him. The Dean [of the Faculty of Sciences], who was a close friend of my Patron, has neither a word of regret nor of thanks. He barely shakes my hand to tell me that our interview is over before it has begun. I will never have an explanation of that very disappointing attitude.

Hammel had one pleasant surprise, however, when another professor, who "had nothing of the hero and was politically rather rightwing," bade him farewell publicly, in front of a group of thirty students, and added that, "for him, the Jews are French like the others and . . . he bitterly regrets that the '*Statut*' is depriving the university of my services."[34]

Few non-Jews were so courageous; there were few public protests. On the contrary, public demonstrations of approval were frequent. Pierre Weill Raynal's father Étienne, for example, previously a popular history teacher at the Lycée Voltaire, was booed and insulted when forced to leave. Raynal himself later recalled that in the endless discussions of the racial laws between professors and students at his own lycée, Louis-le-Grand, most people justified the new legislation. However, Raynal, like Frédéric Hammel, did remember some teachers who discreetly showed sympathy.[35] Raymond-Raoul Lambert received a touching letter of sympathy from his former commanding officer.[36] Dr. Robert Debré, as seen, received a promotion by unanimous vote. But few expressions of support were so public.

Leaders of the Christian churches remained equally silent. Not a single Catholic bishop and only one regular priest—the Jesuit Father Gaston Fessard, during a sermon at the Church of Saint Louis in Vichy in December 1940—publicly protested the racial laws of October 3. Among Protestant clergy, Pastor Marc Boegner, president of the National Protestant Federation, did more, writing private letters of protest on March 26, 1941, to Grand Rabbi of France Isaïe

Schwartz and to Admiral François Darlan, the vice-prime minister.[37] But even Boegner admitted in his letters the existence of a "massive immigration problem" and asked only for a reform of the statutes. Also, his protest was intended to remain private. The letter to the grand rabbi became public inadvertently and was published in the anti-Semitic journal *Le Pilori* in an attempt, not entirely successful, to embarrass the pastor.[38]

Indeed, Jews themselves rarely protested the racial statutes publicly. Almost no one followed the example of Lucien Vidal-Naquet, who, according to Raymond Aron, "protested publicly, they told me, in front of the *Palais de Justice,* defying his colleagues who were passively applying the Vichy ordinances."[39] Equally few followed the opposite step, as exemplified by a Jewish professor who publicly declared that the racial laws had no great importance and that he would never protest them in order not to add to the confusion reigning in France.[40] Most Jews regarded the laws as of earth-shattering importance but either suffered in silence or wrote dignified private letters of protest. One outstanding example of the latter was Pierre Masse, a former deputy, senator, and cabinet minister who, upon learning that Jews could no longer serve as officers in the French army, wrote a scathing letter to Marshal Pétain. The letter said in part:

> I would be grateful if you could inform me whether I must take away the military stripes from my brother, a second lieutenant in the 36th infantry regiment, killed at Douaumont, in April 1916; from my son-in-law, a second lieutenant in the 14th regiment of *dragons portés,* killed in Belgium, in May 1940; from my nephew, J.-F. Masse, lieutenant in the 23rd colonial, killed at Rethel, in May 1940.
>
> May I leave with my brother the military medal won at Neuville-Saint-Vast, with which I buried him? My son Jacques, second lieutenant in the 62nd battalion of Alpine *chasseurs,* wounded at Soupir, in June 1940, may he keep his stripes?
>
> Am I in fact assured that the medal of Saint Helen will not be taken away from my great-grandfather?[41]

Tragically, Pierre Masse's part in the story of the persecution of Jews in France did not end with his letter. He and his brother Roger, a colonel of the artillery and a veteran of both wars who had lost his son in combat in 1940, were among the 743 French Jewish men arrested in their homes in Paris on December 12, 1941. This was the same early German-conducted reprisal raid against Jewish citizens that had netted René Blum. At the age of sixty-two, Pierre Masse was deported from Drancy to Auschwitz on September 30, 1942, where he was gassed upon arrival.[42] Fifty-seven-year-old Roger preceded him on June 5, in the second convoy to leave France for the death camp. Regular mass gassings had not yet begun at Auschwitz, so he was admitted. He soon died from deprivation.[43]

The months that followed the first Statut des Juifs witnessed a long series of anti-Jewish regulations from both the Germans and the French. On October 18, the Germans published a second ordinance for the occupied zone, requiring Jews to declare their possessions at police headquarters and establishing a system for nominating "temporary administrators" of Jewish businesses for the purpose of selling them to non-Jews or liquidating them. Also in October, a specially constituted *Einsatzstab* under the direction of Alfred Rosenberg in Germany began the systematic pillage of Jewish homes and the confiscation, among other items, of scores of private art collections. On April 26, 1941, another German ordinance added to the Vichyite list of occupations prohibited to Jews all employment in hotels, insurance, navigation and transport, travel agencies, banks and other financial institutions, real estate, schools, and numerous other fields involving contact with the public at large.

The French response to the German ordinances was prompt. Soon after the October 18 property decree, the Vichy government set up the Service de contrôle des administrateurs provisoires (SCAP) to ensure that all "temporary administrators" of Jewish businesses in the occupied zone would be French and to enforce the Aryanization provisions quickly in order to preempt German interference. On March 29, 1941, a French law created the Commissariat général aux questions juives (CGQJ), a government bureau of Jewish affairs.[44] The Germans had requested such an agency for the occupied zone, but Vichy officials, ever anxious about questions of sovereignty and unity of administration, extended it to both zones. Then on July 22, the French government voluntarily extended the German program of economic expropriation of Jewish property, both French and foreign owned, to the unoccupied zone.[45]

Under the leadership of Xavier Vallat, the first commissioner of the CGQJ, the Vichy regime produced a second Statut des Juifs on June 2, 1941, replacing that of October 3, 1940.[46] Addressing the thorny question of who was to be considered Jewish, the new statute came up with a slightly different solution. As before, it declared that anyone with three grandparents "of the Jewish race" was Jewish regardless of possible conversion, as was anyone with two Jewish grandparents who was married to someone similarly half Jewish.[47] It then added that a person with two Jewish grandparents was, despite his spouse, also to be considered Jewish unless he could produce a baptismal certificate dated before June 25, 1940. By refusing recognition of nonconfessional status in cases of individuals with two Jewish grandparents, this new definition encompassed many more children of mixed marriages and exceeded that of the Nazis, who defined a Jew as one with three Jewish grandparents and classified individuals with two Jewish grandparents but no personal Jewish affiliations as *Mischling*. Overnight, many who had been exempt from the racial laws lost their rights.

The new law also extended the list of private occupations prohibited to Jews to coincide more or less with that issued by the Germans on April 26. It broadened exemption policies slightly for some positions by extending the possibility to individuals who could prove five generations of French ancestry and past family service. Finally, the statute declared that prefects could intern French Jews as well as foreigners and required a census of Jews in the unoccupied zone. As a result, about 140,000 Jews obediently delivered written declarations of their identity, profession, and possessions to their respective prefects.[48] Unlike Jews in the occupied zone, however, Jews in the south were not required to receive a "*Juif*" stamp on their identification cards until December 1942, a month after the German occupation of the southern zone.

A series of subsequent Vichy decrees affected thousands of Jewish students and professionals. Throughout France, Jews could no longer be publishers or editors. Jewish writers could have their work published only with special authorization. Jewish painters could not exhibit their work at the Salon d'automne. The production of plays by Jewish authors and the playing of music by Jewish composers was strongly discouraged and reduced to a minimum on the radio. A law of June 21, 1941, imposed a *numerus clausus* of 3 percent on Jewish university students.[49] On July 16, 1941, a similar decree placed a limitation of 2 percent on Jewish lawyers admitted to the bar.[50] In Paris alone, an estimated 250 people were removed and only 47 were retained.[51] Then on August 11, the same provision was applied to Jewish doctors.[52] At least 726 eventually closed their offices in Paris, and fewer than 200 continued to practice.[53]

The racial laws of 1941 were greeted with the same public silence as those of 1940. The French remained, for the most part, indifferent. Most had other problems. They worried about the one and a half million French prisoners of war in Nazi Germany—fathers, brothers, husbands, and sons who had been expected home after the armistice but who now seemed unlikely to be freed. They worried about scarce food, clothing, and fuel supplies, inadequate transportation and communications, job security, the formidable demarcation line, which often divided families, and the increasingly hostile behavior of the German occupier. If they were at all disposed to think of others, they focused on the troubles of friends or neighbors, war widows and orphans, or, in rare cases among people of goodwill, the indigent in general. Official censorship deprived them of information about specifically Jewish hardships, while the anti-Semitic press continually reminded them of the "Jewish problem."

Among churchmen, however, consciences were beginning to stir. The indefatigable Pastor Boegner wrote two more private letters of protest, this time to Pétain himself, during the summer of 1941. He also encouraged Pierre Cardinal Gerlier, the Catholic archbishop of Lyon and primate of the Gauls, to deliver to the Marshal in September a similar private note protesting the second racial statute. Meanwhile, about fifteen young Protestant pastors and social workers met in September at Pomeyrol, near Tarascon (Bouches-du-Rhône), to discuss the role and responsibilities of the Church under the current circumstances. They adopted a manifesto of eight theses. Thesis 7 raised "a solemn protest against any statute rejecting the Jews," and thesis 8 declared that the Protestant churches "considered resistance to any totalitarian and idolatrous influence to be a spiritual necessity."[54] A group of conservative pastors prevented the manifesto from becoming official Protestant policy in France, but the document circulated among the faithful and began to make an impression.

Among Catholics, too, there were stirrings. In June, four professors of theology at Lyon, Fathers Joseph Chaine, Louis Richard, Joseph Bonsirven, and Henri de Lubac, prepared a text condemning the racial laws. While it never received official approval, the document nevertheless began to circulate in the region. In July in Paris, Father Riquet delivered a note to the Assembly of Cardinals and Archbishops asking that it condemn the racial laws as "a scandal for the Christian conscience as well as a defiance of the French intelligence." The assembly not only rejected his request but issued a call for "a sincere and complete loyalty to the established power."[55] The Church hierarchy had its own agenda of benefits expected from the new conservative regime and had no intention of jeopardizing it through political criticism. But on an individual level, discomfort with the racial laws was growing.

As one of the final anti-Jewish measures of 1941, the Vichy government on November 29 announced the establishment of a national Jewish council called the Union générale des Israélites de France (UGIF), with separate branches in the northern and southern zones.[56] The measure, a response to a German ultimatum for such a council in the occupied zone, had been evolving throughout the year. Toward the end of 1940, SS Captain Theodor Dannecker, chief of the Gestapo's Jewish Office (Judenreferat) in France, had begun demanding that Jewish charitable organizations in the occupied zone come together under a single coordinating committee. The result was the creation in Paris on January 30, 1941, of the Comité de coordination des oeuvres de bienfaisance du Grand Paris (Coordination Committee of Jewish Relief Organizations). Most local French and immigrant Jewish relief groups affiliated with the committee to avoid dissolution. It was superseded by UGIF in November.

Under the Vichy measure, UGIF membership became compulsory for *all* Jews in France, both French and foreign. The organization technically replaced all existing agencies except purely religious associations and assumed their assets. UGIF's role and structure developed gradually and separately in the northern and southern zones and altered considerably during the course of the occupation. Generally speaking, however, UGIF-North remained legal to the end, operating openly and meeting most German demands. Structurally the successor of the Parisian Coordination Committee, and led primarily by French Jews, it lacked roots among Jewish immigrants and Communists who might have pushed it more firmly into clandestine activity. Physically, also, it remained in Paris, easily accessible to pressure from Nazi anti-Jewish agents.

Until the Liberation, UGIF-North supplied desperately needed food, cooked meals, clothing, medical care, and financial subsidies to indigent Jewish families, literally keeping them alive but inadvertently hindering their perception of their precarious status and security. It also operated hospitals, old-age homes, and orphanages for Jews who could not use "Aryan" facilities. Much less positively, UGIF-North delivered tons of food and clothing to prisoners at Drancy and deportees bound for Auschwitz—material that eventually fell into German hands—and took elaborate measures to ensure that prisoners released from Drancy for temporary care in its medical and social institutions did not escape. Unlike some Jewish Councils (*Judenräte*) in East Europe, which operated under far greater pressure, it never directly selected individuals for internment and deportation. On the other hand, it rarely warned Jews of raids it knew to be in preparation, furnished information about the consequences of deportation, or advised people to hide. It discouraged its component agencies, not always successfully, from engaging in clandestine rescue activities. It provided little leadership, imagination, or wisdom to a community desperately in need. Its wartime role was and remains a subject of enormous controversy.[57]

Throughout the occupation, UGIF-South remained far more independent of German control, more loosely organized, and more deeply rooted in the Jewish community as a whole than UGIF-North. Although most of the largest prewar Jewish social service agencies were legally dissolved throughout the country in the spring and summer of 1942, they were preserved by being incorporated with little alteration into UGIF-South and permitted to function autonomously under different names. Thus, they were able to maintain structural and financial integrity and continue prewar social services under a legal cover.[58] As will be seen, that relative autonomy and legal cover also allowed some agencies to drift more and more completely into clandestine and illegal rescue work after August 1942, even while UGIF-South remained officially committed to strict obedience to the law.

Like their counterparts in the north, leaders of UGIF-South who opted for a strict legality were severely criticized after the war. While they offered social services that were indispensable to indigent families, they also kept offices open where many clients and employees were arrested, maintained lists of names and addresses liable to German seizure, and created false illusions of normality. The criticism is legitimate—mistakes were made, and leadership was often uncertain and misguided. Raymond-Raoul Lambert, the director of UGIF-South, seems never to have understood that the Nazis intended to deport *all* Jews in France, and that any deals or concessions obtained were therefore temporary. But despite the intentions of some leaders, and with the eventual tacit agreement of others, the UGIF cover provided its component parts with the time and the funds needed to define a new clandestine role. In that new role, the component parts rescued several thousand Jews in need of help.

4

Internment Camps in the Unoccupied Zone, 1940–1941

Among the saddest tales in the tragic history of internees in unoccupied France in 1940 is the saga of 6,538 German Jews expelled by the Nazis from their homes in Baden-Wurttemburg, including the cities of Mannheim, Karlsruhe, Heidelberg, Fribourg-en-Brisgau, and Constance, at 7:00 on the morning of October 22.[1] Men, women, and children, many either very young or very old, were given only a few minutes to prepare a maximum of two bags each before they were carted off to congested assembly points and then to local railroad stations. Crowded into seven special trains, they were sent off on a forty-eight-hour trip to the southwestern corner of unoccupied France. Theirs and the simultaneous expulsion of 1,125 Jews to France from the Palatinate and the Saar were the only wartime Nazi deportations to the *west*.[2]

The Baden Jews disembarked at Oloron-Sainte-Marie, thirty-three kilometers southwest of Pau in the Pyrenees, on the night of October 24. In a frigid autumn rainstorm, they were loaded onto trucks for the ten-kilometer journey to Gurs. Originally an internment center for refugees from the Spanish Civil War, Gurs had held 9,771 female enemy aliens and their children, 3,695 Spaniards, and 1,329 French political dissenters during the summer of 1940. All but about 3,309 of these had been released or transferred, however, before the arrival of the Jews from Baden, and many of the others left before the end of the year.[3]

After the war, the president of the Jewish community of Mannheim described his group's arrival:

> Soaked by the rain, shivering with cold, exhausted by the long voyage, the flock was pushed in indescribable disorder into empty barracks, without benches, without straw, without mattresses. Collapsed against their bundles, many old people spent the night. Barracks 25 meters long and 5 meters wide . . . would shelter, during the long months ahead, 75 women or 80 men, according to the haphazard distribution of that first night.[4]

Hastily built on a barren, windswept plateau, Gurs was a forbidding place. The American Young Men's Christian Association (YMCA) representative, Donald Lowrie, later described it as surrounded by "two eight-foot barbed wire fences, fifteen feet apart, with armed guards patrolling between the rows of wire. Atop the fence at a dozen places were weather-beaten wooden towers where watchmen were stationed at night."[5] A horrified internee who arrived in September 1940 added, "The double rows of barbed wire encircled a sea of mud, itself surrounded by infinite rows of barracks . . . not a tree, scarcely a few tufts of grass." He concluded, "If Auschwitz was hell, Gurs was surely purgatory."[6] A non-Jewish French pacifist and political prisoner at Gurs for a short time wrote of it: "The camp had been set up on swampy ground which was transformed into a sewer when it rained. I remember remaining eighteen days without being able to step outside, I would have sunk in up to my stomach. We built a bridge of boards to reach the WC's."[7]

The internment of the Jews from Baden was the predictable response of harassed bureaucrats. The deportees were without resources, contacts, or visible means of support. They had no valid passports, visas, or identification cards; no way to obtain ration cards; and no legal right to work or even live in France. And they were, after all, former citizens of a former enemy country—Germans, additionally stigmatized as Jews. They could not, thought security-minded officials, be allowed to wander about freely. Unoccupied France was in disarray. Hundreds of thousands of refugees from northern France, including well over 100,000 French and foreign Jews, were looking for homes and work and competing with demobilized soldiers in the process. Many were destitute and desperate. The new arrivals were another headache, conveniently solved by Vichy's new law of October 4 authorizing prefects to intern any foreign Jews in their departments, as they saw fit. Bureaucrats seized the opportunity.

With regard to the Jews from Baden, the crime of the Vichy regime was not primarily their initial internment—as seen, thousands of other foreign Jewish and non-Jewish refugees without documents or money had preceded them. The most serious crimes lay elsewhere. First, although they were interned provisionally as enemy nationals, it soon became evident that they would be held permanently as *Jews*. In early July 1941, Admiral François Darlan, in his capacity as minister of the interior, sent a circular to all prefects that read in part, "I have decided that no foreigner of the Israelite race will henceforth be freed from lodging or internment centers if he did not live in France before May 10, 1940. . . . The same applies to foreigners in the [forced] worker companies."[8] Thus, most of the Jews from Baden, along with the Jewish (but only the Jewish) refugees who had fled from the German army in Belgium, were sentenced to remain where they were, regardless of their past histories as anti-Nazis, their ability to support themselves, or the existence of free family members who might help. Darlan, anxious to get Jewish refugees out of France, emphasized that repatriation or other forms of emigration were to be encouraged, but not freedom within France. Vichy officials never bothered to facilitate "other emigration," but when "repatriation" became possible—when the Nazis called for the expulsions of foreign Jews from the unoccupied zone in August 1942 for deportation to the east—foreign Jews still in internment camps were the first victims. Vichy officials asked few questions about the purpose of repatriation.

In addition, foreign Jews in internment camps in the unoccupied zone suffered under appalling conditions of neglect and deprivation—conditions that revealed not mere bureaucratic indifference but active and deliberate ill will. About 3,000 Jews died in the camps. They were the first casualties of the Holocaust in France, and they died because of French, not German, persecution.[9]

As a result of the Darlan circular, only 1,710 of the 21,794 people who passed through Gurs from October 24, 1940, to November 1943 were officially released to live in France or return to their countries of origin.[10] Another 755 successfully escaped, and 1,940 were able to leave the camp after assembling the documents necessary for emigration.[11] Men planning to emigrate were sent to the camp at Les Milles, near Aix-en-Provence, to await their ship; women were placed in the detention hotels in Marseille. Of the 1,940, 30 percent (580) ultimately failed to leave France and were returned to Gurs.[12]

In addition, 2,820 able-bodied men were transferred from Gurs to the forced-labor units run by the French government. Many of them were later transferred to the Todt Organization, where they worked directly for the Germans. Finally, 1,950 internees, mostly women, children, and elderly, went temporarily, with internees from other camps, to more comfortable but still supervised centers called *centres d'accueil*.[13] These men, women, and children remained under government jurisdiction until August 1942, when many were called back to Gurs for expulsion to the occupied zone. That some avoided returning and deportation was due not to the politicians in Vichy but to the clandestine interference of some civilians, both Jewish and non-Jewish, with government policy.

Meanwhile, conditions at Gurs barely supported life. Again statistics tell the sorry tale. In October 1940, the 6,538 deportees of Baden were among the least prepared candidates for internment. Mostly from hard-working and law-abiding urban middle classes, they had remained in their homes in Germany until the bitter end and thus had no practical or psychological preparation for their coming ordeal. More than 60 percent were women; 39.2 percent were over sixty, and 9.7 percent were over seventy-five.[14] They were thrust into a camp totally unprepared to receive them, at the beginning of what was to be the coldest winter of the war. Barracks were filthy, unlighted, and overcrowded, with leaking roofs, sealed windows, rats, lice, and fleas. Food and medicine were inadequate. Of the 6,538 people, 820, or 12.5 percent, eventually died at Gurs, compared with an overall death rate among the total of 21,794 who passed through from October 1940 to November 1943 of about 4 percent. About 62 percent of the total of 1,038 victims there died during the first winter of the occupation, from starvation and exposure.[15] They still lie in the cemetery at Gurs.

Even in that first winter, there were some men and women who cared. Madeleine Barot was the indomitable young secretary-general of CIMADE (Comité inter-mouvements auprès des évacués), a Protestant youth group organized in September 1939 initially to assist residents of Alsace and Lorraine evacuated from the war zone by the French government. She gained access to Gurs as early as May 1940, set up a residence in a small barracks, and brought in a much needed nurse, Jeanne Merle d'Aubigné. Together the two women organized a relief agency called Secours protestant, funded by international Protestant charities.[16] Other groups soon followed. Secours suisse arrived on December 20, 1940, with more dedicated nurses and with milk for children and pregnant women.[17] The Société des Amis des Quakers américains (American Friends Service Committee), known familiarly as the Secours Quaker, began work on December 28, 1940, with a large distribution of beans, rice, lentils, lard, and other urgently needed foodstuffs.[18] Yet the situation remained desperate. Jeanne Merle d'Aubigné later wrote of thirty deaths a day from hunger during the winter of 1940–41; of men and women dying of typhoid on the floor of the quarantine barracks, without medicine or beds; and of a man walking in front of her one day who simply fell over and died of hunger.[19]

Jewish relief organizations in France had been profoundly disrupted by the great exodus from north to south in the summer of 1940, by the dispersion of personnel and the destruction of lists of clients for security reasons, and by the overwhelming and more visible need to assist thousands of Jewish refugees outside the camps. Rabbi René Kapel visited Gurs in November 1940, however, and immediately launched an effort to mobilize aid for the camp.[20] Under the impetus of Andrée Salomon, the Oeuvre de secours aux enfants (OSE), a child welfare organization, received permission to send a medical team in mid-February 1941.[21] At about the same time, Organisation pour la reconstruction et le travail (ORT), which specialized in job training, opened sewing workshops to teach a trade, help inmates clothe themselves, and fill the hours of adults and adolescents who had literally nothing to do.[22] HICEM, which worked to help Jews emigrate, also established a presence. Other groups and individuals, including especially Rabbi Kapel, brought spiritual comfort, much needed extra supplies, and cultural relief in the form of a library, a theatrical group, and schools for the children.

While Gurs was the largest internment camp for foreign Jews in the unoccupied zone, it was far from the only one. The others were so numerous that only a few can be mentioned here.[23] Saint-Cyprien, a few kilometers from Perpignan, held, among others, 7,500 German and Austrian Jewish and non-Jewish men who had fled from Belgium in May 1940 and been promptly arrested in France. Their women had been sent to Gurs.[24] The 1,400 German Jewish refugees expelled from Bordeaux in the occupied zone in early August were also sent to this forlorn strip of beach between a lagoon and the Mediterranean. The horrified Rabbi Kapel described it as "a veritable desert of sand."[25] Gret Arnoldsen, the Viennese refugee from Belgium, remembered it as "a hedge of barbed wire. . . . Behind it . . . extended the barracks, the rows of barbed wire, followed by more barbed wire, followed by still more."[26] Men lived at Saint-Cyprien in abominable conditions, in barracks with dirt floors and no electricity, without adequate food or medical care. The camp was, predictably, destroyed by storms and flooding in the autumn of 1940. The men were eventually moved to Gurs, where conditions, needless to say, did not improve.

Another large camp was Rivesaltes, ten kilometers from Perpignan in one of the most mosquito-infested regions of France. Originally also a camp for fugitives from the Spanish Civil War, Rivesaltes after May 1940 held enemy alien men, the male counterparts of the women at Gurs—the political, racial, economic, and mere tourist refugees caught in France when the German invasion began. In October, 1,125 Jews expelled from the Palatinate and the Saar in Germany at the same time as those from Baden were also interned there, as well as about 1,000 Spanish women and children transferred from Gurs. In the spring of 1941, 1,226 Jewish children and their parents from Gurs were also sent to Rivesaltes, along with others from the nearby camps of Argelès (Pyrénées-Orientales) and Agde (Hérault). At that point, Rivesaltes contained at least 3,000 children and was considered a family camp.[27] Its lack of fitness for children is seen from a contemporary description by the French Jewish social worker Vivette Samuel:

> The entire length of the barracks, on both sides, two levels of bunks separated . . . by old blankets, compartments where whole families milled about, father, mother, children, sometimes grandparents . . . in an undescribable promiscuity. It was dark, cold and humid and there was no heating. And seizing you by the throat upon entering, a bitter odor of human sweat which floats in this den which is never aired out.[28]

Mortality rates reflected conditions, for of a total of 140 babies at Rivesaltes, 60 died during a two and a half–month period.[29]

Other internment centers included Noé and Récébédou (both in

Haute-Garonne, not far from Toulouse), hospital-camps for the sick and elderly; Rieucros, with about 1,500 women in November 1940; Septfonds (Tarn-et-Garonne), with 1,000 demobilized volunteers from the Foreign Legion; Le Vernet, a "repressive camp" with 4,500 prisoners, of whom about 50 percent were foreign Jews; Les Milles, a holding camp for those awaiting emigration documents, with about 3,000 in November; and the above-mentioned Agde and Argelès.[30] Of all the camps, Noé received the most favorable descriptions. Gret Arnoldsen, who arrived there in February 1941, marveled at barracks that were sturdy and clean, walks of gravel rather than mud, and actual flower beds. Even the camp director seemed sympathetic. Arnoldsen wrote of him, "For the first time, we saw the hidden face of France, entirely unknown, that of its goodness."[31] But the director was soon replaced, and conditions deteriorated.[32] An individual could make a difference.

Intriguingly different was the *centre d'hébergement* (lodging center) of Brens (Tarn) near Gaillac, outside Toulouse. During the exodus in May and June 1940, the "rose-colored city" had received far more than its share of refugees, Jewish and non-Jewish alike, and had been hard-pressed to care for them. In October 1940, the Israelite Welfare Committee of Toulouse, coordinating local Jewish welfare agencies, actually requested and received permission from Vichy officials to open a camp at Brens, to feed and shelter destitute Jewish and other refugees. On November 20, 1940, there were 3,000 residents at Brens, of whom 65 percent were Jewish.[33] The camp had no barbed wire. Internees entered voluntarily and could come and go at will during the day. Private welfare agencies could focus their efforts more efficiently on refugees concentrated in one place, while government subsidies could also be obtained. Yet the line between shelter and internment camp was a fine one, and no one noticed when it was bridged. Brens was dissolved in March 1941. The old and sick were moved to Noé, where medical facilities were better. At least 793 Jewish children and their parents were moved, gently and humanely, to Rivesaltes, and other adults were sent to Gurs.[34] The objective was to continue services, not to imprison. But Rivesaltes and Gurs were surrounded by barbed wire, and inmates could not come and go at will. In August 1942, when the Germans demanded and received Jewish victims in unoccupied France for deportation, many who had voluntarily entered Brens were still in custody.

At these other camps, the efforts of private welfare agencies replicated those at Gurs. Madeleine Barot declares that CIMADE maintained two or three social workers—all young, unmarried, healthy, German-speaking, and usually female because of the fear of labor roundups for men—in about a dozen camps.[35] Secours suisse and Secours Quaker acted similarly. Catholic efforts would become important by the middle of 1941, especially because of the work of the well-known parish priest Abbé Alexandre Glasberg (1902–81) and the Jesuit Father Pierre Chaillet (1900–72), but remained minimal in this early period. Father Chaillet himself deplored, in a report, "the lack of Catholic charity" and appealed for change.[36]

On the other hand, specifically Jewish relief efforts were mobilized sooner than at Gurs. At Saint-Cyprien, the young Rabbi René Kapel, in nearby Toulouse awaiting demobilization as an army chaplain, visited inmates as early as August 2, 1940, while still in his captain's uniform. Appalled by what he saw, Kapel decided not to seek another rabbinical position but to devote himself to succoring unfortunate internees. He began by drawing the attention of Grand Rabbi Isaïe Schwartz to the suffering of fellow Jews and obtained, through him, 10,000 francs for hospital care at Saint-Cyprien. After taking representatives of the American Jewish Joint Distribution Committee to the camp, he convinced them to provide the Quakers with another 200,000 francs for clothes and blankets for Saint-Cyprien, Gurs, and Le Vernet.[37] More important than any single contribution was the fact that Kapel had sounded an alarm and provoked interest. Rabbi Henri Schilli soon drew similar attention to the camps of Agde and Argelès. OSE sent the first medical team into Agde in December 1940; ORT established workshops for the indigent at Brens about the same time. Sadly but effectively, the efforts of Jewish welfare agencies were significantly reinforced after the promulgation of the Vichy racial laws in October, for many competent trained professionals lost jobs elsewhere and looked for work among their coreligionists.

After October 1940, the camp activities of the major Jewish welfare agencies were coordinated within the Commission centrale des organisations juives d'assistance under the leadership of Grand Rabbi René Hirschler. A month later, the Jewish central commission met with various non-Jewish agencies working in the camps, such as CIMADE, the YMCA, the Quakers, various national branches of the Red Cross, the Secours suisse, the Service social d'aide aux émigrants (SSAE), the Unitarian Service Committee, the Rockefeller Foundation, and others, as well as with representatives of Pierre Cardinal Gerlier, the archbishop of Lyon, to form the Comité de coordination pour l'assistance dans les camps.[38] The American YMCA representative, Donald Lowrie, became the committee's president. Known familiarly as the Comité de Nîmes, from the city where meetings were held, the new coordinating agency was able to channel resources into the camps more efficiently. As Lowrie himself later explained, "As the anti-Semitic influence in Vichy became more dominant, there were frequent instances where Jewish organizations working alone were refused permission for new projects but where collaboration in the Committee made these possible."[39] With its international connections and consequent ability to embarrass France abroad, the committee was also able to pressure Vichy for concessions. It almost immediately obtained permission to establish small teams of medical and social workers in every camp, unhindered by personal and bureaucratic vagaries at the site. It later won other concessions, such as the right of internees to receive mail and packages, develop schools and workshops, meet with Protestant, Catholic, and Jewish chaplains, and protest against abusive camp personnel.

In the long run, perhaps the most significant work of the Committee of Nîmes involved the establishment of centres d'accueil, the supervised residences outside the camps where internees could live with greater comfort and dignity. The idea was first focused on children and was discussed in the monthly committee meetings in December 1940 and January 1941. Not all members were enthusiastic. In a debate revealing the absence of any sense of a danger of deportation, some argued that it would be more efficient and economical to direct the committee's limited financial resources toward improving conditions in the camps themselves, rather than toward establishing special homes outside for only a portion of the internees.[40] Others added that transferring the children would place a further burden on interned parents and increase general demoralization.

Under the leadership of its social service director, Andrée Salomon, and its medical advisor, Joseph Weill, however, the Jewish children's organization OSE pressed fiercely for the release, under supervision, of all children in the camps. OSE was already operating homes for orphaned, impoverished, and refugee children in the unoccupied zone, and such a release seemed logical. The question was ultimately resolved in OSE's favor. Representatives from the Committee of Nîmes negotiated successfully with Vichy delegates for permission and found three Vichy bureaucrats from the department of Hérault, Prefect Benedetti, Secretary-General Ernst, and an official named Fédérici, to sign the necessary local residence permits.[41]

Estimates of the number of children released from the camps vary, but it seems likely that as many as 2,800 may have found their way into supervised residences on the outside. According to the records of the Committee of Nîmes itself, at least 1,340 Jewish and non-Jewish children had been released by October 31, 1941. About half of these had been placed in the care of OSE; 500 had gone to the Polish Red Cross, 70 to 100 to the *Secours suisse,* and 70 to a Czechoslovakian welfare group.[42] About 2,100 children remained in the camps; 1,800 of these were in Rivesaltes.[43] By the end of May 1942, just three months before the expulsions of foreign Jews from the unoccupied zone began, only about 580 non-Jewish youngsters and few if any Jewish children under age fifteen remained in the camps.[44] They were often from families whose parents did not want them to be separated.

Children were not the only beneficiaries of the Committee of Nîmes's centres d'accueil program, however, for many social workers and organizations focused on the release of adults as well. One of the most outstanding individuals in this respect was Abbé Alexandre Glasberg, the colorful vicar of Notre-Dame in Saint-Alban, one of the poorest parishes in the suburbs of Lyon. Abbé Glasberg was a Ukrainian immigrant and a Jewish-born Catholic convert. The Russian Jewish social worker Nina Gourfinkel, the Quaker activist and government social service administrator Gilbert Lesage, and other friends and colleagues who worked closely with him throughout the war unanimously described him as a big and rumpled man, warm, energetic, "spontaneous to the point of anarchy."[45]

As early as the summer of 1940, Abbé Glasberg began hiding German-speaking political refugees in his church and home to protect them from being turned over to the Nazis under the terms of article 19 of the armistice. At the beginning of the next summer, he asked Archbishop Gerlier of Lyon to intervene with Vichy authorities for permission to open a center for up to sixty foreign refugees from the camps. By the end of November 1941, with help from his brother, Victor Vermont (his Resistance nom de guerre), Nina Gourfinkel, Jean-Marie Soutou, David Donoff, Dr. Joseph Weill of OSE, Ninon Weyl-Haït from EIF, and some others, he had found a site at Chansaye (Rhône) and secured permission from the relevant prefect, subprefect, mayor, gendarme chief, and other Vichy bureaucrats.[46] He had also obtained the release from Gurs of more than fifty adults. In addition, he had received permission from Vichy to organize the

Direction des centres d'accueil (DCA) to establish and supervise not more than one center in every department in the unoccupied zone, and he was hard at work opening two other residences.[47] As Gourfinkel herself remarks, only in chaotic times would so many diverse bureaucrats have recognized the authority of so amateur a social worker.[48]

By the time of the expulsions in August 1942, Glasberg and Gourfinkel had opened centers in the departments of Rhône, Drôme, Hautes-Alpes, and Cantal and were in the process of opening another in Gers. The fortunate men and women chosen to leave the camps and live in these centers were, in Gourfinkel's words, "manual laborers or intellectuals whose past work, state of health, and age permitted the hope that they would take up an active life again after the war." They tended to be young, between the ages of twenty and forty-five. About two-thirds were Jewish, "conforming," as Gourfinkel explained, "to their percentage in the camps."[49] To finance Glasberg's centers with a minimum of dependence on the charities of the Committee of Nîmes, one out of every three residents was chosen because he could afford to pay room and board for himself and two others.[50]

Nina Gourfinkel estimates that about one thousand internees passed through Abbé Glasberg's centers. Their stays were not without conflict—paying guests sometimes refused to share household chores, internal quarrels developed, and residents chafed at scarcities and at the strict prohibitions against working locally for pay, straying beyond a five-kilometer radius, and purchasing on the black market. Some problems were less predictable: for example, a Jewish woman refused a room near the pig sty until an orthodox rabbi assured her that it was permissible.[51]

In addition to Abbé Glasberg's centers, there were, by the spring of 1942, at least four others operated by the Protestant youth group CIMADE. Three of these—the Coteau Fleuri, a former hotel in Le Chambon-sur-Lignon (Haute-Loire); Le Mas du Diable at Pomeyrol near Tarascon (Bouches-du-Rhône); and the home at Vabre (Tarn)—were in strongly Protestant areas that would later provide refuge for thousands of French and foreign Jews alike as they sought to escape deportation. A fourth CIMADE home was the Foyer Marie Durand in Marseille.[52] Residents of these centers were often Jewish and tended, more frequently than the residents of Abbé Glasberg's homes, to be in family units with young children. Meanwhile, the

Vichy administration itself opened several homes for internees cate-
gorized by nationality. Thus, special centres d'accueil emerged for
German, Austrian, Dutch, Polish, and Italian refugees.[53]
The centres d'accueil permitted several thousand foreign refugees,
both adults and children, to leave internment camps and live openly
and legally with greater comfort, cleanliness, and dignity. Many non-
Jewish residents, free from the danger of deportation, remained in
the centers until the Liberation. For them, the system represented un-
mitigated good fortune. For Jews, the improvement was more temporary. Unknown numbers were sent back in August 1942 to the
camps from which they had come, to join their coreligionists being
expelled to the occupied zone and deported to Auschwitz. For them,
the centers constituted but a brief respite. Not all were called back
immediately, however, and the delay enabled many to be warned and
to seek hiding. Had they been in the camps at the moment of danger,
they would have had no possibility of escape. The charitable organizations working together under the Committee of Nîmes established
the centres d'accueil with no inkling of the horrors to come, but in so
doing, they made possible the future rescue of many.

In addition to facilitating the release of internees to supervised
centres d'accueil, social workers affiliated with the Committee of
Nîmes brought help to foreign men working in forced-labor units,
the compagnies (or groupements) de travailleurs étrangers (CTE, or
GTE) throughout the unoccupied zone. Estimated at as many as
60,000 at the end of July 1941, these workers at first were primarily
refugees from the Spanish Civil War, demobilized foreign volunteers
in the French army and the Foreign Legion, and male enemy nationals arrested in the autumn of 1939 and May 1940.[54] Their ranks
were later swollen by foreigners, both Jewish and non-Jewish, arrested by Vichy police in late 1940 and 1941 under laws granting
prefects such authority. Many arrestees, including a large proportion
of Jews, passed briefly through the internment camps before they
were transferred to a labor unit.

Each forced-labor company consisted of about 250 men, commanded by a reserve officer of the French army assisted by junior officers. Companies were initially organized on the basis of nationality,
but the separation of "Aryans" and "non-Aryans" within units
became increasingly formal and rigid until actual "Palestinian companies" appeared. Small company subdivisions were scattered
throughout unoccupied France, working in mines, factories, or, most
commonly, farms. Working conditions tended to vary considerably,

depending especially on the commanding officers. In most cases, however, food, shelter, and medical care were inadequate, discipline was severe and even brutal, and men unable because of age, health, or past experience to perform manual labor for long hours at a time were forced to do exactly that. A common cause of demoralization and despair was the separation of workers from their families. Jews in particular were also terrorized by the constant possibility of transfer to a German labor unit of the Todt Organization.

Social workers from agencies coordinated by the Committee of Nîmes obtained some improvements. They gained access to many of the larger, less remote work camps and managed to increase supplies of food, clothing, and medicine. In some cases, families were able to join their men, or their young children were transferred to more suitable children's homes. In other cases, communications at least improved. In other important ways, however, the committee failed: transfers to the Todt Organization in the occupied zone did not cease, and foreign Jews in the CTEs could not be protected from deportation to Aushwitz after August 1942. Nor were forced laborers released, despite evidence that they could find work on their own.

After the war, the ever-critical and outspoken Nina Gourfinkel attacked the Committee of Nîmes, which, in her opinion, "normalized the nightmare" of the camps and played Vichy's game. She charged, for example, that instead of protesting the terrible location, scarcities, and filth of Rivesaltes, committee personnel worried about getting schools and playing fields for children too weak from hunger and disease to study or play and allowed a cantine for debilitated children to be placed two and a half kilometers from the Jewish children's section, too far for a sick child to walk. She concluded bitterly, "The charities never raised the number-one question, that of the very existence of the camps. They accepted that existence without discussion."[55]

Gourfinkel may have had a point, but it is probable that a noisy protest about the camps' very existence would have damaged the committee's ability to accomplish anything at all. That it did achieve some improvements is clear. The advantages of the centres d'accueil for some have been seen. Within the camps themselves, on the most fundamental level, the death rate never again approached that of Gurs during the first winter of the Vichy regime, despite the drastic increase of official anti-Semitism, not to mention wartime scarcities, in 1941 and 1942. Furthermore, although deficiencies remained glaring, the mere presence of outsiders who cared was immensely re-assuring to internees who feared that a world preoccupied with war had forgotten them. The judgment of Joseph Weill, admittedly a participant in the committee but also a dedicated and sensitive physician and social worker, seems valid:

> We can affirm, without fear of exaggeration, that the activity of [the Committee of Nîmes] constitutes a particularly important page in the history of charity and in the history of occupied France. Side by side, in an atmosphere of equality and reciprocal confidence, the most diverse organizations, with differing goals, constituted a unique front of moral and material resistance. . . . [The committee's] efficiency was great; its radiance throughout the country and its echo throughout the entire world were greater still.[56]

And yet, the question is more complicated. A noisy protest against the very existence of the internment camps in 1941 might not have been the answer, but why did the social workers affiliated with the Committee of Nîmes not encourage and help internees to escape? Most camps were surrounded by barbed wire and guardhouses, but the fences were not electrified, there were no dogs, ditches, or floodlights, and escape was relatively easy. Prisoners caught trying to escape were sometimes punished, but they were not tortured or executed. Furthermore, some internees went in and out of their camps or centres d'accueil daily, on their own promise to return. Why did social workers not encourage more of them to "disappear" discreetly and furnish them with the false documents essential for such a step?

And there are other questions. How could the Israelite Welfare Committee of Toulouse in October 1940 actually *request,* as seen, a government "accommodation center" for indigent Jews at Brens? How could well-intentioned social workers have argued at a meeting of the Committee of Nîmes in January 1941 that it would be better to employ limited resources to improve conditions in the camps for all rather than send some to centres d'accueil? How could representatives of the Quakers in France suggest in July 1941 that the $500 required to allow one child to emigrate to the United States might be better spent to maintain one child in a camp for a whole year?[57] Why, for that matter, did not every foreign Jew in France, if not every French Jew as well, try to escape, legally or illegally, from both the unoccupied and the occupied zone?

Asking these questions sheds valuable light on the reality of the French camps as they existed and as they were perceived in 1940 and 1941. We understand today that the persecution of Jews in France during the first two years of the war—the racial laws, economic expropriations, arrests and internments, vicious anti-Semitic rhetoric—was irrevocably linked to what followed, to the roundups, deportations, and exterminations. We see Gurs, Rivesaltes, Le Vernet, and the other camps as obvious antechambers to Auschwitz. It is difficult to see the internment camps as they were viewed at the time—as uncomfortable, neglected, shameful creations of an antiforeign and anti-Semitic regime, but *not* as way stations on the path to extermination. Internees, and especially families with children, did not escape when they had the opportunity because they had nowhere else to go. Even the camps were better than a French prison in the event of recapture. And the idea of deportation to death never occurred to them.

Long after the war, Rabbi René Kapel, a dedicated internment camp chaplain, social worker, and Resistance fighter, addressed this subject most poignantly:

> Of course, now that we know the atrocities committed in the Nazi extermination camps, we realize that we should have acted differently. We were too inclined to respect a certain legality, in the hope of better serving the interests of the internees. Without doubt we should have silenced our scruples and bribed the Vichy officials, the internment camp directors, the chiefs of the Legion and the *Milice*, agents of the Gestapo and the German security service. We should have furnished false identity cards to a larger number of internees, and done everything to facilitate their escape. We should have acted [earlier] as we [later] did beginning in 1943, when we had to hide the Jews who were outside the camps, to save them from Hitler's clutches.[58]

Despite his pride in the accomplishments of the Committee of Nîmes, Dr. Joseph Weill agreed. As early as 1946, he wrote, "To work to improve the camps, even if one is exclusively preoccupied with the interests of the internees, is to come little by little, unconsciously, to tolerate, then to admit the camps as conditions of life for certain categories of people. . . . It was necessary to help the internees live from day to day; but above all they should have been freed."[59]

So much depended on what they knew and believed of Nazi and Vichyite intentions, and before the summer of 1942, despite occasional rumors of starvation in the ghettos of Poland and mass murder in Russia, they knew and believed very little. Events in the east seemed irrelevant to civilized France. And who could imagine that Frenchmen would freely deliver foreign Jews into German hands? We should have known, declared an anguished Dr. Weill: "If we had directed a more vigilant attention to the great lines of the policy of the conqueror and to the historic laws directing them, rather than concentrating our efforts on improvement in the camps, we would have grasped at the very beginning the interdependence of the coercive measures and their inevitable result, the deportation and the collective assassination."[60] But he is too harsh on himself. The interdependence was not apparent because it was incomprehensible. In this light, Rabbi Kapel's tragic lament rings true: "It is certain that, if we had known that the deportees were sent to certain death, we would have reacted differently, we would have adopted another system of defense and rescue."[61]

5

Roundups and Deportations, May 1941–June 1942

DURING THE FIRST WINTER OF THE OCCUPATION, THE DAILY EXISTENCE of the roughly 185,000 Jews in the northern zone was not radically different from that of Jews in the south. Racial laws and economic controls applied in both zones. Jewish shops were assigned "Aryan" supervisors. Anti-Semitic propaganda was heavier in the north, and Jews there who had responded to the census had a "*Juif*" stamp on their documents and a "Jewish Business" sign in their shop windows. But the dreadful internment camps for foreign Jews were in the south, and Vichy officials pursued foreigners, especially Jewish foreigners, more vigorously there than did their German and French colleagues in the occupied zone. With the exception of some individuals harassed by anti-Semites or arrested for minor infractions, Jews in the north, including foreigners, lived peacefully throughout the winter.

That relative tranquillity came to an abrupt end in the spring of 1941. Between May 9 and May 14, 6,494 Polish, Austrian, and Czech Jews throughout Paris, all men between the ages of eighteen and sixty and most of them wage workers or artisans, received from the French Prefecture of Police a small green card bearing their name. The hand-delivered card read:

Mr. ____ is invited to present himself in person, accompanied by one member of his family or by one friend, at 7:00 in the morning on May 14, 1941, for an examination of his situation.

He is asked to provide identification.

Those who do not present themselves on the set day and hour are liable for the most severe sanctions.[1]

A nervous and busy French policeman delivered a green card to David Diamant in his apartment at 5:00 P.M. on May 13. The recipient later remembered, "There was not the slightest doubt about the meaning of this convocation."[2] He, along with about 2,747 others, did not obey. The other 3,747 men reported to one of the five centers specified on their cards.[3] Some arrived as early as 6:00 A.M., hoping to complete the formalities and get to work on time. Others arrived late because they had received their summons only an hour or two before. Conveniently enough for the authorities, the late delivery deprived recipients of the time necessary for consulting family and friends about what to do.

Why did so many Jews obey their summons? As with the census, it seemed safer to obey than disobey. Most had valid residence permits, and foreign Jews living legally in Paris had not yet been arrested without cause. There was no absolute certainty that a change was imminent. Disobedience, on the other hand, required flight, and flight to these men meant endangering their families and abandoning everything they had struggled for since arriving in France: homes, jobs, and possessions. Marcel Skurnik testified after the war, "I decided to present myself because the rumor was that those who did not go to the convocation would harm their families, who would be mistreated and seized in their place."[4] Lucien Lazare recalled, "My father was not stupid. He was not a sheep, but he went to protect us!"[5] But many were suspicious and fearful. Céline Stene later remembered the moment at 6:00 A.M. when her husband, whose papers were in perfect order, assured her that he had to report and went to say goodbye to their sons. "I followed him and I saw that his face was bathed with tears. The children clung to him and would not separate from him, as if they had a presentiment that they would never see him again."[6] Indeed they did not, for their father died at Auschwitz with so many others from the roundup of May 14.

As the 3,747 men arrived at the assembly points, French municipal police lined them up in alphabetical order and confiscated their identity cards. The person accompanying each prisoner was sent for light clothing, a blanket, and food for two days. Buses then carried the men to the Gare d'Austerlitz, where four trains were waiting. Each car was guarded by a French gendarme. Prisoners were taken to camps in the small villages of Pithiviers and Beaune-la-Rolande (Loiret), both about fifty kilometers from Orléans and a little more than eighty kilometers from Paris.

Prisoners arriving at Pithiviers that same afternoon walked from the railroad station to the camp through the very center of town, in full public view. Most local residents had never seen a Jew. They would soon see thousands of others. Within a month, the wives and children of prisoners learned where their men were being held and came to Pithiviers and Beaune in an attempt to see them. They tried to throw bundles of food and clothing over the double row of barbed wire until the French guards finally relented and permitted the delivery of two packages a month. Eventually, personal visits also became possible. Residents of Pithiviers and Beaune witnessed a continual stream of Jewish visiters until, a year later in July 1942, many of those same women and children were imprisoned in the two camps.

Life at Pithiviers and Beaune was particularly hard at first. The barracks, built in the autumn of 1939 to house captured German soldiers, were dark and flimsy. Camp guards and administrators, all French, were often incompetent and corrupt. Annette Monod, a young French Red Cross volunteer who won permission to work at the camps, observed immediately that a French manager was stealing food. Her colleague reported the abuse to the local subprefect and promptly lost her job, so Miss Monod tried another approach. She resolved to eat only what the men were eating. After one week, she went to see the prefect. In his office, she nearly fainted and burst into tears. The camp manager was replaced, and she was able to distribute increased supplies of bread and even chocolate.[7]

As the weeks passed, life at Pithiviers and Beaune was organized into a bearable routine. The men were gradually allowed to work among themselves as tailors, shoe repairmen, barbers, gardeners, and cooks. A local newspaper appeared, and a group at Pithiviers opened an infirmary and a library with some help from Annette Monod and other Red Cross workers. During the summer of 1941, some men worked for five francs a day on nearby farms; in November, they served as woodcutters in forests north of the Loire. Men from Pithiviers also volunteered for work in local sugar and molasses factories. Others from Beaune drained swamps in the region.

Work outside the camps offered some men an opportunity to run away, and an undetermined number took it. A surprising number, however, did not. Others took a brief, unofficial "furlough" to visit their families and then returned voluntarily. Marcel Skurnik, who fled in the summer of 1941, explained, "Some people who escaped from Beaune-la-Rolande, after seeing the situation in Paris [in August, when thousands of other foreign Jewish men were being rounded up], returned voluntarily either to the camp of Beaune-la-Rolande or to Pithiviers, because, in comparison to Drancy, they were a paradise."[8] Raymond Kamioner escaped, but with no money, no possibility of work, and no knowledge of an organization to help him, he also returned in 1941. Fear of deportation to the east was not yet a consideration, and life in hiding, with its loneliness, danger to families, and economic hardship, seemed less desirable than life in internment. "Yes," he later admitted, "it was stupid, but that's how it was. If at that time there was a certain resistance, if I had been able to reach it, I would not have acted as I did."[9] Kamioner was deported to Auschwitz in June 1942 but survived.

Internment at this early stage did not seem a total isolation from the broader society. Despite the bitter realization that camps were run entirely by the French and that most local residents in Pithiviers were indifferent, surviving prisoners remember examples of support and assistance. Léon Grinberg, who also survived Auschwitz, recalled, "At the Gare d'Austerlitz, the French railroad workers saluted us with raised fists."[10] Raymond Kamioner spoke of Doctor Cabanis, the mayor of Beaune, who helped prisoners obtain extra bread; of a Miss Rolland, a Red Cross social worker who brought medicine from the local hospital; and of nuns who cared for the sick. Arnold and Bernard Bilder remembered a baker woman from Vannes who, with help from a friend at the post office, received and delivered mail for prisoners in the area who were not allowed that privilege. Aron Garbaz told of non-Jews who helped him escape. Zalman Kornblut provided details about a peasant who hid two fleeing prisoners under a pile of garbage.[11] Raymond Kamioner summed up the situation succinctly:

> At every commemorative ceremony, I remember that, beside the French who put themselves at the service of Vichy, at the service of the occupiers, there were people like Doctor Roux, Doctor Cabanis, Miss Rolland, and the population of Beune-la-Rolande [sic] and Pithiviers. And that, I do not forget, I mention it each time I

have an opportunity and for me, it is a sacred duty to make that distinction.[12]

Already it was apparent that a nation physically cut in two was divided spiritually as well. Already some French men and women were acting upon their private disapproval of government policies.

The next three months passed without another roundup, but disaster struck again in Paris on August 20. At 5:30 in the morning, French police blocked all streets and closed all métro entrances in the eleventh arrondissement, an area north and east of the Place Bastille, that was heavily populated by foreign Jews. Between 6:00 A.M. and 2:00 P.M., police arrested as many male Jews between the ages of eighteen and fifty as they could find, except Americans. Armed with census lists and expecting to find 5,784 in the arrondissement, they combed buildings and pounded on apartment doors. By the end of the day, they had caught at least 2,894 men, most of whom were immigrants.[13]

German military authorities had ordered the raid, apparently in reprisal for Communist agitation in France following the invasion of the Soviet Union. Dissatisfied with its initial results, they insisted that it continue for several days. French police therefore scoured other arrondissements in Paris and arrested more than 1,000 additional men. Among them were about 200 French Jewish intellectuals, including many prominent lawyers from the Paris Court of Appeal and the Council of State, the highest administrative court in France. The Germans, holding them responsible for the agitation, had specifically ordered their arrests.[14] By August 25, 4,230 men had been taken by bus to a camp in a town on the outskirts of Paris that was soon to become a familiar and dreaded word in Jewish households: Drancy.

Roger Gompel, the director of the Trois Quartiers department store in Paris, was arrested in December 1941 and sent to Drancy the following March. He described its physical structure:

The word "camp" evokes an image of barracks or tents spread out in a rural setting. Here, nothing of the kind. In one of the most dreary suburbs of Paris, a huge lot has been set aside for cheap housing. Arranged in a horseshoe pattern around an immense courtyard covered with cinders, the constructions are still unfinished. The concrete-slab carcass is divided into seven strictly identical buildings, served by 21 stairways. It is an entire city which will [between 1941 and 1944] sometimes contain up to six thousand internees.[15]

The buildings on three sides of the courtyard consisted of four stories above the ground floor. Each stairway gave access to one large unfinished room on each floor, but prisoners could not pass from room to room on a given floor without going downstairs to a different stairway.[16] Most rooms had windows that looked outward; the young Simone de Beauvoir was one of many non-Jews (the trip was prohibited for Jews) who traveled to Drancy to stand at the barbed wire and search the windows for a glimpse of a friend.[17] Sylvain Kaufmann, arrested and confined at Drancy on June 24, 1942, remembers that prisoners sent out messages in Morse code by flashlight.[18] From the top-floor landing, prisoners could see the skyline of northern Paris, dominated by Sacre Coeur, the Church of the Sacred Heart in Montmartre. Escape was prevented by guardhouses and a double row of barbed wire that surrounded the entire complex.[19]

Until June 1943, the Drancy camp was guarded entirely by French gendarmes. Supplies came from the prefecture of the Seine, and the administration was also French. During the first months, food scarcities at the camp were appalling. More than thirty people had died by early November 1941—a period of scarcely two months after the camp's opening, and before the onset of cold weather. French bureaucratic neglect and contempt for human life had reached criminal proportions. German military authorities actually ordered about 800 prisoners released for health reasons.[20] Many were rearrested in July of the following year.

While the chief targets of the May and August roundups were foreign Jews, the victims in December were French. As Gompel later wrote of the predawn raid on December 12, there were, "in the dark of night, three quick blows on the door of my room. I leaped up, dazed by the beam of a flashlight full in the face. German police!" Gompel was given a few minutes to prepare a bundle of clothing, blankets, toilet articles, and food for two days. He was permitted to bring some money but no paper, pencils, or pens. A military car driven by a German soldier deposited him at the mayoral headquarters of the fashionable sixteenth arrondissement, where the SS took over. He was taken to the École militaire, not far from the Eiffel Tower. At both stops, other prisoners were waiting. From their demeanor and fine clothes—"city suits, correct and neat"—it soon became apparent that "the raid had been directed primarily against the 'notables.' The order of the day seemed to have been to strike at the head. A majority of the men were over fifty."[21]

Unlike the roundups of foreign Jews in May and August, the December operation against citizens was conducted by Germans, with a few French translators. Nevertheless, Vichy officials never protested. Altogether, 743 men, nearly all French and middle-class, were arrested throughout the city that morning. In addition to Gompel, other "notables" included René Blum, Pierre and Roger Masse, the historian Jacques Ancel, the playwright Jean-Jacques Bernard, the physician Georges Wellers, and the husband of the novelist Colette, Maurice Goudeket.[22] The Nazis had apparently ordered the action in reprisal for a series of anti-German attacks by the emerging French Resistance and timed it to follow closely upon the American entry into the war after the Japanese attack on Pearl Harbor. At about the same time, they imposed a fine of one billion francs on the Jewish community in the occupied zone. Then at the fortress of Mont-Valérien outside Paris on December 15, the Germans executed 95 hostages, also as a reprisal. At least 53 of the 95 were Jewish; about 44 of the 53 had been transferred from Drancy the preceding day. Many of the 44 had been arrested on August 20.[23]

The 743 men were assembled at the École militaire. Since the Germans apparently wanted to make an example of 1,000 Jews, they promptly arrested 54 others in a random document-checking operation in the neighborhood of the Place d'Étoile and then added about 300 mostly foreign internees from Drancy to the group.[24] That dark and rainy evening, 1,043 men, including 390 businessmen, 322 artisans, 91 engineers, 63 dentists, 33 pharmacists and chemists, 31 students, 16 lawyers, 11 professors, and others, were driven by bus across the city to the Gare du Nord.[25] Roger Gompel evoked the poignancy of the ride when he later wrote: "Across the dead city, with lights extinguished, boutiques closed and blinds drawn, we had much difficulty figuring out our route. In passing we could make out the heavy mass of the Arch of Triumph, silhouetted against the somber sky. Avenue Wagram, outer boulevards, Gare du Nord."[26]

From there, the prisoners traveled for about two hours in third-class train compartments to Compiègne (Oise), about eighty kilometers to the northeast. There, at 1:00 A.M., they marched two kilometers through town from the station to the camp. Some might have escaped in the confusion at the stations or during the night march, but, according to Jean-Jacques Bernard, "wives, children, parents, dear ones from whom we had been torn, were, even from far away, more powerful guards than the armed and screaming soldiers." "A good half," he continued, "wore the ribbon of a war veteran, the *croix de guerre,* or the *Légion d'honneur.*"[27]

In December 1941, the German-operated camp of Royallieu at Compiègne was divided into three separate sections of barracks, each surrounded by a double row of barbed wire. The entire ensemble was also encircled by a double row of barbed wire and a wall. The Jews were placed in one section, while 3,000 to 4,000 French Communists and numerous Russian prisoners of war were isolated in the other two. Somewhat later, yet a fourth section was carved out for American prisoners. The barracks themselves lacked furniture, running water, heat, and electricity. The two last deficiencies were particularly devastating in winter, when the sun set early and prisoners faced nearly sixteen hours of total darkness in bitter cold. Food and medical care were inadequate, and Jews, unlike French Communists and Russians, could receive no packages. Prisoners did not have to work, but two or more interminable roll calls a day in the frigid courtyard soon sapped their strength. Seventy-three men were released as early as December 20 because they were either over sixty-five or seriously ill. Those remaining at Compiègne suffered throughout the winter.[28]

Change, when it came in March, was for the worse. On March 19, the Germans released 178 Jews over the age of fifty-five to the French. Handcuffed in pairs, men like the Masse brothers and Roger Gompel were marched back through the town to the station. Gompel remembered, "In the streets of the town with the low houses, the mute inhabitants stopped to watch us pass as if it were a funeral convoy." The French took the men to Drancy, where they arrived at 11:00 P.M. to endure a long wait and search. "The first contact with the [French] *gendarmes* of Drancy, brutal and crude, left us with a bitter taste," Gompel recorded. "Under the German authorities, we had been permitted to smoke and to dispose of six hundred francs of pocket money. Here we could only keep fifty francs, and cigarettes were forbidden."[29]

For most of the Jews remaining at Compiègne, however, a still more terrible fate awaited. At 2:00 P.M. on March 26, about 640 men were assembled in the courtyard. Of these, about 80 who were married to non-Jews were removed and returned to the barracks. One of them, Doctor Georges Wellers, remained at Compiègne until April, when he was transferred to Drancy. The others, about 558 men gravely weakened from three and a half months of hunger, were marched through town the following day to board a train already containing 554 Jews from Drancy. Many of the latter had been arrested in Paris on May 14 and August 20.

The train of March 27, 1942, was the first convoy to leave France for Auschwitz. Of it, Wellers later wrote:

> It was the first deportation where I was present. I saw about sixty others, but I have a particularly devastating memory of that one. Maybe because most of the deportees were such good people, very dear friends, maybe because it was the first deportation that I saw, maybe also it was because we husbands of "Aryans" had escaped so unexpectedly. I think the principal reason was that, of the 558 deportees, there were certainly not 50 who were not seriously ill, after three and a half months at Compiègne. Seeing that faltering column leave the camp, I had the piercing sensation of being present at a monstrous holocaust. Later, at Drancy, I had the same stifling sentiment, but rarely with the same dramatic intensity.
> I was not mistaken.[30]

The 1,112 men traveled to Auschwitz in third-class passenger cars—a rare alternative to the horror of sealed and pitch-dark boxcars. They arrived on March 29. Since mass gassings had not yet begun at the camp, all were admitted. One thousand and eight of them died from exhaustion, starvation, and abuse within five months. An estimated total of 23 men survived.[31]

Slightly more than two months passed before additional convoys left France for Auschwitz, but on June 5, 22, 25, 28, and July 17, a terrifying succession of five trains carried most of the victims of the May, August, and December 1941 roundups, and some other Jews, to their deaths. Each train carried approximately 1,000 people. The train on June 22 included 66 women—the first Jewesses to leave France for Auschwitz. Another 34 women were on the train of June 28, and 119 on that of July 17. All deportees from these five trains were admitted to the camp. Since most were between the ages of eighteen and fifty-four, the much vaunted Nazi pretext that deportation was for labor seemed to be vindicated. Nevertheless, of the 1,000 men admitted from the June 5 train and another 1,000 from that of June 22, 783 and 814, respectively, were dead by August 15. The others fared no better. At war's end, the estimated numbers of survivors from the five trains were respectively, 41, 34, 59, 55, and 45.[32]

Well over 1,000 of the 6,078 deportees in the first six convoys to Auschwitz were French citizens, yet the Vichy regime uttered no word of protest.

During the first six months of 1942, the noose tightened imperceptibly around the Jews in France. Hundreds of men and women throughout the occupied zone were arrested for infractions of the racial laws or for attempting to cross the demarcation line illegally. No more mass roundups occurred in Paris until July, but in the Orléans region, 34 women and 73 men, many of them French, were arrested by French police to fill the quota of 1,000 Jews to be deported from nearby Beaune-la-Rolande on June 28.[33] Tension mounted as word of the deportation trains trickled out. Fear then reached into every Jewish home with a new German ordinance on May 29. Beginning on June 7, 1942, French and most foreign Jews over the age of six in the occupied zone were required to wear a six-pronged yellow star of David clearly visible and solidly sewn to the upper left side of their outer clothing.[34] The star, outlined in black, was the size of a man's fist. The word "*Juif*" was printed in bold black Gothic letters in its center. Available at police stations, each star cost one coupon of a monthly clothing ration.

More consistently than the racial laws, economic confiscations, or even the roundups of 1941, the devastating impact of the yellow star decree is evoked in every survivor's testimony. Annette Muller Bessmann remembers that her mother Rachel, a Polish Jewish immigrant, sewed the star on the best outfits of her four children and walked proudly and defiantly through the streets with them. "Poor mama and her useless courage," the daughter adds bitterly. "Wouldn't it have been better to have thrown the star into the garbage and fled far away with her children? Two months later, she was dead. She was not yet thirty-four."[35] Rachel Muller was arrested in the July 1942 roundup in Paris and murdered at Auschwitz.

A survivor identified only as Colette recorded that her father sewed all his medals from the First World War around his star and also wore it with pride. Neighbors greeted him warmly as he walked down the street. His daughter recalls, "A stranger even got off his bicycle to shake his hand."[36] Colette's French-born parents were deported in June 1944. Fourteen-year-old Maurice Rajsfus's Polish immigrant parents also walked with him through the Parisian streets wearing the star. They told him how wonderful France was, he recalls, because wearing the star publicly in Poland or Russia would have led to endless fights.[37] Like Mrs. Muller, the Rajsfuses were arrested in the July roundup and murdered at Auschwitz.

On the first day the star was required, the father of sixteen-year-old Léon Tsevery also told his two sons, "We are going to go out and you are going to walk in the streets like me, your heads high." Tsevery later spoke movingly of that day:

> We lived in a working-class neighborhood, rue de la Chapelle in the 18th *arrondissement*. It was in May, it was a beautiful day. We were walking down the street when an elderly man, well dressed, with a cane, wearing gaiters, approached us and said, "I am ashamed for France," and shook all three of our hands. This gesture greatly moved and comforted us. It was men and women like him who permitted us to survive and struggle in very difficult conditions. During the period from '42 to '44, I had many chances to meet people like that, who helped us as much as possible. But the opposite situation also occurred.[38]

Although French political and religious spokesmen remained silent, and police in the north helped distribute the star and enforce the German ordinance, some ordinary citizens voiced their disapproval. As the persecution of the Jews intensified and became more visible, the French became increasingly divided.

Despite the courage with which it was worn, the star caused profound anguish. Integrated Jews who had long thought of themselves as French above all else were suddenly not only subjected to discriminatory laws but forced to look physically different at all times. As the law obviously intended, they now had to obey every anti-Jewish measure absolutely. They had to respect the 8:00 P.M.–6:00 A.M. curfew, imposed upon Jews in February 1942. After another German ordinance on July 8, they could go to no public places—no parks, cinemas, theaters, libraries, museums, cafés, or restaurants—and they could shop only during limited hours: 11:00 A.M. to noon for food, and 3:00 to 4:00 P.M. for other items, by which time most goods had been sold and many stores were closed. Russian-born Anne Wellers, the non-Jewish wife of Georges whose two children, ages six and eleven, had to wear the star, recorded that they could not even cross the Luxembourg Gardens, although a sympathetic guard said that of course they should.

One hot day, Mrs. Wellers remembers, she asked a café owner for glasses of water for the children, to be drunk on the sidewalk. The man said indignantly, "I'm the boss here—they can come in," but she prudently declined. "It became," her husband Georges concluded, "practically impossible to live in the 'occupied zone' without breaking some prohibition."[39] Ginette Hirtz, then a young French Jewish student at the Sorbonne, remembered, "Each time I came up out of the *métro* station Saint-Michel, I was seized with a sort of anguished paralysis."[40] She feared denunciation by an unknown anti-Semite for a fictitious infraction, or arrest for breaking a regulation unintentionally. If she had not worn the star, she could have been denounced by anyone who knew she was a Jew.

The suffering of children, suddenly singled out as different from their peers, was perhaps the sharpest of all. "It is hard at age eleven to wear a distinctive mark," a man named David later told an interviewer. "I was not like the others, or at least they wanted to make me believe it."[41] Maurice Rajsfus found some consolation in the initial reaction of his schoolmates, who eyed his star curiously and exclaimed, "Vive le Sheriff!" Only a few insulted him, but he, humiliated and mortified, voluntarily withdrew from games at recess. "I never became used to it," he admits. "The worst was to endure the silence, the pitying looks of my comrades, the condescension of the teachers."[42]

For some it was even worse. Lucien Lazare, then nine years old, recalls being teased by students and even teachers in Paris. He declares, "I have never forgotten that the police officers who [later] came to get us were French police officers, that my teachers did not once try to shield me from the taunts of the other children, not to mention actively defend me."[43] Raphaël, age eight when he wore the star, agrees, saying, "Every recreation the children would bully me, the teachers looked on without intervening, I went home beaten up."[44] Robert, a thirteen-year-old student in the Dordogne, later declared, "At almost every recreation, a gang of country children would pick on me."[45] Eight-year-old Annette Zaidman was often surrounded at recess by a group of little girls singing, "She is a dirty Jew, she is a dirty *youpine* [foreign Jew]."[46] She was happy when she was ignored.

Some had more positive experiences. A child identified as Maurice, then age eight, had no trouble with schoolmates in Paris, although he was the only one in his class to wear the star.[47] Polish-born Fania Elbinger Ewenczyk states that other children were always kind to her fifteen-year-old younger sister who wore the star in school and rode quite naturally with her in the last car of every métro train when that became obligatory for the Jews.[48] Those who received support from teachers remember it with particular warmth. Rajsfus recalls that the director of his school, a Pétain supporter, nevertheless informed his students that anyone troubling a child wearing a star would have to reckon with him.[49] Ginette Hirtz declares that although some former friends at the Sorbonne abandoned her, a professor of philosophy was especially kind after he had seen her star.[50] And Annette Muller Bessmann, whose friends also stopped visiting her home when she had to wear the star, remembers a teacher who announced to her class on the first day of the decree, "Two of your comrades are wearing a star. Be kind. Nothing should change between them and you."[51]

The sympathy sometimes shown by teachers was demonstrated by other French men and women as well. The historian Léon Poliakov recalled, "Hundreds of Parisians were anxious to turn the latest harassment into an object of derision by making fanciful stars for themselves. A newspaper saleswoman hung a star around the neck of her dog, an employee made a sign which read 'Goy,' an architect announced his origin as an 'Auvergnat'; 'Buddhists,' 'Papuans' [from New Guinea], and even 'Swing' proliferated throughout the streets of Paris."[52]

Alice Courouble, a non-Jew interned briefly at Drancy for such activities, remembers other non-Jews arrested with her:

> There was Liliane . . . who had worn a rosette of yellow ribbon crossed with a brooch with the portrait of Joan of Arc.
>
> There was also a young man of eighteen, arrested for having worn a yellow handkerchief in his breast pocket.
>
> Josephe had done better. In addition to the star sewn upon her chest, she had made a belt of eight yellow paper stars, each bearing one letter of the word "Victory."
>
> And then there was Paulette . . . who, like me, had accompanied a Jewish friend in the street and worn the star.[53]

Georges Wellers saw about twenty young non-Jewish French men, mostly students, arrive at Drancy in June, and some women, previously held at Les Tourelles, in August.[54] Among them, he mentioned Josette Cardin, who helped comfort the thousands of children who arrived in mid-August. The Red Cross worker Annette Monod knew a woman physician named Adelaide Hautval who worked with the sick.[55] These non-Jewish prisoners were treated much like everyone else and forced, like the Jews, to wear a yellow star. Their star, however, was crossed by a white band reading "friend of the Jews." Their numbers were not great, but as Wellers remembers, "The appearance in the camp of the 'friends of the Jews' produced a discreet but immense joy and a profound gratitude."[56] In the last analysis, however, the non-Jews received supremely different treatment, for most were released at the end of August.

Other French men and women showed their sympathy in different ways. Some, as seen, made a point of shaking hands with unknown Jews wearing stars or gave up seats in the subway for them. The latter "problem" was solved when the Germans decreed, a few days later, that Jews could only ride in the last car of the trains. Furthermore, according to Wellers, the star provoked only a few anti-Semitic incidents, despite Jewish fears.[57] On the contrary, German reports from throughout the occupied zone in June suggest that most French men and women were uncomfortable with the measure. One report read, "A lively and unanimous indignation has been provoked by the Jewish stars. *Even the anti-Semites condemn this measure,* especially because children have to wear the star." Another, from Bordeaux, declared, "The measure is welcomed among small shopkeepers and artisans," but, it continued, "The masses, almost without exception, take the part of the Jews." And a third report, from Nancy in eastern France, claimed, "The disapproval shown vis-à-vis [the star] can be found among almost all classes of the population."[58]

In another indication of the unpopularity of the star measure among French non-Jews, it was never decreed for Jews in the unoccupied zone. Even the Germans did not impose it there after they occupied the southern zone in November 1942. Instead, a French law in December 1942 required all French and foreign Jews in the southern zone to have the word "*Juif*" stamped on their identity and ration cards, as had been necessary in the northern zone since 1940.[59]

Historians disagree about when the extermination of the Jews became official Nazi policy. Certainly the idea had festered in the mind of Adolf Hitler from his student days in Vienna. Certainly the *removal* of Jews from the Third Reich was Nazi policy from the moment of their rise to power in 1933. Jews were encouraged to leave Germany and, later, Austria, Bohemia, and Moravia. When war broke out, schemes for the removal of the Jews were extended to the newly conquered lands. Plans were considered for forced emigration to some vague oriental reserve or, between the spring of 1940 and the early winter of 1940–41, to Madagascar, a French colony. The latter destination seemed feasible after the fall of France, when the defeat of Britain and a permanent peace treaty were considered imminent. But Britain did not fall, and widespread starvation and fear of epidemics in the ghettos of Poland in the winter of 1940–41 reinforced growing pressure among Nazi leaders for a comprehensive policy toward the Jews.

The German invasion of the Soviet Union in June 1941 opened up vast new spaces in the east and incorporated millions of additional Jews into territories occupied by the Third Reich. Nazi plans for the wholesale liquidation of Communists and Jews in the Soviet Union were prepared in the spring before the invasion. They were duly carried out by SS *Einsatzgruppen,* special SS mobile killing units, as the German army advanced. Human life daily became cheaper; murder became an ever more feasible solution to the problem of removing an unwanted population. Plans crystallized on July 31, 1941, when Reich Marshal Hermann Göring instructed SS Lieutenant General Reinhard Heydrich, SS Chief Heinrich Himmler's deputy and head of the Reich Central Security Office (RSHA), to make "all necessary organizational, functional, and material preparations for a complete solution of the Jewish question in the German sphere of influence in Europe."[60]

Göring did not spell out what he meant by the term "complete solution," but in the months that followed, brutal experiments with mobile gassing units began. Permanent killing facilities were constructed at Belzec, Sobibor, Treblinka, and Auschwitz, all in Poland, between November 1941 and the spring of 1942. Systematic murder of Jews in fixed installations began in February or March 1942. The first victims were Polish, but West Europeans were not far behind.

On November 29, 1941, as the construction of permanent killing facilities was beginning, Heydrich invited German SS and government leaders to a special "Final Solution" conference in Berlin. The meeting, the infamous Wannsee Conference, finally materialized on January 20, 1942. To his assembled guests, Heydrich explained that emigration had failed to solve the Jewish problem, and that henceforth all European Jews were to be transferred to the east. He was vague about what would occur there, but he spoke of vast labor camps where most would be removed through a "natural decline," and where the rest would eventually be subjected to a "special treatment." He specified the number of Jews to be removed from each European country. For France, the figure was a preposterous 865,000, broken down into 165,000 for the occupied zone and

700,000 for the unoccupied zone. Heydrich set no timetable, but he clearly expected SS leaders of special Jewish offices throughout occupied Europe to prepare their plans. In France, that responsibility fell to SS Captain Theodor Dannecker, chief of the Gestapo's Jewish Office (*Judenreferat*) in Paris.[61]

Dannecker approached his task with relish. On March 27, he personally accompanied the first convoy of 1,112 Jews deported from France to the east, remaining with the train as far as Auschwitz. In May, he worked intensely with Major General Otto Kohl, the German army director of railroads in occupied France, to ensure the availability of trains for future deportations. Also in May, he issued the star decree and had 136 Jews from Beaune-la-Rolande and 153 from Pithiviers transferred to Compiègne. As seen, they and about 700 others departed on June 5 on the second French convoy for Auschwitz. Then, at a meeting on June 11, 1942, with SS Lieutenant Colonel Adolf Eichmann, his direct superior in Berlin, Dannecker promised a delivery from both zones of France within the next eight months of 100,000 Jews between the ages of sixteen and forty, regardless of nationality or sex. Ten percent could be incapable of work.[62]

The age limit was a result of Himmler's express orders to disguise these earliest deportations as labor convoys, to test public opinion and avoid widespread panic. In his zeal, however, Dannecker had promised to deliver *all* the estimated Jews in France within the specified age range, with no allowance for escapes or for adverse public opinion. Practical difficulties soon forced him to focus on the deportation of 39,000 Jews in the next three months and to extend the age limit to fifty-five, but the numbers and problems remained huge. Since his own forces in the occupied zone were far too small for such a task, while in the unoccupied zone they were nonexistent, his next task became one of ensuring the cooperation of the French police.

Before the summer of 1942, French police in the occupied zone had arrested some Jews for specific violations and had twice, in May and August 1941, had participated in roundups of Jewish men who were mostly, but not entirely, foreigners. They had also condoned the shooting or deportation of some of these men in reprisal actions. In the unoccupied zone, French police had arrested Jewish women and children as well as men, but they had limited that action, again, mostly to foreigners. In the occupied zone, police acted as they did from an acceptance of the inevitable, from a desire to maintain the illusion of autonomy, and, in many cases, from a genuine conviction that adult male Jewish immigrants, like Communists, represented disloyal and politically dangerous factions that should be purged. In the unoccupied zone, police acted upon the population's and the government's perception of the large influx of unwanted foreign Jews as a drain on the economy, a competition for scarce resources, a source of disorder, and a possibly disloyal or radical element in an otherwise homogeneous society. With a few exceptions, however, French police in the occupied zone before the summer of 1942 had not yet arrested Jewish women and children. In the unoccupied zone, they had not yet touched French Jews or delivered Jews to the Nazis in the north, with the exception of some German political dissenters demanded under article 19 of the armistice agreement. Clearly these restraints would have to end if Dannecker's goals were to be met.

During the spring of 1942, a series of personnel changes occurred within the Vichy regime that were conducive to Dannecker's purposes. On April 16, Pierre Laval, whom Pétain had removed in December 1940 and replaced with Admiral François Darlan, returned to a greatly enhanced position of power. He became prime minister (*président du conseil*), rather than vice-prime minister as before. Now fully the head of government, he was also minister of the interior, information, and foreign affairs. Two days later, Laval named thirty-three-year-old René Bousquet, formerly the prefect of the Marne and then the regional prefect of Champagne, as secretary-general of the national police. Bousquet in turn appointed his friend and colleague Jean Leguay as his representative in the occupied zone. Finally, on May 6, the virulently anti-Semitic Louis Darquier de Pellepoix replaced Xavier Vallat as head of the CGQJ.

Laval returned to an office laden with problems. The French people were growing increasingly restive at the failure of the Vichyite "new order" to solve their most fundamental difficulties—the severe scarcities of food, clothing, and fuel, the refusal of the Germans to release the million and a half French prisoners of war, and the division of the country. Meanwhile, German demands, far from decreasing, were becoming more onerous. France was required to deliver ever larger amounts of agricultural and industrial products and, most seriously, manpower for labor in Germany. To survive in office, Laval needed to resolve these problems while reasserting the authority of the Vichy government in both zones. Bousquet entertained the similar objective of reasserting the authority of the French police in both zones. For both men, the Jewish question represented a potential bargaining chip and a possible obstacle. At best, Nazi demands for the Jews might be met in exchange for German concessions on other points. At worst, Nazi demands for the Jews, however unpleasant or unpopular, could not be allowed to obstruct future collaboration and understanding on other issues. In any case, the Jews themselves, and especially the foreign Jews, were of decidedly secondary importance.

A series of complex negotiations ensued in June and early July between Bousquet and Leguay for the French and, on the German side, Dannecker; the RSHA chief in France, SS Colonel Helmut Knochen; the overall SS and military police commander in France, SS Brigadier General Karl Oberg; and Oberg's chief assistant, SS Major Herbert Hagen. To meet Dannecker's commitment to Eichmann, the Germans insisted that the French deliver 10,000 Jews from the unoccupied zone within the next few months, and that the French police conduct a roundup of about 22,000 Jews in the Paris region in mid-July. Not only were German police in Paris too few to conduct such an action, but their chiefs were unwilling to risk the anger of French civilians at the sight of men in German uniform arresting women and children.

For his part, Laval was initially willing, even eager, to empty internment camps in the unoccupied zone by delivering foreign Jews to the Germans for "repatriation." Darlan's circular to the prefects a year earlier had used that word and ordered that "foreign Israelites presently in lodging centers or concentration camps not be allowed to integrate themselves into the national collectivity and that everything be done to achieve their departure from France."[63] That priority had not changed. Indeed, when Heydrich visited Paris in May 1942, Bousquet, learning of the pending deportations but as yet knowing little of German plans for the unoccupied zone, actually asked the RSHA chief if foreign Jews already in camps in the south might be included.[64] By the end of June, Bousquet appeared somewhat more reluctant on this point, but at a meeting with Knochen, Oberg, Hagen, and others on July 2, he declared the willingness of Pétain, Laval, and himself to deliver 10,000 foreign Jews from the unoccupied zone, including those already in camps and others to be arrested for that purpose by the French police.[65]

Although he was willing to arrest foreign Jewish men and women in the unoccupied zone, where the fiction of an independent, autonomous French police force acting on its own initiative could be maintained, Bousquet at first refused to participate in roundups in occupied Paris. There he feared that his forces might appear to be German tools. Furthermore, while Dannecker, in part on principle and in part from a realistic appraisal of the numbers available, insisted that 40 percent of the Jews arrested in Paris be French, Bousquet categorically refused to touch French citizens. At the meeting on July 2, he clung to his two refusals for a time. After a lengthy lecture, however, in which the irate and increasingly anxious Knochen informed him that a French refusal to cooperate would be viewed as a direct affront to the Führer, Bousquet yielded on the first point. He agreed to permit French police to conduct a large roundup of Jews in Paris. He stuck only to his second point. French police would not arrest French citizens. They would fill the quota by arresting more foreigners.[66]

If Vichy officials balked at arresting French Jewish adults, however, they were far less squeamish about the children of foreign Jews, most of whom were French by parental declaration at birth. To his everlasting shame, Pierre Laval, in a meeting with Dannecker on July 4, actually proposed, in Dannecker's words, "that, during the evacuation of Jewish families from the unoccupied zone, children under sixteen also be taken away. As for the Jewish children in the occupied zone, the question did not interest him."[67] Laval even seemed proud of his position, for on July 10 he told the assembled Council of Ministers, in Pétain's presence, that, in the words of the official French meeting transcript, "in the interest of humanity [he] has obtained— contrary to the first German proposals—that the children, including those under 16, be allowed to accompany their parents. They [the Germans] now accept."[68] Laval exaggerated a bit; Dannecker had not yet received permission from Berlin for the deportation of children. But no one at the Vichy council meeting objected.

It is not clear why Laval took such an initiative. Perhaps he merely wished to show the Nazis that he was as cold and ruthless as they, and as committed to the removal of foreign Jews from France. He may have believed that the sight of small children being wrenched from their parents and maintained in French orphanages would outrage public opinion more than their transfer with parents to the east. He may also have been concerned about the French capacity to care for the children discreetly and out of public view. He seems not to have regarded the children as French citizens. Perhaps he simply wanted bodies, to fill his quota of Jews easily without having to touch the "real" French.[69]

Inevitably the question arises as to what Vichy officials actually knew or believed about the Final Solution in May, June, and July 1942, when they were agreeing to supply the Germans with foreign

Jews. They surely knew that deportation would be an excruciating hardship that children and the elderly might not survive. That in itself is reason to condemn their policy unequivocably. But did they know that it meant certain death for the vast majority? In all probability, they did not know at that time, although partial information was available. As early as August 1941, Radio Moscow had begun broadcasting into France the news of systematic mass murders of Soviet Jews by invading Nazi soldiers. From early July 1942, the British Broadcasting Corporation (BBC) spoke frequently of mass murders and large-scale evacuations of Polish Jews from ghettos to sinister camps. The information was furnished by agents of the Jewish Labor Bund in Poland and the Polish government-in-exile in London. On July 2, the *New York Times* published an account of a Bund report and referred to the mobile gassing units employed since December at Chelmno.[70]

Although Laval surely knew about the Soviet massacres, he may well have dismissed the worst reports from Poland as anti-German propaganda by the enemy. Furthermore, none of these early reports spoke of gas chambers permanently installed at death camps, of mass selections of murder victims upon arrival at the death camps, or of any deliberate plan to murder *all* Jews from *all* countries systematically. Indeed, although mass gassings of Polish Jews had begun at Chelmno in December and continued against Polish, Slovakian, and German Jews at Belzec and Sobibor in the spring of 1942, it was not applied to deportees from France until July 21, and not consistently until the beginning of August.

Patterns became clearer in August, when the expulsions of foreign Jews from the unoccupied zone were in full swing. Among other sources of information, Dr. Gerhart Riegner, the representative of the World Jewish Congress in Geneva, received a message at the end of July from a reliable German industrialist who traveled to Switzerland to report Nazi plans to kill all the Jews of Europe. Riegner relayed the message to the American and British foreign offices, where it was slowly digested, checked, confirmed by other sources, accepted, and released to the world in November.[71] In France itself on August 25, the Consistoire central des Israélites de France delivered a formal protest to Pétain, among others, that seemed remarkably well reasoned. Since the Nazis have accepted Jews of all ages and work capacities from the unoccupied zone, the protest read, it is clear that "it is not for purposes of labor that the German government is claiming them, but with the intention of exterminating them methodically and without pity."[72] Vichy officials may initially have been skeptical about the report. Indeed, Consistoire leaders themselves probably did not grasp its full dimensions and meaning. But as government officials, much more than Jewish or non-Jewish civilians, received information about systematic extermination from other sources, they could not have dismissed it entirely.

Among other sources of information was U.S. Secretary of State Cordell Hull, who met in Washington with the French ambassador to the United States, Henri Haye, on September 16. According to Haye's report of the meeting, Hull denounced Vichy's deliveries of refugee Jews to the Germans, who, in Haye's words, "have announced and in great part carried out their intention to mistreat, enslave and, eventually, exterminate these unhappy human beings in conditions of extreme cruelty."[73] But again, this was information from opponents of the Third Reich, and thus dismissable as enemy propaganda.

Furthermore, Hull's warning, like the earlier Radio Moscow and BBC reports, formed part of a wealth of rumors and assertions, many of which turned out to be as false as the allegations of German atrocities against civilians during the First World War had been. We cannot assume that information proven with hindsight to be correct should have been recognized as such at the time. The Germans vehemently denied extermination reports, presenting photographs, films, and the correspondence of Jews who were comfortable in deportation. Cold logic also contradicted the reasoning of Consistoire leaders. Why would the Nazis, who desperately needed workers, commit strategically important trains to transport people simply to murder them? In the face of such contradictions, Pétain, Laval, and the people around them, anxious to rid France of unwanted refugees and pleased to grasp the opportunity available, continued for some time to believe what they wanted to believe.

Reports of extermination kept coming from diplomats and churchmen, however, and Vichy officials' deliberate denials became much more difficult by mid-1943. Scholars generally conclude that, in the words of one, "the French state had no more and no less information than most other states on the reality of the 'Final Solution,' fragmentary for much of 1942, converging and in ample supply in 1943."[74] Léon Poliakov believes that Vichy officials did not know about the gas chambers in 1942, but that they surely learned much more around mid-1943. They received information from the clergy, he maintains, who learned because "the Vatican was well informed."[75]

Maurice Rajsfus also declares, probably correctly, that "they may not have known about the gas chambers, but by mid-1943 they knew everything else."[76]

These statements, however, all address the question of factual knowledge rather than emotional belief. To his own statement, Poliakov adds tellingly, "I did not believe it myself until April 1945!"[77] But Poliakov and other civilians had more limited access to information than did Laval and his aides. Also, as Jews in France saw loved ones and colleagues shipped off to an unknown destination, and as they increasingly understood their own danger, they had every reason to hope that the "facts" might not be true. Vichy officials had fewer psychological barriers to belief. By mid-1943, they surely knew and believed that large numbers of Jewish deportees were being killed in the east.

Until Laval's proposal for their deportation, Nazi intentions for Jewish children from France had been vague. Certainly Dannecker expected that they would ultimately be deported, but he was reluctant to arouse public opinion and preferred to maintain the impression that deportation was for work. Even as late as July 7 at a meeting of German and French officials planning the roundup of foreign Jews in Paris, it was stated that "children [under sixteen] will also be assembled at a single site, where they will be taken in charge by UGIF and transferred to shelters."[78] Dannecker was in fact in a quandary. He did not wish to appear less zealous than Vichy officials, and he was well aware of the problems that internment of a predicted 4,000 children would cause him. Since Laval did not care what happened to the children of foreign Jews in the occupied zone, Dannecker informed Eichmann of that fact on July 6 and asked urgently if he could eventually "evacuate" them. He repeated his request on July 10, stressing that UGIF would be unable to care for more than about 400 children, and that the prolonged "promiscuity" of contact between Jewish and non-Jewish children at French public assistance agencies was undesirable. On the eve of the July 16 roundup, he had still received no response from Berlin.

And so the stage was set.

6

The July Roundup, Paris, 1942

ON THE WARM, QUIET EVENING OF JULY 15, ADAM RAYSKI, A YOUNG
Polish Jewish immigrant and Communist Resistance worker, returned to Paris by train from a political assignment outside the city.
For security reasons related to his Resistance work rather than to his
Jewishness, he lived in a rented maid's room far from his wife and
child. As he walked slowly from the station to his room, he passed
mothers watching their children, and old people peacefully soaking
up the last sun of the day. From a local *brasserie* perpetually filled
with German officers and their French companions, the odor of
sauerkraut, unpleasant to a Parisian in summertime, followed him to
his very door. He thought contentedly of his family, for he carried in
his pocket the false identity cards and baptismal certificates that
would allow them to live without the star. He could not know it, but
at that very moment, his wife Jeanne, forewarned of the raid to
come, was desperately fleeing with their son through other Parisian
streets.

The next morning, Rayski's first appointment was at the Passy entrance to the métro. He describes what followed:

I was descending the stairway leading to the quais, when I saw,
below me, buses turning in the direction of the Grenelle bridge,

today the Bir-Hakeim bridge. Their unusual appearance struck me instantly. On their back platforms, you could see policemen surrounded with packages, suitcases and all sorts of bundles. . . .

Before crossing the bridge, the buses slowed down and I could see some faces. No more possible doubt, simply from the grief of their expressions I knew what was going on. My knees buckled under my body, I had to lean against the rail.

The comrade I met at the meeting place confirmed it. "Yes, it is a massive roundup."[1]

The French historian and author Annie Kriegel also remembers that July 16 morning vividly and with horror. Then fifteen years old and wearing the star, she had been taking her examinations for the *baccalauréat,* the French lycée diploma necessary for university admission, the previous day. Her mother arrived suddenly to tell her not to return home that night. There had been rumors of a roundup. Annie found shelter but left early the next morning. All seemed quiet, but when she rounded a corner onto the rue de Turenne in the old Jewish quarter,

I saw a policeman in uniform who was carrying a suitcase in each hand and crying.

I distinctly remember those tears running down a rugged, rather reddish face because you would agree that you do not often see a policeman cry in public. He was going down the street followed by a little indistinct flock, children and old people mixed together and carrying bundles. . . .

It was the roundup. I nevertheless went on my way until, at the crossing of the rue de Turenne and the rue de Bretagne, I heard screams rising to the heavens: not cries and squawks such as you hear in noisy and excited crowds, but screams like you used to hear in hospital delivery rooms. All the human pain that both life and death provide. A garage there was serving as a local assembly point, and they were separating the men and women.

Not knowing what to do, the young girl just sat down on a bench and waited. "It was on that bench that I left my childhood."[2]

The nightmare of *Jeudi noir* (Black Thursday), July 16, 1942, began at 4:00 A.M., when about 4,500 French policemen, nearly always in teams of at least two, began knocking on doors throughout Paris and the surrounding suburbs. They carried handfuls of a total of 27,388 carefully prepared index cards with the names of Jews to be arrested. The victims were men between the ages of sixteen and sixty, and women between sixteen and fifty-five. All were either stateless or from Germany, Austria, Poland, Czechoslovakia, or the Soviet Union; all were immigrants who had not become naturalized French citizens. Exempt within those categories were women about to give birth or with children under two; wives of prisoners of war; Jews with proof that they were married to non-Jews, plus widows and widowers of the same; Jews married to someone of a non-deportable nationality; Jews with special UGIF cards; and the children under age sixteen of the exemptees. Expressly not exempt were the sick, as well as the children over age two of those arrested, even if they had been born in France and naturalized by parental declaration at that time. Children were to accompany their parents unless a family member, such as a grandparent over the age of fifty-five or sixty, remained at home. They were not to be left with neighbors.[3]

Police instructions were minutely detailed. Jews were to bring their identification and ration cards, food for at least two days, and specific personal supplies: one pair of shoes, two pairs of socks, two shirts, one sweater, sheets, two blankets, a mess tin and drinking glass with fork and spoon, and toilet articles. They were to be allowed no more than two normal-sized suitcases per person. Police were to check that electricity, gas, and water were turned off. Keys were to be left with the concierge or with a neighbor. Pets were to be left with the concierge. Pets, at least, were not to suffer.[4]

Those arrested were to be taken for processing to designated assembly points—police stations, schools, or gymnasiums in each arrondissement or suburb. Fifty city buses were reserved to collect prisoners at the assembly points and take them to Drancy, if they were without children under sixteen, or to the Vélodrome d'Hiver, a glass-covered sports stadium in the rue Nelaton in the fifteenth arrondissement, if they were accompanied by children. Police instructions, otherwise so detailed, did not impart the reason for the two separate destinations. Those without children were expected at Drancy, up to its capacity of 6,000, so they could be immediately deported. Those with children were to go from the Vel' d'Hiv', as it was called, to Pithiviers and Beaune-la-Rolande, to await final authorization for their deportation. Police did receive details about the buses, however. All windows were to be closed, and only guards were to ride on the back platforms. Parisians were to be spared the sorry sight as much as possible.

As might be expected, policemen on July 16 and 17 obeyed their orders with various degrees of zeal. Some knocked down doors and searched apartments thoroughly; others left apartments where no one opened the door, with obvious relief.[5] Most bustled their victims efficiently out the door; a few, especially in the rare cases where they operated alone, told families to prepare and that they would return in fifteen minutes, thus giving individuals a chance to escape.[6] Some policemen insisted on taking every child in the apartment; others declared that they would take only children born outside France. Some took the sick and even the dying; a few left invalids behind. The majority, however, performed their unpleasant duties with neither zeal nor compassion. Maurice Rajsfus notes that one of the two policemen who came to his parents' door was a neighbor but treated them with the cold indifference of a complete stranger.[7] No more than two or three policemen resigned as a result of the roundup.[8]

Non-Jewish friends, neighbors, and even total strangers displayed similarly varied reactions, and most individual survivors testify that they witnessed the whole range of possible behavior. The policeman who arrested her family allowed nine-year-old Annette Muller, for example, to go out to buy a comb when she could not find hers. He apparently hoped that she would not return. A kind shopkeeper then urged her to escape, but she obediently went back. She recalls, however, that other passersby expressed approval of the roundup. In addition, the concierge, who knew her family well, pillaged their apartment after their arrest.[9]

Eight-year-old Annette Zaidman had similar experiences. She was living with her aunt and cousin at the time. The policeman who knocked on their door gave them fifteen minutes to prepare, and then left. He was downstairs looking into a shop window when the three of them, still in nightgowns, ran across the street to a neighbor's apartment. "It is impossible that he did not see us," she declares. Yet his compassion was countered by the viciousness of the concierge, who told another policeman where they were hiding the next morning. They escaped a second time, but barely.[10]

Seven-year-old Odette Meyers was fortunate to have known Marie Chotel, a totally different type of concierge. At 5:00 A.M., Marie pulled Odette and her mother out of bed with a warning that the police were coming. Mother and daughter hid in Marie's broom closet while she assured the policemen that they had gone to the country. She proceeded to entertain the men with wine and anti-Semitic comments to keep them from going upstairs to look at the freshly abandoned apartment. When the police left, Marie's husband Henri took Odette to a Catholic family in a small village, where she hid for the remainder of the war.[11]

Adam Rayski's wife Jeanne found kindness even from total strangers. While others on the eve of the roundup debated what to do, she acted instantly. Tearing off her star, she fled, holding her child on her left side to cover the telltale stitches. She spent the night in a small hotel, but the next morning the hotelkeeper tried to put her out. She saw people outside being rounded up and began to cry with terror. Other customers loudly berated the hotelkeeper, and he relented. When she finally left, he would accept no payment.[12]

For all concerned, July 16 was a day of terror. Many, especially mothers with small children, quietly obeyed the police, but others fled across rooftops or tried to hide with neighbors. Some succeeded, but many did not. Unknown numbers attempted suicide. A woman on the rue Poitou threw her two small children from the window of her fifth-floor apartment and then leaped herself. All three died. Another woman hesitated before jumping with her small son, giving firemen time to put out a net that saved them. Both survived to die in the gas chambers at Auschwitz.[13] Others also chose suicide by leaping from windows, throwing themselves down stairwells, administering poison or lethal injections, or other means.

By the end of the raid at 5:00 P.M. on July 16, 11,363 Jews had been arrested. By 5:00 P.M. on the following day, the total was 12,884, including 3,031 men, 5,802 women, and 4,051 children.[14] The preponderance of women and children was striking even to contemporaries. SS First Lieutenant Heinz Röthke, soon to replace Dannecker as chief of the Gestapo's Jewish Office in France, explained that "during preceding raids, we took principally men and . . . [on this occasion] clearly more men than women have hidden in time."[15] The numbers of those who hid are suggested by the gap between those arrested and the 27,388 originally listed on the police index cards.

Many had been warned. Hundreds of policemen, as well as the bureaucrats and office workers who had sorted file cards, organized schedules, and read police circulars, had learned of the roundup several days in advance, and some had warned Jewish friends. Even Jewish UGIF workers had been employed before the event in making name tags for the children. They suspected trouble and warned a few acquaintances.[16] Only the luckiest minority received precise details of the raid, but many heard general rumors. Meanwhile, at least one

Communist pamphlet and one clandestine newspaper, passed from hand to hand, advised people to flee.

The statistics indicate that many people heeded the warnings, but others, terrified, without resources, or simply skeptical of the danger, did not. Hélène Elek, a Hungarian Jew ineligible for arrest in July, learned of the roundup from a friendly policeman in the fifth arrondissement, where she lived, and warned a Polish family. Refusing to hide, all were arrested. As they marched through the streets to the assembly point, the parents refused to let any of their four children escape to Mrs. Elek. They had dismissed the warnings. Like thousands of others, they could not believe that anyone would harm women and children. After their arrest, they failed, like most others, to grasp the horrors that lay ahead. It seemed best to remain together.[17]

Maurice Rajsfus recalls that his parents had also heard talk of a raid, but "so many false warnings had already reached us that we did not attach the necessary importance [to this one]." In addition, they regarded arrest as "a reasonable possibility which they finally had to resolve. An adversity they could no longer escape."[18] The father's two brothers had been arrested in May 1941, and their own arrests seemed unavoidable. Quite reasonably, they expected to be interned near Paris, as the brothers had been so far, for the duration of the war.

Some other families acted but limited their precautions to the men. Fania Elbinger Ewenczyk, then living in Paris with her mother and younger sister, recalls that ten foreign Jewish men came to their apartment to sleep on the night of July 15 because they had heard rumors of the raid. They believed it to be only for men, as those in May, August, and December 1941 had been, and they felt safe in a home with only women. Arrests of men for work in Germany were conceivable; arrests of women and children were not. Fortunately enough, the apartment was not raided.[19]

Annette Muller Bessmann records that her parents also heard rumors and assumed that the roundup would be only for men. Her father slept elsewhere that night and escaped arrest. His wife Rachel and their four children were seized. The children all miraculously avoided deportation, but Rachel, who had walked so proudly through Paris with the star, died at Auschwitz. Mr. Muller, who had previously escaped from Gurs and who, after the July roundup, managed to save all his children, never forgave himself for his wife's death.[20]

* * *

After their arrests, whole families walked through the streets of Paris to the local assembly points, in full view of curious spectators. One survivor later described her experience:

People stared at us, but I could not make out what they were thinking. Their faces seemed blank and indifferent. At Place Voltaire there was a small crowd, and one woman started shouting: "I'm glad! I'm glad! Let them all go to the devil!" But she was the only one. The children clung to me tighter. As we passed the group, a man turned to the woman who had shouted and said, "It'll be our turn next. Poor things." She blushed and walked away. The policemen told us to walk faster.[21]

Few Parisians remained unaware of the day's events. The twenty-eight-year-old novelist Claude Mauriac wrote in his journal on the evening of July 16: "In various spots in Paris and at different times of day, I came across buses where three French policemen guarded Jewish prisoners, going toward what fate? . . . The heart tightens, one is ashamed to be there, to be present at such ignominious sights and remain silent."[22]

At the assembly points, documents were checked and a few lucky individuals were released. Fourteen-year-old Maurice Rajsfus and his sister were among them. In their case, the local police commander at Vincennes, just east of Paris, decided that children over fourteen born in France should be freed. Mrs. Rajsfus did not hesitate an instant. She gave her daughter all the money she had and pushed them out the door. The parents were murdered at Auschwitz.[23] Maurice was fortunate to escape the same fate, for children over age two of Jews eligible for deportation were supposed to remain with their parents.

An additional fortunate few, usually children, managed to escape during the confusion at the assembly points. Rachel Muller, for example, found a sympathetic policeman at the site and, while talking to him, pushed her two oldest sons, ages ten and eleven, out the door.[24] A woman named Mrs. Soral similarly pushed her ten-year-old son out of a center at a police station near the Panthéon, in the fifth arrondissement, and a Mrs. Landau herself walked out of the center in the town hall of the tenth arrondissement.[25] Most centers, however, were carefully guarded, and prisoners were usually overwhelmed with confusion and terror. Most remained, awaiting the buses that would take them to the next stop.

For 4,992 men and women without children under sixteen, the next stop was Drancy. Buses filled with prisoners began arriving at the camp as early as 7:00 A.M. on July 16 and continued all day. New arrivals waited hours in the courtyard for processing. Dorothée and Samuel Epstein described conditions at Drancy at that time in a letter to their daughter Nathalie:

> Filth of a coal mine. Straw mattress full of lice and bedbugs. Horrid overcrowding. Eighty-six women, six water faucets, you don't have time to wash. There are paralyzed women, women who have had breast operations and can't move their arms, pregnant women, blind women, deaf mutes, women on stretchers, women who have left their small children all alone. Old women of 63. You can't go to the toilet more than once every 16 hours.[26]

Most new arrivals remained at Drancy for only a few days. Deportations began on July 19 and recurred on July 22, 24, 27, and 29. Each convoy left from Le Bourget train station, a five-minute bus ride from Drancy, and ended at Auschwitz. Each train carried about 1,000 people. Most of the deportees were foreign Jews arrested in Paris on July 16 and 17, but 172 were victims of a simultaneous raid in Bordeaux. Of the 172, 38 were French.[27]

Passengers on the July 19 convoy were the first from France to undergo selection on the Auschwitz arrival ramp rather than automatic admission to the camp. As they descended from the train on July 21, 375 men were separated from the others and gassed, only five days after their arrests in Paris. Prisoners on the convoy of July 29 also experienced a selection; 216 women were promptly gassed. All other prisoners on the five trains were admitted—a policy that changed drastically in August. Nevertheless, at the end of the war, only 47 of these approximately 5,000 deportees were known to have survived.[28]

The families arrested on July 16 and 17 with children under sixteen did not go directly to Drancy but were taken to the Vélodrome d'Hiver, near the Eiffel Tower. Despite the detailed plans for the raid itself, few preparations had been made at the Vel' d'Hiv' for an internment that was, in many cases, to last nearly a week. French bureaucrats had again demonstrated a horrendous indifference to human life. More than 8,000 people, including 1,129 men, 2,916 women, and about 4,000 children, were crowded into a glass-covered stadium that was poorly ventilated and stiflingly hot. The glass itself, painted blue for camouflage in the event of an air raid, created a constantly dim and dreary interior light.

Young and old slept on the hard bleachers or on the ground. For several days, prisoners had only the food they had brought with them, supplemented by inadequate supplies of soup from the Red Cross and the Quakers. Since the water in the sinks had been turned off, prisoners could not wash and had almost nothing to drink. Several bathrooms were closed because they had windows that could serve as escape routes. The remaining toilets promptly jammed. People were forced to relieve themselves in corners or where they stood. In all survivor testimony of the Vel' d'Hiv', the most regularly recurring theme is the unbearable and degrading stench, which overwhelmed prisoners and guards alike. Descriptions also focus on the constant noise, absolute lack of privacy, and insufficient medical care.

A team of twelve to fifteen volunteer nurses and a few doctors tried to care for elderly people with heart conditions, women giving birth, children running about freely with measles and mumps, individuals with intestinal problems caused by the vile food, people who went insane from despair, and several suicide attempts, some of which succeeded. Only a few of the most desperately ill were evacuated, usually to the Rothschild Hospital where they either died or waited, under close French guard, until they could again be interned and deported.[29]

Eyewitness testimony to the horror at the Vel' d'Hiv' abounds. André Baur, the director of UGIF-North, was permitted to enter the stadium on the evening of July 16. He wrote at the time: "There is no trace of even the slightest organization, no direction, no chief or too many of them. . . . A woman who went crazy is tied to a stretcher; another tried to kill her child with a bottle. Another child was brought in, the veins of his wrist lacerated by his mother."[30] A Red Cross nurse later recalled: "The atmosphere was stuffy and nauseating: nervous breakdowns, shouting, weeping of children and even of adults who were at the end of their tether. Several deranged individuals spread panic. All was helter-skelter, it was impossible to sleep, there were no mattresses, people were piled one on top of the other."[31] And Sarah Castel, then age five, later described her memory of the Vel' d'Hiv': "Those cries of grief, of horror, of fear, in my spirit as a young child, the memory is of those cries, that horrible odor, the tears of children and that constant blue light day and night."[32]

Profiting from the confusion at the entrances and exits of the Vel' d'Hiv', a fortunate few, with luck, ingenuity, and in some cases police connivance, managed to escape. A Mrs. Linen covered her fifteen-year-old son Nat's star with a coat and sent him away from the bus before entering the stadium. She herself died at Auschwitz. Fourteen-year-old Louis Pitkowicz slipped out while a group of angry mothers was arguing with a police guard. A Mrs. Lichtein helped her little daughter to walk out; questioned by a guard apparently inclined to give her the benefit of the doubt, the child said she was simply visiting. The mother herself then also escaped. She was turned back several times at different exits by angry guards, until she finally found one who would look the other way. And Mrs. Ida Nussbaum also hung around an exit, explaining that her baby son needed fresh air, until she saw her chance.[33] But such cases were exceptional, made possible by the improvised nature of the internment center and the occasional goodwill of a guard.[34]

Some fathers, mothers, and young children left the Vel' d'Hiv' for their next destination within three days, while others remained at the stadium for nearly a week. As they climbed into the same green and beige Renault buses that had brought them in on July 16, many prisoners must have hoped that their next stop would be more comfortable. That was not to be. Most were taken to the Gare d'Austerlitz, where they boarded trains for the journey to Pithiviers and Beaune-la-Rolande, emptied by the deportations of prisoners a few weeks before. At these two camps in the Loiret, prisoners suffered the same hunger, filth, and degradation as at the Vel' d'Hiv'. Then, beginning on July 31, a new and incomparably more horrible nightmare began. Permission to deport young children had not yet arrived from Berlin, and so, to keep the trains filled, authorities decided to send parents and children over fourteen first. Younger children would follow within a week or two. In the meantime, they would have to fend for themselves.

Annette Muller Bessmann, then nine, later described the result at Beaune:

Everyone was assembled in the center of the camp. The children hung on to their mothers, pulling on their dresses. They had to separate us with rifle butts, with truncheons, with streams of icy water. It was a savage scramble, with cries, tears, howlings of grief. The *gendarmes* tore the women's clothing, still looking for jewels or money. Then suddenly, a great silence. On one side, hundreds of young children, on the other the mothers and older children. In the middle, the *gendarmes* giving curt orders.[35]

Annette never saw her mother again.

On July 31 and August 3, 5, and 7, more than 4,000 parents and their older children were marched through Pithiviers and Beaune-la-Rolande, in full view of local residents, and loaded onto four trains for Auschwitz. From the first train, all 1,183 people—693 men, 359 women, and 131 adolescents—were admitted to the camp. Sixteen were alive at the end of the war. Passengers on the other three convoys experienced selections for mass murder; about 2,000, including at least 500 adolescents, were promptly gassed. The others—about 1,150—were admitted to the camp. Nineteen of them are known to have survived.[36]

By the evening of August 7, exactly three weeks after the July 16 roundup, nine efficiently operated trains had transported more than 9,000 mostly foreign Jews from French soil to Auschwitz. Left behind, however, were about 3,500 of the weakest and most helpless victims of the roundup—the children under fourteen. Their story can only be told by the adults who saw them leave, for not one child returned from deportation. The story of the children is the most horrifying, heartrending episode of the Holocaust in France, and the most shameful.

The bewildered and terrified children were left at Pithiviers and Beaune with a few mothers and a handful of Red Cross volunteers. They slept on a layer of straw on the floor, in overcrowded and always noisy rooms. Most had diarrhea from the cabbage soup and rutabaga that was all they were given to eat. Their overworked attendants could not keep their clothes clean; as soon as pants were washed, they were soiled again. Many children did not even know their own names—a reality that belied the official claim that they were to be sent east to be reunited with their families.

Permission for the deportation of children to Auschwitz was finally issued from Berlin in early August.[37] The Red Cross worker Annette Monod Leiris remembers the day when the children were consequently taken to the railroad station, to be shipped in groups of about 1,000 each from Pithiviers and Beaune-la-Rolande to Drancy:

We were standing only two hundred yards from the station, but that is a long way for small children hampered by clumsy bundles.

I noticed one *gendarme* take the bundle of a boy of about four or five to help him walk. But he was immediately reprimanded by an adjutant, who told him rudely that a French soldier did not carry the bags of a Jew. Sheepishly the soldier handed the little bundle back to the boy.

. . . Many of the children were too small to climb into the freight cars without the help of a ladder, so the bigger boys would climb in first and help the younger ones pull themselves up. The *gendarmes* lifted the babies who were hardly weaned and handed them to the women, nursing mothers, or the children who were already on board.

. . . Jacquot, a little five-year-old of whom I was particularly fond, started shouting for me: "I want to get down, I want to stay with Mademoiselle. . . ." The door of the car was shut and bolted, but Jacquot pushed his hand through a gap between two planks and continued to call for me, moving his fingers. The adjutant mentioned above hit him on the hand.[38]

Other witnesses remember the arrival of these same children at Drancy. Georges Wellers recorded:

The children climbed down from the buses [that had brought them from the train station] and instantly the older ones took the little ones by the hand and did not leave them during the short trip to their rooms. In the stairways, the older ones took the smallest ones in their arms and, out of breath, carried them to the fourth floor. There, they stayed one against another, like a frightened little flock of lambs, hesitating a long time before sitting on the disgustingly filthy mattresses. Most of them no longer knew where their bags were. . . . When the buses were unloaded, the children went down into the courtyard to look for their things. The little bundles without names were really difficult to recognize, and for a long time children of four, five, six years wandered among them hoping to find theirs at any moment. . . . After many fruitless attempts, they gave up and remained in the courtyard not knowing what to do. Those who wanted to go back to their rooms often did not know where to go. Then, very politely, with soft and pleading voices, they said: "Sir, I don't know where my little sister is, maybe she is afraid to be all alone."[39]

Soon after the end of the war, Odette Daltroff-Baticle, an adult prisoner at Drancy in the autumn of 1942, also recorded the arrival of the children:

The buses arrived. We took the small creatures from them in an unimaginable state. Clusters of insects surrounded them, as well as a terrible odor. They had travelled from Pithiviers in sealed box cars for days and nights, 90 in a car, with a woman who in general had 2, 3, or 4 of her own children in the group.

They ranged in age from 15 months to 13 years, the filth was indescribable, three-quarters of them have pus-filled bruises all over, and impetigo. . . .

With great cowardice, we told them that they would be reunited with their parents, and that way they could bear up to anything.

I will never forget the faces of those children; endlessly they parade before my eyes. They are serious, profound, and, what is extraordinary: in these little faces, the horror of the days which they are living is branded. They have understood everything, like adults. Some of them are accompanied by their little brothers and sisters, and take admirably good care of them. They have understood their responsibilities.

They show us their most precious belongings: the pictures of their mothers and fathers which their mothers gave them when they parted. Hastily the mothers wrote a tender inscription. We all have tears in our eyes; we imagine that tragic instant, the immense pain of the mothers.[40]

The children were jammed, in groups of about 100, into bare rooms that served as dormitories. They slept on a thin layer of filthy straw. Each room opened onto a stairwell, where a sharp and rusty bucket served as an inadequate toilet for children racked with diarrhea and dysentery. A few harassed volunteers tried to improve food distribution, cleanliness, and comfort, but it was a hopeless task. The children were too disoriented, too often ill, and above all, too numerous.

They did not remain long at Drancy. Within a day or two, preparations for their departure to the east began. Some child in the camp referred to their mysterious destination—the place where they would be reunited with their parents—as "Pitchipoi," and the name stuck. Money and jewelry were not permitted in Pitchipoi. French guards searched the bundles of children as young as two or three, seizing bracelets and earrings from little girls. In one case when an earring did not open easily, a French inspector simply tore it from the ear of a terrified ten-year-old.[41]

Lists of up to 500 children each were drawn up, to be deported in seven convoys with an equal number of adults, total strangers who nevertheless helped maintain the illusion that the children had not been condemned to face their fate alone.[42] Then, in the words of Georges Wellers, who witnessed the scene:

> On the day of their deportation, the children were awakened at 5:00 A.M. and were dressed in the semi-darkness. It was often cool at 5:00 A.M., but almost all the children went down into the court-yard very lightly dressed. Awakened in the night, groggy with sleep, the little ones began to cry and little by little the others copied them. They did not want to go down into the courtyard, they struggled, they did not let themselves be dressed. It happened sometimes that a whole room of one hundred children, seized with uncontrollable panic and bewilderment, no longer listened to the soothing words of the adults who were unable to make them go downstairs; then they called the *gendarmes* who brought down children in their arms who were screaming with terror.[43]

The children were again loaded into buses for the short ride to Le Bourget station. There they, like the adults who had preceded them, were packed into cattle cars, and the doors were sealed for the three-day journey to Auschwitz. The scene inside those overcrowded cars can scarcely be imagined. The lack of light alone was enough to cause panic among toddlers still afraid of the dark. There was no food or water, only an overflowing bucket for a toilet, and only straw for a mattress. Brothers and sisters were often separated, and babies as young as two or three found themselves totally alone. In theory, each car contained from one to ten adults, usually women, to reassure forty, sixty, and, in some cases, over ninety terrified young-sters. In such circumstances, reassurance was not possible.

Between August 17 and 31, seven trains left Drancy for Auschwitz carrying about 1,000 people each. Between one-third and one-half of the passengers in each train were unaccompanied children—the chil-dren from Vel' d' Hiv'. We do not know how many of them died alone in the boxcars during the journey. Nor do we know how they were unloaded at Auschwitz. Did they panic at the incomprehensible barking of orders in German? Did they weep when they lost their bundles, their last memories from home, or when they were sepa-rated from siblings, friends, or attendants? Did they obey orders to disrobe and wait patiently in front of the showers that were the gas chambers? Did they scream when the lights went out, when they died in total darkness? Were they actually asphyxiated, or were they tram-pled to death in the mad struggle within the chamber to reach the last bit of oxygen near the ceiling? How many survived the gas chamber, trapped in a tiny pocket of oxygen beneath a pile of dead bodies, only to be thrust alive into the crematorium? We do not know. Even asking such questions is unbearable. We do know, however, that none of the deported children from the Vel' d' Hiv' returned to the France that had betrayed them.[44]

7

Expulsions from the Unoccupied Zone, August–September 1942

IN EARLY AUGUST 1942, AS PARENTS AND ADOLESCENTS WERE BEING separated from younger children at Pithiviers and Beaune-la-Rolande and shipped to Auschwitz, French police in the unoccupied zone prepared to deliver 10,000 foreign Jews to the Nazis. On August 5, a confidential dispatch from René Bousquet, the secretary-general of the French police, to the regional prefects of the unoccupied zone provided detailed instructions for that delivery. With the exception of eleven precise categories, all Jews from specific countries who had entered France after January 1, 1936, were to be rounded up and transported to the occupied zone before September 15, whether or not they had been naturalized. The countries or areas of origin included Germany, Austria, Czechoslovakia, Poland, Estonia, Lithuania, Latvia, Danzig, the Saar, and the Soviet Union.

Specifically excluded from arrest and expulsion were elderly Jews over age sixty; unaccompanied children under eighteen; parents with a child under five; pregnant women; people incapable of being moved; veterans (and their families) of combat or of at least three months' military service with the French army or former allied armies; men or women with French spouses or children, or with spouses from countries other than those eligible for delivery; and adults with jobs in the national economic interest or with a record of special service to France. Exemptees could, however, choose to remain with nonexempted family members. All individuals eligible for expulsion were to be prevented from emigrating, even if they already held exit visas. Finally, in a clause that became critical later, the dispatch stated that "parents with children under eighteen could, if they so desired, leave them in the free zone."[1]

Although details were unclear to the public, the likelihood of a massive delivery of Jews from south to north had been suspected for weeks. Theodor Dannecker, the chief of the Gestapo's Jewish Office in France, visited internment camps and forced-residence hotels in the unoccupied zone in July, compiling statistics and consolidating plans. During the last days of July, Vichy officials ordered directors of internment camps to restrict visits and reinforce security. They informed prefects that trains carrying foreign Jews would pass through their departments and instructed gendarme officers to prepare escorts to accompany trains as far as Drancy. Grand Rabbi René Hirschler learned on July 20 that the government had decided to deport recent Jewish immigrants and traveled to Vichy to learn details. He was not successful.[2]

Throughout July, foreign Jews trapped in internment camps, the most certain targets for expulsion, became increasingly apprehensive. Ria Rosenthal's memory of Gurs applies to other camps as well. "In the camp, the agitation began a week before the deportations. Everyone knew a little of what was happening, but no one knew anything precise. Everyone had packed his bags."[3] Some succeeded in escaping. Outside the camps, foreign Jews in supervised residence or still living freely with legal papers began to wonder whether the danger applied also to them. The secret police dispatch of August 5 stated that the recent immigrants among them were to be arrested and expelled, but only a few with special connections shared that inside information.

One of the first camps to be affected by Vichy's expulsion order was Gurs. On August 6, only a day after the final dispatch explaining the event to the regional prefects, about 1,003 Jews with last names beginning with the letters A through M were crowded into sealed boxcars and sent to Drancy. On August 8, 600 with names beginning with N to Z followed. As the list of names was read out loud, Rosenthal remembers, "there reigned the silence of death. Many women had fits of weeping in the barracks."[4] Several people attempted suicide, while a few hid in attics, shacks, or latrines. But according to Franz Soël, a prisoner who witnessed the events, those hiding numbered only about 15. He explains, "We did not know that we were to be deported to Poland. We knew only that we were leaving on German orders and we thought that the whole camp would be evacuated." French gendarmes carefully explained that internees were to be reassembled in a special camp for Jews near Besançon in the occupied zone. Some individuals, unwilling to abandon a parent, spouse, sibling, or child, volunteered to go. Soël commented, "The people were very courageous, perhaps because they did not suspect what awaited them or perhaps because they had already become a little tougher."[5]

Most of the first to be expelled were the same German Jews who had been deported from Baden to France in October 1940. They had been shipped west, only to be turned around two years later to be murdered in the east. Many exceeded Vichy's age limit of sixty. Witnesses speak of old women unable to carry their bags in the suffocating late afternoon heat on the slow, two- or three-hour walk to the local station. Soël recalls, "One woman had two heavy suitcases and she carried them separately ten meters by ten meters, first one and then the other. Even the guards watched her with a sad air."[6] Guards had orders not to help, but social workers could be present. Representatives from the Quakers, Secours suisse, OSE, and CIMADE distributed fruit, chocolate, and cheese and provided what little comfort they could.

It was the last kindness the prisoners would receive. By delivering them to the Nazis as carelessly as they had handed over German political refugees the year before, Vichy officials in fact sentenced them to death. Those who left Gurs on August 6 arrived at Drancy the following day, only to leave again on August 10 for Auschwitz. About 585 of the 600 in the August 8 train from Gurs, with 161 Jews from Noé, 173 from Récébédou, and 88 from Le Vernet, followed on August 12. Of the August 10 convoy of 1,000, the first to carry Jews from the unoccupied zone to Auschwitz, 760 were selected to be gassed, 240 were admitted to the camp, and one man returned after the war. Of the August 12 train carrying 1,007 prisoners, 712 were gassed, 295 were admitted to the camp, and 11 ultimately survived.[7]

An eyewitness account by Thérèse Dauty written in August 1942 confirms that the first departures of Jews from Noé and Récébédou resembled those from Gurs. About 340 victims from the two camps were assembled in a special isolation block at Récébédou as early as August 3. They were held there in overcrowded and filthy conditions for five days. Like their counterparts at Gurs, they then had to walk to the station, lugging their bags for two hours, in full view of the general public. Miss Dauty continued:

> The saddest cases were certainly the old women, obliged to stop every few steps, with tears in their eyes, no longer even begging for mercy.
>
> The guards who supervised the move in great numbers could not keep from expressing their amazement at the treatment inflicted on these people, and many of them took it upon themselves to carry their baggage.
>
> The approaches to the station were surrounded by a large contingent of police, some mounted and the others armed with machine guns. Their number probably reached several hundred.[8]

Several hundred armed French police guarded 340 often old and feeble Jewish immigrants who had sought asylum in the country of the rights of man. The government of that country was now turning them over to the Nazis for slaughter.

About 120 of the internees from Noé and Récébédou joined 400 from Rivesaltes on yet a third train to Drancy on August 11. At the station of Sorgues-Chateauneuf-du-Pape (Vaucluse), they picked up an additional 260 people from Les Milles.[9] En route to Drancy, the train stopped for forty-five minutes at the station in Lyon. Somehow, Quakers and members of the Consistoire israélite lyonnais learned of its presence and tried to give prisoners food and desperately needed water. French police barred public access to the quay where the train was standing. Only a few railroad and postal workers were able to get through with water, bread, and fruit. The reaction of the police to this breach of orders was typically mixed. Most pretended not to notice, while a few threatened offenders with punishment and turned them away.[10]

Three days later, about 750 of the 780 recent Jewish immigrants expelled from the unoccupied zone on August 11 joined 238 arrested in the Paris area, including more than 100 children under sixteen and some others, in another convoy from Drancy to Auschwitz. The train of August 14 was the first to carry children under age twelve. Upon arrival at Auschwitz, at least 875 people, including all the women and children, were gassed. All 115 men on the train between ages 18 and 42 were selected for work. One man returned in 1945.[11]

Like the prisoners from Rivesaltes, Jews from Les Milles left for Drancy on August 11, but their ordeal had begun several days before. According to some witnesses, the camp director, Robert Maulavé, far from happy with his orders, urged internees to escape on Sunday, August 2.[12] They had little time to decide, however, for early the next morning gendarmes and *gardes mobiles* (police of the Groupes mobiles de réserve [GMR]) sealed the camp and refused to grant the usual exit passes for errands in town.[13] Other gendarmes began bringing in women and children from the forced-residence hotels in Marseille, the Bompard, Terminus, and Levant, as well as men from nearby forced-labor camps. The women, rendered immobile by lack of money or contacts and by responsibilities for small children, had little chance to escape. Men in the labor camps were sometimes more fortunate.

Some survivors testify to the sympathetic attitudes of their forced-labor group leaders. At Miramas, according to two witnesses, someone announced on the evening of August 2, "Everyone still here tomorrow will be delivered to the Germans." Similarly, at Saint-Cyr-sur-Mer, La Ciotat, and Salin-de-Giraud, foreign Jewish workers were warned several hours before departure that they were to be returned to Les Milles, giving them time to disappear. Fifty of sixty-two men at the first camp, thirty of sixty at the second, and several others at the third managed to escape.[14] Flight, of course, brought the risk of future detection, arrest, and, it was thought, more certain and severe punishment. And while escape itself was not difficult, hiding was virtually impossible without help. Those who fled on August 2 and 3 found shelter with farmers, priests, and villagers in the region of Aix-en-Provence and Marseille. Thousands of other fugitives would soon do the same.

Not all supervisors, of course, allowed their Jewish workers to escape. Hans Fraenkel, a journalist and a Jewish convert to Protestantism, wrote that his isolated group at Corconne and Aulas (Gard) received no warning. When their guard mentioned Poland as they were leaving for Les Milles, Fraenkel and the other workers attributed it to the man's usual sadistic humor.[15] Throughout the day of August 3, cars and buses brought in 200 to 300 men from scattered work sites and farms in Provence.[16]

The screening at Les Milles of internees, women and children from the Marseille hotels, and forced laborers began immediately. Aided by representatives of various Jewish and non-Jewish social organizations, camp personnel checked each individual's documents for age, country of origin, date of immigration to France, service record, and family connections. Parents with sons in or previously in the Foreign Legion or the regular French army tried desperately to provide proof and often sent religious or social workers scurrying about the country for proper documentation.[17] Spouses of French citizens sought similar proof. Many prisoners requested medical certificates stating inability to travel; from a Dr. Raybaud at the camp, some women even obtained papers stating falsely that they were pregnant.[18] Some candidates for deportation were practicing Christians classified as Jews because of the religion of parents or grandparents. Searches for baptismal certificates became more urgent than ever, and some pastors and priests issued false documents.[19]

The most wrenching cases involved the children. By August 8, Julien Samuel, OSE director of Marseille, aided by Grand Rabbi Israël Salzer, the French Protestant pastor Henri Manen, and others, had begun a campaign to persuade parents to leave their children under eighteen behind, as the expulsion order allowed. The youngsters would be delivered to Quaker or YMCA workers who would assign them to Jewish or non-Jewish children's homes in France or help them emigrate safely to the United States. In an agony of desperation, all but one parent eventually realized that they had little choice. Virtually no one understood that all Jewish children in the concentration camps in the east were immediately killed, but most knew that conditions there were rigorous in the extreme. Most had heard about Dachau and other Nazi camps and realized that children could not survive there. Separation was best for the children, but for the parents, assigning them to total strangers with the knowledge that they themselves would be out of reach for years, if not forever, was painful beyond words.

On Monday morning, August 10, about seventy children from Les Milles were loaded into buses for the journey back to the Hotel Bompard in Marseille, where many of them had already lived for months with their mothers.[20] There were many witnesses. One remembers:

> The young children, who could not understand the reason for this separation, held on to their parents and cried. The older ones, who knew how great their parents' suffering was, tried to control their own anguish and clenched their teeth. The women clung to the doors of the departing buses. . . . No protest, no cry of indignation or anger was heard. It seemed that after so much suffering, the internees no longer had the strength to rebel against their fate.[21]

Raymond-Raoul Lambert, the director of UGIF-South, also described the terrible scene in his journal:

It was necessary to hold back the fathers and mothers when the buses [with the children] left the courtyard. What cries and what tears, what gestures from the poor fathers who, before the final deportation, caressed the face of a son or a daughter as if to preserve its imprint on their finger tips! Mothers wailed in despair and no one could hold back the tears. . . . I have seen and experienced two wars, but those two cataclysms did not leave in my mind memories more shameful than these days passed in the courtyard at Les Milles.[22]

Pastor Henri Manen left still another poignant eyewitness account in his journal entry for August 10:

Atrocious separations. A big, good-looking, seventeen or eighteen-year-old lad is between his father and his mother. . . . He is not crying. But he leans first toward one, then toward the other, grazing his face against theirs slowly and sweetly with all the tenderness in the world. Not a word. The father and mother weep silently without stopping. That goes on and on. No one speaks. Finally the bus starts. From the biggest to the smallest, everyone bursts into tears. Not a cry, not a gesture. But tense faces which for one last moment want to look for eternity. All around me the police are ghostly pale. One of them will say to me the next day, "I have been in the colonies. I have been in China. I have seen massacres, war, famines. I have seen nothing as horrible as this."[23]

After the children left, devastated parents joined other internees in an interminable afternoon roll call in the courtyard of Les Milles, under the pitiless sun of Provence. Several people fainted; others attempted suicide; many tried to hide or escape.[24] Bulgarian internees, as yet ineligible for deportation because of their nationality, helped many find hiding places. Auguste César Boyer, a camp guard, helped a family with children hide in a loft for two days and then guided them out of the camp at night and sheltered them in his home in the village.[25] At least three other guards helped Jews, and the camp director, Maulavé, refused to participate in the action from disgust and rage.[26] According to Pastor Manen, however, other French police performed their duties with zeal, thoroughly searching the buildings to catch evaders, and stealing prisoners' few precious belongings at the same time.[27] The diversity of French responses at Les Milles reflected that of French men and women throughout the country.

Toward evening, more than 270 Jews with names beginning with the letters *A* to *G* were marched through the village, in full public view, to the nearby railroad station. As Quakers marched up and down the length of the train passing out chocolate, condensed milk, sardines, and olives, the prisoners were loaded into boxcars. One observer later recorded, "They were cattle cars, strewn with bunches of straw. In each car, a jug of water and a bucket to serve as a toilet."[28] The transport of Jews in unoccupied France was as brutal as that conducted by the Nazis.

The doors were sealed, closing out light and fresh air, but the train remained in the station all night in the stifling August heat. Again aided by the camp guard Boyer, a fortunate few escaped through the weak floorboards of one car, but at least 260 departed at 8:00 A.M. on Tuesday, August 11.[29] Three days later, as we have seen, 236 of them were among the 1,015 Jews sent from Drancy to Auschwitz. Their train carried 100 children from the Paris region but none from Les Milles or Rivesaltes. For some parents, the only consolation as they gazed at other people's children was the knowledge that they had been allowed to leave their own children behind.

Back at Les Milles, on Wednesday, August 12, 538 more internees with names beginning with the letters *H* to *Z* waited all day under the blazing sun and marched to the station in the evening.[30] The guard, tripled from the earlier train, now numbered 4 officers and 129 men. Police brutality also increased. One onlooker recalled, "The relative calm of the day before had been transformed into a much more brutal attitude. The guards harassed the column, which was not moving as fast as they wished, reinforcing their commands with a kick of a boot. A gendarme captain hit a deportee with his fist."[31] The second sealed train from Les Milles also remained at the station all night, finally leaving for Drancy at 8:00 A.M. on August 13. The onlooker continued, "Not a cry, not a protest came from the boxcars, where the faces were pressed against the window bars. And this silence, this quiet courage to the very last minute, was more heartbreaking than tears."[32]

On August 17, yet another convoy from Drancy to Auschwitz carried 301 mostly German, Polish, and Austrian men and women from Les Milles. Also on the train, which bore a total of 997 people, were 530 children from Pithiviers—the first large group of children under twelve from the Vel' d'Hiv', traveling to their deaths without parents. The presence of adults from the unoccupied zone was intended to mask the fact that the children were alone and to deceive any French guards, railroad workers, and casual onlookers who cared about such matters. Upon arrival at Auschwitz, 65 men and 34 women were selected to enter the camp. The rest, including all the children, were gassed. Of those selected, three are known to have survived.[33]

The next convoy from France left Drancy for Auschwitz on August 19 with another 237 predominantly German and Austrian Jews from Les Milles, along with 85 internees, mostly men, from Le Vernet, 497 prisoners from the Vel' d'Hiv', via Pithiviers, including 373 children under twelve, and enough others to total 1,000. The horror repeated itself: 817 people were gassed, including all the children. One hundred thirty-eight men and 45 women were selected to live for a time. Five are known to have survived.[34]

The fate of the Jews in the first four trains from Gurs, Noé and Récébédou, Rivesaltes, and Les Milles to Drancy, sent there by Vichy officials between August 6 and August 13, can thus be traced clearly. Approximately 3,436 people were delivered, and 3,380 of them were among the roughly 5,000 deported to Auschwitz in five convoys within a few days.[35] The machinery of death was running with perfect efficiency. Those who arranged it—Pétain, Laval, Bousquet, Leguay, and all the officials who obeyed their orders more or less willingly—may have known little about the gas chambers in the late summer and autumn of 1942. They certainly knew, however, that Nazi camps were horrible for all, and deadly for the sick, the weak, the old, and the young. Preoccupied and concerned to meet their expulsion quota, they did not care.

On August 25, well after the first deliveries of prisoners from Gurs, Noé, Récébédou, Rivesaltes, Le Vernet, and Les Milles, yet another train carried 1,184 foreign Jews to Drancy from various large and small camps throughout the unoccupied zone. Many of the 1,184 were forced laborers and their families, brought in from isolated work sites to Les Milles on August 16 and 21 and to other major internment camps, such as Noé, Récébédou, and Rivesaltes, around the same time.[36] Others were men, women, and adolescents who had previously been granted permission to live in the centres d'accueil—such as those from Lastic à Rosans (Hautes-Alpes), run by Abbé Glasberg, who were brought to Les Milles on August 22.[37] Most of the transferred internees were included in convoys that left from Drancy for Auschwitz on August 26, 28, and 31.[38] With them on those three trains were the last large groups of young children from the Vel' d'Hiv', deported without parents.

After the August 25 train carried its 1,184 victims from the unoccupied zone to Drancy, internment camps and forced-labor sites in the south were empty of foreign Jews eligible in age, nationality, marital status, and date of arrival in France for delivery north. Vichy had transferred about 4,620 Jews but had promised at least 10,000. Where were the others to be found? Certainly all Jews eligible for expulsion who were currently in local prisons in the unoccupied zone for infractions such as illegally crossing the demarcation line, black market activities, carrying false documents, or violations of curfews or racial decrees, would be delivered. Their numbers, however, were not enough to meet the quota. Foreseeing this difficulty, Pierre Laval and René Bousquet assured the Germans as early as August 3, before expulsions of Jews already in internment camps had even begun, that they would conduct a vast roundup of recent Jewish immigrants in the unoccupied zone. The arrests would occur as soon as local internment camps were empty enough to receive newcomers.[39]

Elaborately detailed plans for the raid, ultimately scheduled for August 26, were developed in the days that followed. At the same time, exemption categories were restricted. Jews with the same national origins as those listed in the August 5 dispatch were to be arrested, although pressure to include those born in Belgium and Holland was building. For married men and families, the crucial date of arrival in France remained January 1, 1936, but for male bachelors between the ages of eighteen and forty, unless they had served in the military or rendered special services to the country, it was extended to January 1, 1933. Visibly pregnant women (the August 5 dispatch had not required visibility) and their spouses, individuals unable to be moved, those over age sixty, and those with French spouses or children remained exempt, but the age limit for young children and their parents who were to be excluded was cut from five to two. Unaccompanied children also remained exempt, but the age limit was reduced from eighteen to sixteen. Most tragic of all, "the option of leaving children under eighteen in the free zone is suppressed," according to instructions from Bousquet to the regional prefects on August 18.[40] As the police intendant in the Limoges region wrote to departmental prefects and subprefects on August 22, "It is essential to observe strictly the principle of the non-separation of families. Consequently, when the Israelites have children in other regions of the free zone, every effort must be made to return them to the camp of their parents."[41]

The huge raid throughout the unoccupied zone began in the early morning hours of August 26 and continued for several days. As one observer described it in Lyon, sinister black cars carried teams of three or four municipal policemen, gendarmes, or *gardes mobiles*, all provided with lists of names and addresses, from house to house. Trucks circulated more slowly, picking up victims and freeing police to go on to the next stop. Those arrested were taken to the nearby camp of Vénissieux or to the fort of Paillet, where they were screened.[42] Police and security forces did most of the work. General Robert de Saint-Vincent, the commander of the Lyon military region, refused to permit his troops to guard a convoy of Jews departing for the occupied zone, as requested by Police Intendant Marchais on August 29. The general was retired within forty-eight hours by General Jean Bridoux, Pétain's minister of war.[43]

The French police operated similarly throughout the unoccupied zone. In Marseille, a Swiss correspondent wrote of what he saw on August 26:

> The entire police force was mobilized for checks on buses, trams, in stations and at the entrances to all small villages and towns. I had to take a bus trip for my work and, in the space of two hours, had my papers checked five times. Foreigners not only had to show their papers but were also asked what their religion was. However, one good thing came out of this as it allowed many people to see that such things do go on. . . . On all sides people in danger are being offered and assured of help and refuge. Priests have been remarkable in their readiness to help the refugees.[44]

The police were scrupulously thorough. They and their superiors had been so ordered, in no uncertain terms. Bousquet instructed the regional prefects on August 22: "In the days that follow the projected operation, I ask you to have important police forces conduct extremely severe checks and identity verifications in order to liberate your region totally of all the foreign Jews whose regroupment is provided for in my letter of August 5 and subsequent correspondence."[45] In the same document, Bousquet asked that all "indiscretions, passivity, or ill will" on the part of Vichy officials be immediately reported. In Limoges, at least, his request was forwarded the same day. The regional prefect in Limoges ordered his departmental prefects and subprefects to report by telegram "all persons who, by their acts or attitude, obstruct or attempt to obstruct the assembling of the Israelites, so that I can propose, without delay, their administrative internment."[46]

Examples of police zeal abound. A young foreign Jewish mother with a five-year-old son had taken refuge from Paris in a small village near Toulouse. She later told an interviewer, "A seamstress by trade, I earned a modest living. I declared myself [in the special Jewish census] as a Jew. The villagers liked me very much." Sensing trouble or perhaps forewarned, like many others, she knocked on the door of a widowed woman neighbor at 11:00 P.M. on August 26 and asked if she and her son could spend the night. The neighbor agreed. When the police came, they knocked long and loud on the mother's door and finally entered and searched the house. Finding it empty, they could have left in good faith. Instead, they searched the neighbor's house, found the boy, and discovered his identity. The mother, confident that the police would not deport a child alone, remained in hiding. She almost lost her wager. The following morning as police were loading the boy onto a truck, the mayor of the village intervened and asked that he be left in his care. Perhaps the police finally remembered their orders that unaccompanied children under sixteen were not to be interned. They agreed to the mayor's request, and the child was saved.[47]

Similarly, Miriam Silberberg was just a few days over the age of two in August 1942. She lived on a farm in the Lot-et-Garonne where her parents, dressmakers who had fled Belgium for France in May 1940, had found work with a kindly peasant. Her parents thought that their child's age would protect them. After all, children up to five had been spared in the first two weeks of August, and even now, although they may not have known it, the police order said two years, and Miriam was barely over two. But the police had their orders, and they did not spare Miriam's family. The child survived only because a French doctor in the assembly camp in the Lot-et-Garonne saw her there, sleeping beside her mother, and arranged to sneak her out and care for her until her parents' return. When camp guards discovered the child's absence the next day, they threatened and terrified the poor mother so thoroughly that she gave them the doctor's name and address. He had to hide his wife and children as well as Miriam, and he himself joined the Resistance.[48]

Despite the determination of the French police and the intensity of the August 26 raid, the action did not yield the expected results. According to a Ministry of Interior report on September 1, 6,701 foreign Jews were arrested in the unoccupied zone on August 26, of whom 5,293 were retained after screening. Another 592 were arrested in the following days.[49] Between August 28 and September 5, 5,259 Jews were transferred to Drancy on seven trains; the total rose to 6,392 Jews in twelve trains before the end of October.[50] While these statistics are appalling, they represent just about half of the 12,686 foreign Jews eligible for expulsion who were believed to be in the unoccupied zone in August 1942.[51] Bousquet, who was well aware of the gap, sent several reminders to his police between August 29 and 31, reminding them to retain children, check identification documents scrupulously, and intensify searches.[52] His agency also prepared a memorandum on September 1 that examined the possibility of producing 7,000 Jews from the unoccupied zone, as demanded by the Nazis for deportation to the east in the last two weeks of September. The writer of the memorandum concluded that police could hope to catch only 2,000 of the roughly 6,000 believed to remain. The other 5,000 needed would have to be supplied by changing the exemption category and moving the date of immigration to France back from 1936 to 1933 or 1931.[53]

A perfect example of what Bousquet did *not* want to happen occurred at the makeshift camp at Vénissieux, a suburb of Lyon, where some 1,200 to 1,500 foreign Jews arrested in the area on August 26 had been dumped into abandoned barracks. The screening took place throughout the day and evening of August 28, in what the OSE representative Georges Garel remembered as "an indescribable confusion. So many instructions and counter-instructions had been given out that no one knew what to do."[54] Swamped by the numbers of prisoners and the pressure of time, desperate camp officials permitted representatives from OSE, EIF, and Amitiés chrétiennes, a joint Catholic-Protestant Jewish-assistance group, to help identify those exempt from expulsion.[55] Social workers interviewed prisoners in their barracks, with the electricity flickering on and off to add to the confusion. In frequent darkness, they advised, urged, indeed even pressured parents to leave their children behind. Garel later recalled:

> Seeing that time was passing, we became more and more authoritarian and, instead of asking if parents wanted to confide their children to us, we declared: we have come for your children. . . . But this authority was not always sufficient . . . and in some cases we had to remove children from parents in spite of their physical resistance. When a mother clung to her child, we had to take him from her—in a manner as civilized as possible.[56]

Parents destined for expulsion ultimately agreed to leave at least 84, but probably about 108, children behind.[57] "They knew where they were going, those families, those fathers and mothers," wrote Jean-Marie Soutou, a Catholic delegate from Amitiés chrétiennes who remembers the anguish as he helped persuade parents to leave their children. "Otherwise would they have confided their children to us, to total strangers?"[58] Officially, camp director Marchais turned the children over to Abbé Alexandre Glasberg of Amitiés chrétiennes and Gilbert Lesage of the Service social des étrangers, a Vichy government agency connected with both the Ministry of the Interior and the Ministry of Labor and charged with the delivery of social services to foreigners in France. The two men immediately arranged for the children to leave on the same buses that had originally brought prisoners into the camp. At dawn on August 29, Abbé Glasberg and Lesage, both in official black government Citroëns, accompanied the little procession out of Vénissieux. They also secreted additional children, often slightly over the age limit, onto the buses or hid them in Abbé Glasberg's car, an exact replica of that of the local prefect. As Lesage explains, "No one ever checked a black car; they just saluted it."[59]

Accompanied also by Claude Gutmann of the EIF, most of the children were taken, with full knowledge of the Vénissieux authorities, to the local headquarters of the Jewish Boy Scouts at 10, Montée des Carmelites, in the Croix-Rousse section of Lyon.[60] On Saturday morning, August 29, a train carrying 544 adult Jews left Lyon for Drancy. Most were sent on to Auschwitz three days later. Also on August 29, the Lyon police intendant was informed that there had been a mistake and was ordered to produce the children. To his great embarrassment, however, the children were no longer at Vénissieux, and after frantic telephone calls to Lesage and to EIF social workers, the regional prefect learned that they had left for an "unknown destination."[61] Vichy had lost at least 84 bodies to fill the quota, and police and prefect officials were furious.

It is unclear how such a thing could have happened. Bousquet's secret telegram on August 18 declaring that the "option of leaving children less than eighteen years old in the free zone [was] suppressed" had been sent to all the regional prefects, but in his report on the matter, the regional prefect in Lyon claimed to know nothing about it. He explained that he had based his authorization for the release of the children on August 28 on earlier instructions from Bousquet that did permit such a decision.[62] However, since the change of orders on August 18, many additional reminders in the form of secret telegrams and telephone calls had gone out from national police headquarters to regional prefects, local police commanders, and camp directors. Apparently none had reached the region of Lyon.

One last-minute telegram prohibiting adults expelled to the occupied zone from leaving their children behind did finally get through to Marchais's office at Vénissieux on the evening of August 28, at the very moment the children's departure was being prepared. Had Marchais seen it, he probably would not have released them. It is quite clear what happened to that particular document. Marchais was out and Gilbert Lesage and Abbé Glasberg were waiting in his office when a young orderly delivered the message. As Lesage looked on, Abbé Glasberg, disheveled and myopic, quietly picked up the telegram and sequestered it somewhere deep in the folds of his great black cassock, where he kept letters, money, and jewelry from prisoners for delivery to their families or friends.[63] Marchais never learned of the change of orders, and the children were released.

It was indeed a miracle. Dr. Jean Adam, a young medical student at the time, was one of four doctors sent to Vénissieux to grant exemptions for health reasons. He later testified that Vichy officials had strongly pressured doctors to release no one. He added that even Belgians, not included in the list of eligible nationalities, were delivered from Vénissieux to Drancy. Against all instructions, Dr. Adam was able to hold on to about 120 people. He even gave small doses of poison to some prisoners, to make them temporarily ill. But he acted at some risk, and against considerable pressure.[64]

Expulsions of newly arrested foreign Jews occurred at several other camps in the unoccupied zone at the end of August. A train carrying 446 foreign Jews, including 25 children, left the camp of Nexon (Haute-Vienne) for Drancy on August 28, the day before the departure of the 544 from Vénissieux. Another train with 620 prisoners arrived at Drancy from Nice on September 1.[65] That same day, yet a third train headed north with 960 prisoners, including, among others, 501 from Gurs, 170 from Noé, and 250 from Le Vernet. Of it, a gendarme captain named Annou wrote, in terms horribly similar to descriptions of Nazi deportation convoys: "The mass [of people] was parked on straw humid with urine. Women unable to satisfy their natural needs out of the sight of strangers were desperate. Those who fainted from the heat and odors could not be treated."[66] Annou's report differed in one important respect, however, for he dared to add, "The spectacle of this train strongly and unfavorably impressed the non-Jewish French population which saw it especially in the stations."[67]

Again the fate of most immigrant Jews delivered to the Nazis can be traced. Most from Nexon, Vénissieux, and Nice went on to Auschwitz on September 2.[68] Most of the 960 from Gurs, Noé, and Le Vernet, with a few others, followed on September 4.[69] They had remained at Drancy less than two days. Thirty men returned from the September 2 train; 25 men and 2 women survived from that of September 4. No children returned.

During the same period at Les Milles, between 1,300 and 1,500 new prisoners were brought in after roundups in the Marseille and Aix-en-Provence region on August 26. Another haphazard and exhausting screening procedure in the camp courtyard lasted throughout the hot afternoon of September 1 and on into the damp early morning hours of the next day. At least 500 people finally left for Drancy at 8:00 A.M. on September 2; they paused along the way to pick up another 250 victims from Rivesaltes.[70] Unlike at Vénissieux, children were not spared. Forty-seven youngsters between the ages of two and sixteen at Les Milles were included.[71] Of their ordeal during the interminable screening, Pastor Manen wrote poignantly:

> The smallest children stumbled from fatigue in the night and the cold, crying from hunger, clutching piteously at their parents to be carried, but their parents had their arms full of packages and baggage; poor little fellows five or six years old tried valiantly to carry a pack as big as themselves but then fell asleep and dropped to the ground with their packages, shivering in the dew of the night in a wait which for some was prolonged for hours; the young mothers and fathers cried long and silently at the confirmation of their helplessness before the suffering of their children; then came the order to leave the courtyard and depart in the train.[72]

Raymond-Raoul Lambert, present at the train's 8:00 A.M. departure, later recorded with indignation that the Marseille regional police intendant and his chief aide, enraged at the sight of two unfilled boxcars, simply threw in another sixty prisoners at random, regardless of their eligibility for expulsion. Still in their nightclothes, they were given no time to gather precious possessions.[73] Pastor Manen also wrote of the expulsion of several Foreign Legion volunteers. One young man who especially interested Manen had been living in Switzerland when the war broke out but had come to France expressly to fight the Germans. Thinking he was safe, he had remained in the unoccupied zone after demobilization. In August 1942, he was arrested and turned over to the Nazis by the nation he had hoped to serve.[74]

Two more trains from the unoccupied to the occupied zone followed in rapid succession. On September 4, one arrived at Drancy with 899 Jews, including 200 from Septfonds (Tarn-et-Garonne), 300 from Chasseneuil (Lot-et-Garonne), 150 from Saint-Sulpice (Tarn), and at least another 150 from miscellaneous or unknown camps. The next day, an even larger train arrived with 1,041 prisoners, of whom 621 were from Rivesaltes, 280 from Montluçon (Allier), and the rest unknown.[75] It was probably either this last train or a subsequent one that arrived with 650 Jews from Rivesaltes on September 15 that a Jesuit priest, Father Roger Braun, described indignantly years later: "I saw two Austrian Jews deported from the camp of Rivesaltes wearing in their buttonholes the red ribbon of the French Legion of Honor."[76] After September 5, however, the pace slowed somewhat, for in addition to the September 15 train, just four other small transports occurred before the end of October. These carried 190 from Rivesaltes, Le Vernet, and Brens who arrived on September 25, 70 from Rivesaltes on September 30, 117 from miscellaneous camps on October 6, and 106 from Rivesaltes on October 22.[77]

The ultimate fate of most of those expelled to Drancy between September 2 and October 22 is as brutally clear as that of those who left earlier. On September 7, most of the 47 children who had spent the night on the ground at Les Milles, plus scores of other children, were among the 488 deportees from Les Milles, 283 from Rivesaltes, and 106 from other southern camps to be deported to Auschwitz.[78] On September 9, 588 of the 650 Jews delivered from Septfonds, Chasseneuil, and Saint-Sulpice to Drancy on September 4 were among the roughly 1,000 in the next convoy to the east. On September 11 and 14, 570 of the 621 from Rivesaltes and 140 of the 280 from Montluçon delivered to Drancy on September 9 followed. Six hundred fifty additional Jews arrived at Drancy from Rivesaltes on September 15; 571 of them were among the 993 prisoners sent to Auschwitz the very next day. And so it went for the smaller trains from the unoccupied zone at the end of September and in October.[79]

On November 11, 1942, four days after the Allies landed in North Africa, the German army occupied southern France in flagrant disregard of the 1940 armistice. Vichy collaboration with the Nazis entered a new phase. Before that date, however, French government officials had allowed seventeen trains to carry 11,012 foreign Jewish men, women, and children from independent French territory to the occupied zone. Deportation to Auschwitz within a few days of arrival at Drancy can be clearly traced for 9,383 of those expelled from the unoccupied zone; nearly all the others followed the same route on undetermined convoys. Only between 100 and 200 returned from deportation.

The French case was almost unique. In all occupied countries except Denmark, native non-Jews in varying proportions collaborated with the Nazis to hunt down and deport Jews. Among the unoccupied, autonomous, or semiautonomous allies of the Third Reich, however, only the Slovaks and the French delivered Jews from their established heartland to the Nazis. Romanians, Bulgarians, and Hungarians subjected Jews in areas acquired since the First World War to an atrocious fate—in Bessarabia and Bukovina in Romania, in newly annexed areas of Thrace and Macedonia in Bulgaria, and in Ruthenian and Yugoslavian acquisitions in Hungary. But they did not permit deportation from their prewar territories while unoccupied. Italians, on the other hand, also allied to the Third Reich, not only prevented the deportation of native and foreign Jews from their country as long as it remained unoccupied but actively intervened to protect foreign Jews in Italian-occupied areas of Greece, Croatia, and southern France. And the Finnish government, like the Italians an ally of the Third Reich, obstinately and successfully refused Nazi demands for its 2,000 Jews.

Vichy officials defined their problem differently. Slovakian authorities had for a time collaborated in the deportation of *all* Jews, native and foreign alike. Vichy authorities, however, claimed to be defenders of native-born Jews. French Jews could be subjected to onerous and demeaning racial laws but theoretically not turned over to the Nazis. Recent Jewish immigrants in France, on the other hand, were to be treated as aliens and simply sent home again. Their ejection from France was portrayed as no different from any expulsion of undesired foreigners. The victims themselves were defined as an unassimilable element in a country under stress, an intolerable burden on a strained economy, a security risk, and a source of black market and other criminal activities.

The fallacies in the Vichy position are obvious. First, native-born Jews were *not* consistently protected. The Germans in the occupied zone had arrested and deported hundreds of adult Jews by November 1942, and Vichy officials rarely protested. On the contrary, French police under Vichy orders often assisted in the operations. Furthermore, thousands of children of foreign Jews had been born in France and were French citizens but were deported along with their immigrant parents after July 1942. Third, foreign Jews in France were hardly disruptive. Most who had chosen to immigrate before the war were, like most French Jews and non-Jews, honest, hard-working, politically uninvolved, and patriotic. The minority who had either fled from the advancing German army in May 1940 or been expelled from the Third Reich to France the following October were admittedly displaced and dependent, but they constituted no threat to the society. The articulated reasons for their delivery to the Nazis for deportation were mere excuses. The real reasons involved the anti-foreign sentiments, anti-Semitism, xenophobia, and demagoguery of Vichy officials. Hoping to win concessions on other matters from the German occupiers of the north of their country, French bureaucrats yielded to Nazi demands for a specific number of Jews and then filled the quota with foreigners.

The most deadly deception of the Vichy policy was the myth of deportation to countries of origin, or for labor. The euphemisms eased the fears of victims and the consciences of French officials. These myths could not, however, have been fully believed for long by anyone who objectively sought the truth. No effort was made in France to sort out Czechs, Poles, Russians, Germans, and Austrians and to send them back where they had come from. Did French officials really believe that the Germans would make that effort once the deportees arrived on their soil? And when the old, the sick, and the very young were thrown in with the able-bodied, did the French really believe that deportation was solely for labor? For that matter, did the victims themselves fully believe it?

Extermination, of course, was not the only, or the most probable, alternative. Despite the rumors of massacres in Russia and starvation in Poland that everyone had heard, the idea of the organized mass murder of hundreds of thousands of prisoners remained inconceivable. Most people in France, Jews and non-Jews alike, probably believed that Jewish deportees would be sent to a vast and horrible reservation in the east, where adults would work and care for the weak among them. Since the Germans desperately needed workers, such an explanation seemed logical. And yet, the explanation had gaps. Annette Monod Leiris later observed, "We saw little children who did not even know their last names deported without parents and without name tags. How could it have been for 'family reunion?'"[80] But few wanted to question reality so closely. Few wanted to know the truth.

8

Attitudes toward the Jews, 1942

ON A TRAIN TO LYON IN JULY 1942, A FORMER SOCIALIST DEPUTY, Jean Pierre-Bloch, overheard a Parisian and several men from Bordeaux condemning the recent roundup of foreign Jews in Paris. The travelers were particularly angry about the arrests of pregnant women and young children. Pierre-Bloch later wrote, "I am happily surprised by the burst of verbal solidarity they all showed toward the Jews. The anti-Semitic propaganda of Vichy and the Germans has not succeeded in corrupting all the French."[1]

Pierre-Bloch had reason to be surprised. Former friends had been supportive during his visits to Vichy in 1940 and 1941, and even the ardently Pétainist deputy Philippe Henriot had assured him, "You know perfectly well that we are only thinking of the Jews, and not of the French of Israelite religion."[2] But there had been virtually no public protests against the racial laws, the internment of foreign Jews in the unoccupied zone, the atrocious conditions in the camps, the arrests of Jews in the occupied zone in 1941, and the first deportations in March 1942. Of the few private protests that had occurred, most French men and women knew nothing.[3]

Most of the conservative Catholic press—widely read because of censorship and the banning of opposition journals—joined Vichy publications in the unoccupied zone and the anti-Semitic collaborationist press of the occupied zone in endorsing measures against the Jews.[4] These Catholic journals were often encouraged by the church hierarchy.[5] Pierre Cardinal Gerlier, archbishop of Lyon and primate of the Gauls, welcomed Pétain during a visit to Lyon in November 1940 with the well-publicized words, "Pétain is France and France today is Pétain." About the same time, during an interview with Jews who had come to inform him of prisoners dying of starvation and neglect at Gurs, Gerlier lectured on the abuses of Léon Blum and spoke of the need for expiation.[6] However, Gerlier sent a private protest on conditions at Gurs to the minister of the interior in Vichy in December 1940.[7] In September 1941, he wrote another private letter of protest against the racial laws. Then during a speech at Fourvière on January 1, 1942, he made a veiled public allusion to official anti-Semitism and called on Christians to refrain from stirring up hatred and vengeance.[8] But again, these discreet measures were known to very few.

The silence of the Church hierarchy in the face of the persecutions of Jews before July 1942 had a counterpart on the Left, in the Resistance press. According to two historians, the major clandestine Communist paper, *L'Humanité*, referred to Jewish matters only eight times between June 1940 and May 1941 and said nothing at all about German anti-Semitic ordinances in the occupied zone or about Vichy's racial laws.[9] On October 3, 1940, it welcomed the confiscation of the property of Maurice de Rothschild, predictably calling for a similar policy against all capitalists and declaring, "Those who oppose these measures, whether done under the guise of anti-Semitism or under other pretexts, are no more than the watchdogs of capital."[10]

L'Humanité finally attacked anti-Semitism as such in May 1941, when it described the arrests of Jewish workers in Paris. After the German attack on the Soviet Union in June 1941, it did much more, mentioning attacks on Paris synagogues in October, the conditions of Jewish prisoners at Compiègne and Drancy in May 1942, the star decree in June, and the July roundup in Paris in a special August–September edition. But still, it referred to Jewish matters only nine times between May 1941 and September 1942, and not at all between September 1942 and the end of the war.[11] Most French Communists, particularly non-Jews, adhered to the party line: anti-Semitism was an unfortunate by-product of capitalism and a distraction from the class struggle. It and all forms of racism, they believed, would inevitably disappear with the triumph of the workers' revolution.

More specialized Communist newspapers, such as *L'Université libre,* a publication of Parisian intellectuals, and *Notre voix (Unzer Wort* in Yiddish) and *Solidarité,* representing foreign Jews, mentioned the racial persecutions much more frequently than did *L'Humanité.* Also, the Trotskyite newspaper *La Verité* was apparently the only major Resistance journal to oppose Vichy's first racial laws as early as November 1940.[12] But these journals were limited in circulation and impact, as were the many simple, anonymous pamphlets that also occasionally denounced the persecutions of the Jews.[13] More often read but far more reticent were non-Communist clandestine publications, such as *Pantagruel, L'Arc, Libération-Sud, Le Franc-Tireur,* and *Défense de la France*, which inveighed against anti-Semitism only occasionally.[14]

A tiny minority of French non-Jews, usually professional social workers or individuals physically at the scene by chance, tried to ameliorate the lot of Jews in 1941 and early 1942. A few people tried to bring desperately needed supplies into the camps or to arrange the supervised release of inmates; others living near Pithiviers and Beaune-la-Rolande tried to aid Jewish men arrested in 1941. Many demonstrated their objection to the star decree. But personal acts of assistance and support were unpublicized and unknown to most French men and women. There were few public spokesmen—few leaders to encourage people to think for themselves and evaluate independently the government's Jewish policy. As a result, as so often happens, most people took that policy for granted, without giving it much thought. They personally knew no Jews, saw few of the consequences of the policy, read even less, and had other troubles.

Among Christian activists, there were a few refreshing exceptions. During the autumn of 1941, a group of Catholic priests and Protestant pastors in and around Lyon founded a clandestine Christian Resistance journal entitled *Cahiers du Témoignage chrétien.* The initiative came from Father Pierre Chaillet, a priest and teacher of German theology and philosophy at the Jesuit school at Fourvière. Father Chaillet, described as a "demanding and reserved intellectual" and later known and honored for his rescue work with Jewish children, received help and support from the Jesuit fathers Henri de Lubac and Victor Fontoynont, and several others from Fourvière; the Protestant pastor Roland de Pury from Lyon; and two Catholic laymen, Alexander Marc and Louis Cruvillier.[15]

The first issue of *Témoignage chrétien,* a seventeen-page volume entitled "France, prends garde de ne perdre pas ton âme," appeared in November 1941. Written by Father Gaston Fessard, the Jesuit who had denounced the racial laws from his pulpit at Vichy in December 1940, the volume was printed in only 5,000 copies and distributed, like all subsequent issues, clandestinely. It declared the fundamental incompatibility between National Socialism and Christianity and called upon all Christians to make a choice and resist. With regard to the Jewish persecutions, it protested specifically against the internments of Jews at Gurs, the film *Le Juif Süss,* and the anti-Semitic campaigns in the collaborationist press. It reminded readers that the Holy Office had condemned anti-Semitism in 1928, and that Pope Pius XI had declared in 1938, "Spiritually we are Semites."

Three of the next four issues of *Témoignage chrétien*—"Les Racistes peints par eux-mêmes" (April 1942, 31 pages, 10,000 copies); "Antisemites" (June 1942, 32 pages, 20,000 copies); and "Droits de l'homme et du chrétien" (August 1942, 32 pages, 25,000 copies)—focused almost exclusively on anti-Semitism, declaring it incompatible with Christian doctrine and unacceptable to the French. In "Droits de l'homme et du chrétien," Father Chaillet described the terrible roundup in Paris on July 16 and revealed that the Vichy regime was preparing to deliver foreign Jews from the unoccupied zone to the Nazis. "The Church can not disinterest itself in the fate of man, wherever his inviolable rights are unjustly threatened," he reminded his readers. "When one member [of the human race] suffers, the entire body suffers with him."[16] Every bishop received a copy of each issue.

During the same months when *Témoignage chrétien* was being organized to fight collaboration in general and anti-Semitism in particular, other Christians specifically interested in social and economic assistance to Jews were establishing a body to coordinate their activities and work directly with Jewish welfare agencies. *Amitiés chrétiennes* was initially proposed by Gilbert Beaujolin, a silk merchant from Lyon, and Olivier de Pierrebourg, a young student.[17] Abbé Alexandre Glasberg and Father Chaillet soon became involved, and Pastor Marc Boegner and Cardinal Gerlier agreed to be honorary patrons. Other participants included Jean-Marie Soutou, Germaine Ribière, and Annie Langlade among the Catholics, and Pastor Roland de Pury, Suzanne Chevalley, and Denise Grunewald among the Protestants. Also involved was Jean Stetten-Bernard, who established printing facilities that over the course of three years produced more than 30,000 identity cards, about 50,000 ration cards, and thousands of other documents in French and German—all false.[18] Three Jewish observers facilitated coordination with Jewish welfare agencies, while the American Jewish Joint Distribution Committee and several French Jewish organizations provided funding.

Until the German occupation of the southern zone in November 1942, Amitiés chrétiennes operated openly and legally from its head-quarters in Lyon, distributing food and other aid to Jews in and out of the internment camps. In some cases, as at Vénissieux in August 1942, it became a front organization for a secretly coordinated effort when Vichy authorities discouraged or even prohibited the interven-tion of Jewish groups. As recent Jewish immigrants were being ar-rested and expelled during the late summer of 1942, Amitiés chréti-ennes became more and more involved with illegal activities—with producing and distributing false documents, contacting Christians willing to shelter and hide Jews, and escorting Jews to Switzerland. The story of clandestine Christian rescue work belongs to another chapter. The relevance of Amitiés chrétiennes here is as a shaper of public opinion. Along with *Témoignage chrétien*, its activities en-couraged growing numbers of nonpolitical people of goodwill to look beyond their daily problems of existence and question the gov-ernment's Jewish policy.

Nevertheless, public opinion in France before July 1942 remained largely either indifferent or hostile to Jews, as demonstrated by the regular departmental reports that prefects were expected to send to the Ministry of the Interior during the war. The reports, it might be emphasized, covered a broad range of issues and attitudes; most often, the Jews were not mentioned at all. However, "measures taken against Freemasons and Jews have provoked few reactions," wrote the prefect of the Var in October 1941, after a year of racial laws, economic expropriations, and internments of foreign Jews.[19] A month later, the prefect of Bouches-du-Rhône, which includes Aix-en-Provence and Marseille, reported:

> The Jewish question seems of less lively interest to opinion, despite the considerable number of Israelites presently installed on the Coast.
>
> In my opinion, comprehensive measures intended to check Jew-ish attempts at monopolizing the totality of command posts in the nation should be promulgated and enforced with rigor as rapidly as possible; opinion will applaud it unanimously.[20]

Such reports may say as much about the personal inclinations of the prefects as about opinion within their departments, but indifference, if not hostility, toward Jews was reflected in other reports as well during 1941 and the first six months of 1942. "Measures removing an important number of Israelites and foreigners to supervised residence continue to be approved by the population of this department," wrote the prefect of Alpes-Maritimes, which includes Nice, in August 1941.[21] "Still very numerous, the Israelites continue not to benefit from sympathy in Lyon," declared the prefect of the Rhône in April 1941.[22] A few months later, an official in the same department added, "Measures taken against the Jews have been favorably received. Those who demand a still more complete purge are numerous."[23]

Such reports might be dismissed as opportunist attempts by prefects to pander to Vichy authorities by telling them what they wanted to hear. Indeed, descriptions of public attitudes toward Marshal Pétain are subject to the same charge. During 1941 and early 1942, most officials in the unoccupied zone reiterated the fact that the Marshal was immensely popular. The French "always show the same sentiments of admiration and enthusiasm for his person," wrote the prefect of the Var in May 1941.[24] "The Chief of State possesses, in spite of all foreign propaganda, an immense prestige among our people, and the majority of opinion, despite its instinctive or calculated preferences, will defer to any decision which he firmly declares to be in the interests of France and French Honor," declared the prefect of Haute-Garonne.[25] Frenchmen grumble about the state of affairs, stated the prefect of Bouches-du-Rhône in November 1941, but "this discontent is never directed toward Marshal Pétain"[26]

Suspicions of possible falseness and opportunism in prefects' descriptions, however, are weakened by the remarkably frank and less ingratiating treatment of other subjects in the same reports. For example, the prefect of Bouches-du-Rhône added, in his November 1941 report, "The policy of collaboration is making little progress in public opinion."[27] In June 1942 he repeated, more dramatically, "A major part of the population is clearly opposed to the idea of French-German collaboration."[28] "The masses who remain very Germanophobic continue to think that collaboration with Germany is a one-way street, and its opponents are becoming much more numerous than its advocates," wrote the prefect of the Var in May 1941.[29] A year later, he too repeated, "The word 'collaboration' has never been welcomed with enthusiasm."[30] "Despite the absence of precise reactions, opinion continues to show itself hostile to the policy of collaboration," echoed still another prefect in November 1941.[31] "The idea of collaboration is combatted strongly by a great number of Frenchmen," warned yet a fourth in February 1942.[32]

French men and women in the unoccupied zone also appeared to be singularly unimpressed with Vichy's National Revolution. As one official from the Var wrote frankly in October 1941, "The Nation is certain, and appearances make it difficult to prove otherwise, that the Government is totally uninterested in it on a domestic level; in effect, the social reforms have had and continue to have virtually no repercussions."[33] "Unanimous opinion has stated that the government and its representatives find themselves without direct lines to the country," the prefect of the Var added in June 1942.[34]

Unhappy with collaboration and contemptuous of the National Revolution, most French men and women focused on their day-to-day troubles. As one prefect wrote in November 1941, "The greatest concern of the French at present—one might almost say the only one—is the food supply."[35] "The state of public opinion is a function of the state of the food supply," echoed another.[36] Other prefects mentioned additional grievances—the continued detention of French prisoners of war in Germany, the scarcity of labor, and, somewhat later but then with increasing frequency and vehemence, the German forced-labor programs. French non-Jews were clearly grumbling and criticizing their government, but they were not questioning the Jewish policies. Not one prefect report before August 1942 mentioned public sympathy for the Jews.

In Paris in the occupied zone, public opinion toward the Jews seems to have been similar. As one official report declared on October 4, 1941, the day after seven synagogues in the capital were attacked by a group of Nazis and French collaborators:

> The general Parisian public does not like the Jews, but it tolerates them. Shopkeepers especially wish to be rid of the Israelites because they compete with them. In fact, the severe measures taken against the Jews by the German Authorities and the French Government have not raised protests within the mass of the population.

However, unlike most reports from the unoccupied zone, this one from Paris warned that hostility and indifference might have their limits. "Many people find excessive the violent anti-Semitism of the

Parisian press, which exceeds in effect and by a great deal their own antipathy for the Jews. . . . The opinion of many people, and particularly in Catholic circles, is that the opponents of the Jews generalize too much and that in unleashing such anti-Semitism, regrettable errors will be provoked."[37] Prophetic words.

July and August 1942 marked a crucial turning point in what French non-Jews knew and thought about the Jewish persecutions. As Pierre-Bloch's experience in the train suggests, news of the roundups inevitably circulated by word of mouth. French authorities took great pains to disguise the persecutions—arrests often occurred at night or early in the morning; trains were loaded and sealed at those times as well; the public was kept away from train stations when convoys passed through. But arrests were necessarily public, and internment camps, for ease of transport, were usually located near towns or villages. In Paris and other cities in the occupied zone where Jews were arrested, in every city and village in the unoccupied zone where mothers, children, and old people were dragged from their homes and thrown into trucks or buses, and in villages throughout France near camps like Pithiviers, Beaune-la-Rolande, Les Milles, and others where families were visibly torn apart, there were policemen, guards, and civilian witnesses who did not like what they saw and who talked about it. Word spread.

The interest and concern of the clandestine Resistance press were finally aroused. In the late summer of 1942, Jewish Communists initiated two new publications, *J'accuse* in the occupied zone and *Fraternité* in the south, specifically to inform non-Jews of racial persecutions.[38] *Libération-Sud, Libération-Nord, Combat, Le Franc-Tireur, Le Populaire,* and other newspapers joined *Témoignage chrétien* and the Jewish Communist publications in describing and denouncing the July 16 roundup in Paris and the expulsions of Jews from the unoccupied zone. The press stressed the arrests of women and children, expressing indignation and often calling upon French non-Jews to help their persecuted neighbors. In addition, between the beginning of August and the end of September, the BBC mentioned the arrests in its French news broadcasts at least eight times and called upon non-Jews to help.[39] Those broadcasts had a large audience. As one Vichy official lamented in the autumn of 1942, "Although the police operations were conducted with the maximum of discretion, the news diffused by the radio from London has been rapidly known by the whole population."[40]

Of more impact on the general public than the clandestine press, however, were the protests of some church leaders. For a time in the summer of 1942, objections remained private. Soon after the Paris roundup in July, cardinals and archbishops in the occupied zone met and decided against a public protest but authorized Emmanuel Cardinal Suhard, archbishop of Paris, to address a private letter to Marshal Pétain in their name. The letter referred directly to the July roundup and conditions at the Vel' d'Hiv'. It articulated "a protest in favor of the inviolable rights of the human person," and issued "an anguished appeal for pity for the immense sufferings, especially for those which are affecting so many mothers and children."[41] All bishops in the occupied zone were charged with communicating the text of the protest to priests in their dioceses.[42] Then on August 19, as Vichy officials were delivering foreign Jews in the south to the Nazis in the north, Gerlier wrote a similar private letter to Pétain in the name of Catholic archbishops from the unoccupied zone. He asked that Jews in the south, "if it is possible," be spared further suffering.[43] A day later, Pastor Boegner also wrote another private letter, protesting both the expulsions from the unoccupied zone and the inhuman conditions in which they were being conducted. He added, "I beg you, *Monsieur le Maréchal,* to impose the indispensable measures so that France does not inflict upon herself a moral defeat whose weight would be incalculable."[44] Again, wise and prophetic words; again, unheeded.

The first *public* protest came in the wake of the expulsions of foreign Jews already in internment camps in the unoccupied zone, but before the massive arrests there on August 26. It was issued by the frail and elderly Archbishop Jules-Gérard Saliège of Toulouse. The letter, to be read during masses in all churches of his diocese on Sunday, August 23, said, among other things:

> That children, women, fathers and mothers should be treated like animals, that family members should be separated and sent off to an unknown destination, it has been reserved for our time to witness this sad spectacle. . . . In our diocese, moving scenes have occurred in the camps of Noé and Récébédou. Jews are men. Jewesses are women. Foreigners are men and women. All is not permitted against them, against these men, these women, these fathers and mothers. They are part of the human race. They are our brothers like so many others. A Christian cannot forget it.[45]

Officials at the prefecture of the Haute-Garonne learned of Saliège's letter about noon on Saturday, August 22, and tried frantically to head it off. When Saliège refused to withdraw it, officials prohibited its public reading and sent telegrams to all mayors in the department advising them of the ban.[46] Most priests, ignoring orders from local mayors, obeyed their archbishop. In parishes where the letter was not mentioned on August 23, it was read on August 30.

Within a few weeks, at least four other French bishops in the unoccupied zone followed Saliège's example. Bishop Pierre-Marie Théas of Montauban (Tarn-et-Garonne) wrote a letter to be read at all masses in his diocese on August 30, four days after the onset of the arrests in the unoccupied zone. His message read in part:

> In Paris, Jews by the tens of thousands have been treated with the most barbarous savagery. And now in our region we are witnessing a heartrending spectacle: families are being dislocated; men and women are being treated like animals and sent toward an unknown destination, with the prospect of the gravest dangers.
>
> I declare the indignant protest of the Christian conscience and I proclaim that all men, Aryan or non-Aryan, are brothers for they are created by God; that all men, whatever their race or religion, have the right to the respect of individuals and States.
>
> The present anti-Semitic measures are a contemptible attack on human dignity, a violation of the most sacred rights of the individual and the family.
>
> May God console and fortify those who are iniquitously persecuted.[47]

Bishop Théas confided his letter to an energetic and courageous Catholic lay worker and *Témoignage chrétien* distributor named Marie-Rose Gineste, who made multiple copies and for four days delivered them by bicycle to priests in even the most remote parishes of the diocese. She was helped by two friends, one a young woman and the other a former officer from Lorraine and father of six children.[48]

Cardinal Gerlier in Lyon and Archbishop Jean Delay in Marseille wrote somewhat less forthright letters of protest to be read in their dioceses on September 6. Both men alluded to the right of the state to resolve "a problem" (Gerlier) and to "protect itself against those who, especially these last years, have hurt it so much" (Delay).[49] Both, however, strongly condemned the persecutions of innocent men, women, and children simply because they were Jews. Bishop

Moussaron issued a less equivocal protest in Albi on September 20, and representatives of the National Council of the Reformed Church of France (the principal Protestant organization in the country) produced a similar letter on September 22, to be read from all pulpits on October 4.

The pastoral letters caused what the unhappy regional prefect in Toulouse called "a considerable stir" throughout the unoccupied zone.[50] The messages of Saliège and Théas, in particular, were reproduced in Resistance pamphlets, read over the BBC, and distributed in Catholic bookstores.[51] The interest of parishioners in local Catholic publications was suddenly aroused. "I was in Toulouse during the war," recalls the historian François Delpech. "I was still a child, but I remember very well. . . . Never had *Semaine Religieuse* been so read."[52] The regional prefect with jurisdiction over Marseille and Aix-en-Provence declared on October 7 that "the pastoral letter read in the churches of the department on Sunday, September 6, has certainly produced profound and lasting consequences." Both he and the prefect reporting for Lyon declared that the emerging sympathy for foreign Jews was most apparent among the comfortable Catholic middle classes.[53]

Thanks to the clandestine press, the BBC, the pastoral protests, and simple word of mouth, most French citizens in the unoccupied zone knew by the end of September that foreign Jewish men, women, and children were being arrested and delivered to the Germans. A smaller percentage had also heard of the massive roundup in Paris. Bishop Théas was the only bishop to refer precisely to it, but the BBC, *Témoignage chrétien,* and other Resistance publications also mentioned it. In the occupied zone, where information circulated with more difficulty, most also knew of the Paris roundup and other arrests. A somewhat smaller proportion of the population in both zones was also vaguely aware of deportations eastward. Before evaluating the public response to this knowledge, however, it is useful to focus again on what people did *not* know.

Most people in the autumn of 1942 did not know where deported Jews were being sent, much less what was happening to them upon arrival. "Unknown destinations" were perceived as huge ethnic regrouping centers and horrible work camps somewhere in the east, where lingering death, but not immediate murder, awaited the weakest. As Robert Lévy, an Auschwitz survivor, later wrote, "We expected to work very hard in the factories, coal mines, quarries, but we did not think that our destruction had been decided and was going to be carried out in cold blood."[54] Further knowledge was rare and uncertain. Indeed, as seen, systematic, methodical selection on the arrival ramp at Auschwitz of victims for immediate gassing had not begun for Jews from France on a regular basis until the beginning of August.

Presumably, French men and women in the autumn of 1942 had access to the same sources of information mentioned with reference to Pétain and Laval: the Radio Moscow broadcasts of 1941, clandestine Jewish Communist tracts and newspapers intended primarily for foreign Jews and referring vaguely to extermination by mid-July 1942, and BBC broadcasts after early July 1942 that spoke of mass murders in Poland.[55] Presumably, after July some had seen the Jewish Communist publications *J'accuse* and *Fraternité,* founded, as mentioned earlier, especially to inform non-Jews about the deportations. Both papers promptly began to question the nature of the "unknown destination," and on October 20, *J'accuse* declared for the first time that 11,000 deported Jews from France had been gassed.[56] But Communist journalists in France had already made sweeping allegations of other types of atrocities, and their credibility was low. Furthermore, regarding mass gassings of Jews, even the journalists were not absolutely certain. Adam Rayski relates that, in fact, the publishers of *J'accuse* suffered agonies of indecision that October about whether to print news of gassings. They trusted their source— apparently a Communist veteran of the Spanish Civil War released from Gurs for forced labor and sent to Poland with the Todt Organization. But they were not sure they believed it. Rayski recalls, "And if it was not true, as we hoped deep in our hearts?"[57]

Among all their sources of information, French men and women were probably most inclined to believe the public protests of their bishops, but those letters were vague about deportation. Saliège and Théas spoke of the deportees being sent to an "unknown destination," and Théas added, "with the prospect of the gravest dangers." Cardinal Gerlier, who was the best informed about the reality of deportation, referred only to a "cruel dispersion." Only Archbishop Delay declared that Jews were being sent "perhaps to their deaths."[58]

Did religious leaders, both Jewish and Christian, have any special knowledge about the Final Solution toward the end of 1942? Without identifying the precise nature or source of his own information, Grand Rabbi Jacob Kaplan later claimed that he knew about the systematic extermination of deported Jews as early as August 1942, and that he advised Cardinal Gerlier of it at a meeting on August 17.[59] Two days later, the cardinal sent his private protest to Pétain. The Consistoire central also seemed informed by the late summer of 1942, as seen by the protest letter sent to Pétain on August 25 that spoke of methodical and pitiless extermination.[60] Members of the Consistoire agreed to send copies of the same protest to all rabbis and presidents of Jewish communities, as well as to the papal nuncio, Pastor Boegner, the president of the Red Cross, and various priests, pastors, government ministers, prefects, and journalists.

Although Consistoire members articulated the awful reality of methodical extermination, it seems doubtful that they actually believed it, for two reasons. First, their knowledge had several fundamental limitations. Unlike the publishers of *J'accuse* in October, they based their claims in August on the logic of deporting the young, the old, and the weak rather than on reliable eyewitness testimony. They had no idea of the scope of Nazi intentions. They did not realize that the objective was the deportation and extermination of *all* the Jews of France, foreign and native alike without exception, and that *all* Jews should be warned and hidden. And they expressed no knowledge of the gas chambers. They did not seem to know the manner of death at all, and that lack of fundamental detail diminished certainty. They could still hope it was not true.

Second, like government and religious leaders throughout the world with partial knowledge of the mass murders being committed in the east, Consistoire members did not necessarily understand emotionally what they knew intellectually. That failure of imagination was not limited to 1942, when facts were still scarce; it continued until the end of the war. The full and unique reality of the Holocaust—members of civilized societies engaged in the carefully planned, methodical, systematic, orderly, disciplined destruction of men, women, and children—can be comprehended today with the help of thousands of haunting personal testimonies, documents, photographs, and physical remains of gas chambers and killing centers. During the war it was almost inconceivable.

Consistoire members' failure to believe in systematic extermination in August 1942 is indeed vividly apparent in their protest itself, making it a curious and tragic document when read with hindsight. The authors argued at first, quite correctly and logically, that the deportation of so many people who were unfit for labor proved the Nazis' intention to exterminate them without pity. They ended, however, by requesting that if it was not possible to stop the expulsions of foreign Jews from south to north, at least the French government should maintain the exemptions of war veterans and their families, isolated children under eighteen, parents of children under three, pregnant women, and, "especially, young girls for whom these deportations risk having the most revolting consequences."[61] Their imaginations, as opposed to their logic, seem to have extended as far as sexual depravities. Mass murder remained unimaginable. Indeed, a full year later, when the president of the Consistoire, Jacques Helbronner, received a copy of a letter from papal nuncio offices in Munich describing the crematoriums and mass executions of Jews, he still found it unimaginable and sought verification from Jewish agencies in Switzerland.[62]

The social workers and churchmen who composed the Committee of Nîmes, charged with coordinating relief efforts for foreigners in internment camps, demonstrated the same failure to comprehend during the late summer of 1942. They knew that Jewish war refugees and recent immigrants were being delivered to the Germans in the occupied zone, and that they were subsequently being deported. At their monthly meeting on September 9, however, they talked of regaining contact with deportees, of going to Poland to check on them, and of the possibility of future deportations of Spanish refugees as well.[63]

The postwar testimony of hundreds of survivors, many of whom had seen Resistance tracts and heard BBC reports throughout the war, reveals similar incomprehension. Vivette Samuel, for example, whose husband Julien, an OSE director, was arrested in May 1944 and escaped from a train en route to Drancy, declares, "We did not know everything about deportation, but we knew it was terrible and to be avoided at all costs. Julien, knowing that I had not been arrested, chose to risk his life by jumping from the train." But she goes on to tell about Julien's sister Nelly, in the Vosges, who knew much less about the consequences of deportation. The wife of a Jewish prisoner of war, Nelly and her three children were relatively safe from deportation until her husband was released as the father of a large family. Upon his return, he declared, "Now our troubles begin." A local teacher came to them to offer to take in the children, because a roundup seemed imminent. Nelly, now pregnant with her fourth child, refused to let her family be separated. All were arrested in March 1944. Nelly and the children were gassed at Auschwitz on April 16, 1944. Her husband died there on October 30.[64]

Raymond Aron, who spent the war years with the Free French in London, where information circulated freely, later wrote:

> We were not unaware of acts of resistance, nor of Gestapo repression, nor of the deportation of Jews. But to what extent did the organizations of Free French in London know that the transfer of Jews to the east had a different meaning from the deportation of resistance fighters captured by the Gestapo? . . . What did we in London know of genocide? . . . As far as direct awareness was concerned, my perception was something like this: the concentration camps were cruel, ruled by prisoner-guards chosen from among the common criminals rather than the political prisoners; mortality was high, but the gas chambers, the industrial assassination of human beings—I must confess that I did not imagine it, and because I could not imagine it, I did not know.[65]

Unlike Raymond Aron, Dr. Georges Wellers, arrested on December 12, 1941, and permanently confined until his own deportation to Auschwitz on June 30, 1944, did not have direct access to the BBC or the clandestine press. As a medical worker and social assistant on the Jewish service staff at Drancy for nearly two years, however, he was able to speak with every prisoner who passed through and to keep in touch with the outside world. In the courtyard of Drancy, he also personally witnessed the assembling of prisoners for more than sixty deportations to the east. He saw the tiny children who did not know their own names and were traveling without parents. He saw the old and the sick, carried to the trains because they could not walk. He later recalled: "I was one of the best informed about the mental state of several dozens of thousands of internees, future deportees. I can affirm categorically that they had no suspicion of the systematic assassination which the Jews actually experienced at the end of their deportation journey." What did he think it was all about?

> I spent long hours, alone or with friends, trying to understand the sense of these events . . . whose essence always seemed: the exploitation of Jewish manpower by a Germany more and more short of labor, an exploitation aggravated by the wish to isolate the Jews in an immense and miserable ghetto. The most somber imagination went no further.[66]

Wellers was convinced that most of the Jewish leadership in France equally failed to understand the consequences of deportation.

At various times at Drancy he spoke with David Rapoport, a founder and director of the Comité rue Amelot, a welfare and rescue group in Paris; with the UGIF officials André Baur and Armand Katz; with Fernand Musnik of the EIF; with UGIF's German liaison agent and translator, Israël Israëlovitch; and with many others. None spoke to him of imminent death. On the contrary, sixty-year-old Rapoport, born in the Ukraine, spoke of his hopes of getting help in deportation from Ukrainian and Polish Jewish social workers. Baur, Katz, and Is-raëlovitch all saw their wives and children join them at Drancy, and "none of them acted like men who knew that they were witnessing a death warrant issued against their dear ones."[67]

Wellers speaks for men who did not survive to bear witness to what they knew, but other insiders confirm his claims. Robert Debré, the pediatrician who lived in Paris and hid Jewish children in the last years of the occupation, later declared that although he had listened regularly to the BBC, he never believed rumors of gas chambers.[68] Henri Krasucki, an eighteen-year-old leader of Jeunesses communistes in Paris who was presumably fully aware of the contents of the Jewish Communist press, later recorded of his arrival at Auschwitz in 1943: "We knew that terrible camps existed. . . . We had a certain idea of what might happen. What we did not know was the degree of the savagery and especially the existence of the gas chambers. It was necessary to arrive there to know that."[69] Henry Bulawko, a young foreign Jewish Resistant who worked closely with David Rapoport's Zionist and Socialist group, also remembers his arrival at Auschwitz. He experienced the selection on the train platform and entered the camp. His barracks chief greeted the new arrivals brutally. "You have just seen smoke rising to our right. They are burning your women and children, your parents and sisters. Do you understand?" They still did not believe it. Prison barbers confirmed it, and then other prisoners.[70]

Georges Wellers was at Auschwitz for three days before he learned the truth. At first, prisoners refused to answer his questions. Then he met a Dr. Garfunkel whom he had known at Drancy and who had been deported earlier with his wife and two children. Wellers asked what had happened to his family. Dr. Garfunkel explained that at the selection, his wife and daughter had been sent one way and he and his tall, strapping fourteen-year-old son had been sent the other. Thinking that the women and children would have an easier time, the father asked an SS guard if his son, still a child despite his appearance, could go with them. The guard agreed, very politely.

And so all three were murdered. Thus Wellers learned the truth.[71]

For Marc Klein, deported to Auschwitz from France in 1944, understanding took even longer. He recalls that he did not grasp the meaning of the selection process on the arrival ramp. A French prisoner explained it to him. Two weeks later, he met Grand Rabbi René Hirschler, who also told him of deliberate murders. He still did not fully comprehend. He saw huge piles of possessions left by recently arrived Hungarians, and he wondered. Finally, he met a prisoner who had seen the whole process—the selections, the waiting lines, the gas chambers, the crematoriums. Thus, he says, incidentally explaining why other prisoners had trouble believing: "After four weeks, I was convinced that a number, determined in advance, of new arrivals was exterminated daily at Birkenau; but in front of my comrades, who had left their families on the arrival ramp, I always pretended with conviction that I did not believe those horrible stories."[72]

During the summer and autumn of 1942, many French non-Jews, partially informed as they were, underwent a gradual but significant change of opinion about their Jewish neighbors. In the occupied zone, the shift dates from the July roundup. Vivette Samuel puts it succinctly: "After July 1942, after seeing even children deported, the French attitude changed. Yes, some had been anti-Semitic even toward French Jews, but there is a big difference between anti-Semitism and agreeing to deportations."[73] "The measures taken against the Israelites have rather profoundly troubled public opinion," declared a police report from Paris on July 17. "Although the French population is overall and generally quite anti-Semitic, it does not judge less severely these measures which it perceives as inhumane."[74] "In more than one case, the French population has expressed its compassion for the arrested Jews and has felt sorry for them, especially the children," wrote Heinz Röthke, the chief of the Gestapo's Jewish Office in France, to his superiors on July 18.[75] Alarm was by no means widespread; on July 25, a German SS officer reported the arrests of forty-three Jews in the departments of Haute-Marne, Marne, and Aube, and declared, "The action has had no particular effect on the attitude of the population."[76] But concern was growing.

It was the same in the unoccupied zone. In the Var, where the prefect had written in October 1941 of public indifference to the problems of the Jews, not much changed. "In my department, the regrouping of foreign Israelites has caused little public unrest," he wrote a year later.[77] He scarcely mentioned Jews again. And from Limoges the regional prefect wrote, "The operations of the night of 25 to 26 August have taken place without notable incidents."[78] But prefects from departments with the largest concentrations of foreign Jews reported more public concern. According to the regional prefect with jurisdiction over Marseille and Aix-en-Provence:

> The administrative measures taken against the stateless Jews have raised an unquestionable emotion among the population which has judged them with severity. . . . The rights of people, the international rights of asylum have been violated, and delivery of foreign Israelites to the Germans is considered by many as a "national disgrace."

The regional prefect went on to stress that the concern was based on the nature of the persecution, and not on the fact of persecution itself:

> Not that the Jews are viewed with favor, far from it, they are on the contrary violently criticized for their desire for lucre and their blackmarket practices, but opinion is almost unanimous in thinking that they should have been stricken only by economic and social measures which separated them from positions where they were not wanted, and not by bullying policies which, in attacking women and children, cannot fail to shock popular sentiment profoundly.[79]

Many other prefects echoed that view. Throughout 1941, the prefect of Alpes-Maritimes, which includes Nice, mentioned popular hostility against wealthy Jewish refugees living comfortably along the Riviera. In August 1942, however, while still referring to the same resentment, he wrote: "The arrests of Jews from countries occupied by Germany . . . have undeniably shocked public opinion. . . . Opinion which would have accepted with a sigh of relief the internment of these Jews in France has been surprised that they are being delivered to the Germans."[80] A prefect official from the Rhône, which includes Lyon, wrote on July 5, 1942, of more and more marked public hostility against the Jews, but on September 5 he declared, "Although no demonstration has occurred, an important fraction of the public, especially in Catholic circles, is expressing a certain irritation [against the arrests of foreign Jews]. Because of [those Catholic circles], the departure of several hundred Jews for Germany, which occurred on

August 27, has not passed unnoticed."[81] And a prefect official from the Haute-Garonne, which includes Toulouse, wrote in October that although the public had demonstrated little concern for foreign Jews before that date, opinions had changed dramatically: "The spectacle of a train composed of boxcars in which women fainted from the heat and from the odors of straw soaked with urine strongly and unfavorably impressed the French non-Jewish populations which went to see them, especially in the railroad stations."[82]

In a country where life was difficult for all, the emerging concern for the Jews did not remain long in the forefront. The Germans occupied the southern zone on November 11, 1942, following the Allied landings in French North Africa. Shortages of food and fuel worsened, most prisoners of war still did not come home, and resistance and political repression increased. Nearly every family had its own troubles—a family member in political trouble or in prison, a labor center, or a prisoner-of-war camp; a child without proper nutrition; an old person without medicine; a home without heat. People complained about low salaries, the gradual move toward conscription of labor for Germany, and the abuses of Fascist fanatics in Jacques Doriot's Parti populaire français (PPF).[83] French men and women observed, with both pleasure and trepidation, the course of the war—the defeat of German General Erwin Rommel at El Alamein by November 4, the Allied landings in Algeria and Morocco on November 8–11, and especially the surrender of the German Sixth Army at Stalingrad in February 1943. They realized that, while the Germans might lose the war, the fighting would come to France after all.

In such circumstances, it was difficult to think about others, and especially about foreign Jews for whom many French men and women harbored lingering suspicions and prejudices. At the same time, the official persecution of the Jews, with some notable exceptions, grew more discreet. Roundups were smaller; deportation trains were fewer and farther between. People focused inward, but they did not forget what they had seen and learned in August 1942. The prevailing climate shifted subtly from one of ignorance, indifference, or sullen hostility toward Jews to one of mild benevolence. That new climate, however, made all the difference for those who needed to hide, and for the minority of Jews and non-Jews who actively helped them.

9

Arrests of Foreign Jews, September 1942–February 1943

On September 14, 1942, two months after the roundup of July 16, French police in Paris launched another carefully planned house-to-house raid on foreign Jews. In the intervening period, arrests of foreign and French Jews alike had continued for specific violations of the racial laws—for carrying false papers, curfew infractions, improper wearing of the star, or being in banned public places—but individuals had felt fairly secure in their homes. Now policemen carrying lists with the names of 607 Parisian and 101 suburban residents again knocked on private doors. This time the intended victims were Dutch, Latvian, Lithuanian, Estonian, Bulgarian, and Yugoslavian Jews between the ages of sixteen and fifty-five for women, sixteen and sixty for men. Children were to be taken with their parents. Some exemptions existed: visibly pregnant women, mothers nursing a child or with a child under age two, war widows, wives of prisoners of war, those married to non-Jews, and those carrying UGIF cards.[1] More than 200 victims were found at home, arrested, and imprisoned at Drancy.

On September 24, it was the turn of Romanian Jews. Like Italy, Hungary, and Bulgaria, Romania was an ally of the Third Reich, and its citizens were not subject to deportation without the expressed consent of their government. But in September the Romanian government relinquished protection of its Jews living in France, and the unsuspecting victims became immediate targets.[2] In the well-organized roundup in Paris and surrounding suburbs, only one exemption was defined—for furriers and their families, provided with special yellow identification cards proving that they were producers of warm clothing for German soldiers at the front.[3] That Romanian Jews were not only unsuspecting but unwarned is suggested by the large number of victims caught in their homes. At least 1,594 people were arrested and dragged off to Drancy.[4]

Five days later, French police turned against Belgian Jews. Meanwhile, at homes in the provinces throughout the occupied zone, similar arrests occurred. By the end of October, French police outside the Paris region, with some German help, had caught at least 1,700 foreign Jews eligible for deportation. They included 617 from around Poitiers, 236 from Nancy and the eastern departments of Meurthe et Moselle, Meuse, and Vosges, 294 from the Angers area, 135 from Bordeaux, 122 from Dijon, and under 100 from Rennes, Châlons-sur-Marne, Saint-Quentin, Rouen, Melun, and Orléans.[5]

On November 5, police throughout the occupied zone focused on Greek Jews, immune until then. Permission for the arrests had been forwarded from Berlin on October 12. Most of the intended victims lived in Paris; only about 200 were estimated to be living in the provinces. Again, only Parisian furriers working for the Germans were exempt, along with their families. There were no exemptions for age, state of health, or marital status, although the pregnant and the very ill were usually sorted out at Drancy and sent, at least for a time, to hospitals. Also, those married to non-Jews or prisoners of war were not usually deported.

The early morning raid on Greek Jews was astonishingly effective. By 9:00 A.M. in the department of the Seine, which includes Paris, 1,060 people had been caught from a list of 1,416. With immense satisfaction, Heinz Röthke, chief of the Gestapo's Jewish Office in France, reported to his superiors in Berlin, "One has the impression that this time the French police effectively kept the news of this action secret until the last moment, as they had been instructed to do."[6]

Between September 14 and November 7, 1942, well over 4,500 foreign Jews were arrested in the occupied zone alone. The fate of most of them can be clearly traced. On September 16, two days after their arrest, 25 Latvians, 88 Lithuanians, 40 Bulgarians, 14

Yugoslavs, and 38 Dutch Jews, totaling 205 people, joined nearly 800 other deportees, most of them from the unoccupied zone, for the trip to Auschwitz. On September 25, 729 of the 1,574 Romanians arrested two days before made the same deadly trip, with another 275 Jews from Drancy. On September 28, an additional 594 Romanians, with 310 others, followed. Thirty-eight Belgians arrested September 29 and 55 Dutch arrested September 14 made up part of a small convoy of 211 deportees on September 30. Most of the 1,745 foreign Jews from the provinces traveled east, with others, on November 4, 6, 9, and 11. The Greeks were moved out on November 9 and 11. Of approximately 6,766 deportees on these eight convoys, about 97 returned.[7]

Also throughout the autumn of 1942, and especially in Paris, municipal police continued to apprehend individual Jews in the streets, usually for minor violations of the racial laws. After the arrests of these unfortunate victims, more specialized anti-Jewish police often sought out their entire families in their homes and sent them to Drancy as well. Other individuals were arrested for black market activities or, outside Paris, for illegally crossing the demarcation line. Many served prison terms before being sent to Drancy.

Meanwhile, however, there were no large raids on French Jews in Paris or in any other major city. Nazi Jew-hunters certainly tried. As early as September 21, 1942, for example, Röthke informed his superiors of his elaborate plan for a huge roundup in Paris of 5,129 specific prominent French Jews and their families, to be followed within a few hours by a thorough police search of six arrondissements and the indiscriminate arrests of anyone found wearing a star, plus their families. The raid was to take place the following day; 3,000 French police were to be mobilized by the German SS that very evening, bypassing Vichy police chiefs René Bousquet and Jean Leguay entirely. For an indefinite period following the initial roundup, police in Paris were to continue to arrest everyone found wearing the star.[8] The situation in Paris, in other words, would come to resemble that regarded, much later, as the standard Holocaust condition: any and all Jews could be seized on sight.

Helmut Knochen, Röthke's immediate superior in the RSHA in France, was fearful of the impact of a large-scale arrest of French Jews both on public opinion and on those Vichy officials whose collaboration he needed in other security matters. Not only was he uncertain about whether French police would obey German orders without explicit permission from their own chiefs, but he was reluctant to provoke an embarrassing confrontation. As a result, he promptly prohibited the roundup. Acting independently, a furious Röthke and two French assistants arrested seventy-six Jews in two Parisian apartment buildings on the night of September 22. Fifty-eight of the seventy-six were French. All were of modest means, in contrast to the prominent Jews originally scheduled for arrest.[9] But Röthke then turned his attention to the Romanian Jews, who were arrested en masse on September 24. In the months that followed, he never received the permission that he desired for the indiscriminate roundup of French Jews in Paris.

Meanwhile, in a situation difficult to comprehend today in the light of knowledge of persecutions in other European countries, many Jews, especially French citizens, moved openly about Paris and elsewhere, hoping for the best. Some illegally changed residences or at least slept away from home, but children wearing stars nevertheless attended public schools until the end of the academic year in 1944—just two months before the Liberation in August. Adults attempted to earn a living. Those in need frequented Jewish social service agencies in Paris and certain other cities until well into 1944. Many synagogues remained open and busy until at least the spring of 1944, and some even until June. French police rarely had carte blanche to arrest at will every Jew they spotted regardless of nationality, as Röthke so desired. When they did have it, permission was limited to a specific place and time (as in Rouen and Marseille in January 1943) or to a particular institution (as in a raid on a hospital or social service agency, when all present, even if only by chance, could be seized). With these and a few other important exceptions, most French police would only arrest Jews whose names appeared on a list, plus those guilty, or alleged to be guilty, of an infraction.

As the months passed, it became increasingly dangerous and difficult for Jews in major cities to live legally at home, for several reasons. First, as seen, specific nationalities became eligible for deportation without warning, and unsuspecting victims in their homes were rounded up by police with lists of names. Second, law-abiding Jews wearing stars fell prey to vicious neighbors or unknown anti-Semites in the streets, who accused them falsely of disregarding some regulation and had them arrested. Third, German SS agents, while generally few in number and reluctant to make arrests and attract public attention as the persecutors of French citizens, but increasingly frustrated by the foot dragging of the regular French police, occasionally did stage indiscriminate raids of the type that Röthke had wanted in

Paris in September. On those rare occasions, they seized every Jew in sight. The largest and most terrifying example was the Nazi action in Nice in September 1943, as will be seen.

Finally, by late 1943, small numbers of French and foreign Jews alike were detained indiscriminately and arbitrarily each day, not by regular police but by specialized Jew-hunting units such as the Permilleux service in Paris and the Milice or groups of individual French thugs working with local Gestapo agents elsewhere.[10] Such outfits operated in coordination with German SS police in a freewheeling manner not tolerated by the regular French police, and they represented an enormous threat to Jews attempting to live openly in both urban and rural areas. In recognition of the increasingly generalized danger of arrest, most Jews in France did at least change residences by early 1944, but surprising numbers, especially among French Jews and especially in large urban areas where anonymity was greater, remained discreetly at home and ventured into the streets as little as possible. Many paid for that decision with their lives, but in Paris, about 30,000 Jews are believed to have remained in their legally declared residences until a month or two before the Liberation.[11] Most of these hid only during the final chaotic weeks.

Maurice Rajsfus and his sister are examples of Jews who decided to remain legal and succeeded. As seen earlier, they and their Polish-born parents were arrested in the July 1942 roundup in Paris. Their parents were deported and did not return, but, in an exception to the usual procedure, they, born in France and citizens by parental declaration at birth, were released. They returned to their apartment to find the concierge rummaging through their cupboards. Representatives from UGIF urged them to report to a children's center, but they ignored the invitation—a decision that may well have saved their lives, for Jewish children's institutions later became easy targets for raids.

Rajsfus and his sister lived legally and openly in their apartment until June 1944, when they were warned of possible arrest and went to live with friends and contacts until the Liberation. Rajsfus supported his sister by working as an apprentice for a non-Jewish jeweler. He went to work every day, wearing his star, and had very little trouble. His sister remained at her lycée until June 1944, also wearing the star. He admits that they were lucky. They could have been denounced at any time by the hostile concierge, and the police would have been obliged to arrest them. Or they could have been denounced on the street for a real or imagined offense, or picked up arbitrarily by the Permilleux service. They were in constant danger, but as Rajsfus explains:

> There was never a massive roundup of French Jews in Paris, except the one in December 1941. It was not worth the trouble to go door to door. The susceptible Jews were those in groups, in orphanages, nursing homes, or hospitals, who could be picked up easily when Brunner had room at Drancy or needed to fill a train. No one should ever have remained in a group. All should have been dispersed.[12]

Maurice Rajsfus and his sister were lucky, but many were not. Mrs. P. Dachs later declared, "I was arrested *in my home* in Toulouse *on June 28, 1944,* with my two children, aged three and five years."[13] The three were deported on July 30 or 31, 1944, directly from Toulouse to Ravensbruck. They were fortunate only in that they all survived.

Also unlucky, but at a much earlier date, was the young Jewish rescue worker Henry Bulawko. Although he was engaged in clandestine work, producing and distributing false documents to Jews in hiding as early as 1942, Bulawko was arrested by pure chance for an alleged infraction. As he left the Paris métro at the Père Lachaise exit on the afternoon of November 19, 1942, he ran into a policeman who had made no arrests that day. The man accused him falsely of covering his star with a book and a raincoat that he was carrying over his arm. "I was his only 'client' of the day and he had no intention of releasing me," Bulawko remembers.

The policeman turned out to be a stupid and vicious anti-Semite. He accused his prisoner of not fighting for France in 1940. Bulawko replied that he had been too young—his class had not yet been called up. And in 1914? He had not yet been born. "The Jews always find good excuses," the policeman concluded. Bulawko was sent to Drancy, from where he was deported to Auschwitz on July 18, 1943. He was among the 52 survivors of his convoy of 1,000.[14]

The Rajsfus children, Mrs. Dachs, and Henry Bulawko lived in cities, but Jews in rural areas had to make similar decisions about hiding, often with less information. Gaby Cohen, for example, tells of her parents, Mr. and Mrs. Wolff from Alsace, who moved to a small town west of Vichy in the spring of 1940. They remained reluctant throughout the war to believe rumors about the death camps. "My mother's reaction," Mrs. Cohen recalls, "was, 'How can they tell such stories?' We knew the German people, we knew they were like everyone else. How could it be true?" When the Germans occupied the town in November 1942, Mrs. Cohen's cousin, an older man who had served in the German army before Alsace was returned to France in 1918, regularly stopped soldiers in the street and proudly described his military service. He and his entire family were eventually arrested and deported.[15]

The Wolff family had many friends in the town who advised them to hide. Her father refused to carry false papers and continued to work discreetly in a factory. Mrs. Cohen explains, "We French Jews felt it was for foreign Jews but not for us." After a specific warning, however, her parents did hide for a short time and survived. They also agreed to send their two sons, ages five and ten, to Switzerland.[16]

Similarly, Denise Caraco Siekierski tells of her parents, French Jews who left Marseille in January 1943 when they realized that citizens as well as foreigners were being arrested there. They rented a house in a village about ten kilometers from Avignon. Being law-abiding citizens, the Caracos insisted upon registering as Jews in their new place of residence. The local mayor, aware of the danger and absurdity of such a step, refused to process their registration, claiming that he did not have the proper forms. The elderly couple then walked to a village six kilometers away, in the middle of winter, where they could register as the law required. When they later changed houses, they made the same trip again. The Germans did not come for the Caracos until the summer of 1944. They were out visiting at the time, and their shutters were tightly closed against the summer heat. Neighbors told the police that they had left days before, and they survived. They lived out the remaining days of the war in hiding, finally using the false papers that their daughter, a teenager active in a Jewish rescue network, had secured for them at the end of 1942, before they had even left Marseille. Until the summer of 1944, they had simply kept the papers in a drawer.[17]

The numbers of Jews who decided to remain entirely legal must not be exaggerated. They represented a distinct minority of French Jews, and a far smaller proportion of foreigners. Most lived in large cities, especially Paris, where the nature of the danger was different from that in small villages. Most were French, lulled by the fact that their names rarely appeared on police lists until 1944 (and in Paris, not even then). Many, especially in the later period, were the most helpless—children, women alone with children, or the elderly, set in their ways and therefore, as Léon Poliakov described them, "uncamouflageable."[18] Thus, while they based their decisions on a mixture of ignorance, fear, fatalism, and deficiencies of imagination, resources, and sound options, their inaction was hardly representative of the community as a whole. On the contrary, most of the 76 percent of the Jews in France who survived did so in part because they eventually took some steps to hide. Also, as will be seen, Jews in France organized themselves as early as 1941 into Resistance and self-rescue groups to a degree that was perhaps exceptional in wartime Europe. They were hardly passive.

The decision of a minority to remain legal, then, must be accepted at face value as a risky option that succeeded for some and failed for others. More usefully, it should be examined for the invaluable light it sheds on the nature of the Jewish persecutions in France. It indicates, for one thing, the degree to which some Jews in France misread the danger signals. Lulled by the apparently "normal" periods between roundups, initially deceived by the limitation of arrests to particular national groups, and uninformed because of censorship about raids in other cities, many Jews failed for a long time to understand that the Nazis ultimately intended to deport them all. Members of a threatened national group, if they survived the first raids, usually went into hiding, but others continued to delay. French citizens, whose names rarely appeared on French police lists for large roundups before 1944, were particularly and understandably slow to read the signs. That the Vichy regime would expel "undesirable aliens" was conceivable; that it would abandon citizens was not. It was illegal for Jews to travel or change residences without permission, not to mention live on false documents, and those caught disregarding the regulations were sure to be arrested and deported. Many who opted for legality, like the Caracos, did so because they felt safer that way. They did not understand, or they understood too late, that observing the legalities was not a guarantee of safety.

The very possibility of survival in one's legal residence in late 1943 and 1944 also reveals the scarcity of personnel and facilities allocated to the hunting of Jews. With only a small German SS staff at his disposal, Röthke depended upon French police cooperation. For roundups of native-born Jews, such help was difficult to obtain. When required to meet a quota, French police deliberately focused on foreigners. Also, as Rajsfus pointed out, they vastly preferred to concentrate on institutions, where they could make a quick and large haul without attracting much public attention. They increasingly disliked going to individual residences, where pickings were slim and where hundreds of other apartment dwellers could observe arrests.

There never was an "open season" throughout the country on all Jews during which they were to be rounded up whenever and wherever they were discovered. Röthke's forces were always too limited, the French police too legalistic, and non-Jewish public opinion too unreliable, for such an action. Another reason was purely technical. Primarily because of problems with the availability and scheduling of trains to the east, Jews awaiting deportation had to pass through Drancy. They could be held temporarily at Compiègne, Pithiviers, Beaune-la-Rolande, several camps in the southern zone, or various municipal prisons, but ultimately they had to come to Drancy, which had a limited capacity. This constraint necessitated careful planning and discouraged the launching of a single, indiscriminate Jewish roundup throughout the country.

The decision to attempt to live openly also suggests the dangers and difficulties of hiding. As mentioned, detection meant certain arrest, and hiding in the face of that certainty required enormous courage. Hiding also required money. Families who took in Jews often had to be paid, if only for food and supplies. Non-Jewish institutions like schools and convents usually required payment for room and board. Money was also needed to obtain false documents and to pay guides to cross the demarcation line or the frontier into Switzerland or Spain, unless rescuers were willing and able to provide such services free of charge.

Hiding also involved contacts, either with Jewish rescue agencies, about which French Jews usually knew little, or with non-Jews, often unknown to foreigners. And last but by no means least, hiding often involved breaking up family units. Children were placed with strangers; old people were left in institutions; adults joined the Resistance, or lived from hand to mouth, or chose legality to maintain others in hiding. The agony of making choices upon which life itself depended was nearly unbearable, while day-to-day living without news from loved ones was perhaps the greatest burden of all.

Finally, the possibility of surviving legally says something about the attitudes of French non-Jews. That Jewish children wearing their stars could go to public schools in Paris and elsewhere in the north (stars were never required in the south) throughout the occupation while their similarly marked parents worked and shopped suggests an atmosphere of limited tolerance. That they could remain in apartments where all their neighbors knew them suggests the same. Any informer could denounce them to the police, and in such cases, police felt obligated to make arrests. Thus, the consequence of denunciation was always Drancy. And there were in fact many informers. But far more French non-Jews saw Jews regularly and left them alone—a phenomenon inconceivable in much of Eastern Europe. It was a mild tolerance, certainly, often not much stronger than indifference. It was perhaps unworthy of praise, but it was clearly worthy of notice. It created a climate conducive to rescue efforts by a minority of Jews and non-Jews.

The growing danger of arrest and deportation that threatened foreign Jews in the north spread into most of the unoccupied zone when the Germans invaded it on November 11, 1942. Until then, it will be recalled, Jews in the south who had arrived in France after 1933 or 1936, regardless of whether or not they had been naturalized, had been delivered to the Germans. Thousands of less recent immigrants, however, remained. After November 1942, foreign Jews of nationalities eligible for deportation were in as much danger in the south as in the north.

There was, however, one bright spot in the darkness. The Italian army marched into eight departments east of the Rhône River at the same time that the Germans moved southward, and Italy's different policy toward Jews was soon evident in its zone.[19] The Vichy government decreed on December 11 that every Jew in France must have his personal identification and ration documents stamped with the word "*Juif*." Despite the fact that Vichy technically retained jurisdiction throughout the country, Italian military and diplomatic authorities promptly prohibited such a stamp in their zone. Vichy police also continued to arrest individual French and foreign Jews throughout the country and to herd foreign Jews not yet arrested into supervised residences. Warned by an Italian Jew named Angelo Donati of Vichy's anti-Jewish activities in their zone, Italian authorities prevented local arrests, released many already arrested, and saw to it that those placed in supervised residence were not transferred by the French to the German zone.[20]

Jews were not slow to grasp the advantages of life under Italian rule, and thousands migrated into the southeastern corner of France. An unhappy Röthke reported that an area that before the war had contained 15,000 to 20,000 Jews held 50,000 in July 1943. He added:

> The attitude of the Italians is, and was incomprehensible. . . . In the last few months there has been a mass-exodus of Jews from our occupation zone into the Italian zone. The escape of the Jews is facilitated by the existence of thousands of flight-routes, the assistance given them by the French population and the sympathy of the authorities, false identity cards, and also the size of the area which makes it impossible to seal off the zones of influence hermetically.[21]

Most refugees gravitated to Nice, where they received the necessary residence permits and ration cards. From there, Italian authorities sent many to supervised residence in villages in the interior.

The testimony of new arrivals in the small Italian zone sheds light on conditions in the German-occupied area of France as well. Sixteen-year-old Adam Munz, a refugee from Poland by way of Belgium, had previously been disguised as a non-Jew in a boarding school in Villefranche-de-Rouergue (Aveyron), near Montpellier in southwestern France. He remembers his arrival to join his father at Saint-Martin-Vésubie (Alpes-Maritimes) in the Italian zone in the summer of 1943:

> The constant fear during the German occupation of France is something difficult to describe. It cannot be exaggerated. It was everywhere. People were terrified.
>
> Saint-Martin in the Italian zone was like paradise. There were so many Jews living peacefully and openly there! *Carabinieri* [Italian national police] and soldiers would smile and say hello. We invited them to our parties and concerts, and they came![22]

Alfred Feldman arrived at the same village about the same time, also to join his father, who had escaped from a French labor camp for foreign Jews. His mother and sister had already been caught and deported. Like Munz, his reactions contrasted dramatically with his sense of oppression in the German-occupied zone:

> I arrived at Saint-Martin toward evening and I saw something that I had not been accustomed to seeing for a long time; Jews were passing peacefully through the streets, sitting in the cafés, speaking in French, German, some even in Yiddish. I also saw some *carabinieri* who passed through the narrow streets of the town with their characteristic Napoleonic hats, and even a group of *bersaglieri* [Italian elite light infantry] with their black plumes.

Everything seemed to be happening freely, there were no particular regulations concerning relations between refugees. Discussion flourished with the greatest liberty.[23]

Needless to say, Italian protection of the Jews in their zone enraged both the Nazis, who saw it as an embarrassing and incomprehensible challenge from an ally, and Vichy officials, who hoped to deport foreign Jews throughout France to ease pressure on native Jews. Pierre Laval himself expressed the official Vichy position perfectly when he informed officials at the Italian Embassy in Paris that, in the words of the Italian report, "our intervention on behalf of Jews of Italian nationality is entirely understandable. He cannot however see what moved us to intervene on behalf of the foreign Jews."[24] The Germans protested more firmly, finally sending Foreign Minister Joachim von Ribbentrop to Rome in late February to discuss the situation with Mussolini himself. Hans Georg von Mackensen, the German ambassador to Italy, also had at least two conversations with the Duce on the subject. Mussolini apparently told the Germans everything they wanted to hear, agreed to instruct Italian occupation authorities to give French police a free hand against the Jews, and sent a former police inspector, Guido Lospinoso, to Nice in March to establish the Commissariat for Jewish Affairs. Lospinoso's assignment was to enforce a Jewish policy more compatible with German aims. Yet nothing changed.[25]

In the early months of 1943, the terror Munz and Feldman described in German-occupied France still was experienced primarily by foreign Jews like themselves. It is difficult to know exactly how many French Jews were arrested, usually for specific or alleged offenses, in 1942, but on January 21, 1943, Helmut Knochen informed Eichmann in Berlin that there were 2,159 French citizens among the 3,811 prisoners at Drancy.[26] Many had been at Drancy for several months. They had not been deported because, until January 1943, there had usually been enough foreigners and their children to fill the forty-three trains that had carried about 41,951 people to the east. There had been a few exceptions. A majority of the 1,112 men deported on the first convoy from France, on March 27, 1942, had been French citizens, most of them arrested in Paris on December 12, 1941. A train on June 22 had included 435 French men and women, and another on September 23, 540. Most other convoys in 1942 contained smaller groups of French adults scattered among much larger contingents of foreign Jews. Vichy officials did not protest those exceptions. On the contrary, French police aided the Germans in supervising convoys and guarding them as far as the frontier.

By January 1943, however, foreign Jews were increasingly aware of the danger and difficult to find. Nazi pressure for the arrests of French Jews and the deportation of those already at Drancy increased accordingly. Thus, when Knochen reported the presence of 2,159 French citizens among the 3,811 prisoners at Drancy on January 21, 1943, he also asked Eichmann for permission to deport them. There had been no convoys from Drancy in December or January, and Röthke was pressuring Knochen to resume them. Röthke also wanted to empty Drancy in order to refill it. Despite Vichy officials' past disapproval and Eichmann's own prior discouragement of such a step, permission for the deportation of the French Jews at Drancy, except for those in mixed marriages, was granted from Berlin on January 25.[27]

Röthke immediately arranged for three trains to leave Drancy for Auschwitz on February 9, 11, and 13. When French police officials learned that the last of the three trains was to carry citizens, they actually offered to conduct another large roundup in Paris of foreign substitutes.[28] The result on February 10 and 11 was an action suggested, planned, and conducted entirely by the French. The challenge was daunting, for most able-bodied foreign Jews in the city who were eligible for deportation had changed residences by February 1943. The obvious targets were therefore the most helpless—young children in orphanages, the sick in hospitals, and the elderly in old-age homes.

The victims of the February 10–11 roundup numbered 1,549, of whom 1,194 were over the age of sixty.[29] On February 10, French police seized 12 sleeping children from the orphanage of the Rothschild Foundation, 22 from the Centre Lamarck, and 10 from the Centre Guy Patin. The next day, they returned to the Rothschild orphanage for 4 more. They also tore 30 sick patients from their beds at the Rothschild Hospital and another 30 elderly people from the Rothschild nursing home.[30] It was perhaps the lowest moment in the ugly history of French police collaboration in the destruction of the Jews. In the absence of other prey, the young and the old were the primary targets in a raid initiated by the French themselves.

Knochen greeted the news of the arrest of 1,549 foreign Jews to take the place of French Jews, with the remark, "Obviously both categories of Jews will be deported in this case."[31] And so it happened. Most of the old people and children arrested on February 10 were deported to Auschwitz the next morning.[32] Two days later, 1,000 French Jews whom the police had hoped to protect, most of them arrested for minor or alleged breaches of the racial laws, followed. Despite their warnings to the contrary, French police helped with the loading and accompanied the train to the frontier.[33] Eight prisoners escaped from the train. Seventeen others also survived.[34]

At 11:10 P.M. on February 13, just three days after French police had combed Jewish institutions in the city for deportable foreigners, two German Luftwaffe officers were assassinated in Paris as they returned to their hotels from their offices. In reprisal, German authorities demanded that the French police arrest and deport 2,000 foreign Jewish men between the ages of sixteen and sixty-five.[35] Again reluctant to arrest French Jews and aware of the extreme difficulty, if not impossibility, of finding 2,000 foreign Jewish men of specific ages in Paris alone, police arranged a nationwide roundup. Prefects particularly in newly occupied departments in what was now called the southern zone were requested to supply lists of residences and workplaces of foreign Jewish men. A fearful manhunt began on Saturday, February 20.

During the lull that departments in the south had enjoyed since the roundups of August and September 1942, many foreign Jews had continued to live openly. Those who had entered France before 1933 (if young male bachelors) or 1936 (if women or married men) and been spared expulsion in August 1942 felt somewhat secure; so too did large numbers of foreign war veterans who had volunteered to fight for their adopted country, been decorated, wounded, or even invalided in that service, and usually been exempted from expulsion. Hundreds of men were now caught. In the Italian zone, Jews arrested by French police were held locally but eventually released on the intervention of the occupation authorities. In the much larger German zone, however, victims were assembled in local camps, such as Noé, Le Vernet, and Nexon, and then transferred to Gurs. At the latter camp, they joined some long-term inmates who had been spared expulsion in August but were now eligible for deportation. On February 26, 957 men were shipped north from Gurs to Drancy. On March 2, at least 770 others followed.[36]

Two convoys left Drancy for Poland on March 4 and 6, carrying almost exclusively foreign men between the ages of sixteen and sixty-five. The trains went to Chelm, near Lublin and the extermination camps of Sobibor and Majdanek. The precise fate of the 2,000 passengers is not recorded, but only 9 are known to have survived the war.[37]

10

No Holds Barred,
January–December 1943

ALTHOUGH FRENCH POLICE TRIED TO PROTECT JEWISH CITIZENS IN Paris and throughout the country in February 1943, one of the first general roundups of French and foreign Jews alike had already occurred in Rouen on January 13–16. Under orders from the occupation authorities in reprisal for the killing of a German officer at the railroad station, French police had arrested 222 Jews, of whom 170 were French.[1] A few days later, at the opposite end of the country, another reprisal action began in Marseille. Between Friday, January 22, and Wednesday, January 27, the Germans evacuated and destroyed the Vieux Port, the old central harbor and market section of the city. At the same time, German and French police combed the city for indésirables—Communists and other political dissidents, common criminals, prostitutes, illegal aliens, and Jews regardless of nationality. On the first day of the raid, Jews were simply picked up in the streets when routine checks revealed the deadly stamps on their identification documents. On the second day, house-to-house arrests began, as described by Raymond-Raoul Lambert, the director of UGIF-South:

All Jews, French or foreign, were systematically arrested. The authorities prepared this police operation scrupulously and with the greatest rigor. Locksmiths were requisitioned to open the doors of homes where tenants pretended to be absent. . . . Women were taken away in police buses, without having time to dress; the ill were forced to leave their beds; old people were taken away by force and parents were separated from their children.[2]

In the days that followed, police barricaded entire neighborhoods. People in trains, buses, shops, and movie houses were thoroughly searched. Altogether, 5,956 people were arrested, of whom more than 3,000 were eventually released. Many of those retained were held in prisons in Marseille, but 1,642, including prostitutes, convicted criminals, illegal aliens, and about 800 Jews, were sent by train to Compiègne on January 24. The Jews included 211 born in metropolitan France, 254 born in North Africa, 120 naturalized citizens, and about 215 foreigners.[3] Dr. A. Drucker, already a prisoner at Compiègne, viewed their arrival on January 26: "Everyone nearly in rags, many barefooted, in night shirts, arrested in their beds and sent off that way."[4]

Dr. Drucker saw the Jews from Marseille leave Compiègne in mid-March. They were transferred to Drancy and deported with others on March 23 and 25. Among the total of 994 deportees on March 23 were 570 French Jews; among 999 on March 25, the French numbered 580. The comparative immunity of French Jews from deportation had ended. The two trains went not to Auschwitz but to Majdanek and Sobibor. From the first train, no one returned; from the second, 5 survived. None of the 800 Jews sent from Marseille to Compiègne on January 24 returned.[5]

On February 9, just a few days after the Marseille roundups and one day before the mass arrests of foreign Jewish children and old people in Paris, the local Gestapo chief, SS First Lieutenant Klaus Barbie, acting without authorization from Paris or Berlin and without help from French police, raided UGIF offices in the rue Sainte-Catherine in Lyon. His men arrested 86 social workers and clients who were unfortunate enough to be present that day. Of the 86 Jews arrested, 28 were French and 58 were foreign. Two men escaped, and 84 were sent to Drancy. Seventy-eight of the 84 were deported to Auschwitz, and 3 of the 78 survived.[6]

Of the first three Nazi moves against Jews without regard to nationality, the roundups in Rouen and Marseille were reprisal actions and the Sainte-Catherine affair was Barbie's personal and unauthorized initiative. Gradually, unofficially, and almost imperceptibly during 1943, however, the danger of arrest broadened to include

French Jews on a regular basis. About 535 Jews were arrested in Paris and sent to Drancy in March, of whom 388 were previously exempt foreign furriers. The others were local residents, often French, arrested in the streets for real or alleged legal infractions. Approximately 600 additional Jews were arrested in March throughout the country.[7] In April, about 411 Jews were arrested in the Paris region, and about 150 in the rest of the country. Many of the 150 seized outside the Paris region, as well as many of the 371 arrested in Paris in May along with 250 throughout the country, were French. Of those arrested outside the Paris region, Raymond-Raoul Lambert wrote in his notebook in mid-May, "Since April 19, the German authorities have proceeded with massive arrests of French Israelites in the region of Nîmes, Avignon, Carpentras and Aix."[8]

On May 6 in Marseille, German SS police raided the UGIF headquarters at 58 rue de la Joliette and seized, without distinguishing their nationalities, 16 men, 52 women, and 6 children. Again, the raid was a reprisal for an anti-German incident on May 1; again the target was an institution, a quick and easy objective.[9] Other Jews, French and foreign alike, were caught during searches of trains in the Marseille area in May. Indeed, with 260 Jews seized in April, May, and June 1943, Marseille was second only to Paris in the number of Jews arrested. Other cities with high arrest rates included Nancy with 120, Toulouse 110, Lyon 70, Poitiers 45, and Bordeaux 35.[10]

Arrests continued in a piecemeal fashion throughout the summer of 1943: about 257 in Paris and 365 in the provinces in June, about 200 in Paris and apparently very few in the provinces in July, and about 400 in Paris and 160 in the provinces in August.[11] Only a few personal cases can be cited here. Lambert recorded in his diary that 18 Jews were arrested in Aix-en-Provence in June, of whom 8 were released upon his intervention and guarantee.[12] The sixty-year-old, Ukrainian-born David Rapoport, a founder and director of the Comité rue Amelot, was arrested by the Gestapo in his Paris office on June 1, 1943, and deported to his death at Auschwitz on October 7.[13] André Baur, the thirty-nine-year-old, French-born director of UGIF-North, was arrested on July 21 as a result of his courageous protests to Vichy officials against conditions at Drancy. With his wife Odette and their four children, he was deported on December 17, 1943, and murdered at Auschwitz.[14] Then on July 30, police arrested 50 people at the UGIF headquarters in the rue de la Bienfaisance in Paris, without regard for nationality or for the exemptions enjoyed by UGIF workers and their families. And on August 21, forty-nine-year-old, French-born Raymond-Raoul Lambert was arrested with his wife Simone and their four children. Deported to Auschwitz on December 7, 1943, none of the six returned.[15]

Despite the increasingly frequent piecemeal arrests of French Jews, the Nazis maintained the official fiction of respect for adult Jewish citizens throughout the summer of 1943. Except briefly in Rouen and Marseille, large-scale roundups of French Jews did not occur, for the Germans lacked the manpower to conduct them alone and French police were reluctant to participate. Meanwhile, as foreign Jews became increasingly difficult to find, deportation rates slowed. In marked contrast to the summer of 1942, when twenty-five trains left Drancy for Auschwitz, just three departed during the summer of 1943. Those three, however, included large numbers of French Jews. About 382 adult citizens were among the 1,018 deportees on June 23.[16] Nationality statistics then became less precise, for after SS Captain Aloïs Brunner, Röthke's aide, assumed management of Drancy from the French on July 2, deportation lists no longer mentioned birthplaces.[17] Survivor testimony and investigations of the personal backgrounds of listed prisoners, however, indicate that many French Jews were included on the trains of July 18 and 31, as on all subsequent convoys.[18]

Unable to dissipate French distaste for the arrests of Jewish citizens, Nazi Jew-hunters tried two different tactics during the summer of 1943. First, as seen, they and Vichy officials bombarded the Italians with demands for the arrest of foreign Jews in their zone, where 20,000 to 30,000 potential victims lived openly and legally. If released by the Italians and unwarned, they could have been seized in huge numbers by French police in a single, well-planned lightning raid. But despite the pressure, Italian authorities refused to cooperate. The Allied invasion of Sicily in July, Mussolini's subsequent fall from power, and his replacement as head of government by Marshal Pietro Badoglio ended any lingering hopes of the French and German authorities that the Italians would release foreign Jews in their zone and ease the pressure on Vichy officials to arrest Jewish citizens. Jews lived openly and securely in the Italian-occupied zone throughout its entire existence—until, that is, the announcement of the Italian armistice with the Allies on September 8, 1943, and the immediate withdrawal of Italian forces from France.

As a second tactic, Germans pressured Vichy officials throughout the spring and summer to rescind the citizenship of foreign-born Jews naturalized since 1927 or 1932—an act that would have made most of them instantly eligible for arrest. In June, Pierre Laval actually signed one version of such a law, affecting about 16,600 Jews naturalized since 1927.[19] Heinz Röthke eagerly planned a vast roundup of denaturalized Jews and their families, to coincide precisely with promulgation of the law. As the summer wore on, however, Vichy officials became increasingly less cooperative. Laval finally decided at the end of July that the law would not be promulgated. He explained to the outraged Röthke on August 14 that he had not understood that denaturalization would be inextricably linked to deportation. He hinted that, after consultation with the Council of Ministers and with Pétain himself, he might endorse a more moderate denaturalization procedure. Meanwhile, he urged the Nazis to pressure the Italians more firmly for the release of foreign Jews in their zone.[20] His final refusal was nonetheless clear. With that single decision, Laval prevented Röthke's pending roundup and saved thousands from certain death, at least temporarily.

Had Laval similarly resisted German demands the summer before, he could have saved thousands of foreign Jews with equal impunity. A year later, the Nazis continued to lack not only the necessary manpower but also the will to act alone. Röthke and Brunner were dedicated fanatics with a single job to do—to arrest and deport all Jews from France—but Helmut Knochen, Röthke's chief at the RSHA, was responsible for security throughout the country. As he had demonstrated by his veto of Röthke's planned roundup of French Jews in Paris in September 1942, Knochen was unwilling to jeopardize collaboration with the Vichy regime, further alienate French public opinion, and compromise security and economic stability by permitting a huge, visible, anti-Jewish roundup throughout the country conducted solely by German police.[21]

Laval changed his mind about the denaturalization law for several reasons. The first involved the course of the war itself. In the summer of 1942, when Laval had cooperated with the expulsion of recent immigrants from the unoccupied zone, German victory still seemed certain. In Laval's view, the most opportune course for France was to prepare for a role as a partner in the new European order. The delivery of foreign Jews, especially the recent refugees whom he wanted removed in any case, was for him an easy price to pay. A year later, the future was less predictable. Allied landings in North Africa in November 1942 had been followed by major German defeats at Stalingrad and in Tunisia. In July, during the very period when Laval was debating the denaturalization law, British and American troops

Victor Fajnzylberg, age thirty-four, with his children. Like her father, the daughter, who is over the age of six, is required to wear the star. The son, under six, is exempt. Victor Fajnzylberg lost a leg fighting for France at the beginning of the war, and was decorated for his valor. He was nevertheless deported to Auschwitz on February 10, 1944. Because of his handicap, he would certainly have been among those gassed upon arrival.

Courtesy of Centre de documentation juive contemporaine, Paris

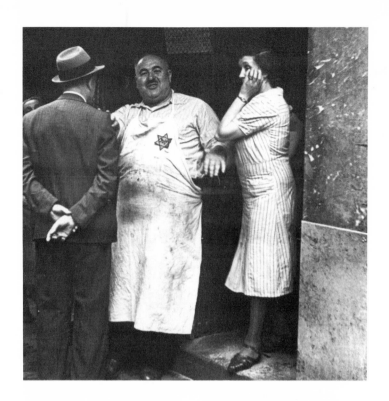

June 1942 street scenes in the rue des Rosiers, the center of a Jewish neighborhood in Paris where many immigrants first settled. The pictures were taken on the day the wearing of the Jewish star became obligatory.

Courtesy of Bibliothèque historique de la ville de Paris.

The first major roundup of Jews in Paris, May 14, 1941. French police summoned 6,494 foreign Jewish men; 3,747 duly reported. Jews here are at the Gare d'Austerlitz, on their way to internment at the camps of Pithiviers and Beaune-la-Rolande. Many of them were deported to Auschwitz the following year.

Courtesy of Centre de documentation juive contemporaine, Paris

A view of the internment camp of Pithiviers. In the foreground, a French gendarme stands guard.

Courtesy of Centre de documentation juive contemporaine, Paris

The internment camp at Gurs, in the unoccupied zone. More than 60,000 Jews and non-Jews, most of them foreigners, passed through Gurs between April 1939 and August 1944. Of the 18,000 foreign Jews in the camp between October 25, 1940 and October 31, 1943, more than 1,000 died of starvation and disease. Vichy officials delivered 3,907 Jews directly from Gurs to the Germans, for deportation to Auschwitz. Many of the others were transferred but handed over from other locations.

Courtesy of Centre de documentation juive contemporaine, Paris

An elderly internee, coping with the mud at Gurs.
Courtesy of Centre de documentation juive contemporaine, Paris

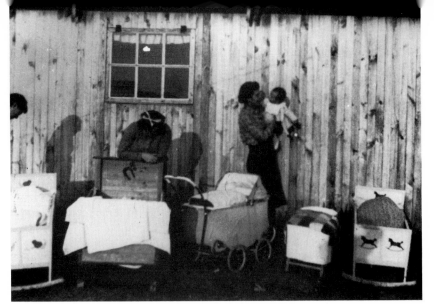

A "nursery" at Gurs. Social welfare agencies tried to provide cribs, layettes, and milk for interned Jewish children.
Courtesy of Centre de documentation juive contemporaine, Paris

A makeshift school for interned Jewish children at the "family camp" at Rivesaltes.
Courtesy of Centre de documentation juive contemporaine, Paris

The courtyard of an unfinished low-cost housing complex at Drancy, on the outskirts of Paris, which served as the last stop before the journey to Auschwitz for at least 62,000 of the more than 75,700 Jews deported from France.
Courtesy of Centre de documentation juive contemporaine, Paris

Adult male internees at Drancy.
Courtesy of Centre de documentation juive contemporaine, Paris

Men and boys interned at Drancy.
Courtesy of Centre de documentation juive contemporaine, Paris

Girls at the UGIF children's home at Saint-Mandé, wearing the star. Gestapo agents arrested sixteen of them, with at least one adult supervisor, during the night of July 21–22, 1944, and sent them to Drancy. Deported to Auschwitz on July 31, fifteen were gassed upon arrival. One fourteen-year-old girl was selected for forced labor, and survived.
Courtesy of Centre de documentation juive contemporaine, Paris

The arrival gate at Auschwitz-Birkenau, the end of the journey.
Courtesy of Centre de documentation juive contemporaine, Paris

Eyeglasses at Auschwitz, left behind by the millions who died there.
Courtesy of Centre de documentation juive contemporaine, Paris

landed in Sicily. Also in July, the Soviet army launched a major offensive along the entire eastern front. With the Germans in retreat, Laval began to reconsider the best policy not only for France but for himself.

Second, and related to the first, by the summer of 1943 Laval knew much more about the fate of deported Jews than he had a year previously. If he had received nothing but reassurances from the Nazis in France, he was nevertheless increasingly aware of mass murder and gas chambers from church reports, Allied and Resistance newspapers, and the BBC.[22] He may not have comprehended the entire devastating horror of the gas chambers, but unlike potential victims, he had no psychologically self-protective reason to dismiss the stories. And given the new possibility that he might have to account for his deeds to the victorious Allies, he needed to proceed cautiously.

Finally, Laval changed his mind about the denaturalization law because he realized that a large-scale roundup of former citizens would be unpopular. Remembering the public disapproval of the arrests and expulsions to the north of foreign Jews in August 1942, as reported by the prefects, he could only have expected greater condemnation of arrests of large numbers of denaturalized Jews—men and women to whom France had granted the protection of citizenship. Laval also recalled the loud public protests by French bishops in the autumn of 1942 against those same expulsions. The more limited and discreet arrests that followed had not evoked similar protests, but the possibility, especially in the event of a large-scale roundup, remained. Indeed, Monseigneur Chappoulie, writing on behalf of the Assembly of French Cardinals and Archbishops, clearly threatened a repetition when he wrote on August 21, 1943, to Jean Jardel, secretary-general to Pétain, "Today, any new deportations would provoke an increased wave of emotion and grief among Catholics, and it is probable that the Bishops would believe themselves obliged to make their voices heard once again."[23] If Laval had any lingering inclination to yield to German demands, such a threat would have discouraged him.

This is not to imply that support for the Jews was a predominant sentiment in France in 1943. Most French non-Jews throughout the war were personally unacquainted with Jews and only dimly concerned about their plight. Non-Jews who witnessed the brutal roundups and expulsions in the summer of 1942 or heard their priests condemn them often forgot about them as they became rarer and less visible. Departmental prefect reports after the autumn of

1942 rarely mention Jews as a popular concern. They instead list a host of other complaints. The Service de travail obligatoire (STO), the obligatory German labor service introduced in February 1943 for French young people born in 1920, 1921, and 1922, was, in the words of one prefect in April 1943, "the measure which, indeniably, has had the greatest repercussions on the spirit of the population."[24] Léon Poliakov, disguised as a non-Jew and working in a paper mill at the time, witnessed the impact of the STO and called it "a monumental psychological gaffe: exasperating opinion, it carried at its breast its clandestine child, the *maquis*."[25] Prefects also mentioned complaints about shortages of food, fuel, and clothing and about the increasing abuses of power by French Fascist paramilitary units.

By 1943, large numbers of French men and women clearly harbored, as another prefect wrote, "dissatisfaction against the policy followed by the Government."[26] To impatience with the discomforts of daily life was added, above all, a growing hatred of the Germans and the war itself. The Germans had invaded the south and deprived the Vichy regime of its justification for existence. They had imposed the hated STO, and they were rightly judged responsible for food shortages. And most seriously, they now appeared to be losing the war.

As the Vichy regime and the German occupiers grew less popular, Pétain and Laval became more cautious and sensitive to public opinion. They were now unwilling to risk renewed criticism of their Jewish policy. As Pétain himself put it when he refused to sign the denaturalization law, "The occupation authorities ceaselessly insist on the necessity of maintaining Order [*sic*] in France. The French Government has so many difficulties in this respect that it must avoid measures which would profoundly shock the French and further complicate the task."[27]

Röthke understood the situation perfectly. He reported to Knochen on August 15: "In effect, with or without promulgation of the denaturalization law, we can no longer count on the collaboration of the French Police in the arrests of Jews *en masse*. Unless the German military situation clearly improves within the coming days or weeks."[28] And so, average French men and women contributed indirectly to sparing thousands of recently naturalized citizens from deportation. They did so not because they were overwhelmingly and consistently supportive of Jews, but because they had expressed some disapproval of large, brutal, and very visible anti-Jewish actions in 1942 and because, by 1943, Pétain and Laval could no longer afford to antagonize them unnecessarily.

In certain other countries, hatred of the Germans and the war did not operate in favor of the Jews as it did in France. In Poland, for example, most non-Jews hated the German occupier and many fought bravely in the Resistance, yet few exhibited any sympathy for Jews. Nor did knowledge of who would win the war necessarily benefit Jews. In Hungary, more than 437,000 Jews were deported with the full cooperation of local police in May, June, and July 1944, when the outcome of the war was almost certain.[29]

Nor did public opinion in other countries always influence government policies toward Jews. In Italy at the end of 1943, for example, the population rarely demonstrated anti-Semitic sentiments, generally disliked the war, and understood that the Germans were losing. Nevertheless, Mussolini's puppet government, reinstated in September when the Germans occupied the country after the armistice, officially abandoned native and foreign Jews alike in a sweeping manner that never occurred in France. The political manifesto of the new Italian Social Republic, better known as the Republic of Salò, declared on November 14, 1943, that "all those belonging to the Jewish race are foreigners," thus depriving of citizenship not only recently naturalized individuals but also Italian Jews whose families had lived in the country since before the birth of Jesus.

Two weeks later, on December 1, 1943, a police order declared that *all* Jews residing in Italy were to be interned within the country until the end of the war.[30] Such an unrestricted police order was never enacted in France. Those in control at Salò, firmly supported by the German occupiers, were more fanatically Fascist than Laval; clearly there were French Fascists who would have acted like their Italian counterparts if permitted.   But Nazi officials other than Röthke and Brunner preferred to keep Pétain and Laval in power, to maintain order without having to commit large numbers of German troops. Pétain and Laval needed some popular support, and massive anti-Jewish roundups were decidedly unpopular.

Although many recently naturalized Jews were spared loss of citizenship and certain arrest in July and August 1943, however, they and other French Jews had by that time lost all but a remnant of their special status. As if to prove the point, another 450 Jews born in France or Algeria were deported from Drancy to Auschwitz on September 2, along with about 550 foreign Jews. Of the total, 21 returned.[31] Röthke warned on August 19 that if Vichy officials did not sign the denaturalization law, he would no longer respect differences between French and foreign Jews and would organize large roundups in both zones.[32] The French did not give in, but Röthke lacked the manpower to carry out his threat. A turning point had nonetheless been reached. Röthke stopped trying to influence French denaturalization policy and directed his efforts elsewhere. His first victims were the Jews of Nice.

At 6:30 on the evening of September 8, 1943, U.S. General Dwight David Eisenhower announced to the world that the Badoglio government in Italy had signed an armistice with the Allies and withdrawn from the war. "By nightfall," one observer recalled, "Nice was one huge party. It was like the fourteenth of July [Bastille Day]. Women were kissing Italian soldiers, accordions were playing, couples were dancing in the streets."[33]

The only surprise about the announcement was its timing. The armistice had been signed secretly on September 3, but rumors had begun circulating well before that date. With permission from the occupation authorities, Angelo Donati and others had been organizing trucks and buses to bring 3,000 to 4,000 foreign Jews from forced residences in mountain villages throughout the Italian zone back into Nice, where the Italian army was expected to take a stand. Jews living in Cannes, Antibes, and other coastal towns west of the Var River fled eastward into Nice for the same reason. They clustered together and registered openly in local hotels. Because dissimulation was not necessary under the Italians, they had no false papers and few local contacts. They became perfect targets.

Meanwhile, since Mussolini's fall and replacement by Badoglio on July 25, Donati had traveled to Rome several times in a frantic attempt to arrange a rescue operation for the Jews in Nice. A remarkable French Capuchin monk named Father Marie Benoît, who had already found hiding places for many Jews in Marseille before his transfer to Rome in June, introduced Donati to influential individuals at the Vatican. They included Sir Francis Osborne and Harold Tittmann, the British and American ambassadors to the Vatican. After lengthy negotiations, Donati obtained the concessions he needed on the morning of September 8. The Italian government would provide four ships, the British and Americans agreed to permit 30,000 Jews from Italian-occupied France to land in North Africa, and the American Jewish Joint Distribution Committee offered to finance the vast move. The operation would take two or three weeks, but announcement of the armistice was not scheduled before October.[34]

The Italians themselves hoped to hold a small area that, excluding the kingdom of Monaco, extended along the coast from the east bank of the Var to their own frontier. Like the French departments of Haute-Savoie and Savoie in the Italian-occupied zone, Nice had been part of the kingdom of Piedmont-Sardinia until 1860. Eisenhower's premature announcement of the armistice, however, caught the Italians completely off guard, and the result was chaos. Confused, demoralized, and without clear government instructions, the army headed home to an Italy now falling under German occupation. Germans began to enter Nice the very evening of the announcement. Within hours, German police occupied bus and train terminals, blocked harbors, roads, and rail lines, and sealed the frontier, seizing thousands of retreating Italian soldiers. Jews who for a few glorious moments had believed that they were in Allied territory were now trapped, with little hope of escape.[35] In a region around Nice of some 250,000 inhabitants, they numbered between 25,000 and 30,000. About 15,000 of them were foreigners.

Two days later, Aloïs Brunner entered Nice with his own team of about fifteen highly trained SS police. He had been waiting eagerly in Marseille for this opportunity to destroy a large community of Jews who, as he saw it, had been deliberately taunting the Nazis by living openly in the Italian zone. His victims were concentrated in one area and nearly helpless, but Brunner also had certain disadvantages. First, he could expect no help from the French police, who would not participate in an unauthorized raid that made no distinction between French citizens and foreigners. Second, unlike the organizers of previous roundups in France, he had no complete lists of Jewish families and residences. And third, Jews in the former Italian zone had no revealing "*Juif*" stamp on their personal documents, for the Italians had not permitted it. With these three handicaps making it difficult to determine who was Jewish, Brunner's tactics were necessarily brutal.

The story of the Nice roundup, among the most vicious episodes of the Holocaust in Western Europe, is best told by those who experienced it. Léon Poliakov, who arrived in Nice at the end of August with the hope of helping Jewish refugees, later remembered:

Those official black Citroëns cruised the streets of Nice, and passengers attentively scrutinized passers-by. At any moment, a pedestrian would be asked to get into a car. No useless questions or identity checks. The car went to the synagogue. There the victim was undressed and, if he was circumcised, he automatically took his place in the next convoy to Drancy.

The famous SS Aloïs Brunner had come in person to direct operations. The official black Citroën method was not the only one. Other teams raided hotels, pensions, and furnished rooms, and took away entire Jewish families. Members of the *Milice,* those jackals of the Gestapo, checked apartment buildings and made lists of names that sounded Jewish. Improvised physiognomists were posted in the stations.

Poliakov estimated that the German police searched about 10 of the roughly 170 hotels in Nice each night. He recalled, "Every night at the Hotel de Lausanne, I told myself before going to bed that I had about one chance in seventeen of being raided. . . . Ah, those nights in Nice."[36]

Eight-year-old Serge Klarsfeld, his sister Georgette, and their Romanian and Russian Jewish parents, Arno and Raïssa, also spent those nights in terror. Thirty-eight-year-old Arno, a French army volunteer cited for valor in combat and an escaped prisoner of war, had prepared a hiding place in their apartment at 15 rue d'Italie, not far from Brunner's headquarters at the Hotel Excelsior. He built a false wall at the back of a closet, with a small access panel. Clothes hanging on a rack blocked the wall from view. The Germans pounded on their door about midnight on September 30, the night before school was to begin. Quickly, mother and children made their beds to disguise their presence and climbed into their hiding place. Arno remained to open the door, to convince the intruders that his family was in the country. As his wife Raïssa later remembered, he had declared, "I can stand a concentration camp. I'm strong." She added, "We didn't know about the gas chambers then."[37] Arno Klarsfeld was deported to Auschwitz on October 28, 1943, where he died from hard labor, starvation, and exhaustion.[38] His family found a new hiding place and survived.

Police raids on hotels, boardinghouses, and apartment buildings were not always by chance. More frequently than in other large roundups, Brunner made use of paid informers in Nice. Though never rare, denunciations elsewhere had less value—they were sometimes inaccurate and usually dispensable in situations where police already had carefully prepared lists of Jewish names and addresses. In Nice in September 1943, however, where German police had no lists, saw no stamped identification documents, had no French police assistance, and could not recognize typically Jewish names, informers were more useful. Acknowledging that reality in his report of September 4 on preparations for roundups in the Italian zone, Röthke suggested that informers be paid 100 francs per victim.[39] That reward increased to 1,000—and occasionally 5,000—francs.

Informers in Nice were a danger to Jews, partisans, illegal aliens, labor conscription evaders, and other individuals in hiding. For East European Jews, however, the greatest threat came from White Russian and Ukrainian refugees, who had been numerous in Nice since the 1917 Revolution. More easily than the French, Russian non-Jews could distinguish Jewish immigrants from other Poles and Russians. Jacques Neufeld, a young Jewish Resistant in Nice in 1943 and 1944, remembers Serge Majaroff, a former officer in the Tsarist army who shared a superb villa with about thirty German officers. Majaroff, who spoke Yiddish as well as any East European Jew, headed a deadly group of anti-Semitic informers. His chief aide was a Ukrainian named Georges Karakaieff. Neufeld's Resistance unit, an urban *groupe franc* of the Armée juive (founded and led by Zionists), made a practice of sending small wooden coffins with letters of warning to known informers. When such steps did not discourage Majaroff and Karakaieff, Resistants attacked in the late spring of 1944. Despite their private security measures, Majaroff was severely wounded and removed from action, and Karakaieff was killed.[40]

Other informers, however, continued their dirty work. Small teams of French collaborators checked names on mailboxes for those that sounded Jewish. Self-styled "physiognomists" claiming that they could recognize a Jew by his physical appearance also did their bit. Philippe Erlanger, who hid in Nice for several days during the roundup, noted some of their mistakes, such as the French Fascist arrested because of his beard, and the Catholic nurse seized because her name was Esther.[41] Poliakov remembered others, like Abraham Goukassov, an Armenian oilman and owner of a pro-Tsarist newspaper, arrested and sent to Drancy because of his first name and his circumcision.[42] Despite their incompetence and absurd pseudoscientific claims, "physiognomists" and other "experts" did immense damage.

Nor were all informers necessarily paid and premeditating. From naïveté, ignorance, or sheer terror, a concierge or any other apartment building resident could tell German police about strange, foreign-looking tenants and do as much damage as any calculating collaborator. Most did not do so, but each one who did destroyed lives.

The number of informing, collaborating, or merely cooperative non-Jews in Nice will never be known. About 1,800 Jews were caught, however, from a population of 25,000 to 30,000. Since most

Jews had not troubled to disguise their identities during the Italian occupation, and since so many were foreign and thus obviously "different" to even the most uninformed observers, the small proportion arrested would suggest that informers were not numerous. The increase in the reward from 100 to 1,000 francs, and sometimes even more, has a similar implication. Nevertheless, even a small number of informers could wreak havoc, sentencing to certain death whole families and even larger groups hiding together.

In addition to the thorough combing of buildings at night and the daily haphazard arrests in the streets, Brunner's men tried to search every train, bus, and car leaving the city. Philippe Erlanger, still in hiding, discovered the danger when he asked a non-Jewish friend to travel out of Nice on a train and come back to report to him on its safety. Everything appeared quiet and normal at the station, and at first the friend thought Erlanger's fears absurd. He soon thought differently, however, and returned pale and shaken, declaring, "If I hadn't seen it, I never would have believed it." Erlanger recorded his friend's description:

> The five o'clock train left the station normally. It was jammed with refugees who thought they could escape that way. The Germans were clever enough to let them depart peacefully. Then after a few minutes, when they had assembled all their victims, they stopped the train.
>
> They scarcely bothered to verify the identities of travellers. Many Aryans found themselves mixed into the flock of Jews who were beaten with truncheons, searched from head to foot, kicked in the face, regardless of sex or age, and finally loaded like cattle into trucks which had been carefully hidden.[43]

For three interminable days and nights, Erlanger waited in a shabby little pension for the fatal knock on his door. He claims that he had no illusions about deportation and carried a vial of poison around his neck. Losing it was his greatest fear. Each night through the flimsy wall of his room, he could hear the sobbing of an Austrian Jewish woman who had fled there with her husband, both with only their sleeping clothes. Erlanger wrote farewell letters to his friends, and the owner of the pension obligingly mailed them. He read and reread the only magazine he had, in which, ironically, an article he had written was published under a false name. He pondered the highlights of his young life. Finally, on September 14, desperate from tension and boredom and feeling "all the anxieties of a hunted criminal," as he put it, he let his friend talk him into leaving Nice by public bus. The bus before his was thoroughly searched, as was one an hour later. His bus was not searched, and he escaped.[44]

Many were not so lucky. Men who were seized were immediately disrobed, for as one witness declared, "The Germans maintained that circumcision was absolute proof of Jewishness. Thus, all documents lost their value."[45] Erlanger, agreeing that the Germans assumed that most documents were false, added: "They classed them as Jews and non-Jews according to whether or not they were circumcised. That allowed the sons of some agnostic Israelites to be released. On the other hand, a good number of Moslems and Catholics, having undergone the operation for reasons of hygiene, went to die at Auschwitz."[46]

The humiliating examination took place on the street, in the synagogue, or at Brunner's headquarters at the Hotel Excelsior, conveniently near the railroad station. Those designated as Jews were held at the Excelsior, sometimes for weeks, while the SS tried to collect family members. Women were classified as Jews on the basis of a family relationship to a circumcised man.

Greater horrors awaited at the Excelsior. Prisoners were interrogated by Nazis trying to extract information about family members not yet arrested. Dr. A. Drucker, sent to the hotel from Drancy to give medical attention to Jews there during a three-month period, describes their condition afterwards: "Day and night, the greatest number of prisoners needed medical care: bandages for bullet wounds in the thigh, leg, buttocks; gashes in the scalp; an ear detached by a gun butt; multiple swellings and bruises all over the body; broken teeth; split lips; abrasions on the face; broken ribs; sprains; etc." One prisoner, tortured horribly, begged Drucker for a lethal injection and, when he did not obtain it, threw himself from a window. Another man, beaten into a coma, was refused hospitalization and died.[47]

Brunner terminated his on-the-scene supervision of the Nice roundup on December 14 and returned to Paris. During the three-month period of his direct involvement, about 1,100 Jews from Nice, another 300 from along the coast, and 400 from villages in the interior of the former Italian zone were shipped to Drancy on twenty-seven separate trains. Three hundred fifty-nine people left on six trains in September, 593 on nine trains in October, 735 on nine trains in November, and 132 on three trains in December.[48] From Drancy, of course, the prisoners inevitably proceeded to Auschwitz—on two deportation trains in October, one in November, two in December, and others in 1944. Few returned.[49] The Pétain government, which had not permitted the involvement of French police in an action that did not distinguish between citizens and foreigners, nonetheless made no protest when Germans did the dirty work.

Although deeply tragic, the statistics of the three-month roundup suggest that Brunner was actually unsuccessful in Nice. The total of about 1,800 men, women, and children arrested and sent to Drancy represented 6 to 7 percent of the Jews in the area. They tended also to represent the most vulnerable. Many were foreigners, easily recognizable as different and with few resources or local contacts. In addition, they and other refugees, including citizens from the north, were unpopular in an area already strained by food shortages and inflation.[50] They were the easiest prey. About 93 percent of their more fortunate co-religionists escaped Brunner's intense searches.

Brunner's roundup was statistically unsuccessful in part because, with few German agents, no French police help, and no lists, it was uncoordinated and inefficient. But above all, it failed because most non-Jews did not support it. French observers were offended by the concentrated and visible brutality, unusual in a country where Jews were generally arrested in carefully planned operations by police bearing lists. Then, because that visible brutality was conducted entirely by Germans, it was even more unpopular than it would have been if it had carried the Vichy stamp of approval. Fresh memories of the Italians' very different treatment of the Jews influenced attitudes as well. As Philippe Erlanger later wrote, "It is necessary to underline, to the honor of the people of Nice, that the majority of them, compensating for the disgrace of the *miliciens* and other collaborators, were occupied rather in hiding the Jews. Catholic circles did their best to protect children."[51] Erlanger overstated his case. An unidentified Jewish Resistant put it better. "As a general rule," he reported in December 1943, "the population shows sympathy to the Jews and shelters and hides a good number. This sympathy however does not exceed the passive stage: no manifestations, nor evident opposition."[52]

The majority of the people of Nice were *not* involved in hiding Jews. As elsewhere in France, rescue was the work of a small minority of dedicated Jews, Catholics, Protestants, and political activists, working both separately and together in complex ways that will be explored in subsequent chapters. The success rate of active rescuers, however, was dependent upon the passive support of the majority of average French men and women—shopkeepers, innkeepers, bus drivers, train conductors, landlords, apartment dwellers, village residents—who could tell at a glance that a customer or newcomer was different and probably a fugitive, and chose to keep silent. The combination of active rescuers and a vaguely benevolent populace kept people alive in Nice, in the face of the Nazi onslaught.

While Brunner's agents focused on Nice in September 1943, German police were not inactive elsewhere in the former Italian zone. They were also often joined by Vichy police, who had been angered by the long period of restraint imposed by the departed Italians and were anxious to arrest foreign Jews to ease pressure on French citizens. The objective was to catch foreign Jews in forced-residence hotels and boardinghouses in small resort villages before they had time to secure false papers and hiding places. Angelo Donati, as seen, had transferred many of those Jews to Nice at the last moment, but some remained. They became instant targets after September 8, and many were seized.

As foreign Jews in mountain villages north of Nice became aware of their danger, many looked toward the Italian frontier. There, they thought, peace had come at last. Between September 8 and 13, about 1,000 foreign Jewish men, women, and children gathered in the village of Saint-Martin-Vésubie (Alpes-Maritimes), about sixty kilometers north of Nice and just a few kilometers from northern Italy. Following the Italian army, they then made a harrowing trek through mountain passes at more than 2,400 meters above sea level. Starved and exhausted, they arrived in the little Italian villages of Valdieri and Entraque in the province of Cuneo, southwest of Turin, only to find that the German army was occupying Italy as well. Local villagers offered food and shelter, but the German SS ultimately caught 349 of the refugees. Of these, about 330 people, foreign Jews who had been eluding the Nazis for years and who had found both hardship and help in the France that had seemed their last hope, were deported back to Nice. In November they were sent to Drancy; from there the destination was Auschwitz. No more than 9 are known to have survived.[53]

Nor were larger towns and cities exempt. Rabbi René Kapel writes of the terror that struck Grenoble (Isère), southeast of Lyon, in the autumn of 1943. He held services for Rosh Hashanah and Yom Kippur in a Protestant church and a Catholic hall, with a Catholic parish priest, Father Vermoral, standing watch outside.[54] Rabbi Kapel exercised extreme precautions, carried false papers himself, and worked endlessly to secure similar documents for his acquaintances. Many other rabbis were less conscious of the danger. Most synagogues remained open until at least January 1944, when an assembly of French rabbinical leaders, after much deliberation, finally authorized individual rabbis to close their institutions if they believed that "circumstances warranted it."[55]

Raids were not limited to the former Italian zone but intensified throughout the country. Jurisdictional disputes seem also to have flourished. In Toulouse, after more foreign Jews were arrested on the night of September 8, the regional prefect refused to allow them to be transferred to the north.[56] In Rouen, after German security police directly ordered French gendarmes to arrest 56 French Jews on October 21 and they obliged by seizing 29, the regional prefect ordered the prisoners released. The Germans ordered them arrested again; the regional prefect refused; the order was repeated; the order was again refused. What the prefect called "the German authorities in Paris" seem to have sided with him. In what was undoubtedly an understatement, the prefect concluded, "In this matter, the local German authorities, who seem to have wrongly interpreted the instructions from Paris, showed a certain irritation."[57]

Despite such confusion, the terror was immense, as the statistics reveal. About 285 Jews were arrested in Paris and 315 in the provinces (excluding Nice) in September; 420 and 597, respectively, in October; 528 and 877 in November; and 279 and 421 in December.[58] Each statistic represents a personal tragedy. On October 20 at the Château de la Verdière, a UGIF children's home in Marseille, Gestapo agents seized at least 29 children with their director, Mrs. Alice Salomon. All were deported to Auschwitz.[59] The following day in Lyon, police acting on Brunner's orders arrested seventy-year-old Jacques Helbronner, president of the Consistoire Central, and his wife Jeanne, the same age. A prominent French citizen, Helbronner had written several letters to Pétain and Laval protesting the treatment of his coreligionists. The Helbronners were deported to Auschwitz on November 20, on the same train as Alice Salomon.[60] Like her, they did not return.

The last month of 1943 witnessed several raids in large cities, conducted, as in Nice, solely by Nazis making no distinction between French and foreign Jews. In Bordeaux on December 20, without advising the local prefect, German police arrested 108 Jews. They were sent to Drancy ten days later.[61] The victims had felt secure in Bordeaux and, unlike Jews in many other parts of the country, had not left their homes to hide. Neither Pétain nor Laval protested the arrests or the German failure to consult them.

In Marseille on December 22, Gestapo agents arrested employees at the local UGIF center, which had remained open despite the devastation all around it. Also on that day in the same city, three Gestapo agents arrested thirty-eight-year-old Grand Rabbi René Hirschler, who had worked for months with foreign refugees in southern France, and his thirty-three-year-old wife Simone. The Hirschlers, both French, had taken certain precautions: they had false papers, they no longer worked or slept at home, and they had hidden their three young children in the countryside. When arrested at the home of their secretary, they were holding train tickets for a move to a hiding place in Lyon.[62] Beaten, insulted, and terrorized by Gestapo agents exultant at having caught a rabbi, they were deported first to Drancy and then, on February 3, 1944, to Auschwitz. They did not return.[63]

More than 17,000 Jews were deported from France in seventeen convoys in 1943, as opposed to about 42,000 in forty-three convoys in 1942. Although the year's total had decreased, the last four months revealed a significant intensification of arrests and a tendency for German police to act alone. The Nazis by now made arrests with no regard for nationality, while French police were still reluctant to participate in large-scale arrests of their own countrymen simply because they were Jewish. That too would change in 1944.

11

The Final Abandonment, 1944

IN THE FIRST FOUR MONTHS OF 1944, MORE JEWS WERE ARRESTED IN France than in any comparable period in 1943, including the peak months of the Nice roundup. The year opened with fearful raids in several French cities—in Laon, Saint-Quentin, and Amiens on January 4, Bordeaux on January 10, Reims on January 27, and Poitiers on January 31. In most cases, the actions were effective not only because of the intensity of the German effort but because of yet another swing in French policy. On German insistence, Joseph Darnand, chief of the Milice, replaced René Bousquet as national police director at the end of December. Under Darnand's influence, Pierre Laval permitted French police to participate in Jewish manhunts that were not justified as reprisal actions and made no distinctions between citizens and foreigners.[1] It was the final abandonment.

The consequence of the change in the provinces was made dramatically clear in Bordeaux, where, of 473 French Jews designated for arrest, 228 were caught by French police on January 10.[2] The proportion was nearly 50 percent, compared with 6 to 7 percent in Nice and the surrounding area in the autumn of 1943, when German police had acted alone without lists. Then on January 27, the Germans ordered the regional prefect of Poitiers to arrest Jews in his area. After demanding and receiving authorization from his French superiors, he obeyed with a vengeance on January 31.[3] From a list of 633 victims, French police caught 484—an astounding 76 percent.[4] Clearly most French Jews in the Bordeaux and Poitiers regions did not yet feel threatened and were not hiding. Equally clearly, no warnings were issued from French police headquarters.

Among many other roundups that month, German police accompanied by French gendarmes also descended upon villages in the Ardennes around Rethel, southwest of Sedan, on January 5 and 6, in search of foreign Jewish agricultural workers. More than 450 foreign Jewish men with at least 100 women and children, most of them from the Paris region, had volunteered for that labor between November 1941 and October 1942, hoping to escape urban roundups and find a way to support themselves. Leaders of UGIF-North had encouraged them to volunteer, expecting that such evidence of Jewish willingness to work would ease German demands for internment and deportation. UGIF officials promised to protect and assist families left behind in Paris—promises they may have made sincerely but were unable to honor.

On January 5 and 6, police with empty trucks visited farms employing foreign Jews and arrested all they could find. There are no complete statistics of arrests, but more than 160 volunteer farmhands were among the 1,147 Jews deported from Drancy to Auschwitz on January 20.[5] Scores of others, warned of approaching police by sympathetic country folk, had time to flee. Many hid themselves or their children among their local acquaintances. After interviewing several farmers, escapees, and survivors from deportation, Maurice Rajsfus drew an interesting conclusion about this previously little known incident:

> When the roundup began, certain French witnesses . . . were able to telephone to nearby villages to warn of the imminent arrival of the German police and their French auxiliaries. It seems that under the circumstances the peasants of the Ardennes clearly behaved better than most residents of the Paris region or of the large provincial cities who were present at the major roundups of 1942 and 1943 without really reacting.[6]

Similar roundups of French and foreign Jews, many of whom were still living at home, continued throughout the provinces in February and March: in Troyes (Aube) on February 3; in Bordeaux against forty elderly Jews, spared in January because of their age, on

February 5; in the region around Dijon (Côte-d'Or) on February 24; and in the Moselle, Meuse, and Meurthe-et-Moselle departments, where the major city is Nancy, on March 2 and 3, to mention just a few. Some roundups, as in Dijon, were conducted by French police; others were carried out by German security police bearing lists of names and addresses delivered to them by French prefects, with specific authorization from Vichy officials.[7]

The attitude of non-Jews to the arrests of Jewish citizens—the reaction that had concerned Laval a few months earlier—is not always clear. A prefect official wrote from Bordeaux on February 2, "The arrests of January 12 provoked in the department an emotion so much sharper because no particular reason explained it and because French police participated, under conditions which the population knows nothing about but interprets unfavorably."[8] A police official reported from Nancy on March 2 that anti-Jewish operations had "provoked some public assembly, but had not caused any incidents."[9] Ginette Hirtz, age twenty-two when she and her younger sister and brother barely escaped the 6:00 A.M. roundup in Amiens on January 4, 1944, in which her parents were seized, later observed, "With some rare exceptions, the indifference was general when a roundup occurred, and certain people even profited from the situation by robbing and pillaging." She added, "For the most part, the population was not interested in our fate. When the final roundup swept down like lightning upon the last French Jews of the region, not a protest, not a ripple troubled the surface of public opinion."[10]

Ginette Hirtz was, however, quick to note the exceptions: "Few in number but very courageous and effective were those who loved and helped us." She wrote of a woman who gave them clothes and brief shelter despite her husband's objections, an employee at the prefecture who gave them false papers, and a peasant family that hid her for a few days—"Theirs were the humane and pacific values of the peasants of the north, reputed to be 'cold.'" She also wrote of a man at the Amiens train station on January 4 who saved an unknown Jewish woman by pulling her out of line and pushing her under a train car standing nearby, so quickly that no one noticed. She concluded:

In spite of the Nazi terror and the murderous anti-Semitic propaganda of the Pétain government, there existed that man's vigorous arm. The hand which falsified identity papers in a bureaucratic office also existed. And there existed the cry of revolt of the woman who gave us her own child's clothes. It was a spontaneous resistance, from people with heart. We must not be silent about it. Unorganized, it existed and comforted us. It even undermined the implacable regime.[11]

Meanwhile, smaller actions occurred in towns and cities throughout the country. In Limoges (Haute-Vienne) on the evening of January 19, Gestapo agents and French *miliciens* raided an OSE office and arrested Jews with suspicious or illegal documents. They spared, at least that day, those with legal documents bearing the *"Juif"* stamp, thus reinforcing doubts about the wisdom of clandestinity. When the police appeared, Vivette Samuel, a young OSE worker and child rescuer, had just left her office to go to a shop before it closed. Her father had arrived to accompany her home. Her father was arrested because his papers, like Vivette's, were not stamped. He was deported and did not return.[12]

In Chambéry (Savoie) on February 8, Gestapo agents raided the OSE office that had become the national headquarters a year earlier because it was in the safer Italian zone. They arrested the director, Alain Mosse, seven staff members, and numerous visitors.[13] On Mosse's orders smuggled out of prison, OSE ceased all legal operations after the incident and broke all links with UGIF-South. Other Jewish social welfare institutions, however, remained open and easy targets. In Saint-Étienne-de-Crossey near Voiron (Isère) on March 23, police seized 18 youngsters at La Marcellière, a home for orthodox Jewish children run by the Association des Israélites pratiquants (AIP).[14] At Brive-la-Gaillarde (Corrèze) and Périgueux (Dordogne), the Gestapo attacked local UGIF offices on April 3 and 4. They did the same at Vichy on April 11.

About 1,520 Jews were sent to Drancy from the French provinces, excluding the Paris region, in January 1944, 2,080 in February, 1,060 in March, and 2,000 in April.[15] Arrest levels in February and April far exceeded those in any month in 1943. Among the February group was the French surrealist poet Max Jacob (1876–1944), a friend in better days of Jean Cocteau, Pablo Picasso, Guillaume Apollinaire, and Sacha Guitry. Jacob was arrested in hiding at Saint-Benoît-sur-Loire, near Quimper (Finisterre) in Brittany, on February 25. His brother, sister, and brother-in-law had already been deported. A Catholic convert considered Jewish under the racial laws, he was sent to Drancy, where he died of pneumonia on March 5, before he could be deported.

The largest numbers of victims in the first four months of 1944 from outside Paris came from Toulouse, Lyon, Marseille, and Nice. Among the April group from Nice was sixteen-year-old Simone Jacob (not related to Max Jacob) and her family. Later Simone Veil by marriage, she would become famous as the minister of health in the government of Valéry Giscard d'Estaing in the mid-1970s, and as president of the European Parliament. The Jacob family, all French citizens, had remained at home during the worst days of the roundup in the autumn of 1943 but had later taken false papers and dispersed. Simone's father André, an architect who lost his job because of the racial laws, lived with one of his former employees; her mother Yvonne and brother Jean were sheltered by local artisans; an older sister, Denise, was in the Resistance; and she and another older sister, Madeleine, stayed with different teachers from their lycée. In November, Simone was asked to leave the lycée—whether for her own safety or for that of the teaching staff was never clear. She continued to prepare privately for the baccalauréat, however, passing her final examinations on March 28. Two days later, she was arrested in the street when Gestapo agents discovered her false documents during a routine check.

The Jacobs all had false documents from the same source, and all except Denise were caught. Simone, Madeleine, and their mother were held at the Hotel Excelsior, sent to Drancy, and deported to Auschwitz on April 13. Mrs. Jacob died of starvation and exhaustion on March 25, 1945, less than three weeks before liberation. Simone's father and brother were deported on May 15 from Drancy to either Kovno (Kaunas) in Lithuania or Reval (Tallinn) in Estonia, where they died from starvation and brutal treatment.[16] Simone and Madeleine returned. Simone was among the youngest French survivors of the death camps.

A week after the arrest of the Jacob family in Nice, one of the most notorious incidents of the Holocaust in France occurred a few score miles to the north. About 9:00 A.M. on April 6, as forty-five children and eight adult caretakers were having breakfast, a Gestapo unit descended upon a large farmhouse in the tiny village of Izieu, near the town of Belley (Ain) east of Lyon. All the caretakers were Jewish, and all but one had been born in Eastern Europe. All but one of the children were also Jewish. Over half had been born outside France; most of the others had been born in France of foreign parents. Seven had been born in Algeria.

The children's personal histories cover the whole range of French

Holocaust experiences. A few had lost their fathers during the arrests in Paris in 1941. Some had lost one or both parents in the July 1942 roundup in Paris. Others were the children of foreigners interned at camps like Gurs, Rivesaltes, and Les Milles in the unoccupied zone who had been expelled to Drancy in August and September 1942 and subsequently deported. They themselves had been among those youngsters ushered out of the camps at the last moment when they were turned over to Jewish and non-Jewish social workers by anguished parents scheduled for expulsion. Other children at Izieu had lost one or both parents in more recent raids, as at Marseille in January 1943. A few had one or both parents living but unable to care for them because they were ill, in hiding, or in the Resistance. Two had a parent on the Izieu staff. All had been turned over to OSE social workers and had found their way to the farmhouse at Izieu, most of them in the spring of 1943.[17] The initial move from an OSE home at Palavas-les-Flots, near Montpellier (Hérault), had been recommended and assisted by two sympathetic local prefect officials there. The secretary-general, Ernst, and his assistant, Fédérici, hoped that the children might reach the relatively safer Italian-occupied zone. Izieu was not quite that far east, but the Italians were in any case long gone by April 1944.

Izieu was a remote and isolated village nestled in hills overlooking the Rhône River valley. It seemed far from the horrors of war and occupation ravaging the big cities. The farmhouse itself should have provoked little suspicion. Formerly a summer vacation home for Catholic school children, it was officially registered as a "Settlement for Refugee Children from the Hérault." It was secretly subsidized by OSE, but for security reasons that information did not appear on the registration documents. Marcel Wiltzer, the thirty-three-year-old subprefect of Belley, and his twenty-nine-year-old assistant, Marie-Antoinette Cojean, knew the truth about the farmhouse at Izieu and were sympathetic. Among other services, these two Vichy officials helped the director, Sabina Zlatin, set up the farmhouse as a refuge, protected its disguise, provided identification and ration cards, attended holiday parties there, and arranged for the children to receive a primary school teacher, Miss Gabrielle Périer.

Villagers, while not always fully informed, were usually kind as well, selling milk and farm produce at fair prices and occasionally donating food to the tiny "refugees." Two local families took in three children too young to live at the farmhouse and successfully protected them during and after the Gestapo raid. Other families employed some of the older boys and paid them much-needed wages. And yet, perhaps inevitably, a few villagers were hostile. Two or three may have served as Gestapo informers.[18]

Despite the appearance of security, adults at the farmhouse at Izieu were uneasy in the darkly ominous spring of 1944. Most other OSE children's homes in the southern zone had been dissolved. The recent arrest of a Jewish doctor a few kilometers from Izieu reinforced the sense of urgency, and Sabina Zlatin was in Montpellier making final arrangements for a move when the raid occurred. Meanwhile, an alarm system had been set up. The house on the hill had a long view of the road and approaching vehicles. Children were to stand watch and ring bells in the event of danger. Everyone was to run to the woods, where some, if not all, might escape. But April 6 was a beautiful sunny day and a Christian holiday, Maundy Thursday. There were no guards, and the alarm system was not activated.

At 8:10 P.M. on the same day, SS First Lieutenant Klaus Barbie, the commander of the Gestapo in Lyon, sent a telegram to his superiors in Paris. It read in part: "This morning, Jewish children's home . . . in Izieu (Ain) was cleaned out. In total 41 children, aged from 3 to 13 years, were captured. In addition the arrest of the entire Jewish staff, or 10 individuals, including 5 women, has taken place. . . . Transport to Drancy will take place on April 7, 1944."[19] In fact, Barbie had counted three of the older boys, ages fifteen, sixteen, and seventeen, as staff. The total arrested included 44 children and 7 adults. One non-Jewish child cared for at Izieu had been released. One adult man, not a staff member but visiting by chance that morning, had escaped into the woods.

The victims of Izieu were transferred to the prison of Fort Montluc in Lyon, where they spent the night. The next morning, they were sent to Drancy. One week later, on April 13, 34 of the children and 4 of the adults were among 1,500 people deported to Auschwitz. Also on the train were Simone Jacob and her mother and sister. Of the group from Izieu, no children and just one adult returned. Ten children and 3 adults from Izieu were deported on subsequent trains on April 29, May 15, 20, and 30, and June 30. None returned.[20]

On April 14, 1944, the RSHA director, Helmut Knochen, issued a new set of detailed instructions for the arrests of Jews throughout the country. "All persons who are considered Jewish according to the law must be arrested without consideration for nationality or other circumstances." Jews in still-valid mixed marriages contracted before

July 1940 remained "temporarily" exempt as long as they did nothing "harmful" against the occupying power. Stateless Jews and those from countries occupied by Germany, including France, were subject to "evacuation to the east." Those with valid passports from neutral or belligerent countries, such as the United States and Britain, were also to be arrested; neutrals could return home, while belligerents were to be interned in France. Their possessions were not to be confiscated.[21]

Bodies to fill the trains to Auschwitz were becoming more and more difficult to find, and Knochen specified in his instructions that Jews were to be seized from children's and old-age homes, hospitals, prisons, and work camps. Four days later, on April 19, police transferred to Drancy at least 137 Jews from Poland, interned at a camp at Vittel (Vosges). They had been spared until then because they held passports from South American countries. Despite that protection, they were deported on April 29. Among them were the poet Yitzhak Katznelson and his son Zvi. Yitzhak's wife Chanah and two other sons had been deported from the Warsaw ghetto to Treblinka in August 1942, but he and Zvi had been sent to Vittel in May 1943 because they held Honduran passports. Now they too were to be murdered.[22]

About 1,400 Jews were brought to Drancy from the provinces in May, but the number dropped to about 425 in June.[23] Just one convoy with about 1,153 Jews departed for Auschwitz in June, and another left with about 1,300 in July.[24] Meanwhile, on June 6, 1944, Allied troops landed in Normandy and began their slow approach to Paris. Simultaneously, Resistance activity began to flourish throughout the country. As order broke down, several hundred other Jews left for the east directly from the southern internment camps of Noé and Saint-Sulpice on July 30 or 31.[25] Two weeks later, another train with about 650 Jews and Resistants from the prison at Fort Montluc left Lyon for the east. It wandered for eleven days before delivering its approximately 308 Jewish passengers at Auschwitz.[26]

A French non-Jewish Resistant named Jeanne Kahn was among the arrivals at Auschwitz from Lyon. Kahn had married a French Jew, and since she was from an anticlerical family, she was not herself baptized. Her claims to be non-Jewish were therefore not believed. Her first glimpse of Auschwitz was the Gypsy section, where half-dressed men, women, and children weak from starvation and sometimes barely able to crawl stared at her from behind barbed wire. Kahn recalled years afterward, "We understood all at once that we had fallen into the kingdom of death." She also remembered the children on her train. To her own children, who had remained in hiding in France, she later said of those others:

> They seemed to have become little old people. They did not cry, but they wore a fearfully resigned expression, as if they understood better than we what was going to happen. . . . And I thought only of you two, I said to myself: "I don't know what will happen to them, but I prefer that they are killed brutally in a bombardment rather than know one day here."[27]

Robert Kahn, Jeanne's husband and a dedicated Resistant also imprisoned at Fort Montluc in Lyon, suffered a different fate. His wife had been among the last prisoners to leave the city. The bombings that preceded the Allied landings on the Mediterranean coast on August 15 destroyed the Lyon train station and the local airport at Bron. On August 17, Robert was among the 50 Jews taken from Montluc to repair the airfield. Among them also were forty-six-year-old Alfred Lévy with his sixteen-year-old son Jean (the youngest in the group) and his seventeen-year-old nephew Raymond. Others included a Polish physician, an Austrian toymaker, a hatmaker, a furrier, and a rabbi who had had no news of his four children. At the end of their workday, all the men except their interpreter were marched to a large pit at the edge of the airport, shot in the back, and buried in a shallow grave. Twenty-three other Jewish prisoners shared their fate and their grave the next day; 37 non-Jewish Resistants were also shot and buried nearby. The 109 bodies were discovered after the German evacuation a few days later. For months afterward, the dead men's personal effects—a handkerchief, socks, a belt buckle, glasses—rested on 109 individual chairs in a special room at the prefecture, along with 109 envelopes giving specifications—height, weight, hair color, estimates of age. Jeanne somehow found the strength to go there after her return from Auschwitz. She identified her husband from a handkerchief she had embroidered for him.[28]

The martyrs at Bron were far from alone. The executions in June and July of Marc Bloch, Jean Zay, and Georges Mandel, the latter two by the Milice, have been mentioned. They had been preceded by the murder on January 10, also by the Milice, of eighty-year-old Victor Basch, the president of the Ligue des droits de l'homme, and his wife Hélène, the same age. These victims were the most prominent, but there were hundreds of others. At Bourges on July 24, Gestapo agents aided by one French milicien shot 28 Jewish men and 8 women and threw their bodies into a well, finishing off those still alive by throwing large rocks down upon them. Throughout the spring and summer of 1944, about 600 Jews and Resistants were taken from Montluc to be executed in small groups in lonely spots in the country-side. At the fortress of Mont-Valérien in Paris during the war, 1,137 people were executed, of whom at least 133, or nearly 12 percent, were Jewish. Most prisoners at Mont-Valérien were there because of Resistance activities. They were shot either as a direct punishment or in reprisal for incidents elsewhere. Jewish hostages were often among the first to be selected for reprisal executions. Overall, at least 1,100 Jews were executed in France during the war.[29]

In Paris itself during the first six months of 1944, arrests of Jews continued at a heavy pace—approximately 730 in January, 840 in February, 360 in March, 200 in April, 350 in May, and 425 in June, dropping to 55 in July.[30] Except in April, they constituted between 20 and 50 percent of all Jewish arrests in the country. Roundups in Paris, however, differed in one significant respect from those else-where, for they continued to be directed almost exclusively against foreign Jews. An estimated 30,000 mostly French Jews went on liv-ing at home and even appearing on the streets wearing their stars.

Foreign Jews in Paris and its suburbs, on the other hand, experi-enced fearful raids in 1944. On the night of January 21, French po-lice arrested more than 643 foreign Jews and their French Jewish spouses and children, from a list of 1,679 names. Of these, 529 were among the 1,214 prisoners deported to Auschwitz on February 3.[31] Another 525 mostly Polish Jews, of 2,231 sought, were arrested on the night of February 3; 469 of them were brought to Drancy, and most were among the 1,500 deported on February 10.[32]

Nor were French Jews in Paris really secure, for individuals con-tinued to be detained throughout the spring at the rate of roughly ten to twenty a day. These arrests usually occurred when Gestapo agents supplied police in the French Permilleux service with specific names, generally based on denunciations, and ordered that those individuals and their families be seized. Occasionally, Aloïs Brunner's security police also made arrests, again concentrating on specific individuals and their families. The Nazis were sometimes accompanied by one or more French-speaking Jewish prisoners from Drancy, usually Aus-trian like Brunner himself, who were used to translate and verify the identity of new victims.[33] The prisoners were usually threatened with immediate deportation unless they cooperated.

It is difficult to understand why Nazi Jew-hunters resorted to such painstaking efforts to arrest individuals when they might have simply launched a concerted raid against French Jews in Paris. As Maurice Rajsfus explains, "They arrested according to the rhythm of necessity." When Brunner had a train to fill—an increasingly less frequent circumstance toward the end of the occupation, when the Germans had other uses for their trains—he sought out a particular number of victims. Arrests of French Jews were unpopular, but individual arrests following a denunciation could be justified on the grounds that the victims had committed some crime. Furthermore, Rajsfus adds, "There was a peculiar Nazi logic, which maintained the fiction of the unity of the family."[34] Even in mid-1944, Brunner tried to convince Parisians that Jewish workers were being transferred to the east for their labor and were accompanied by their families for the well-being of all.

By July, however, as the Allies drew ever closer to Paris, Brunner realized that time was short, and he initiated more brutal measures to seize as many Jews as possible. Tragically, the most accessible victims were children, often orphans, in eleven UGIF homes in the Paris region. Most of the children had been arrested with their parents but for various reasons, including their own poor health or crowded conditions at Drancy, had been turned over to UGIF by the Germans on the understanding that they would be returned on demand. They were officially classified as *enfants bloqués,* or "blocked children." Other children in the same homes were known as *libres,* or "free." They had never officially fallen into German hands but had been placed in UGIF homes by parents, relatives, or other caretakers unable to support them.

In contrast to most social workers for OSE, EIF, and other Jewish children's homes in the provinces, most UGIF workers in Paris refused to take special measures to protect either the blocked or the free children in their care.[35] Their motives have remained the subject of bitter controversy. Some undoubtedly refused to believe, despite all evidence to the contrary, that the Gestapo would seize and destroy small children. They believed in good faith that children would be safer in a legal situation than in illegal hiding places; they did not want to turn their charges over to unknown lawbreakers posing as rescuers; in some cases, they did not want to break promises made to parents that the children would remain in a Jewish environment. Furthermore, dissolving the children's centers would have jeopardized all UGIF relief activities, such as providing subsidies, food, and health care to indigent Jewish families still at large.

Other interpretations of UGIF workers' motives are less charitable. According to them, UGIF leaders demonstrated a blind and unpardonable arrogance. They believed that German promises made to *them,* men of prominence and influence in the Jewish community and, before the war, in the non-Jewish world as well, would be kept, even when those made to the Jewish masses and their foreign leaders were not. Especially after the arrests of their most courageous leaders, such as André Baur, the remaining UGIF directors and employees were weak and terrified of breaking the law. UGIF personnel, usually French but occasionally foreign, carried special cards guaranteeing them and their families immunity from arrest and deportation. Also, they realized that French Jews in Paris were not usually arrested unless they acted illegally. Dissolving the homes for mostly foreign children would have destroyed their own special protection as UGIF employees, placed them in the category of lawbreakers, and forced them to give up their possessions and go into hiding. It might also have provoked reprisals against the thousands of French Jews still living openly in Paris. It seemed better to gamble on legality.[36]

The gamble failed. Between July 21 and 25, less than one month before the liberation of Paris, Gestapo agents raided eight of the eleven UGIF children's homes in the Paris region and seized about 258 children and about 30 adult caretakers.[37] Many were *enfants bloqués* technically under Nazi jurisdiction; others were *libres* and could have been hidden without any direct abrogation of a specific Nazi-UGIF arrangement. Thrown into Drancy, all but about 10 of the children were part of the last large convoy to leave for Auschwitz on July 31 with about 1,300 victims. They did not return.[38]

Allied troops, drawing ever closer to Paris during the first two weeks of August, finally liberated the capital officially on August 25. During the chaos and confusion of the last days, Brunner, with the single-minded concentration of a fanatic, focused on one final objective—the deportation and destruction of the Jews remaining at Drancy. He did not succeed entirely. On the morning of Thursday, August 17, he turned the camp over to the German army and fled. The army in turn handed Drancy over to the Swedish consul general, Raoul Nordling, who visited it with the Red Cross worker Annette Monod that same afternoon. They found 1,518 famished and terrified Jews who had been living under the constant threat of a last-minute deportation.[39] The liberated prisoners lacked identification cards and ration books, not to mention food, clothing, and a place to stay. Since fighting continued in Paris, most agreed to remain at Drancy for a few days, until their immediate needs could be met and their safety assured.[40]

Tragically, however, Brunner did not leave Drancy alone. Through great effort, he managed to secure three cars on a train headed east. He and his SS police used two, but he filled the third car with fifty-one special Jewish prisoners. More than half were known Resistants, including Rabbi René Kapel, Jacques Lazarus, Henri Pohorylès, and Ernest Appenzeller.[41] They had eluded the Nazis for months, if not for years. Appenzeller, for example, a blond "Aryan"-looking Austrian Jew who emigrated to France at the age of twelve and learned to speak French perfectly, had been arrested at home in Nice by the German police on October 15, 1943. He was sent to Drancy where he convinced the notorious Professor George Montandon, the Swiss-born, French-naturalized, and self-appointed expert in the identification of Jews through their physical appearance, that his circumcision was medical in origin. Released from Drancy, he became an active Resistant until he was rearrested.[42]

The fifty-one special prisoners also included several Jewish "notables" and their families. Among them was Armand Kohn, the manager of the Rothschild Hospital and a holder of a UGIF card promising him and his family exemption from internment and deportation. Kohn had scrupulously performed his duties at the hospital, taking all possible measures to prevent the escapes of patients referred there from Drancy. He was arrested on July 17, 1944, with his seventy-five-year-old mother Marie-Jeanne, his wife Suzanne, and their four children, Rose-Marie, Antoinette, Philippe, and Georges-André.

During the interminable journey east, twenty-seven prisoners, including Kapel, Lazarus, Pohorylès, and Appenzeller, escaped. Among them also were twenty-one-year-old Philippe and eighteen-year-old Rose-Marie Kohn. They acted in direct defiance of their father, who feared that escapees would bring deadly reprisals upon those who remained. Twelve-year-old Georges-André wanted to join them, but his father prevented it; twenty-two-year-old Antoinette decided to stay to help her parents and grandmother. The elderly Marie-Jeanne died at Auschwitz, Suzanne and Antoinette at Bergen-Belsen. Armand Kohn returned.

Of the deportees on the last train from Drancy, young Georges-André Kohn suffered perhaps the most terrible fate of all. Admitted to Auschwitz, he was among the twenty children between the ages of five and twelve selected in November 1944 to be sent to Neuengamme, outside Hamburg, for medical experiments. Another child from France, twelve-year-old Jacqueline Morgenstern, was also in the group. Like Georges-André, Jacqueline was French-born. She was arrested in Marseille with her parents Suzanne and Karl, as the result of an informer, and deported on May 20, 1944.[43] The children were joined at Neuengamme by two French doctor-prisoners, Professors René Quenouille and Gabriel Florence, and two Dutch orderlies, Dirk Deutekom and Anton Holzel. Sixty-year-old Professor Quenouille, a radiologist, had been arrested by French police when he tried to shelter British paratroopers. Fifty-eight-year-old Professor Florence, a biologist from Lyon nominated for the Nobel Prize, had been seized by the Gestapo for Resistance activities.

For five months, the children were injected with disease-causing bacteria, especially tuberculosis, while the four adults were forced to keep their medical records and comfort them as best they could. On April 20, 1945, with the approaching Allied guns clearly audible, the children and the four adults were taken to the cellar of the school of Bullenhuser Damm, in the Rothenburg section of Hamburg, and hanged. Philippe Kohn did not learn of his little brother's murder until 1979. Spared the news were his sister Rose-Marie, who died from leukemia in 1949, and his father Armand, who died in 1962. Suzanne and Karl Morgenstern died in deportation.[44]

The war in France did not cease with the liberation of Paris but continued throughout the autumn of 1944. Most of northern France was liberated in September, as was eastern France as far as the Vosges. French troops reached the Rhine River and entered Mulhouse on November 20; others took Strasbourg three days later.[45] But deportations of Jews virtually ceased after the liberation of Drancy in August. One train left Clermont-Ferrand on August 22 with an unknown number of Jewish prisoners, but at least sixty-three. It arrived at Auschwitz on September 8, after an excruciating voyage of eighteen days.[46]

An agonizing waiting period then ensued. Auschwitz was liberated by the Soviet army in January 1945, but during the icy days just before their arrival, the SS moved about 58,000 inmates westward to camps in the Third Reich—to Bergen-Belsen, Buchenwald, Mauthausen, and others. Those who survived those terrible death marches or the train rides through Germany on open cars, in the dead of winter, with no food and only their flimsy prison rags for warmth, waited, and mostly died, until the war ended in early May 1945. Other prisoners too sick to leave Auschwitz were freed and cared for by the Soviets but were unable to move west or even communicate with their families. They traveled slowly through the Soviet Union to Odessa, where they eventually found ships to carry them home when the war ended. Henry Bulawko boarded the British transport ship *Monoway* and reached Marseille on May 10.[47] Léa Feldblum, the only survivor of the fifty-one deportees from the children's home at Izieu—she had been brutally separated from her little ones on the platform at Auschwitz—also returned by way of Odessa, to bear witness to the deaths of the others.[48]

Meanwhile, survivors in the west had no news from deported loved ones, and still no certainty of the nature of the death camps. Everyone dared to hope. Surely the Nazis would have pity on the children, on the old people. Conversely, surely an able-bodied man, a strong young woman, a hearty teenager would survive hard labor. Of a family of five or six, someone would survive. Surely the evil rumors of extermination were exaggerations.

Of that Liberation period after August 1944, a time of joy and rejoicing for most French men and women, Denise Baumann, a heroic young OSE social worker and child rescuer whose parents, sister, brother-in-law, and three nieces were deported to Auschwitz in 1943, later wrote in her memoirs: "Then came the wait without much hope . . . the discovery of the camps, the return of the deportees, the false good news, and then the last cards: the blue cards of the *Ministère des Anciens Combattants* which said 'Died for France in deportation to the camp of Auschwitz.'"[49]

Denise Baumann's family did not return.

French social workers took over the Hotel Lutétia, a "grand hotel" on the boulevard Raspail on the Left Bank in Paris. The building had been requisitioned for German use during the war; most of the staff still employed there had served the occupying forces. The Lutétia was prepared to receive civilians returning from the concentration camps—Resistants, political prisoners, and Jews.[50] Reception tables were arranged in the lobby to process newcomers and determine their needs. A disinfecting room was set up where repatriated persons were to be sprayed with DDT.

For many weeks after the end of the war, volunteers met every train at the Gare de l'Est. They guided former prisoners with no homes or families in Paris to buses that took them to the Lutétia. Loudspeakers in the station, constantly blaring, did the same. Many men and women arrived still in their striped prison garb. "Most of all," says Annette Monod Leiris, "I remember how they walked. They all moved by sliding. They were too weak to pick up their feet."[51]

After registration and disinfection at the hotel, new arrivals received proper identification cards, ration books, a little money, and a new suit of clothes purchased with coupons at the Bon Marché department store nearby. Those who wished could then leave. Others were transferred to hospitals or checked into rooms at the hotel. Rooms were kept very warm even in May, for former prisoners in a weakened state. Social workers set up nursing stations on every floor to provide emergency aid during the night. Special easily digested foods were secured; rich food would kill those still accustomed to only bread and water.

The families of deportees, Jews and non-Jews alike, soon learned of the preparations at the Hotel Lutétia and came looking for their loved ones. The universal agony blurred distinctions, but there was a difference: non-Jews were usually looking for individual adults, while Jews all too often searched for entire families. There in the lobby of the hotel, if not already at the train station, the lucky ones found a returning parent, a child, a spouse. The less fortunate, desperate for a bit of news and a fragment of hope, met returning deportees and bombarded them with questions. Had they come across a red-haired five-year-old girl from Dijon? A man with blue eyes and black wavy hair from Amiens? Did they know this name, or that one? Could they be mistaken? Please could they try to remember?

A huge bulletin board to the left of the hotel entrance carried heartrending notices, often accompanied by photographs from better days, of smiling children, proud parents, whole families that were missing. Had anyone seen the mother photographed with her four children, arrested in Paris in July 1942? Or a father, seized in December 1941? Or a son? Or three, four, or five sons? There were also messages on the board. "When Mrs. Jeanne Kahn arrives, would she call her mother-in-law immediately?" And so Jeanne, returning weak and sick from Auschwitz, realized instantly that Robert was dead.[52] And there were lists of missing persons, long heartbreaking lists that sometimes repeated the same last name eight, ten, twelve times, revealing the destruction of several generations of a single family. Sometimes a deportee remembered a name, a face, a description, but usually the news was horrifying. "Yes, I saw her with her five children, on the train platform at Auschwitz. They were sent to the right. Yes, the line for the showers, for the gas chambers. They waited calmly. They did not know what it was." Or, "Yes, she was with me in the evacuation from Auschwitz, as the Russians approached. She could not keep up. The SS guards shot her. She died in the snow. I am sure." Just occasionally, "Yes, I worked with him in the mines. He was still alive two months ago, but very sick. We were separated. Perhaps there is a chance."

After the Liberation, Jews in France reckoned their losses and slowly, painfully slowly, began to live again. Whole families had been wiped out; the total number of dead was not initially known. Since 1945, however, historians and archival researchers have been able to calculate Holocaust statistics for France with considerable accuracy. The names of 73,853 Jews deported from France in seventy-four convoys between March 27, 1942, and August 17, 1944, have been determined. Of the convoys, sixty-two left from Drancy, two from Compiègne, six from Pithiviers, two from Beaune-la-Rolande, one from Angers, and one from Lyon. All but six of the trains went to Auschwitz; of the six exceptions, four went to Majdanek or Sobibor, one to Kovno and Reval, and one to Buchenwald. Approximately 1,653 men and 913 women, or about 3 percent of the deportees, survived these convoys.

To these 73,853 deportees must be added a minimum of 815 Jews arrested in the French departments of the Nord and the Pas-de-Calais under Belgian-based German military occupation during the war and deported from the camp of Malines in Belgium; about 400 wives and children of Jewish prisoners of war deported to Bergen-Belsen on May 2 and 3, and July 21 and 23, 1944; roughly 360 deported from Toulouse to Ravensbruck and Buchenwald on July 30 or 31, 1944; at least 63 deported from Clermont-Ferrand to Auschwitz on August 22; and at least 230 Jews deported individually or with groups of Resistance fighters. Of these groups, survivors are sometimes difficult to calculate, but they included at least 219 from the prisoner-of-war families and a handful of others. Thus, Jewish deportees totaled a minimum of 75,721. Survivors numbered about 2,800, and the dead—about 72,921.[53]

There were, as seen, other dead. At least 1,100 Jews were executed in France during the war, and an estimated 3,000 died in camps such as Compiègne, Drancy, Gurs, Le Vernet, Noé, Récébédou, Rivesaltes, and others.[54] The death toll, then, reached at least 77,021. From a population of about 330,000 at the end of 1940, nearly 80,000 Jews had been deported or murdered in France. They represented more than 24 percent of the Jewish community.[55]

Breaking these statistics down into their native and foreign components is more difficult. According to Serge Klarsfeld, there were about 195,000 French Jews in the country at the end of 1940, representing about 59 percent of the total Jewish community. There were also about 135,000 foreign Jews, or 41 percent.[56] From lists of deportees (including survivors) and individuals who died in France, Klarsfeld estimated that about 24,500 were French and 56,500 were foreigners. French victims in turn consisted of about 8,000 born in France to French-born parents (including 6,500 born in metropolitan France and 1,500 born in Algeria); 8,000 naturalized citizens; 8,000 children born in France to foreign Jewish parents and French by parental declaration; and 500 unaccounted for.[57] If these admittedly approximate figures are valid, one may conclude that, of the 80,000 Jews who were deported from France or died there during the war, roughly 30 percent were French and 70 percent were foreign—percentages significantly different from the proportions of natives and foreigners in the Jewish population as a whole. Alternatively, and again roughly, it seems that about 12.6 percent of the French Jews, including those naturalized at birth and later, and about 41 percent of the foreign Jews were deported from France or died there during the war.

These different, if always rough, statistics for French and foreign Jews may be interpreted yet another way if the 8,000 deported children born in France to foreign Jewish parents are placed in the foreign category. They clearly *were* French, by declaration at birth, but as seen, they were almost invariably treated as foreigners. Vichy officials who usually refrained from putting the names of French Jewish adults on arrest lists carefully specified that most children of foreign Jews were to accompany their parents. Calculating them as *foreigners,* then, about 16,500 Jewish citizens and 64,500 Jewish foreigners were deported or died in France. Thus, about 20 percent of the victims were French and 80 percent were foreign. Seen another way, less than 9 percent of the French Jewish community was deported or died in France, while 45 percent of the foreign Jewish community suffered the same fate.

These statistics suggest that the Vichy regime partially managed to protect French-born adult Jews. The figure of 6,500 murdered Jews who had been born in metropolitan France to French-born parents is, while always tragic, surprisingly low. Except for a period in early 1944, Vichy officials refused, for the most part, to participate in roundups of French Jews. Had they refused cooperation in roundups of foreign Jews as well, death rates would have been considerately lower.

One-quarter of the Jews in France died during the war for many reasons. Obviously the primary blame rests with the Nazis, for it was they who imposed the policy of the Final Solution in all the countries they occupied and enforced it to the bitter end, often at the expense of the German war effort itself. In France, however, the complicity of the Vichy regime remains paramount. Vichy officials interned thousands of foreign Jews in the unoccupied zone and delivered them directly to the Nazis. Following both French and German orders, Vichy bureaucrats distributed stars of David, stamped documents to reveal Jewish identities, conducted several censuses, and compiled lists of Jewish households. Vichy police seized far more Jews than did the German security police, beginning with massive roundups of foreign Jews, extending to individual arrests of alleged French and foreign violators of racial regulations, and ending in 1944 with roundups in some cities, excluding Paris, of listed French Jews as well. And perhaps most important, the Vichy regime with the much-admired Marshal Pétain at its head set the tone and created a climate in which anti-Semitism was acceptable, and even patriotic, and in which informers could function with impunity and self-respect. Thousands of Jews fell victim to informers who believed they were serving their country because the leaders of their country had told them that Jews were the enemy.

Other factors help explain the more than 77,000 dead. Jews were sometimes slow to go into hiding, for several reasons. Many were lulled by personal prewar experiences in the French Republic that were generally favorable. They were deceived by the clever Nazi policy of enlarging the groups eligible for arrest only gradually from foreign *men,* to certain categories of foreign men and women with their children, to Jews in general. They were deluded by French police reluctant to round up citizens, and by non-Jewish civilians who, for the most part, continued to treat Jews in a friendly manner. They were also reassured by the continued functioning of UGIF and by the synagogues and social agencies that remained open. Information about arrests in other cities circulated slowly, and evil rumors about death camps were dismissed as propaganda. Eluding deportation did not seem a matter of life and death.

In addition, the many foreign Jews in France, impoverished, often unemployed, visibly different, and with few friends and contacts in the non-Jewish community, were especially vulnerable. They were, at the same time, specific Vichy targets. They formed a predictably large portion of the victims.

12

Jewish Rescue Organizations

For eighteen-year-old Denise Caraco, a university student in Marseille, the summer of 1942 was a vacation. Although both her parents were French Jews, Denise had not been greatly troubled by the racial laws. At the university, she was among the few fortunate Jewish students allowed by the *numerus clausus* to continue their studies. In her hometown of Marseille, French Jews were not yet being arrested. Denise was a member of the Éclaireurs israélites de France (EIF), the Jewish Scouts of France. Their founder, Robert Gamzon, asked EIF leaders to spend a month working with younger Scouts. Denise spent her vacation at Lautrec (Tarn) in one of about ten EIF settlements where teenage Scouts lived full-time, farming, studying, and learning a trade.

Some Jewish Scouts residing at Lautrec were French and had joined the group because they were orphans, because their parents could not care for them, or to escape air raids during the first months of the war. Many others were foreigners or the children of foreigners. Some had been born in France; others were refugees from Germany after 1933 or Belgium in 1940. Often their parents were interned in one of the Vichy camps for foreign Jews, and they themselves had been released to the custody of OSE or EIF after the intervention of those organizations on their behalf. In other cases, their parents lived outside the camps but remained in constant fear of internment as foreign Jews. They sent their children to EIF for education, support, and a stable environment. When Vichy officials in August 1942 suddenly started delivering interned foreign Jews of specific nationalities and dates of arrival in France to the Germans, while arresting similar Jews living outside the camps for the same purpose, they also began searching for the children of their victims in the name of "family regrouping."

Warned, usually by local French civil servants, of pending roundups, Scouts in danger of arrest at Lautrec and elsewhere began to leave EIF farms and go into hiding. Denise's first mission at Lautrec was to escort to safety four girls not much younger than herself who spoke little French. She took one to a rabbi in Limoges, where the girl could hide in the temporary safety of a French Jewish home. She took the other three to families in Moissac, Brive, and Tulle. "I did not think of it as Resistance. I had no plans, and no idea of a personal commitment."[1]

Denise's second mission that summer was as a field worker for the Château de Montintin (Haute-Vienne), an OSE home for younger Jewish children. The OSE homes included the same mixture of children as the EIF groups, and some individuals were in similar danger. During the week following August 26, 1942, French police arrested dozens in several homes.[2] Demands for more were expected.

Denise's job was to scour the surrounding countryside for families willing to take a child from the château. There was as yet little hope of disguising identities. The children had no false papers, and everyone knew that the château was a Jewish home. Denise made it clear to families that if the children could not be placed, they would be deported—a fate not yet recognized as the equivalent of murder. She recalls a wide variety of responses, but many children were placed.

As at most other OSE homes, Denise and her directors first hid the children of interned foreigners, since they were already being summoned. The next priority went to those with still-free parents of specific nationalities and post-1936 immigration dates, since they too were expected to be called with their families. Children were moved out gradually over a period of several months and replaced by others in less immediate danger.[3] The directors of the château deliberately kept their official records vague and disorganized. They told police seeking a specific child that he or she had been transferred, recalled by other officials, or reclaimed by a family member. They invented hundreds of excuses. French police, often unhappy with the job of bringing in children, were usually satisfied that they had done their best.

By the beginning of the new school term in the autumn of 1942, Denise was committed to illegal rescue work and considered it too dangerous to return to the university. She soon became involved with the Service André, a Jewish Resistance network in her home city headed by a thirty-four-year-old Russian industrial engineer named Joseph Bass. To protect her parents and herself, she assumed a false name. French police were combing the city for recent Jewish immigrants eligible for expulsion. Denise hid these fugitives with French Jewish families willing to help. "But," she says, "not all French Jewish families wanted to be bothered. Far from it."[4]

To ease the burden on host families with no ration cards for extra mouths to feed, Denise and her friends prepared and delivered meals every day. That activity was not dangerous, for the cooks could explain that their meals were for the families themselves. Meanwhile, the young rescuers began the search for safer hiding places in schools, hospitals, convents, and other non-Jewish institutions. They also sought out clients in need of help. Before the German occupation, Denise explains, foreign Jews in danger of arrest usually gravitated to the synagogue or to local Consistoire or OSE offices, where employees, committed to purely legal activities by the close police scrutiny under which they operated, referred them to her network. She and her friends met people in need in those Jewish centers until the arrival of the Germans made it too risky. Then they met in Catholic and Protestant churches.

With the help of Joseph Bass, Denise met Father Marie Benoît and Pastor Jean S. Lemaire in the late autumn of 1942. Both churchmen not only made their offices available but supplied Jewish rescuers with personal letters of introduction. Armed with her letters, Denise began to search for hiding places in religious institutions first in villages surrounding Marseille and later in more distant areas. Sometimes church men and women turned her away, but more often they either agreed to help her themselves or referred her to families of goodwill within their local parishes. Pastor Lemaire also put Joseph Bass in touch with Pastor André Trocmé in the village of Le Chambon-sur-Lignon (Haute-Loire). Hundreds of Jews were already hiding at Le Chambon. Denise and the Service André would soon send another thousand.[5]

Contacting people in need and finding hiding places for them were perhaps the easiest parts of the job. Much more difficult was moving about with foreigners who lacked proper documents and were conspicuous by their accents and dress. Train and bus stations were closely guarded, trains and buses themselves were often searched, and roadblocks were ubiquitous. False documents and convincing alibis were essential for travel. Then, after fugitives were hidden, they needed regular deliveries of monthly ration cards, food, and money. Scores of assistants, Jewish and non-Jewish alike, helped with these daunting tasks. The assistants were usually young French women— French, because French Jews were not yet being deported, and because foreign Jews disguised as French could be revealed by their accents; women, because Jewish men were too easily discovered by their circumcisions, and because non-Jewish men in certain age brackets were, after February 1943, liable to conscription for labor service in Germany.

Denise Caraco's activities in Marseille during the war reflect in microcosm many aspects of Jewish rescue in France. She herself was typical of the well-educated young women who drifted into rescue activities almost by chance, and who did much of the field work. Her experiences also reveal the close interaction of various Jewish social agencies, especially OSE and EIF, which played a role in a rescue effort that was unparalleled in any other occupied country. Finally, Denise worked with hundreds of non-Jewish host families whose help was indispensable. As she herself declares, "No matter how effective Jewish rescue organizations were in helping people escape the camps, in finding hiding places, in supplying food and false papers and visiting people in hiding, and in obtaining funds, especially from the American Jewish Joint Distribution Committee in the United States, they could *never* have worked without help from thousands of non-Jews. Where else could we have hidden our people?"[6]

Young social workers like Denise Caraco were the last links in several complex child rescue networks organized by Jewish agencies such as OSE, EIF, and MJS (Mouvement des jeunesses sionistes). At the head of one major OSE chain was a young Jewish engineer from Lyon named Georges Garel. As seen, Garel was called to the camp of Vénissieux outside his home city in late August 1942 to help with the screening of foreign Jews recently arrested for expulsion to the occupied zone. While there, he met Dr. Joseph Weill, OSE's director of medical services. During the next two months, Dr. Weill became increasingly aware that the children of recent Jewish immigrants needed to be hidden and serviced in a more structured and organized fashion. Garel, who had never been associated with Jewish welfare agencies and whose name therefore appeared on no official list, seemed the perfect man to supervise a clandestine network.[7]

Garel accepted the assignment. As a first step, his friend Charles Ledermann, the OSE representative at Rivesaltes, and Henri de Lubac (1896–1991), a Jesuit priest and subsequent cardinal, visited Archbishop Jean-Gérard Saliège in Toulouse. The archbishop, it will be recalled, had issued a public protest on August 23 against Vichy's expulsions of foreign Jews. After Ledermann and Father de Lubac's visit, Garel himself called on the elderly prelate in his office in December. Of that meeting, Garel later declared, "From my first contact with him, I knew I was in the presence of a superior person. That man, I can and I must say, had the stuff of a saint."[8] Saliège and his coadjutor, Monseigneur Louis de Courrèges d'Uston, both promptly agreed to help.[9] They convinced Garel not to set up a new organization but to work within already existing local Catholic welfare institutions. They also gave Garel a personal letter of introduction.

Armed with the precious letter, Garel and his agents, usually young Jewish and non-Jewish women recruited and assigned by the OSE leader Andrée Salomon, visited non-Jewish institutions throughout the unoccupied zone. They placed their first twenty-four children with the Oeuvre de Sainte-Germaine, a Catholic philanthropic organization in Saliège's diocese that worked with needy families and young people. They placed other children in private non-Jewish homes, religious and laic boarding schools, orphanages, hospitals, youth hostels, and private homes. They even found spots in institutions operated by Secours national, the Vichy government's welfare bureau.

The need for places never ceased, however, for by the autumn of 1943, most OSE leaders realized that *all* Jews were in danger of deportation. The Germans had occupied the Italian zone and, incensed both by Italian tolerance of Jews and by Vichy's refusal to promulgate the denaturalization law, had unleashed ferocious, indiscriminate roundups there and throughout the country. OSE homes would have to dissolve and hide all their children.[10] At the same time, terrified parents increasingly confided their youngsters to the child welfare agency. Garel and his assistants were busier than ever.

By the end of the war, the number of children maintained in hiding had risen to more than 1,500. Of these, according to Garel, only four were caught. After the Liberation, Garel reported, "In every department or diocese, there was a religious or laic, private or public charity or institution which involved itself in the protection of our children."[11] An official OSE report written in 1946 added that "it was the spirit of solidarity springing out of the major part of the population which made it possible to find [those institutions]."[12] The OSE social worker and child rescuer Gaby Cohen confirms, "Nothing could have been done without the tremendous help we received from those around us."[13]

OSE social workers themselves decided which children could be entrusted to the "Garel circuit." They usually chose those who "could more or less pass as Aryans."[14] Those who were recognizably Jewish by speech, religious practice, or physical features had to be protected in other ways. Younger children were often placed with non-Jewish families, who usually but not always knew they were Jewish. Even if not told beforehand, most families came to suspect the truth about their charges, in large part because the lonely youngsters, in the intimacy of their new environment, revealed themselves either inadvertently or deliberately, from an urgent need to confide in a trusted adult.

Older children more capable of keeping secrets often went to institutions, especially boarding schools, where only one or two directors knew the truth. They were usually disguised as refugees from bombed-out cities in the north whose families had been killed, drafted, or otherwise broken up. As there were many such children in wartime France, the disguises usually passed unquestioned. If challenged, however, the disguises could not be disproved, since archives in the children's "home cities" had been destroyed in the air raids.

Finding hiding places and choosing children for placement were only part of the OSE challenge. Social workers also had to prepare young children, often foreign urban dwellers still unsteady in the French language, for the enormous transition to life with new families totally different from their own. They then had to escort those children to their new homes. They faced trips in closely watched trains and buses and long waits in public stations with children whose accents might betray them, who often had faulty papers, and who were having difficulty remembering their new names. Upon arrival, they had to assess the suitability of the host families, often with the lowest of criteria because of the scarcity of alternatives, and bid the terrified children farewell. Finally, they had to return periodically, delivering monthly ration cards for food and clothing, regular financial stipends for maintenance, extra supplies whenever possible, and, to a limited extent, letters between parents and children.[15] Those visits also enabled social workers to reassure children that they were not forgotten and to check on the treatment they received.

OSE social workers, usually young women, assumed enormous responsibilities under the most difficult and dangerous of circumstances. Denise Baumann, for example, then a twenty-two-year-old assistant at the Château de Masgelier at Grand-Bourg (Creuse), remembered taking a young Jewish girl to a Catholic school where she was to be hidden. The regular escort could not go that day, and Denise was a replacement. The woman director of the school, upset and suspicious of the unfamiliar escort, pretended to know nothing about the case and refused to accept the child. Denise and her charge were stranded. Only with great difficulty could the director be persuaded to change her mind. When asked if she herself ever felt fear, Denise replied quite simply, "All the time. We always had our bags packed at the home, and a plan prepared. We knew which adults would go with which children. The older children could hide in the woods, but the little ones could not."[16]

Jewish Resistants and rescuers bore at least one additional burden that their non-Jewish colleagues did not share: they constantly feared for their families as well as for themselves. Denise Baumann, for one, saved many children but lost her entire family. Her sister Simone and her brother-in-law Albert Weill, both French Jews, were arrested with their three young daughters at their home in Remiremont (Vosges) in January 1943 and sent to Drancy. The youngest child was just ten months old. Denise and Simone's parents, Renée and Léon, sent packages to Drancy, via UGIF, as often as possible. They were themselves arrested at their home in La Ferté-sous-Jouarre, about sixty kilometers east of Paris, in October of the same year and deported to Auschwitz on November 20, before their children and grandchildren. Simone and her family followed on December 17. In a last letter to Denise from Drancy two days before departure, Simone wrote, "We will undoubtedly rejoin papa and mama, I hope we will be in the same camp. . . . It is the trip which bothers me the most, for the little one, because of the cold now." She added, "We leave with courage, for it is not for long."[17]

Denise Baumann risked her life daily to save children but remembered of the Liberation, when she was safe at last, "It is now that I am really afraid, afraid of what I am going to learn, of what deep in my heart I already know."[18]

The Garel circuit was the largest but not the only OSE child rescue network. Another chain, based in Nice, was directed by Moussa

Abadi, a Syrian Jewish student of medieval literature. Abadi had foreseen trouble and begun searching for hiding places even before Aloïs Brunner's raid in September 1943. During that event, he was besieged by terrified parents seeking help. He received significant assistance from Monseigneur Paul Rémond, the bishop of Nice, who provided a letter of introduction, a private office within the bishop's residence where Abadi manufactured and hid false papers, and hiding places for children in several local Catholic institutions.[19] According to Garel, who knew him well, Abadi also worked with two Vichy officials who furnished blank ration cards, and with Maurice Brener, the Joint representative in France who provided financial aid to many Jewish rescue groups.[20] With only two regular assistants, Huguette Wahl and Dr. Odette Rosenstock, both of whom were ultimately deported, and with help from other local Jewish rescue groups, Abadi kept about 400 children safe until the Liberation in Nice, Grasse, Antibes, Cannes, Juan-les-Pins, and other beautiful towns along the Mediterranean coast.[21]

Similarly in Paris, after the massive roundup of foreign Jews in July 1942, fear-crazed parents appeared at a tiny OSE office at 35 rue des Francs-Bourgeois, begging social workers to hide their children. A director of OSE-North, Falk Walk, supervised rescue operations until his arrest in January 1943. He was subsequently deported without return. Dr. Eugène Minkowski, wearing the yellow star required of Jews living openly in the northern zone and with the help of only four or five close collaborators, continued the struggle and managed to hide some 600 to 700 children from the Paris area.[22] Like Garel and Abadi, Dr. Minkowski worked closely with rescuers from other clandestine organizations, Jewish and non-Jewish alike. He acted in deliberate opposition to the policy and preferences of UGIF-North leaders.

Dorothéa Morgenstern was among those desperate mothers who found help at an OSE dispensary in July 1942 and lived to tell how it worked. She and her sons Jackie and Henri had barely escaped the roundup of July 16—she, pregnant at the time, had fainted when French police came to her apartment; Jackie was in bed with a fever; and nine-year-old Henri began to vomit. Perplexed police left with only her husband Léopold, telling Dorothéa that they would return the next morning. She continues:

Very early the next morning we had already left the house. We went to a "dispensaire" where the Organisation OSE was located.

They placed the children, and I did not know where they were and how they were doing until the liberation. Every month a woman doctor, Dr. Breton, went to see how the children were doing, and all she told me was, "Your children are alive, they're alive." I found out only after the liberation that they had been kept hidden in the little village of La Chapelle du Bois de Feu in Normandy, near Evreux.[23]

She secretly gave birth to a daughter and then found shelter in the home of a Mrs. Chatelain, a woman doctor from the hospital. Dorothéa Morgenstern and her children survived. Her husband died from deprivation at Dachau in May 1945, just after the camp was liberated.

Among many other activities, Dr. Minkowski in January 1944 became the OSE delegate on the newly formed Comité d'union et de défense des juifs, a group dedicated to Jewish rescue. For several months before the liberation of Paris, committee members tried unsuccessfully to convince leaders of UGIF-North to dissolve the children's homes and hide youngsters with non-Jews. Those leaders refused, as seen, and German police arrested about 258 children in eight UGIF homes in July 1944.[24] The committee failed them but managed to save many individual children. One who survived, fourteen-year-old Robert Frank, resided at the École de travail in the rue des Rosiers. He recalls that he received a strange letter toward the end of May 1944 asking him to come, without baggage and without telling anyone, to a particular address the following day. With some trepidation, he did as he was told. Committee member Frédéric Léon met him at the designated spot, explained that he was to be hidden, and saved his life. A few days later, children at the École de travail were among the 258 seized by the Nazis.[25]

The clandestine child rescue networks constitute perhaps the most dramatic part of OSE's work during the war, but the agency provided other services as well. In the months before its final dissolution in February 1944, OSE operated nine major and more than four smaller local offices in the southern zone that offered open and legal health care to thousands of families. It also, less legally, distributed subsidies to children hiding more or less securely with their own families, either because their parents refused to separate from them or because they were identifiably Jewish or strictly orthodox in religious practice. Garel explains that among these children, "cases of deportation were necessarily more frequent."[26] OSE workers also worked with other Jewish and non-Jewish rescuers to help children escape to Switzerland.[27] The story of OSE's wartime activities involves hundreds of courageous individuals who should all be honored and remembered.[28] Only a tiny fraction have been mentioned here.

In December 1939, well before the German invasion, Édouard (Bouli) and Shatta Simon of the EIF acquired a large, old patrician house on the banks of the Tarn River in the town of Moissac (Tarn-et-Garonne) to serve as an evacuation center for 350 Jewish children from Paris, Strasbourg, and Mulhouse. These first residents were joined in June by refugees from the north whose parents, French and foreign Jews alike, feared bombardments as much as they distrusted the Nazis. Many of the original children returned to their families, to be replaced by others whose foreign parents were in internment or in fear of arrest. In 1941 and early 1942, after the EIF leader Ninon Weyl-Haït joined social workers from OSE and other Jewish and non-Jewish organizations to help secure the release of children from the internment camps, another 22 youngsters from Gurs arrived at Moissac. Forty girls from the camps settled at an EIF home at Beaulieu-sur-Dordogne (Corrèze), while others went to EIF farms at Taluyers, Lautrec, and Charry.[29] As with the children released to OSE, these young Scouts were to be held in readiness for possible recall.

The house at 18 quai du Port in Moissac soon expanded into adjoining structures and came to include a children's residence, synagogue, school, library, document center, and artisan workshop. It also served as national headquarters for the EIF movement itself. From there, Robert Gamzon (1905–61), the founder of the Jewish Scouts of France in 1923 and a former lieutenant in the engineering corps decorated for valor in combat against the Germans in 1940, encouraged the founding of about ten farms to be run entirely by older Scouts and their adult supervisors.[30]

The largest and best known of these farms were Taluyers (Rhône), near Lyon, established under the supervision of Frédéric Hammel and his wife; Charry, near Moissac, under the leadership of Isaac and Juliette Pougatch; and Lautrec, about thirty kilometers south of Albi, with help from Robert Gamzon, Léo Cohn, and Gilbert Bloch.[31] As seen, Denise Caraco worked at Lautrec in August 1942. Most of the farms had been abandoned or allowed to deteriorate, and the young Scouts started with very little. Most enterprises grew within a year or two into solid economic units, with cows, hens, and grain production. Many also offered training in manual skills, such as black-smithing and metalwork, carpentry and cabinetmaking, shoe repair and leather work, and sewing and dressmaking. All provided schools and libraries and stressed Jewish religious and cultural education. To the traditional Scout emphasis on morals, service, and discipline, Jewish Scouts added two new concepts, artisan training and Judaic awareness. Their combination of a "back to the land" philosophy with one of "back to the cultural roots" resembled the kibbutzim movement in Israel.

Shortly before the French police roundups of recent Jewish immigrants in the unoccupied zone on August 25 and 26, 1942, Gilbert Lesage, the chief of Vichy's Service social des étrangers, warned EIF leaders that some of their Scouts were in danger of arrest.[32] At Moissac, most of the Scouts were away on a camping trip when police arrived with a list of names. Those not sought returned from the trip, while those on the list quietly disappeared.

German-born Kurt Maïer, who had entered France alone in 1939 at the age of fifteen and found his way to Moissac, was among those in danger. He later related that his group of fifteen boys camped in the woods until October, when it became too cold. At that point, their adult leader, Léon Rosen, turned to the bishop of Tulle, Monseigneur Chassaigne. The bishop gave Rosen the names of directors of six convents, monasteries, and other church institutions willing to hide youngsters and telephoned ahead to prepare them. Twelve Scouts ultimately found shelter in those institutions. The other three boys stayed with a friendly farmer for a time, then went to the monastery of Saint-Antoine-de-Padoue in Brive (Corrèze), and finally were sent to the Collège Saint-Pierre at Courpière (Puy-de-Dôme), east of Clermont-Ferrand. The German Jewish boys passed as Alsatian Protestants. Only a few of their teachers knew their real identities.[33]

Similar warnings of raids occurred at other EIF homes and farms, and Scouts in danger were hidden in the woods and later with French Jewish (for a time) or non-Jewish families or institutions. Frédéric Hammel explains that at Taluyers, where he was expected to keep a list of resident Scouts, he simply recorded those he knew to be in danger of arrest as having departed. Gendarmes arrived apologetically looking for a few boys at a time, enjoyed a brandy, studied the list, and left feeling relieved. They never searched the premises. But Hammel could not depend on continual goodwill. He was himself denounced to the authorities in the autumn of 1942 by a French farmer who envied the farm. Hammel had to report briefly to police headquarters, where officials treated him with sympathy.[34]

Just as illegal rescue networks like the Garel circuit emerged to hide and support OSE's children after August 1942, a group mysteriously called the Sixième (the Sixth) developed within the EIF.[35] Under the direction of former EIF leaders such as Robert Gamzon, Marc Haguenau, Ninon Weyl-Haït, and Henri Wahl, older Scouts affiliated with the Sixième secretly hid and provisioned younger ones in danger—at first, the children of recent Jewish immigrants. Meanwhile, EIF homes and farms managed to remain open for other Jewish children until the autumn of 1943. Frédéric Hammel remembers that after the Germans occupied the southern zone in November 1942, his boys at Taluyers installed an electric warning bell in their second-story dormitory. It was activated near a window in his own first-floor bedroom, which looked out toward the farm entrance. The boys practiced jumping from an upstairs window and escaping over a wall. They were, in effect, willing to risk arrest, for they did not know what deportation entailed. Hammel explains, "Of all the rumors beginning to circulate at this time, we believed only the most optimistic, that is to say the most benign: for example, that the Germans had an urgent need for laborers."[36]

The real change began in the autumn of 1943, when the Nazis began conducting indiscriminate raids independently of French police. Shatta and Bouli Simon recall, "At the beginning of December 1943, Hammel came to Moissac and told us: 'Now, it is time that the centers disappear.'"[37] Some EIF leaders were still opposed, but it was done. At Moissac, all the children were placed within three weeks.[38] Overall, according to Hammel, EIF adult leaders and older Scouts hid 200 to 250 young children within six weeks and arranged with the Sixième to maintain them. Of the non-Jews asked to take a child, Hammel relates, the majority accepted.[39]

Shatta and Bouli Simon, explaining that they preferred to place children in schools so that they could continue their education, confirm Hammel's report:

I must say that Monseigneur Théas opened for us as for others the college de Sorrèze [sic], that of Saint Antoine de Padoue near Brive, other religious secondary establishments, where we were able to place a very large number of young people. . . . I remember that the director of the Protestant theological faculty at Montauban was not so understanding and refused to welcome our youth even when I cited to him the examples of his co-religionists. . . . But his was just about the only refusal we had; in general, all the state, Catholic, or Protestant establishments always responded favorably.[40]

After the younger children were placed, Scouts over sixteen living on the farms had several options. A few rejoined their families, usually in hiding. Others tried to cross the Pyrenees into Spain, from where they could link up with de Gaulle's Free French forces or perhaps reach Israel. Switzerland, surrounded as it was by countries at war, was a less popular choice, for once there, it was difficult to leave. Still other Scouts decided to remain in France, either to join the general French Resistance, an increasingly attractive alternative after the Allied landings in Normandy in June 1944, or to work with the Sixième. As activists with the Sixième, they supported Jewish rescue efforts within France, helped escort refugees across frontiers into Spain or Switzerland, and joined specifically Jewish armed Resistance units.

In all their activities, young Resistants in the Sixième worked closely and often inextricably not only with OSE but with the Mouvement des jeunesses sionistes (MJS), whose clandestine branch was known as Éducation physique. Agents of the Sixième and Éducation physique produced tens of thousands of false papers indispensable for Jews and non-Jews alike—for fugitives from Jewish manhunts and the non-Jewish obligatory labor service, and for members of the Resistance and their families. All kinds of papers were needed at different times—identification documents, working papers, ration books, military discharge statements, releases from forced labor, driver's licenses, and certificates of birth, baptism, and marriage to show "Aryan" lineage. The production of such papers became an art, and "laboratories" flourished in every city in France.

Techniques varied according to necessity. In some cases, preexisting documents were "washed" by experts who, as Hammel explains, could transform "a name too obviously Jewish into one more anodyne: Lévy into Leroy, Marx into Marceau, Cohen into Colin."[41] In other cases, especially in the beginning, blank forms could be purchased at shops, filled in by individual bearers, and stamped with homemade, stolen, or "borrowed" municipal seals. When blank forms were not available for purchase, sympathetic employees at local municipal or prefect offices sometimes delivered them along with government seals, often on a regular basis, for months on end.

Ration books, especially, had to be renewed each month, a dangerous process that exposed the bearers, often non-French-speaking immigrants, to harsh scrutiny. Government documents were often supplemented by false religious certificates furnished by helpful priests
and pastors.

Still another technique involved creating blank forms and official
seals from scratch, with raw materials and printing presses that varied enormously from place to place. Ideally, stamps and forms declared the bearer to be from a bombed-out village where verification
was impossible. Another technique was to choose from a telephone
book or municipal list the name and address of a real person in a distant town. Borrowers risked that police would verify the identity
only superficially, rather than by actually visiting the residence.

Full-time activists in the Sixième and Éducation physique were not
numerous; the former claimed eighty-eight operatives after the war,
and the latter, about fifty.[42] But full-time activists were assisted by
dozens of other young and committed Jewish and non-Jewish volunteers and by scores of printers, photographers, civil servants, and ordinary civilians who knew perfectly well what the activists were
doing but remained silent. Fania Elbinger Ewenczyk, for example, a
nineteen-year-old MJS worker in Grenoble in 1943, recalls her experiences delivering identification cards, ration books, and money to
indigent Belgian Jewish families stranded in tiny mountain villages
after the withdrawal of the Italian occupiers, afraid to move. She visited her families every week or two, traveling by bicycle. A local
baker gave her boxes of cookies and crackers for her "refugees." Another person gave her clothes from a local Catholic charity. She
sometimes gathered up children for delivery to a guide who would
smuggle them into Switzerland. One day she was on a bus with a
group of fifteen children, wondering what to say if stopped. The driver said, "Don't worry, Miss. I am here." He had seen her on her regular route every week and understood perfectly what she was doing.
"Everyone knew," she concludes. "They said nothing. The people
helped us very much. The people of Grenoble and the surrounding
area were very cooperative."[43]

Jewish rescue operations could not have functioned without the
passive sympathy and occasional active support of local non-Jews. It
only took one informer, however, to destroy a network that operated
with the tacit blessing of hundreds of uninvolved spectators. Like
OSE, the Sixième and Éducation physique lost few "clients," but, in
part because of denunciations, casualty rates among full-time

activists were enormous. Thirty of the eighty-eight Sixième workers were either killed in France or in deportation; the figure for Éducation physique reached at least eleven out of fifty.[44]

While OSE, EIF, and MJS helped Jews on a nationwide basis, many smaller groups acted locally. Each has its own complex and dramatic story, but only a few can be mentioned here.[45] In Paris, the Comité rue Amelot was established in June 1940 by representatives of several local immigrant social service centers anxious to continue operations under the difficult circumstances of German occupation. The committee took its name from the location of its central offices at 36 rue Amelot, in the headquarters of La Colonie scolaire, a prewar child welfare agency run by the Fédération des sociétés juives de France (FSJF). Much of its funding came from the ubiquitous Joint. Participating agencies included soup kitchens, health dispensaries, and other welfare centers of the nonpolitical FSJF, the Jewish Socialist Bund, the *Arbeiter Ring* (Workers' Alliance), and three Zionist groups with differing orientations toward Marxism—the right-wing and the left-wing *Poalé-Zion* and the *Hashomer Hatzair*. Among major Jewish immigrant social centers, only Communist groups were excluded, in part because they often gave priority to armed struggle within the general French Resistance. The Comité rue Amelot was concerned above all with Jewish survival.[46]

Originally intended simply to continue the distribution of cooked meals, clothing, medicines, and health care to indigent Jews in the Paris area, the committee drifted gradually into clandestine activity. Through contact first with the impoverished families of men arrested in Paris in 1941 and later with the remnants of families seized in July 1942, social workers from the Comité rue Amelot became increasingly aware that foreign Jews needed to hide. Even before the July 1942 roundup, they began placing needy children with Catholic peasants and supplying them with monthly subsidies and false documents. They ultimately hid and maintained about 1,000 children, as well as numerous adults. At the same time, they continued their open social assistance in Paris, operating, among other activities, six canteens and serving at least 31,000 meals a month until June 1944.[47] Losses among social workers of the Comité rue Amelot were high and included two dedicated founding fathers, David Rapoport and Léo Glaeser.[48]

Also in Paris, a Jewish Communist group called Solidarité offered economic assistance and clandestine rescue. Established in Paris in

September 1940, a year after the French government officially banned the party and its affiliated agencies, Solidarité was clandestine from the beginning. Rather like the non-Communist Comité rue Amelot, it was essentially a regrouping on a local neighborhood basis of individuals, usually immigrants and their families, and their prewar social agencies. Its members collected donations to aid families impoverished by the racial laws or by the internment of their major breadwinners. Activists ran canteens, soup kitchens, and health clinics and subsequently became involved in supplying false papers and hiding Jewish children. Jewish Communist women affiliated with the Union des femmes juives, like Solidarité established as a regrouping of neighborhood activists and agencies, shared its activities.[49]

Two other local Jewish rescue groups, the Service André based in Marseille and the Maurice Cachoud Group in Nice, have been mentioned briefly. The former, in which Denise Caraco worked, was founded in the autumn of 1942 by a flamboyant Russian Jewish engineer named Joseph Bass. All who knew him seem to agree with Léon Poliakov's description: he "was undeniably what the English call 'conspicuous.' Tall and large, he seemed taller and larger than nature. . . . Cordial and noisy, he made a deep impression."[50] The "conspicuous" Bass was perhaps not the most appropriate character to run a clandestine operation, but run it he did. His clients came not only from Marseille but from throughout southeastern and south central France. He claimed after the war that his group ultimately included about thirty activists—Jews and non-Jews, religious and secular, of all political persuasions—and that it hid about 1,000 people in the Protestant village of Le Chambon-sur-Lignon alone.[51] He also worked closely with Catholic priests and monks. Father Régis de Perceval provided a base in a monastery in Marseille, where Bass disguised himself as a Dominican monk, held meetings, and recruited resident monks to help him. He was known among them as Brother André.[52]

The unit later called the Maurice Cachoud Group was founded in Nice about the time of the German occupation to hide and provision fugitive Jews and escort others to Switzerland. It consisted of twenty to twenty-five young men and women, many of whom had their roots in local EIF or MJS organizations. It also worked closely with Moussa Abadi's local OSE network and with the Service André. The group bore the name of Maurice Cachoud-Loebenberg, described by Poliakov as a natural and outstanding leader.[53] Cachoud was an expert in the manufacture of false documents. One of his fellow Resistants, Henri Pohorylès, later estimated that in the six months following September 1943, the group provided 20,000 identification cards and hundreds of other supporting documents.[54]

The history of the Jewish rescue organizations is far more complex than appears here, for the many questions and controversies that surround various groups cannot be explored in a brief general account. About OSE, for example, historians have asked whether directors of children's homes should have foreseen the arrests of the children of recent immigrants in August 1942 and hidden them sooner; whether local offices and homes should have dissolved sooner; whether cooperation with UGIF was beneficial or detrimental; whether concerns for the preservation of institutions and the children's Jewish milieu blinded staff members to the terrible dangers that threatened; whether, in short, OSE might have saved even more lives than it did.[55] Similar questions are asked about EIF. About activists in some of the smaller local groups, critics have complained that they were too independent, too reluctant to cooperate with other agencies, or were careless amateurs who took unnecessary risks with their own and others' lives.

Some of these questions are valid, worthy of the consideration they have received and deserving of further examination. Other questions are petty and trivial. The point here, however, is not that the rescue organizations were perfect and the leaders infallible, not that large numbers of Jews and non-Jews participated in organized rescue, and not even that huge numbers were saved by rescue networks. As will be seen in the next chapter, more people were saved by informal, unorganized measures initiated individually than by organized networks. The point is simply that there were many effective Jewish rescue organizations. Men and women acted, erred, risked their lives daily and often lost them, when they might have focused merely upon their own personal survival. For Jews in wartime France, survival itself was resistance. Concern for the survival of others required exceptional courage, fortitude, and nobility of spirit—the stuff of heroes.

13

Survival and Non-Jewish Rescuers

"**R**OUGHLY FIFTY KILOMETERS FROM PUY-EN-VELAY AND ABOUT FORTY kilometers from Saint-Étienne, there is a little town, Le Chambon-sur-Lignon, the tiny capital of the plateau of the same name, an ancient Protestant village. There you can still find the caves where the Protestants gathered to practice their religion as well as to escape the king's dragoons."[1] Thus begins Joseph Bass's postwar report on a remote village on a pine-studded plateau, about 960 meters above sea level, in the Massif Central west of Valence and the Rhône River. Léon Poliakov, who helped Bass hide Jews there, later described the department of Haute-Loire where Le Chambon is located as "one of the poorest and wildest regions of the Cévennes." Its Protestant inhabitants, he added, "distrust all authority, listening only to their conscience—or their pastors."[2]

Long before Bass and Poliakov arrived there, hundreds of Jewish and non-Jewish refugees had already found their way to Le Chambon. Some had wandered into town as early as the winter of 1940–41. Most came independently at first, advised by friends or casual acquaintances of an isolated village of about 1,000 people, reputedly sympathetic.[3] Newcomers found shelter with village families or with the roughly 2,000 peasants, most of them also Protestant, in the surrounding countryside.[4] Others took rooms in one of more than a dozen hotels and boardinghouses in this popular summer resort area of pine forests, clear streams, and bracing air.[5] Most were trying to escape internment, and most, needless to say, were not legally registered.

During the late spring and early summer of 1942, many foreign Jews and non-Jews released from internment camps to the care of charitable agencies also came to Le Chambon. Local institutions to care for them multiplied, openly and legally. Madeleine Barot and other young Protestant social workers of the CIMADE established a family residence at the Hôtel Coteau Fleuri, outside of town.[6] Quakers, with help from Le Chambon's Pastor André Trocmé, funded a boardinghouse for young children. Older students joined two farm-schools operated by the Secours suisse, or moved into residences of the École Cévenol, a private Protestant secondary school slightly north of the village. Still others were welcomed at the École des roches in the village itself.[7]

In August 1942, French police rounding up recent Jewish immigrants in the unoccupied zone did not overlook Le Chambon. They arrived in the village with three empty buses, demanding that Pastor Trocmé provide a list of resident Jews. Trocmé not only claimed ignorance, somewhat truthfully, of names and addresses but promptly sent his Protestant Boy Scouts to even the most distant farms to warn Jews to hide. Other local residents had undoubtedly already seen the approach of the police up the valley, along a road visible for miles from the plateau. Then and later, that visibility was one secret to security in Le Chambon. Police searched the region for two or three days and returned regularly for several weeks. They apparently netted only one victim, an Austrian who was later released because he was only half-Jewish.[8]

Jews literally poured into Le Chambon after August 1942. By this point, their presence was totally unofficial. They came with the Service André—Bass later reported that the pastor never hesitated to help him—and with OSE and other clandestine networks.[9] Some stayed in Le Chambon only long enough to find a guide to Switzerland, but many remained, hidden with families or in boardinghouses or schools. They kept coming until, as Poliakov observed, "in some hamlets, there was not a single farm which did not shelter a Jewish family."[10] Roughly 5,000 Jews are estimated to have been hidden among the 3,000 native residents, all of whom knew about the refugees.[11]

In his memoirs, Poliakov describes with touching detail his arrival at a local hotel with a group of Jewish children in 1943:

Frightened, they hovered in a corner of the room. The first peasant couple enters: "We will take a little girl between eight and twelve years old," explains the woman. Little Myriam is called: "Will you go with this aunt and uncle?" Shy and frightened, Myriam does not answer. They muffle her up in blankets and carry her to the sleigh; she leaves for the farm where she will live a healthy and simple life with her temporary parents until the end of the war. . . . In a flash, all the children were similarly housed, under the benevolent eye of Pastor Trocmé.[12]

Who was this pastor whose name appears in every account of Le Chambon-sur-Lignon during the war? Born in Saint-Quentin in Picardy in northern France in 1901, André Trocmé studied at the Union Theological Seminary in New York City, where he met his future wife, Italian-born Magda Grilli, in 1925. A pacifist and conscientious objector, Trocmé made no secret of his beliefs after his arrival in Le Chambon in 1934. Indeed, he and Pastor Édouard Theis, the director of the École Cévenol, were equally frank after 1940 about their dislike of the Vichy regime and the racial laws. Trocmé often spoke from the pulpit about the evils of racial persecution; Theis taught the same principles at the École Cévenol. On August 15, 1942, during a visit to the village by the Vichy youth minister, Georges Lamirand, and the departmental prefect and subprefect, several older students at the school presented the officials with a letter protesting the July 16 roundup in Paris and expressing local support of the Jews.

Trocmé, Theis, and Roger Darcissac, the director of the public school in Le Chambon, were arrested by French police in February 1943 and held for a month. At the end of the year, the two pastors went into hiding. During that period, Theis served as a guide for CIMADE, escorting refugees to Switzerland. Magda Trocmé continued her husband's work during his absence; one scholar has judged that she was at least as important as he in saving lives.[13] Mildred Theis kept the École Cévenol open and continued to shelter refugees.[14] The two women had many aides. Bass remembered pastors named Poivre, Leenhardt, Jeannet, Curtet, Betrix, Vienney, and Besson from surrounding hamlets, as well as the Trocmés' good friend Simone Mairesse.[15] Municipal officials also cooperated, if only by looking the other way. And the people of the plateau, often influenced by their outspoken pastors but guided as well by their own sense of justice, continued to protect their Jewish guests until the Liberation.[16] Of them, Bass wrote after the war, "The conduct of the Protestant pastors and men of action of the plateau of Le Chambon deserves to be told to Jews throughout the entire world."[17]

In considering the rescue of Jews in Le Chambon, two questions arise: why was the local population so sympathetic, and why was it so successful? To answer the first, Madeleine Barot stresses the special status of Protestants in France as a minority persecuted by Catholics. Protestants in Le Chambon still told tales of persecution around their hearths on cold winter nights and visited caves where their ancestors had hidden. The memory of persecution made them suspicious of authority, sympathetic to other minorities, and comfortable with clandestine life. In addition, many French Protestants were skeptical about the Vichy regime, in part because authoritarianism often bodes ill for minorities, but especially because, according to Barot, "Pétain dedicated France to the Virgin, and made it an intensely Catholic state."[18] Finally, Christian anti-Semitism notwithstanding, Bible-reading Protestants of the type living around Le Chambon sometimes articulate a special affinity for the Jews, based on a shared reverence for the Old Testament and a common acceptance of God's special compact with his chosen people.[19]

These various factors certainly did not apply to all French Protestants. Many, especially those of the assimilated and highly educated urban classes who were more removed from their historical and cultural roots, were favorably inclined toward the Vichy regime for the same economic and social reasons as their Catholic neighbors, and held the same variety of attitudes toward Jews. But Protestants around Le Chambon cherished their historic memory. That love, combined with the sturdy individualism and independence of mountain people and the leadership of a group of exceptional pastors, made Le Chambon an equally exceptional place.

But why were the rescuers of Le Chambon so successful? Admittedly, even they had their tragedies and their victims. In the spring of 1943, the Gestapo raided the École des roches, seizing many students along with their dedicated director, Daniel Trocmé, Pastor Trocmé's second cousin. Nearly all, including Daniel, died in deportation.[20] But the Germans did not return and thus failed as miserably as the French police to find most of the Jews they knew were there. Why?

Geographic factors were important. The isolation of the area was made even more extreme by the closing of access roads in winter. Any movement on those same approach roads could be seen from the plateau. Thick forests were good for hiding. The Gestapo and the French Milice, busy elsewhere, were reluctant or perhaps afraid to enter a hostile area that, however dedicated by its pastors to nonviolence, was surrounded by armed Resistance fighters. Why stir up a sleeping hornets' nest?[21] French police and gendarmes not only shared that reluctance but were also affected by local sympathies for refugees.

Two witnesses tell amusing stories. Madeleine Barot later declared of her own experience, "When the *gendarmes* in Tence received an order for an arrest, they made a habit of dragging themselves along the road very visibly, of calling a halt at the café before tackling the steep ascent to the Coteau, announcing loudly that they were about to arrest some of those 'dirty Jews.'"[22] Poliakov confirms the description, explaining that when the gendarmes received an arrest order, "they went to the [local] Hotel May and ordered a glass of wine: comfortably seated at their table, they took their papers from their satchels and spelled out 'Goldberg . . . it's about someone named Jacques Goldberg.' Unnecessary to add that when they arrived at Goldberg's domicile half an hour later, the latter was long gone."[23] Poliakov adds that when a more serious danger approached in the form of the Gestapo or the Milice, a telephone call of warning usually preceded them from the valley

Barot's and Poliakov's accounts both allude to the most important factor in the rescue success rate in Le Chambon—the determination of local residents to protect their guests. The people of Le Chambon lived in a state of constant alertness, with a warning system prepared. Their solidarity also made it difficult for potential informers to act. To whom could they safely leak information? Municipal authorities sympathized with the majority, as did, it appeared, many of the police. Even local censors of mail were likely to prevent a denunciation. In such a situation, a careless informer might even put himself in danger. In addition, it was psychologically more difficult for a solitary anti-Semite or opportunist to express his bile in a region where he was bucking an obvious majority. He could not so easily convince himself that he was acting as a "good and loyal Frenchman." And in any part of France—where so many individual arrests of Jews by preoccupied and understaffed local Gestapo units were prompted by denunciations—the reluctance of informers was decisive.

The solidarity of the people of Le Chambon-sur-Lignon was exceptional in France and probably in all of Europe. Equally significant, however, and less well known, was the support shown to fugitive Jews throughout the mountainous area of Languedoc known as the Cévennes—a remote region with a large Protestant population that shared the values of coreligionists in Le Chambon, but with many Catholics as well. About 40,000 residents of a particular section of the Cévennes northwest of Nîmes, for example, hid from 800 to 1,000 Jews, French and foreign alike.[24] Although they did not always know the fugitives were Jewish, they certainly knew of the presence of "outsiders." Informers were rare, and warning systems fairly reliable.

As in Le Chambon, some Jews reached villages in the Cévennes independently, advised of a sympathetic local population or invited by non-Jewish friends in Nîmes to live in their vacant vacation homes. After the major roundup of foreign Jews in Nîmes on August 26, 1942, however, many knocked on the doors of Protestant pastors in that city. The pastors in turn referred them to colleagues in the mountains, and a spontaneous informal network emerged. Most fugitives settled not in major towns or administrative subprefectures which tended to have small but dangerous coteries of local Pétain supporters, but in more remote villages or farms. At the same time, they tried to avoid the vicinity of armed Resistants, who inevitably attracted security forces.

Survivors testify to the general warmth of their reception in the Cévennes. They recall local mayors and innkeepers who welcomed them without excessive scrutiny of their documents. Café owners warned of approaching police, mailmen and telephone operators intercepted denunciations and notified victims, and gendarmes were decidedly lacking in zeal. Villagers and peasants befriended them, knowing full well that they were Jews but never referring to it. A French Jewish survivor identified as Juliette B. later said of the family of Anna Laval, a fifty-year-old peasant rescuer, "I don't know what intrigued them more [about me], my Jewishness or my being a city-slicker." Of the pastor who first met her and insisted on carrying her bags, Juliette recalled, "It was not sufficient for him just to save us; he also had the grace to treat us like chosen guests."[25] Many fugitives participated in village activities, sending their children to school and performing a wide variety of odd jobs ranging from farm work and tailoring to medical service and tutoring.

As in Le Chambon, the general attitude of sympathy for Jews in the Cévennes emerged from a Protestant majority, influenced by its own historic memory of persecution and by the courageous examples of its pastors. Unlike Le Chambon, however, the Cévennes also included Catholic villages, whose residents seem to have shared the prevailing values. Montméjean in the commune of Ispagnac, for example, was a Catholic hamlet. Simone Serrière, the local schoolmistress, was a Protestant who, at the request of the pastor of nearby Florac, agreed to hide a foreign Jewish couple. The couple hid in a single room for several months, until school children at play discovered them. Simone had no choice but to tell the entire village the truth. She was heartily scolded for not having confided in the villagers sooner, and for having carried heavy bags of provisions without help. The Jewish couple subsequently mingled easily with the Catholic population, and the man won many friends by helping with the harvest.[26]

Doctor Lucien Simon, his wife, and their two daughters, from Nîmes, also made friends with their neighbors when they took refuge in the Cévennes in the summer of 1943. Auguste, Emma, and Léon Boisson, two brothers and a sister all in their sixties and all "more or less illiterate," welcomed and helped them. The Simons never knew whether their neighbors realized they were Jewish, but when they were obliged to leave and seek a new hiding place early in 1944, they tried to explain their departure. "We want to tell you . . . ," they began. "Don't say anything," interrupted Emma. "We have known it for a long time, but we didn't mention it to you, in order not to worry you." They parted in tears.[27]

The Cévennes region may have been outstanding in the degree of support it gave to Jews in hiding, but conditions were not perfect even there. Survivors recall that a few local people complained that outsiders were the cause of food scarcities and price increases. Fugitives often had to move to more secure quarters, and some fell victim to informers or zealous police. Several dozen, or about 5 percent of those in hiding, were caught—personal tragedies, but a proportion considerably below the national average.

The Cévennes was not the only area in France where whole villages demonstrated support. Survivors from many other regions tell similar stories. Emmanuel Ewenczyk, for example, hid his Polish-born parents during the winter of 1943–44 in an isolated mountain hamlet of about fifteen families called La Ruchère, near Grenoble. He rented a room from a peasant he did not know, explaining that it was for Alsatian refugees. After the war, he learned that the peasant was considered a collaborator, that the whole village had known that the "refugees" were Jewish, and that while they were there, French miliciens had visited the local café to ask if any "foreigners" (nonvillagers) were living in the hamlet. Everyone had replied negatively, and the miliciens departed. Mr. and Mrs. Ewenczyk survived.[28]

Similarly, Claudine Rozengard, a young high school student, stayed with a friendly non-Jewish couple named Caperons in the village of Saint-Girons (Ariège) after her Polish Jewish parents went into hiding in 1942. She stubbornly refused to change her name and take false papers. She recalls, "The whole town of Saint-Girons knew that I was a little Jewish girl." The headmaster of her school assured her benefactors that he would protect her if the Germans raided the premises, and the local leader of the Milice told them, "I want you to know that if they touch a hair of that child's head, I'm the one who'll die."[29] Claudine remained in the town without incident until the Liberation.

The mother, sister, brother-in-law, and young son of Albert and Sonja Haas had a similar experience in the village of Villon (Yonne) in Burgundy, about sixty kilometers southeast of Paris. Albert, a French citizen born in Hungary, and Sonja, from Belgium, performed valuable services for the Resistance before they were caught in the autumn of 1943. Hoping to be deported rather than executed, both admitted separately, by prior agreement, that they were Jews. The Gestapo did not believe Albert. He was deported as a political prisoner to a number of camps, from which he returned after horrible ordeals. Sonja's claim was believed, and she was deported to Auschwitz, from where she too returned.[30] Meanwhile, their family hid in Villon.

According to Albert, the family scraped out a meager existence as makers of charcoal during the war. They went to Villon entirely by chance, to work, knowing no one. Father Vigoreux, the local priest and guiding force in the hamlet, regularly admonished villagers not to be anti-Semitic. He helped when the Haases' son, born in 1942, developed an ear infection, and he promised to hide the boy and his cousin in case of danger. The local mayor broke the law by refusing to register the refugees as Jews and by providing them with ration cards. Everyone in the village knew they were Jews but, in part because of the urging of the priest, no one ever troubled, much less betrayed, them.[31]

Albert and Sonja Haas's story inevitably had its dark side. Sonja's mother, hiding in Nice, was denounced and deported to Auschwitz, where she was murdered. And in La Napoule, on the coast west of Cannes where Albert and Sonja lived for a time, a local priest told his flock from the pulpit that they should denounce Jews.[32] The family experience, then, is representative of the broader Jewish experience in divided France. It included two courageous heroes, two anti-Semites, and an anonymous mass that demonstrated a vague mixture of indifference and goodwill. That mixture enabled those hiding in Villon to survive.

The family of Claude Morhange-Bégué found similarly divided attitudes in the village of Chamberet (Corrèze), fifty-two kilometers north of Tulle and fifty-nine kilometers southeast of Limoges. Claude's parents, both medical doctors, lived in the village before the war; her father died there in an automobile accident. Her mother was arrested in Chamberet early one spring morning in 1944, after the mayor of the village, also a doctor and anxious to get rid of a competitor, denounced her. To make the arrest, the Gestapo asked a little old local woman for directions, and the woman pointed straight at the house. Knowing that the Germans were in the area and aware of her danger, Doctor Morhange had already sent her seven-year-old daughter across the street to the parents of a schoolmate. Instead of hiding her, the frightened parents sent Claude to school with their own daughter, as on a normal day.

The Germans took Dr. Morhange to the same school, where a classroom was available for interrogation. Where was her child? She swore she did not know. Meanwhile, two teachers quietly took Claude from the classroom the instant she arrived and delivered her to a local dressmaker named Marie who knew her family. Marie hid Claude, her grandmother, and her aunt in her house during that day and took them to a barn for the night. At dawn the next day, the local blacksmith escorted Claude out of town to hide with an impoverished peasant couple who shared what little they had with her and of whom she would later write, "It is the time when I discover true Frenchmen: . . . those that are not somewhat Jewish, those who are not a little bit Russian or Polish, those who speak but one tongue which is their own." Later she hid at a château where she remembers being "surrounded by friendly people."[33]

Claude's aunt ultimately hid with a Protestant minister near Castres (Tarn). Also rescued was her grandmother, a woman "from a Russian Jewish middle-class family, a woman who had lived in several European capitals, who had had servants, jewels, furs, an English governess for her three daughters." The old lady was saved by a former patient of Doctor Morhange's. Claude later vividly described the rescuer:

That woman without education and whom one wouldn't have had over for music on a Sunday afternoon in winter-time, unwed mother with a questionable past in the city, an overblown blonde with overly large eyes and overly full lips, turns up during broad daylight and without further ado takes my grandmother by the hand and leads her home to her house, smack in the center of the village, opens a trap door, has her climb up into her attic, almost touching the tower of the village church. In the attic she fixes a bed for her, brings food to her, takes away the water she has used to wash in, sometimes comes up for a chat; in a word, saves her, physically and mentally, and does it without fanfare, without vainglory, naturally, as a matter of course, as if she'd done nothing else all her life, as if heroism were everyday stuff with her.[34]

Claude Morhange-Bégué knew the full range of villainy and goodness in her village, but she recorded little about the majority—the uncommitted or indifferent. In a letter written after the war, another survivor named Hosiasson said more about the 250 people of Beauvezer (Alpes-de-Haute-Provence), sixty-six kilometers east of Digne in southeastern France. About forty French and foreign Jews hid in the remote village after the Germans occupied the former Italian zone. "The population treated them well," Mr. Hosiasson recalled. "The mayor, Mr. Trotabas, and the *gendarmes* regularly answered in the negative all questionnaires from the subprefecture of Castellane inquiring about the number of Jews residing in the commune."[35] The Jews lived in Beauvezer peacefully for several months, occasionally alerted by sympathizers that Gestapo agents from Nice were in the area. At 2:00 A.M. on January 31, 1944, however, the Gestapo arrived without warning, with an empty bus. For two hours they searched the town, pounded on doors, and beat up villagers who would not give information. They made several arrests; their victims were deported to Auschwitz in February. After the war, several people were cited for the help they had given Jews during the raid, including the local postmistress, the secretary of the mayor, and a rural constable. Predictably enough, several others suspected of informing were arrested, and one woman was executed.

The historian Saul Friedländer describes a similar polarization of attitudes in the little town of Néris-les-Bains (Allier) where his parents, refugees from Czechoslovakia in March 1939, settled in 1940. The majority in the town were indifferent, but as for the "real French," in Néris, as everywhere else, only a small fraction of the population divided into two opposed camps. On the one side were the three schoolmasters, fiercely anti-German and anti-Pétain from the very first, as well as a number of "patrician" families of the city. . . . On the other side were members of the *"grande bourgeoisie,"* also half provincial and half Parisian, about whose Pétainist—and anti-Semitic—feelings there was no doubt.[36]

Saul Friedländer, then nine years old, was saved by one of the sympathetic "patricians," a woman whom his parents scarcely knew. As the local librarian, she had befriended him and guided his tentative reading in his new language. She arranged his placement at the Catholic boarding school of Saint Béranger, in the nearby city of Montluçon. Once he was safely placed, his parents attempted the dangerous crossing into Switzerland. They were refused entry. Instead, Swiss border guards delivered them to the French police on September 30, 1942. They were sent to Rivesaltes, from where they were among the thousands delivered by the Vichy government to the Germans in the occupied zone. Jan and Elli Friedländer were deported to Auschwitz on November 4, 1942. They did not return.[37]

Approximately 250,000 Jews living in France in 1940 survived the war. Where and how did they do so? As seen, about 30,000 lived openly in Paris, wore the star, obeyed all regulations, went out as little as possible, and survived with a good dose of luck. Another 50,000, at least, escaped to Spain or Switzerland. Twenty to thirty thousand, mostly children, survived with the help of Jewish rescue organizations that placed them with non-Jewish hosts. The largest group of Jews in France, however—some 140,000 to 150,000—survived in some form of hiding within France, relatively independently and with little organized help.

Of the last seven families mentioned—Simon, Ewenczyk, Rozengard, Haas, Morhange, Hosiasson, and Friedländer—all except possibly Mr. Hosiasson, who does not say, hid loved ones on their own initiative, relying on organizations only for the indispensable false documents.[38] So too did Maurice and Annette Fersztenfeld, who hid their daughters Yvonne and Renée in the convent of Port Saint-Sauveur in Toulouse. They received help from Father Agathange Bacquet, a Franciscan monk whom they knew.[39] In so acting, these families represented the majority of survivors and were atypical only in that a member of each later recorded their deeds. Most independent survivors left few descriptions of their traumatic experiences. Their histories can be reconstructed only partially, and with difficulty. Yet some patterns emerge.

It is clear that tens of thousands of Jewish adults, especially foreigners, opted to separate from their children and elderly parents and to hide them with non-Jews before they themselves went underground. There were many reasons for such a step. First, young children and the elderly often could not interact with the "real world" on a daily basis. They could not adopt a disguise and keep a secret under the close scrutiny of suspicious adults; they were much more likely to break down under questioning. They also usually needed greater stability and comfort than did adults in their middle years. Furthermore, the adults themselves needed flexibility to move from place to place, to cross frontiers, or simply to work in order to support their dependents.

Second, children were easier to place than adults because they often spoke French better than their foreign parents and attracted less suspicion. Also, potential host families were often sympathetic toward children but did not want to be encumbered with adults. Special institutions for children existed, such as boarding schools and orphanages. Jewish children could be disguised as Christians and placed there. For the elderly, a similar option existed in the form of old-age homes. An institutional alternative was much less available for adults in their middle years.

After making the heartrending decision to separate from their children, many parents, as seen, went to local Jewish social service offices, such as those maintained by OSE or, in Paris, by the Comité rue Amelot or Solidarité. Many more, however, went directly to a non-Jew whom they knew or had some other reason to trust. They asked an acquaintance in the country, for example, or a former friend, teacher, employee, employer, customer, or non-Jewish relative by marriage if they could place their children with them. Countless testimonies of Jews who barely escaped a roundup and found themselves in the streets with no place to go repeat the phrase, "I tried desperately to think of someone I knew." Thus, twenty-two-year-old Ginette Hirtz, who escaped with her younger sister and brother through a window of her house in Amiens when the Gestapo came, found shelter at the last moment with peasants she had known before the war.[40] Twelve-year-old Raia Bretnel, who barely escaped when her parents were arrested in Tours on July 15, 1942, and who wandered around the city with her three-year-old brother and two other children after being refused help several times, thought desperately until she remembered a friendly dairy shopkeeper.[41] Faivel Schrager, born in Poland, the holder of a French university degree, an army volunteer in September 1939, and an escaped prisoner of war, wandered all night through the streets of Agen (Lot-et-Garonne) with his pregnant wife after being warned of police roundups of foreign Jews in August 1942. He finally thought of a shopkeeper whose son had been with him in the German prison camp and went there, finding shelter for a week.[42] Claude Morhange-Bégué, as seen, found help at the last moment from her mother's dressmaker and a former patient, and Claudine Rozengard, also in an emergency situation, from friendly neighbors.

Many Jews in trouble, especially foreigners, knew no one to ask for help and had to petition total strangers. The strangers they chose, however, were of a special type—usually men or women of the Church. Priests, pastors, or nuns did not always agree to help them; Estréa Zaharia Asséo records being rejected by nuns at three different church institutions in Avignon when she sought a refuge for her children, an eleven-year-old girl and a four-year-old boy. But she trusted that the nuns would not turn her in.[43]

Far from turning them in, a stranger's request for help from a man or woman of the Church often initiated a long-term commitment to rescue. Father Marie Benoît, for example, relates that he knew nothing about the problems of Jews until June 1940, when a stranger seeking help for a young Jewish relative knocked on the door of his Capuchin monastery in Marseille. "I was a refugee myself," insists Father Benoît, called "Père Barbiche" by his friends, for his great bushy beard. He had recently had to leave his monastery in Rome, for the French had become unpopular among Italian Fascists upon the outbreak of war. "I had no assigned role at Marseille. I could carve out my own niche."[44] Father Marie Benoît spent the next four years protecting Jews and other fugitives in southern France and in Rome, where he returned in 1943 when his activities in Marseille and Nice became too well known.

Like the first stranger who contacted Father Benoît, the father of Annette Muller exhibited trust in the religious when trying to save his two sons Henri and Jean, ages ten and eleven. The boys had escaped from the Paris roundup of July 1942 after being arrested with their mother Rachel, sister Annette, and younger brother Michel. Mr. Muller's first requests for assistance were refused. Finally by chance he saw an unknown nun at the Saint-Lazare train station and impulsively asked her to help. He was luckier than some, for Sister Clotilde of the Sisters of Saint-Vincent-de-Paul agreed at once. She placed the boys in a Catholic orphanage and later helped Annette and Michel escape from the Asile Lamarck, a UGIF home in Paris where children from Drancy were held pending deportation. Posing as their visitor, she simply walked out with them, against all rules. She placed the four siblings together in a Catholic orphanage at Neuilly-sur-Seine, near Paris, and later in a convent in the Auvergne. She saved their lives.[45]

As the Muller story indicates, men and women of the Church could be of great help to Jews if they so desired, for many reasons. First, they were more likely than average laymen to learn about people in distress. Second, they had access to large institutions with extra space and a capacity to absorb and feed newcomers. Third, Jews in those institutions could disguise themselves as students, novices, or laymen on retreat. Even foreigners posed few problems, for religious institutions had always included the faithful from other countries. Thus, fugitives attracted far less attention than in homes in small villages, where local residents instantly noticed every newcomer.

Finally, men and women of the Church had both religious and secular contacts over a large area and knew where to look for help in obtaining hiding places, false papers, extra food, and guides. Thus, informal rescue networks of people who knew and trusted one another sprang up naturally and quickly. The network between Protestant pastors in Nîmes and their colleagues in the Cévennes has been mentioned, as have those between Archbishop Saliège and the priests and Catholic laymen of his parish. Such separation by region and religious denomination was natural; as Germaine Ribière explains, young Christian rescuers like herself tended to look for hiding places for Jews among those they knew personally.[46] There was some crossing of traditional lines, however. Father Marie Benoît of Marseille, for example, referred Jews to Le Chambon as readily as did Protestant pastors.

The openness of Protestant schools in Le Chambon and the experiences in Catholic institutions of Annette Muller, Yvonne and Renée Fersztenfeld, and Saul Friedländer, were typical of what occurred throughout France during the war.[47] Equally impressive is the work of the Order of Notre-Dame de Sion, which ran residences for students before the war, especially in Lyon and Grenoble. During the war, the order sheltered several dozen Jews in their teens and early twenties and referred many others to neighboring schools and training centers.[48]

The sensitive issue of conversion inevitably arises in any discussion of Jewish survival in Christian institutions. Evidence on the subject is scarce and inconclusive, for many reasons: Jews who converted while hiding often do not wish to talk about it; those who resisted conversion attempts are occasionally understandably embittered; and those who claim that they experienced no pressure are sometimes, and often unjustifiably, dismissed as naive. Emotions on the subject run high, and personal accounts vary. Those who survived among Protestants rarely mention conversion attempts. On the contrary, most agree with Rudy Appel, who lived as a student at Le Chambon and later declared that he experienced no suggestion of conversion. In fact, he recalls that he and his coreligionists held their Holy Day services in the local Protestant church.[49]

For Jews in Catholic institutions, the experience was varied. Children separated from their parents naturally wanted to resemble their peers and share the enthusiasms of the group, and some overzealous priests and nuns wanted to "save their souls." Abuses occurred. A survivor named Jacques, for example, later told the former OSE social worker Denise Baumann about one priest he had known: "Every Thursday, he came to show us films on the death of Jesus; he told us at the same time that it was the Jews who had killed him and that our parents had been deported because they had not believed in him. If we would convert, we would be saved. At the age of ten, I was on the verge of conversion!"[50]

Children placed with Catholics by Jewish organizations had some protection against such abuses. They entered schools or orphanages with the understanding that conversion attempts would not occur, and social workers checked and occasionally moved them if the terms were not honored. Liliane Klein-Lieber, who placed and visited children for the Sixième, later reported that she exercised "a constant vigilance" against conversion attempts, especially by the Sisters of Notre-Dame de Sion, an order originally founded to convert Jews and reluctant to change. She visited her charges weekly, giving them care and attention as well as lessons in their religion, history, and heritage. She recorded with satisfaction that "none of them renounced their Jewish identity."[51] Her achievement was repeated by most other Jewish rescuers.

Much more vulnerable were the more numerous Jewish children

hidden with Catholics by their parents without the intervention and supervision of a Jewish rescue organization. In these cases, baptism (in principle, not performed without parental consent) could become a requirement of admission, allegedly for the safety of hiders and hidden alike, but equally often from an excess of zeal to obtain conversions. Desperate parents often felt forced to agree. Thus, Maurice and Annette Fersztenfeld agreed that their daughters at the convent school in Toulouse should become Catholics and even attended their baptismal ceremony. The heartbroken mother finally let her emotions show, fleeing from the church crying, "I sold you, I sold you!"[52]

Long after the war, Denise Baumann examined the experiences of 100 Jewish survivors who had been under eighteen during the conflict and had had at least one parent deported. From her own rescue work with OSE, she also knew many more cases personally. She concluded that flagrant conversion abuses were exceptional.[53] Much more common, however, were subtle attempts to influence the young and steer them in a certain direction. Children in Catholic institutions had to learn prayers and attend mass to maintain their disguises. Fania, for example, prayed to Jesus for the return of her parents. She remembers the kindness of the nuns who knew of her suffering, and she wonders, "Deep inside, did they hope that I would become Catholic? I think that they troubled themselves more about me than about the other students. That is the memory I have: a good memory."[54] Frida Scheps Weinstein also recalls that she and another Jewish girl hidden at a Catholic school always received special love and attention, although, since their parents did not or could not give consent, they were not baptized.[55] The kindness was understandable, given their personal tragedies, but it was perhaps also motivated by hopes of conversion.

Again according to Denise Baumann:

> The cases of conversion encountered in the study [of 100 child survivors] generally resulted from more distant and deeper influences. . . . One girl was converted by the example of an aunt, Catholic well before the war, a survivor, loved and respected. Another child had been baptised before his arrival in France, on his parents' request.[56]

While the observation may be valid beyond the confines of her study, it is surely less true of very young children who lost their parents and could not later remember how they became Catholics. Furthermore, many conversions occurred but did not last, disrupted by returning relatives or Jewish social workers. Finally and most interesting, men and women from the upper echelons of the Church hierarchy often opposed, deterred, or revoked conversions improperly encouraged by overzealous nuns and Catholic lay teachers. A girl named Eliane, for example, told Denise Baumann that Father Pierre Chaillet became furious after the war when he learned that she had been converted at the age of eleven, after her father had been shot as a Resistant.[57] Similarly, a nun named Julie, working among the poor in the 1980s, told Baumann that she had converted in a Catholic orphanage at the age of thirteen, despite the strong opposition of the mother superior and the local bishop, as well as a rabbi.[58]

Annette Muller's story is similar. As seen, Annette was placed with her three brothers in Catholic institutions. All four children were baptized, apparently without parental consent, and became very religious. One brother wanted to become a priest, and she a nun. She fervently prepared to make her first communion, but the night before the ceremony, just after the war, she was told that she could not do so. The nuns' superiors in Paris, accusing them of taking advantage of the children, had written to prohibit it. Annette was devastated at the time but later recorded the incident with understanding and respect.[59]

Saul Friedländer entered his Catholic boarding school with a letter from his father consenting to baptism. He never knew if it had been a requirement for admission. He received first communion and confirmation and thought of becoming a Jesuit priest. He received vague news after the war that his parents were dead, and he remained at the school. One day in January 1946, a Jesuit whom he calls Father L. described Auschwitz to him in full detail and spoke at length about anti-Semitism. Friedländer recalls:

> The attitude of Father L. himself profoundly influenced me: to hear him speak of the lot of the Jews with so much emotion and respect must have been an important encouragement for me. He did not press me to choose one path or the other—and perhaps he would have preferred to see me remain Catholic—but his sense of justice (or was it a profound charity?) led him to recognize my right to judge for myself, by helping me to renew the contact with my past.[60]

Needless to say, not all men and women of the Church showed similar justice and charity, but it is important to remember that many did.

Although German and Vichy authorities were sometimes reluctant to arrest and convict popular church men and women, the decision to help Jews and other fugitives bore definite risks. One of the best known examples is that of Lucien Bunel, who, under his religious name of Father Jacques, was the director of the Petit Collège Sainte-Thérèse, a Carmelite boarding school for about ninety boys in Avon, near Fontainebleau (Seine-et-Marne), about sixty-five kilometers southeast of Paris. In 1943, Father Jacques accepted several Jewish boys at his school. Jacques-France Halpern, David Schlosser, and Hans-Helmut Michel, ages seventeen, fifteen, and thirteen, were referred to Father Jacques by Mother Maria of Notre-Dame de Sion in nearby Melun. Mother Maria kept several Jewish girls at her school but could not shelter boys. Father Jacques admitted the three lads as students.[61] He also accepted two others as workers. Eighteen-year-old Maurice B. and his younger brother were sent to him by Mother Louisa, mother superior of a chapter of Notre-Dame de Sion in Paris. According to Maurice B. years later, Mother Louisa saved more than 500 Jewish children by referring them to several schools and convents.[62]

The three students had suffered severely before their arrival at the school. Jacques-France's parents were deported on August 5, 1942, and David Schlosser's mother on February 13, 1943. David's father was hidden by Father Jacques and survived. Hans-Helmut Michel was seized with his mother in Paris on July 16, 1942, but was released because his grandmother, too old to be arrested, could care for him. Father Devaux, the parish priest at the Church of Saint-Sulpice in Paris, apparently referred him to the nuns in Melun.[63]

On January 15, 1944, at 10:15 in the morning, seven or eight Gestapo agents, alerted by an informer, raided the school and arrested Father Jacques and the three Jewish students. Maurice B. hid in a wood pile, according to a plan he had thought out ahead of time, and escaped with help from local French acquaintances. His brother had left the school a few days earlier.[64] Also arrested that day at their home in Fontainebleau were Lucien Weil, a Jewish teacher fired elsewhere because of the racial laws and employed at the school by Father Jacques, and his sixty-eight-year-old mother Irma and thirty-nine-year-old sister Fernande. The informer, a former student whom Father Jacques had directed into the Resistance and who had been captured and probably tortured by the Germans, had known about Weil too.[65] The three boys and the three members of the Weil family were sent to Drancy. Less than three weeks later, on February 3, 1944, they were deported to Auschwitz, without return.

Father Jacques was sent to Compiègne and then to Sarrebruck, where he saw fifty-six of his sixty-three companions die within three weeks.[66] In April, he was sent to Mauthausen, where he lived for just over one year. Liberated on April 28, 1945, he died in a hospital in Linz on June 2 from the ravages and deprivations of camp life.[67]

Another churchman who suffered grievously for his rescue work was Pastor Jean S. Lemaire, who allowed Jewish fugitives to meet in his church on Sunday afternoons to receive false documents and instructions from Denise Caraco. Pastor Lemaire was apparently denounced in March 1943 by a German Jewish fugitive trying to save himself—an unusual but not unknown phenomenon. Arrested, tortured, and deported to Mauthausen and Dachau, the pastor returned, according to Denise, "in a deplorable state of health; he remained an invalid until the end of his life."[68]

After hiding their children and their elderly, or in many cases after deciding to keep their loved ones with them, well over 100,000 Jews in France—by far the largest grouping of them—simply blended into the population as a whole. And here the trail grows dim. They left few records, and most may have regarded their stories as unremarkable.

Like so many other French men and women, Jews in France became displaced persons, abandoning their homes and moving to cities, villages, or farms where they were not known. Unlike non-Jews, however, Jews did not usually make their identities known at their new places of residence but lived on false papers acquired with the help of local officials, militant Resistants, or Jewish rescuers. To avoid suspicion, they often sent their children to school, with some foreboding about their ability to keep a secret. For the same reason, and with the same foreboding, they made friends with neighbors. Presumably, at a time when it was safer to know nothing, their neighbors asked few questions. But in rural areas, at least, every newcomer was noticed. Investigating police often did not ask precisely for Jews, labor service evaders, or other fugitives but instead sought "outsiders." Under such circumstances, Jews were at the mercy of their neighbors. Some were betrayed, and some were actively protected. Most enjoyed benign neglect or vague goodwill and were able to survive.

Many cases of infamous betrayal and courageous protection have been mentioned throughout this text. Readers have met informers, overzealous Vichy bureaucrats and police, and fanatic anti-Semites. They have also read of non-Jewish rescuers—of Pastor Trocmé, Father Marie Benoît, and Father Jacques; of Madeleine Barot and Germaine Ribière; of Gilbert Lesage. There are hundreds of others whose cases should all be remembered but who cannot be mentioned here—the indispensable active benefactors who provided shelter, false documents, and warnings of police searches. Thousands will never be known—the families and the directors of institutions who took in the uncounted thousands of Jews placed formally by Jewish organizations and informally by their own relatives. Every individual who hid a Jew saved a life and made a difference.

Finally, there was the vast majority of French men and women who remained silent. A compliment for silence or benign neglect is faint praise indeed, and praise is in fact not intended here. But in the historical reality of the Holocaust in France, especially as it applied to native Jews, silence was perhaps the most important factor in survival. In a situation where Jews were not usually physically identifiable as such and where anti-Jewish police units were understaffed, Jews with false papers and ration cards could often survive by living quietly and taking occasional odd jobs. They needed, in most cases, one or two active benefactors, but they equally required the passive goodwill of the neighbors who inevitably knew they were outsiders. The rough total of 250,000 Jews who survived among French non-Jews—a figure that includes those hidden both independently and by Jewish rescue organizations, the 30,000 who lived openly as Jews in Paris, and those who ultimately managed to cross the frontiers—were totally dependent upon that goodwill.

14

Crossing Frontiers

DURING THE AUTUMN OF 1943, AS DIRECTORS OF JEWISH GROUP homes realized that they could no longer remain open safely, social workers placed most residents with non-Jewish families or institutions. Some Jews, however, were difficult to place, for many reasons, including their high visibility because of strict religious observance, language, or physical traits; family insistence on remaining together; their psychological or physical disabilities; or a simple scarcity of hiding places. For these and others who requested it, illegal passage to Switzerland or Spain seemed fitting. Many had preceded them, but now the pressure intensified.

The problems of passage were daunting. Since Jews could not move about without special permission, they required impeccable false documents to travel anywhere. They also needed a convincing explanation for their movements. During any train or bus trip, documents might be scrutinized several times, and explanations demanded. Frequency and attention increased as the frontier approached. Jews caught with false papers were invariably deported.

Every refugee presented a different challenge. Children disguised as campers or pupils on a school trip were moved in groups. With luck, those with distinguishing physical or language traits could pass with the others. Adults without children traveled alone or in pairs,

sometimes with a guide in another compartment, on slow and exhausting secondary rail or bus lines where scrutiny was less intense.
René Nodot described the train he often took with refugees from
Bourg-en-Bresse (Ain) to Bellegarde-sur-Valserine, near the Swiss
frontier, a distance of about eighty kilometers:

> I used a mixed train of eight or nine freight cars and two passenger
> cars. This ultra-slow omnibus, averaging eleven or twelve kilome-
> ters per hour, left the capital of the Bresse [region] at six o'clock in
> the morning to arrive at Bellegarde at noon. At every station [there
> were] interminable manoeuvers to take on or leave freight cars.
> But this train carrying only peasants going to local markets was al-
> most never the object of a very serious search . . . at least until Sep-
> tember 13, 1943 [after the Germans had occupied the former Ital-
> ian zone].[1]

Whenever possible, refugees and their guides avoided hotels, with
their danger of searches. Jews bound for Switzerland from
CIMADE's Coteau Fleuri in Le Chambon-sur-Lignon or from other
refuges in the Cévennes often stopped first in Nîmes, where they
stayed in Protestant presbyteries or private homes. They often went
on to Valence (Drôme), another Protestant center, on the Rhône
River south of Lyon.[2] Jews with Catholic or Jewish guides often assembled in Lyon or Grenoble. Refugees then moved slowly and cautiously toward the northeast. At Annecy, René Nodot, the CIMADE
workers Suzanne Loiseau-Chevalley and Geneviève Priacel-Pittet,
known as Tatchou, and other guides often directed their charges to
Paul Chapal, the local Protestant pastor who hid refugees in his
house, his attic, and even his church. Escorts also depended upon
Abbé Joseph Folliet, the Catholic chaplain of Jeunesse ouvrière chrétienne (JOC) who arranged with monasteries and convents in the department of Haute-Savoie to serve as way stations. While awaiting
special frontier guides and transport, women often stayed at the convent of Chavanod about seven kilometers from Annecy, and men at
the Abbaye de Tamie, above Faverges.[3]

From Annecy, the route to Switzerland divided and became ever
more dangerous. Tatchou and other social workers sometimes directed refugees in the direction of Chamonix and Argentière (Haute-
Savoie), near Mont Blanc and the high alpine passes. This was the
safest route, for the snowfields were not criss-crossed with barbed
wire, and the border patrols remained in the nearest village or stayed

predictably close to their frontier posts. It was by far the most arduous, however, and only the hardiest walkers could attempt it even in the period from May to October when the passes were open. Furthermore, refugees in the mountains were totally dependent upon local guides known as *passeurs,* who were often former smugglers being paid from 500 to as much as 7,000 francs per person. Most passeurs were reliable, but some, once under way, abandoned their charges, demanded more money, or turned them over to the border guards for a reward.

Alternative routes avoided the alpine passes by leading north from Annecy to towns such as Collonges, Saint-Julien-en-Genevois, Annemasse, or Machilly on the Swiss frontier south of Geneva, or to Thonon-les-Bains and Évian-les-Bains on the southern shore of Lake Geneva. There the terrain was less rugged, but surveillance in the towns and at the frontier itself was much greater. Each route became an intricate network, requiring numerous helpers for each lap of the way. Rolande Birgy, for example, a young JOC activist who escorted children's groups for the Sixième, remembers one such network: "Once a week, and sometimes twice, my friends and I took to the parish priest of Douvaine groups of Jewish children who, for the most part, would not see their parents again. We arrived generally by train, at Machilly. There were each time from eight to twelve children, once twenty-three."[4] The parish priest, Abbé Jean Rosay, met the children at the station at Machilly and took them, usually on foot, to his residence at Douvaine, about eight kilometers away. There he fed and sometimes housed them for several days. Suzanne Loiseau-Chevalley recalls of his home, "Nowhere, during the entire war, did I feel so much at home as there. We had to feed the children, find a needle to sew [into the lining of their clothes] the names of the Jewish children who were going to cross the frontier: we found everything."[5]

As soon as it was feasible, Abbé Rosay sent the groups on. They traveled, sometimes by bus, to friendly farmers whose land outside the hamlet of Veigy bordered a stream called the Hermance, separating France from Switzerland. One of those farmers was Joseph Lancon, father of seven children. His daughter Thérèse Neury records: "Sometimes, there were families of three or four people, but often, there were ten or twelve of them, even more. The whole [Lancon] family was mobilized, as well as [neighbor] François Perillat, to carry the luggage, and guide those people to the border crossing spot, which it was necessary to change from time to time."[6]

Abbé Rosay and his helpers accepted no money for their assistance. Their network functioned actively throughout the period of the Italian occupation, and with greater difficulty under the Germans. On the evening of February 10, 1944, however, the Gestapo descended upon Douvaine and Veigy, arresting Abbé Rosay, Joseph Lancon, François Perillat, and Father Figuet, the director of a local orphanage. Father Figuet was released, but the other three men were deported. François Perillat died of pneumonia at a Nazi labor camp on December 18, 1944; Joseph Lancon perished on March 5, 1945. Abbé Rosay died of exhaustion and starvation at Bergen-Belsen in early April 1945, shortly before its liberation.[7]

After the Germans occupied the Haute-Savoie in the Italian zone, it was no longer an easier crossing area than more northern French departments that also bordered Switzerland. At the same time, Jewish children's homes in the former Italian zone had to be closed because of the German presence. New routes had to be found, and several in the Doubs, Jura, and Ain departments began to be used more frequently. Tatchou sometimes took refugees to Switzerland by way of the town of Saint-Claude (Jura), northwest of Geneva, and through the Jura Mountains, but she disliked that route because it involved a difficult hike of some thirty kilometers through the village of Les Rousses to the frontier.[8]

Every alternative required helpers. Tatchou mentions, in addition to Abbé Rosay, the pastor of Thonon. Rolande Birgy sometimes worked with a friend whose farm near Annemasse lay in the no-man's-land between the wires. René Nodot recalls Abbé Marius Jolivet of Collonges—"a man of about thirty, rather tall, thin. His slightly pale face had a great nobility, and his eyes shone with intelligence."[9] Abbé Jolivet personally escorted six-year-old Eva Stein across the frontier to Geneva. Her mother, brother, and sister had previously crossed on foot from Chamonix, after being robbed and abandoned by their passeur while still an hour from the border. The priest aided many other fugitives, including Jews, Resistants, and American intelligence agents.[10]

Father Louis Favre, a teacher at the École Saint-François at Ville-la-Grand on the outskirts of Annemasse, offered a different kind of help. A long curved wall enclosing a garden behind the school bordered directly on Switzerland. Getting refugees to the school itself was the most difficult problem. Children were disguised as pupils, and adults as visiting parents. Once in the school, a ladder led over the garden wall. Hundreds of Jews and Resistants were saved, but

Father Favre was arrested by the Gestapo in February 1944, about the same time as Abbé Rosay, Lancon, and Perillat. He was tortured and shot near Annecy in July.[11]

Once actually at the frontier, refugees faced new problems. Tatchou remembers two rows of barbed wire, several meters apart and about two meters high, along the border south of Geneva. Depending upon the time and place, it was patrolled by French, Italian, or German police on one side, and by Swiss police, sometimes equally determined to keep refugees out, on the other. The French gendarmes were difficult to predict, like their compatriots in general. Some turned a blind eye to refugees, while others did their job with a vengeance. The Italians were usually, but not always, more lenient. German soldiers were the most predictable. They patrolled with dogs that were not fed all day. Those animals, according to one witness, literally tore people to pieces.[12]

At this last lap of the journey, help was essential, if not from experienced mountaineers as at Chamonix, then at least from local residents who knew the habits of border patrols and the locations of gaps in the wire. Tatchou often worked with local teenage Protestant Boy Scouts. Nodot, who had spent summers around Saint-Julien-en-Genevois, was his own guide. In the middle of a field in the shelter of a clump of trees where he had played as a boy, he found his own opening in the wire. Other social workers, less familiar with the area, employed professional passeurs, some of whom were no more reliable than those in the mountain passes. Thirteen-year-old Frida Cohen's passeur abandoned her and a group of small children within sight of the line not far from Annemasse at four o'clock in the afternoon. The terrified children had to wait alone until dark and then crawl under the wire without adult help. Older children carried the babies. One child screamed when her hair became tangled in the wire and nearly betrayed the entire group. An older boy cut her free with his jackknife.[13]

Most fugitives who crossed into Switzerland were helped by organizational escorts and local rescuers. Some, however, and especially strong young adults unencumbered by children or the elderly, managed almost alone. Their stories are the least well known. That of the future French prime minister Pierre Mendes France, however, is recorded. Mendes France escaped from a Vichy prison on June 21, 1941. After several unsuccessful attempts to secure assistance from the still diminutive Resistance, he read in an old newspaper of a local smuggler on Lake Geneva. He made inquiries, one contact led to another, and he eventually found himself disguised as a deckhand on a little fishing boat bound, quite illegally, for Lausanne. He and the fisherman-smuggler rowed until they were out of sight of French soil. Only then did they turn on the motor.[14]

After spending weeks approaching the frontier and finding ways to cross it, refugees faced another period of anxiety when they finally confronted the Swiss border guards. Many have recorded their initial terror, not knowing whether German-speaking, gray-uniformed, armed soldiers were Swiss or German. The real danger, however, was the possibility of expulsion. Throughout the war, Swiss bureaucrats, occasionally anti-Semitic, often antiforeign, constantly afraid of provoking the Germans, but sometimes sympathetic to the victims of Nazism, produced vague and varying guidelines for the admission of illegal immigrants.

On May 18, 1940, as the German invasion of France was driving thousands of desperate refugees toward their frontiers, the Swiss Department of Justice and Police addressed a circular to border police, instructing them that "all civilian fugitives will be sent back except women, children under sixteen, men over sixty, and the disabled."[15] Then on August 13, 1942, at the very moment of the expulsions of foreign Jews from the unoccupied to the occupied zone in France, the same department ordered Swiss police to reject everyone except soldiers, individuals planning to leave immediately for the unoccupied zone, and political refugees. The new order stated explicitly that "those who have fled only because of their race, the Jews for example, should not be considered political refugees."[16]

Even in 1942, however, police were given some authority to examine individual cases. As Nodot states, "The frontier was never hermetically sealed for refugees, as has been claimed."[17] Guards turned away most able-bodied adults but usually accepted parents with children under six, unaccompanied children up to the age of sixteen, and the ill and infirm. But there was never any certainty of policy. Roger Fichtenberg, a Sixième activist who often escorted children on their way to Switzerland, recalls that when he left them with a local passeur he always arranged a meeting place in France in case they were rejected at the border. On December 22, 1942, he delivered eight adolescents to a passeur and found all of them at the Annemasse railroad station the next morning. He had to return them to Moissac.[18] Swiss officials did not encourage police to disregard guidelines for the admission of Jews until early 1944. The guidelines themselves were not changed until July 12, 1944. At that point, the category of political refugee was broadened to include "foreigners truly menaced . . . for political or other reasons."[19] "Other reasons," of course, meant race or religion.

The exact number of Jews turned back is unknown, but it reached several thousand.[20] The Swiss guards who expelled them had various options. Some provided refugees with aid, advice, and even safe transport back. Others simply ordered them to return immediately the way they had come. The majority drove them to a crossing and left them to fend for themselves. A sadistic few actually delivered them to patrols on the other side. Most guards acted with cold courtesy, but some demonstrated deliberate cruelty. Fred Zacouto, then a fifteen-year-old German Jewish refugee alone, without his parents, was turned back despite his age, relatives in Switzerland, pocket money, and three years of study in the country. Guards seized him and about twenty others, including mothers and young children, in the middle of the night, drove them to the border without explanation, struck a frantic mother, and threatened to deliver them all to a German patrol if they did not leave instantly. Zacouto reached Annemasse at five o'clock in the morning, where he met a sympathetic French railroad worker who told him angrily that he saw the same thing every day.[21] Zacouto survived, but hundreds, if not thousands—like the parents of Saul Friedländer—were returned to a French prison, deportation, and death at Auschwitz.

While several thousand were turned away, 28,242 refugee Jews from German-occupied countries, by one estimate, were accepted.[22] Most remained in Switzerland until the end of the war. They lived for the most part in work camps, job training centers, group homes, or special facilities for the ill and elderly. By 1945, 104 such establishments existed. Most refugees had few contacts with Swiss civilians other than employers, often vintners and farmers, and many suffered from a profound sense of isolation. Work conditions and human contacts varied considerably, but most centers were run honestly and maintained adequate living standards.[23] Jews and other refugees lived austerely, and with overwhelming anxiety for their loved ones in occupied Europe. But they lived.

Among the Jewish organizations that guided children into Switzerland, three—OSE, the EIF in its clandestine form known as the Sixième, and the branch of the MJS called Éducation physique—seem particularly outstanding. The three agencies sometimes worked together and sometimes separately; they shared similar non-Jewish offers of hospitality and assistance. Their success rate reached several thousand, and their failures were few. It is the tragedies, however, that should be specifically noted, for their victims paid the ultimate price for their heroism and self-sacrifice.

Mila Racine, born into a Jewish family in Moscow, emigrated to France when she was five years old. In 1943, she was twenty-four. While her parents hid in Nice, she worked with her brother Emmanuel and sister Sacha as a children's guide for Éducation physique. She often brought groups to Annemasse from as far away as Nice and, with the help of a local passeur, accompanied them to the frontier. On the night of October 21, 1943, German soldiers patrolling with dogs caught her and Roland Epstein, another Éducation physique worker, at the wire near Saint-Julien-en-Genevois with a group of refugees. Incarcerated and interrogated for three weeks locally and for another three weeks at Montluc, both young people managed to hide the fact that they were Jewish. Roland was deported to Buchenwald, from where he returned. Mila was sent to a concentration camp for non-Jewish women Resistants at Ravensbruck, and later to Mauthausen. On March 22, 1945, while working as a prisoner, she was killed in an Allied air raid.

Marianne Cohn was born in Mannheim, Germany. Fleeing the Nazis, her parents took her and her sister first to Spain and then to France. In 1940, the family was interned for a time at Gurs. They managed to get to the EIF home at Moissac, where the women helped with the young Scouts and Mr. Cohn taught accounting. After the Germans occupied the southern zone, Marianne, then twenty, moved to Grenoble in the Italian zone and began to work for the Sixième. When Mila Racine and Roland Epstein were arrested, she and Rolande Birgy from Jeunesse ouvrière chrétienne, both skilled in working with children, replaced them.

On May 31, 1944, a German patrol with dogs caught Marianne with a group of twenty-eight children between the ages of four and fifteen, just two hundred meters from the frontier. She was imprisoned in Annemasse with eleven of the older boys and girls. On the intervention of Jean Deffaugt, the town's mayor recently appointed by Vichy but surreptitiously connected to the Resistance, the Gestapo agreed to let the younger children remain in supervised residence in official government institutions. Deffaugt and Emmanuel Racine concocted an escape plan for Marianne, but she refused to use it from fear of reprisals on the children. Early in July 1944, just a few weeks before the liberation of the town, Gestapo agents took Marianne and five other Resistants from the prison to an isolated spot in Ville-la-Grand, outside Annemasse, and brutally beat them to death.

The twenty-eight children for whom Marianne Cohn died survived, thanks to the intervention of Mayor Deffaugt. The local Gestapo chief, Georg Meyer, informed Deffaugt on July 22 that he was about to send the children to Lyon. There, like the children of Izieu, they would have fallen into the hands of the local SS chief, Klaus Barbie, and been deported to Auschwitz. Through an astute combination of pleas for mercy, threats of Resistance reprisals, and promises of postwar protection—promises that he later honored and that enabled Meyer to escape to Switzerland—Deffaugt convinced the Gestapo chief to turn the children over to him. Marianne did not die in vain. Had she agreed to escape, Meyer might well have refused Deffaugt's pleas.[24]

For men in their teens, twenties, and thirties, refuge in Switzerland had one serious disadvantage: surrounded by countries at war, it was a geographical dead end. Children and older people were usually grateful to live out the war in camps or other forms of temporary residence in neutral territory. Those who wished to join the anti-Nazi struggle, however, preferred the Spanish option, in the hope of joining the Free French in London or the Jewish Brigade in Palestine. They were joined by others, Jews and non-Jews alike, who crossed the Pyrenees rather than the Alps simply because they were closer, or because their personal contacts led them there.

The Spanish route involved all the hazards of the Swiss passage, plus some new problems. As with Switzerland, train or bus transportation became increasingly dangerous as the frontier approached. Despite excellent false papers, many Jews bound for Spain were arrested on trains while still as far away from the border as Agen, Montauban, Toulouse, or Montpellier. Claude Vigée was more fortunate. His papers helped him reach Pau, from where he booked train passage on October 26, 1942, to Canfranc, an official port of entry into Spain. At the frontier, where surveillance was naturally the strictest, a friendly Vichy customs official whose father had known one of his relatives overlooked suspicious flaws in his documents.[25] A few days later, the Germans occupied southern France and controlled the entire Spanish border. Crossings became far more difficult. Train approaches to the frontier grew even more hazardous, and the final lap was generally made on foot.

That final lap was, in most cases, a grueling ordeal, impossible for all but the most physically fit. At first, many refugees traveling on foot left from border villages not far from the Mediterranean coast. They crossed the Pyrenees along footpaths· which were difficult but not much higher than a few hundred meters. Vichy police patrolled the footpaths until November 1942. After the arrival of the Germans, however, refugees were forced inland, where French and German patrols were fewer but where the terrain was daunting. Routes leading to Spain out of Oloron-Sainte-Marie (Basses-Pyrénées) or Saint-Girons (Ariège), for example, involved passes at 1,600 meters or more, amid peaks which exceeded 3,000 meters.

In such terrain, blinding snowstorms occurred as late in the season as May. Avalanches and fog were constant threats. Most passeurs were honest local mountaineers, but some were unscrupulous professional smugglers charging from 3,000 (the equivalent of a worker's wage for two months) to 10,000 francs per person, and occasionally 30,000 francs or more.[26] Nor did high fees guarantee performance. Some passeurs, losing patience with slow or weak travelers or taking fright from a storm or nearby patrol, pointed the way vaguely down a mountain and disappeared. Others, wary of being arrested in Spain, left their clients at the frontier but still hundreds of steep meters from easy terrain. Without guides, refugees promptly lost all trace of the meandering shepherds' trails. Men, women, and children froze and starved in mountain huts, awaiting a break in the weather, or fell to their deaths over unexpected precipices.

At least 30,000 Jews are known to have crossed from France into Spain during the war, and many more may have passed through the Iberian peninsula without ever being detected.[27] Several thousand emigrated quite legally, and therefore relatively comfortably, in the summer of 1940, during the panic of the fall of France. A limited but steady stream of emigrants followed, some legally and some illegally, until the summer of 1942, when Vichy's expulsions of foreign Jews caused a renewal of panic. The German occupation of the southern zone heightened Jewish fears still further, and totally illegal emigration continued at high levels until the Liberation.

Most Jewish refugees arranged their trips independently, without the support of formal rescue organizations. Their stories are difficult to reconstruct. Presumably they inched their way cautiously toward the frontier in small family groups, armed with false documents, ready cash, and references from priests, ministers, or personal friends. Maurice Shotland, then age thirteen, remembers such a journey made with his sister, mother, and father, a well-to-do diamond merchant from Belgium. After many adventures despite their good and costly false papers, the family reached Perpignan by train in September 1942 and set out on foot for Figueras in Spain. The boy was impressed with the two guides—Spanish-speaking smugglers with guns on their hips and shoulders, knives in their belts, bandanas, and mountain boots. The group walked over steep terrain throughout the hours of darkness on two successive nights, in pouring rain, resting at daylight in shepherds' huts. They were arrested and jailed in Figueras, but they survived.[28]

While most refugees made their own way, others received organized assistance. Exact numbers are not recorded. At least 313, however, crossed the Pyrenees between May 1943 and August 1944 under the direction of the Armée juive, an armed Resistance group founded and led by Zionists.[29] About 225 of these were adults, including many former Scouts from dissolved EIF centers and other Jewish refugees who had come from the Netherlands with the help of a Dutch Resistance group operating in France. Since these adults were anxious to reach Palestine and join the Jewish Brigade, their military objectives merged with those of the Armée juive. Eighty-eight of the 313 were children from dissolved OSE homes. They were directed toward Spain because they were considered sufficiently strong to cross the Pyrenees, because the flight to Switzerland had become hazardous, and because their only surviving relatives lived in Palestine. The children traveled in groups of no more than twelve. They moved at night along a route that took them into neutral Andorra, where they rested in hotels before continuing to Barcelona by bus. All the children arrived safely. Of the adults, two died in the mountains and six were caught and deported. Two of the latter survived. Of the 313, 272, including 79 children, managed to leave Spain for Palestine in 1944.[30]

Once in Spain itself, many refugees' problems were far from over. As in Switzerland, they faced the terrifying possibility of expulsion or the less agonizing but still demoralizing likelihood of internment. Policies were not always clear or predictable. Generally, however, Jewish and non-Jewish refugees in transit with proper legal documents—with French exit visas and Spanish and Portuguese entry visas—were allowed to pass. Refugees without visas but with valid passports from Allied countries were temporarily detained but released when their consulates intervened. Illegal refugees from German-occupied countries, including all of France after November

1942, enjoyed no consular protection and could be refused entry or detained for long periods. Spanish border guards seem to have made few distinctions between Jewish and non-Jewish refugees. After the summer of 1942, however, all Jewish refugees from France were illegal by definition, for the Vichy regime refused to grant them exit visas.

Spanish policy on rejection or detention of illegal refugees from Nazi-occupied countries varied at different stages of the war. According to Rabbi Yehuda Ansbacher, who escaped from Gurs in 1942 and fled to Spain in 1943, "Until the occupation of Southern France by the Nazis on November 11, 1942, Spanish authorities again and again sent people back when arriving at the border."[31] The problem apparently had a partial solution, however, for if refugees could elude border guards and get into the country before being detected, they were as likely to be interned as expelled.[32] Clandestine crossings of the Pyrenees were arranged accordingly. Furthermore, according to Rabbi Ansbacher, "After [November 11, 1942], with the exception of a few isolated cases, Spain did not turn people down anymore."[33] The record of Francisco Franco's Spain seems to have been at least as lenient as that of democratic Switzerland.

Arrests and internments, however, remained a regular occurrence. Jews and non-Jews without consular protection and with no place to go were often held for a year or more. Many spent some time in city prisons in Barcelona, Pamplona, and elsewhere, where they suffered from overcrowding, poor food, and occasional maltreatment. Before being released to supervised residence in Spain or, for the fortunate few, emigration abroad, most men also passed through a camp at Miranda de Ebro, a small town northeast of Burgos. Of this camp, Thomas Hamilton, a reporter from the *New York Times* who visited it during the war, recorded:

> The huts were not heated, but prisoners were given blankets at least; the food was deplorable, but it was not much worse than that of their guards.
> ... Few prisoners complained about either their treatment or the amount of work they were compelled to do. They suffered most from boredom.[34]

British Ambassador Sir Samuel Hoare also observed:

> The accommodation was neither better nor worse than the ordinary accommodation for Spanish troops. When I complained of its

many inadequacies, for instance the lack of an adequate water supply, I was told that if the improvements that I demanded were permitted, there would be a mutiny in every Spanish barracks, as the Miranda standard would then so far exceed the normal conditions of Spanish barrack life.[35]

Finally, and perhaps most revealingly, a Jewish Austrian author interned at Miranda for twenty-six months later recalled:

While in all the concentration camps of the continent and in North Africa [notably, Vichy French camps] so many of the internees died in consequence of the terrible sanitary conditions, of the miserable food and of ill-treatment, it can be declared and proved that during those two years nobody died in Miranda from any of those causes, and there was no exceptional mortality at all.[36]

Freedom from death by starvation is negative praise at best, and time spent in Spanish camps was time lost in a most unpleasant manner. Another freedom, however—the freedom from threat of delivery to the Nazis—was so immense and so novel to Jewish arrivals in Spain during the war that most accepted discomfort and lost time with dignity and even gratitude.

15

Jews in the Armed Resistance

ON JUNE 23, 1940, FRENCH-BORN RENÉ CASSIN (1887–1976), A DIS-
tinguished lawyer, a professor at the Sorbonne, and a wounded veteran of the First World War, accompanied by his wife, boarded a ship
at Saint-Jean-de-Luz bound for England. After de Gaulle's radio appeal from London, he needed only five days to decide to leave his
mother and brother in France and abandon his career and property
for one overriding objective. He intended to fight for a free France.
He was fifty-two years old and spoke almost no English, yet he remained abroad for more than four years. Among other roles, he
served as a *commissaire national*—in effect, cabinet minister—in de
Gaulle's administrative council in London from 1941 to 1943. His
responsibilities were law and justice, and public instruction.[1]

As a result of the racial laws in 1940, Louis Kahn (1895–1967), a
French-born graduate of the École polytechnique, was retired from
the French naval engineering corps. In 1942, he secretly left France
for London to join de Gaulle. The director of naval construction
with the Free French, he was transferred to Algiers where he helped
prepare the August 1944 landings in Provence. In recognition of his
wartime contributions, he was appointed admiral in 1944.[2]

At the other end of the political and social spectrum was sixteen-
year-old Thomas Elek, born in Hungary to Jewish parents who sub-

sequently settled in Paris and opened a little Hungarian restaurant near the Sorbonne. Thomas attended the prestigious Lycée Louis le Grand, a feeder school for the nation's elite institutions of higher learning. But the young man was restless and determined that the war should not pass him by. He was also deeply offended by anti-Semitic insults at school, the "Jewish Business" sign his parents were forced to put in their restaurant window, and the required wearing of the star of David. He left school and joined an armed Resistance unit of foreign Communist Jews. With his new comrades, he participated in numerous military actions against the German occupiers of his adopted city. He was caught, tried, and shot with twenty-two others at Mont-Valérien on February 21, 1944.[3] Of the twenty-three executed Resistants in Elek's group, all but two were foreigners and at least nine were Jewish.[4]

As the cases of René Cassin and Admiral Louis Kahn on the one hand and Thomas Elek on the other demonstrate, Jewish men and women who wished to join the armed Resistance in France had several options. Many, especially citizens like Cassin and Kahn, joined general Resistance forces, both non-Communist and Communist, where they rarely knew the religious, ethnic, or cultural backgrounds of their comrades. Others, especially newcomers like Elek but including many dedicated French Zionists and second-generation immigrants as well, chose specifically Jewish units, also both non-Communist and Communist. The motives and priorities behind these choices differed considerably, but all Resistants shared an overwhelming desire to defeat Nazism. As the Resistant Léo Hamon later remembered: "There were some Jews who felt themselves French above all . . . and other Jews, foreigners, who had . . . for part of them, the will to create later on a Jewish State. But all were united then by the common combat that they waged against Nazism."[5]

The range of choices reflected the broad diversity of backgrounds and personal priorities of Jews in wartime France. Most non-Communists who had been citizens for generations agreed with Léo Hamon that "we acted as Frenchmen who considered that their country had been violated, that precious provinces had been amputated, that its message had been misunderstood and scorned and that they had, in consequence, an obligation to defend it."[6] Many were not even particularly aware of the special dangers threatening French Jews when they themselves first joined the Resistance between 1940 and mid-1942. Some, like Louis Kahn, lost their jobs as a result of the racial laws—a condition that left them freer and more ready to

join the Resistance—and many had a heightened political consciousness because of personal sensitivity to Nazi and Vichyite anti-Semitism. But they fought as Frenchmen, not as Jews.

Those who joined general Communist Resistance units tended also
to be citizens with little sense of their Jewish cultural or historical
roots. Like non-Communists, they acted as Frenchmen, but they also
fought to defend the international Communist movement and the Soviet Union. Many were immobilized by the irreconcilability of these
objectives before the German invasion of the Soviet Union in June
1941, but after that date the multiplicity of motives was a spur to action rather than a deterrent.

Other Jews, especially immigrants who felt more Jewish than
French, identified with specifically Jewish Resistance groups for a variety of reasons. Zionists joined Jewish non-Communist units from a desire to defeat Nazism and defend France, but also in the hope of proving the effectiveness of Jewish fighting forces while preparing young
men for a future struggle in Palestine. Other young Jews, especially immigrants, joined specifically Jewish Communist units for a variety of
reasons, some, as will be seen, not wholly linked to Marxism. Furthermore, as time went on, many Resistants, Jewish and non-Jewish alike,
joined Jewish non-Communist and Communist armed units simply because they were militarily active and physically proximate. The leaders
and old-timers in those units—committed Zionists in the former case
and equally dedicated Communists with little Jewish consciousness in
the latter—continued to define their groups' ideological orientations,
but the rank and file often varied considerably.

Statistics of the Jewish Resistance are almost nonexistent, for several reasons. Within the general Resistance, participants were never
identified as Jews and were rarely even known as such. In the general
Communist Resistance, theoretically dedicated as it was to international and universal values, such a situation is comprehensible, but
for the non-Communist Resistance it merits some attention. Léo
Hamon explains, "For certain of our comrades, for a great number
of them, we did not know that they were Jews because of the disguising of names, or rather we were not supposed to know—it was an el-
ementary rule of security."[7]

Even among two or three comrades he knew to be Jewish, Hamon
insists, he *never* discussed Jewish questions. There were too many
more pressing issues—problems of immediate survival, as well as
broader questions such as what relations to maintain with the Communists or with other political parties, and whether acts of resistance

in general were worth the price paid in German reprisals. While it is understandable that many Resistants prefer to be remembered primarily as French men and women rather than as Jews, such total lack of concern for specifically Jewish problems seems hard to believe. It was indeed deliberate, as Hamon admits when he says, "In a combat in which the enemy wanted to single out the Jews at any price, we had to affirm, on our side, the unity of the nation, the 'dress without seams.'"[8]

Within the specifically Jewish Resistance, at least, statistics might be expected, but here again problems arise. Initial groupings of armed, Communist, immigrant Resistants in Paris were based not upon religious or national affiliations but upon language. Immigrant Jews joined the Yiddish-speaking group, but many could also be found with Romanian, Hungarian, German, or Polish-speaking units, unidentified as Jews. Even within the primarily Jewish FTP-MOI Second Detachment in Paris, membership levels varied from week to week, activists from other nationalities came and went, and few records were kept. Non-Communist Jewish groups similarly recorded little and included participants with varied religious backgrounds, especially in 1944. In Léo Hamon's opinion, "If one could make, after the fact, a census of the active French Resistance, one would find without any doubt a good number of Jews, proportionately more important than those in the overall French population."[9] Hamon, though Jewish, was not excessively partial, and his impressionistic assessment is probably correct. He was speaking primarily of Jews in the general Resistance, and he explained their overrepresentation in terms of their availability because of the racial laws, their heightened political sense, and their devotion to their country. The specifically Jewish Resistance maintained the overrepresentation, for no other immigrant fighting units were as large in comparison to their overall numbers within the general population.

In 1984, Henri Noguères, a historian and journalist and the president of the Ligue des droits de l'homme, looked back on his days in the general non-Communist French Resistance and recalled:

When I joined the *Comité d'action socialiste,* it never entered my mind that its founder and animator, Daniel Mayer, was Jewish—he was a Socialist. And when I joined *Franc-Tireur,* I knew the real name of its chief, Jean-Pierre Lévy, but it never entered my mind that he was Jewish—he was chief of a Resistance movement.[10]

Surely most Jews in the general French Resistance would want to be remembered as Socialists, Communists, Gaullists, or, above all, patriots. They would not want to be singled out from their fellows because of differences of religion or ancestry. And yet, the story of Jews in the armed Resistance is incomplete without brief mention of at least a few of them. Their histories cover, in microcosm, the entire complex organizational structure of the French Resistance.

Jean-Pierre Lévy, born in Strasbourg, was twenty-nine years old in 1940 when he won the *croix de guerre* for military action against the invading Germans. The following year he became chief of Franc-Tireur, a group founded in Lyon to circulate anti-Vichy propaganda. Franc-Tireur established a clandestine newspaper bearing the same name, an intelligence-gathering service, and sabotage teams called *groupes francs*. In September 1942, Lévy agreed that his organization would cooperate with the two other major non-Communist Resistance groups in unoccupied France, Henri Frenay's more conservative Combat, and Emmanuel d'Astier de la Vigerie's more leftist Libération-Sud. The three groups formed the nucleus first of the Armée secrète (Secret Army) desired by de Gaulle's agent Jean Moulin, and later of the Mouvements unis de résistance (MUR), to which the Secret Army became subordinate. Lévy subsequently served in London as a director of intelligence, security, and supplies for the MUR. He is recognized as one of the most prominent leaders of the non-Communist French Resistance.

Daniel Mayer, a fifth-generation Parisian on his father's side and a descendant of Jews who came to France from Alsace and Lorraine in 1870 on his mother's, was a Socialist journalist who was called up for military service when war broke out. Demobilized in July, he went immediately to Toulouse to consult with Léon Blum on a method for joining de Gaulle in London. Blum urged him to work instead within France. When his mentor was imprisoned shortly afterward, Mayer remained to reconstitute a clandestine Socialist party and become its secretary-general. After serving as a driving force for the coordination of French Resistance groups, including the Communists, under the aegis of the Conseil national de la résistance (CNR), he helped Jean Moulin secure the allegiance of that council to de Gaulle. He insisted upon the separate representation of political parties within the CNR, however, and became his party's delegate. He then successfully led the movement within the CNR to define a program of postwar social reforms.[11]

Léo Goldenberg, referred to above as Léo Hamon, the nom de

guerre he retained after the war, was born in France to parents exiled from Russia after 1905. A lawyer in his early thirties during the early years of the occupation, he was involved with Combat and with Ceux de la résistance, a non-Communist group in the northern zone. In 1943, he distinguished himself by leading five other Resistants into the Service du travail obligatoire (STO) offices in Paris after closing hours and burning an entire card index with tens of thousands of names of young Frenchmen eligible for forced labor in Germany.[12]

As a leader of Ceux de la résistance in 1944, Hamon became one of six directors—three Communists and three moderates—of the Comité parisien de libération (CPL). The committee, the local counterpart of the CNR, was charged with directing a popular insurrection in Paris at the moment of its liberation. Hamon supported such an insurrection but strongly disagreed with Communists who did not want to wait to coordinate action with the approaching Allies.

An uprising in fact broke out prematurely at the Paris prefecture of police on Saturday morning, August 19. At 6:00 A.M. the next day, after borrowing a tie for the occasion, Hamon led a small force of unarmed men into the Hotel de Ville, Paris's city hall, and occupied it in the name of the CPL and the provisional government of the Republic. It was, he explains, "an action heavy with symbolism."[13] Later that same day, he was one of three delegates sent by the CNR to meet with the Swedish consul general, Raoul Nordling, to arrange a cease-fire with the German military governor of Paris, General Dietrich von Choltitz. In the face of bitter Communist opposition to a truce, Hamon convinced most other Resistance leaders to accept it for a time. General Jacques Chaban-Delmas, de Gaulle's military delegate to the Forces françaises de l'intérieur (FFI) in Paris at the time, later recalled, "Thus Paris was liberated without being destroyed or its population massacred, and Léo Hamon is among the small number of men responsible for this immense good fortune."[14]

Gilbert Hirsch-Ollendorf, later known by his nom de guerre Gilbert Grandval, played a more military than political role in the general Resistance. A thirty-six-year-old businessman and pilot in 1940 and a member of a deeply patriotic Jewish family with roots in eastern France, he later recalled, "I was sickened by the capitulation of Pétain and outraged at the brutality of the German occupation and then the annexation of Alsace-Lorraine. I became a resistant immediately."[15] Like Hamon, he began with Ceux de la résistance in Paris. In 1943 in Lorraine, he helped organize the Forces françaises de l'intérieur, the unified internal military Resistance organization and final product of a merger under de Gaulle of the non-Communist Secret Army and the Communist Francs-tireurs et partisans (FTP). In November 1943, Grandval became the military chief of the entire FFI in region C, which included Alsace, Lorraine, Champagne, and the Argonne. Three months later, in a unique fusion of roles, he was named de Gaulle's personal military delegate to the same sector.[16]

Other Jews in the general non-Communist Resistance included Georges Altman, the Socialist editor of *Le Progrés de Lyon* before the war, who became an editor of *Franc-Tireur* and one of Jean-Pierre Lévy's top three assistants when Lévy himself was called to London. Raymond Samuel, later known as Raymond Aubrac, was an engineer from Alsace who planned many acts of sabotage of bridges and railroads for d'Astier's Libération-Sud, served on the staff of the Secret Army, was imprisoned with Jean Moulin in June 1943, and survived.[17] Léon-Maurice Nordmann, a prominent Parisian attorney and Socialist supporter of Léon Blum, was involved with the Musée de l'homme group, named for the museum in Paris where many of its leaders were employed. The group printed and distributed clandestine Resistance literature throughout Paris in 1941. Nordmann was one of seven victims executed for that activity on February 23, 1942. Also involved with the Musée de l'homme group was Renée Lévy, a teacher at the Lycée Victor Hugo until she was fired as a result of the racial laws. After the discovery of the Musée de l'homme group, she continued in other clandestine activities until her arrest in December 1941. She was sentenced to death by a military tribunal in Coblenz, Germany, and executed on August 31, 1943. Her last words were, "I am French and I have done well to serve my country. I only regret that I could not do more."[18] There were hundreds of others, in France, in London, and in Algeria.[19]

Of French Jews who fought with the Communist general Resistance, two, Roger Ginsburger (Villon) and Maurice Kriegel (Valrimont) were especially prominent. Ginsburger, the son of a rabbi, was born in Strasbourg and educated as an architect there and in Paris. He joined the Communist party in 1932. Subsequently known by his nom de guerre, Pierre Villon, he became the head in 1943 of the Front national, a grouping of primarily Communist organizations including the party itself, its trade union sections, and its armed Resistance units. The military arm of the Front national, Francs-tireurs et partisans, was the largest and most important armed Resistance organization in both zones. As the Front national and the FTP coordinated their efforts more closely with non-Communists, Villon became their representative on the CNR. In August 1944, he also served as the most important (because of his concurrent role with the CNR) of three chiefs, known as "the three *V*'s," of the Comité d'action militaire (COMAC), the military action committee for the liberation of Paris.[20] One of the other two chiefs, Maurice Kriegel (Valrimont), was also Jewish and Communist. The third chief, Jean de Vogüé (Vaillant), was neither.

Maurice Kriegel (Valrimont), like Villon from Strasbourg, was a Communist trade union leader before the war. He first entered the armed Resistance with d'Astier's non-Communist Libération-Sud in the unoccupied zone. He became a member of the staff of the Secret Army, and by the time of the liberation of Paris he had come to represent all armed Resistance forces from the southern zone at COMAC.[21] Vaillant represented the same forces from the north. The "three *V*'s" argued strenuously with Léo Hamon and his superiors on the timing of the insurrection in Paris. The events as they unfolded—insurrection, temporary truce, and liberation—were in part the product of that conflict.

Less well known than Villon and Valrimont but fully their equals in commitment and sacrifice were the hundreds of Jews, both French and foreign, who struggled and often died with the general Communist Resistance. Albert Ouzoulias (Colonel André), for example, the son of a French soldier killed in the First World War and himself an activist in the Communist youth movement in the 1930s, made a daring escape from a German prisoner-of-war camp in 1941. He commanded the Bataillons de la jeunesse, armed youth units affiliated with the Jeunesses communistes, until 1944, when he became an FTP commander in Paris.[22] Georges Politzer, an intellectual and longtime Communist militant, founded a Resistance journal in 1940 with his friend Jacques Solomon, a brilliant scientist and also a Communist. The two men were arrested in March 1942, tortured, and shot with other Resistants at Mont-Valérien on May 23 of the same year.[23] Valentin Feldman, born in Saint Petersburg in 1909, a graduate of the Lycée Henri IV in 1927, and a lycée teacher who lost his position because of the racial laws, was also a Communist militant long before the occupation. Like Politzer and Solomon, he produced clandestine publications in Rouen. Arrested in February 1942, he was executed, also at Mont-Valérien, on July 27. Just before his execution, he wrote on the walls of his cell, "My death is the most beautiful success of my life."[24]

Like Valentin Feldman, Joseph Epstein (Colonel Gilles) was a foreign Jew in the general Communist Resistance. Epstein was born in Poland in 1911. He became a Communist during his lycée years, emigrated to France for political reasons in 1932, and studied law at Bordeaux. Like so many of his Resistance comrades, he fought in the Spanish Civil War. During the occupation, he became a military chief of the FTP in the Paris region. He was captured in November 1943 and shot by the Germans at Mont-Valérien on April 11, 1944.[25] Years after his death, Albert Ouzoulias, who knew him well, called him "the greatest military tactician of the entire Resistance."[26]

Parallel to the general Communist Resistance and at times not clearly separable from it were several specifically Jewish Communist groupings. Jewish youth groups, for example, became increasingly militant in the second half of 1941, putting up anti-Nazi posters, distributing political tracts, sabotaging workshops where artisans, often Jewish immigrants, produced goods for the German army, directing older members into partisan units, and occasionally planning armed actions themselves. Many young people paid for these activities with their lives.[27]

For slightly older Communist immigrants wishing to fight the Nazis, the urban partisan units of the FTP-MOI were often an attractive option.[28] At first their assignments, always defined and controlled by the party or the FTP, resembled those of the youth groups. Militants distributed tracts and posters, sabotaged war production, put tacks in the way of German vehicles, destroyed road markers, and attempted to recruit anti-Nazi German soldiers for propaganda and espionage. The urban guerrilla actions in which they ultimately specialized, however, began in the late summer of 1941 and became increasingly frequent in 1942. By the summer of 1942, there were five FTP-MOI units in Paris. Perhaps 90 percent of the fighters in the First (Hungarian-Romanian) Detachment were Jewish, and the figure approached 100 percent in the Second (mostly Polish) Detachment.[29] The Third Detachment was Italian, and the Fourth, a mixed group, was largely Spanish and Armenian. The fifth unit, too small to be classified as a detachment, was Bulgarian.[30]

Until at least the middle of 1942, most foreign Jewish Communist Resistants, like their non-Jewish immigrant comrades, were motivated primarily by politics. Most had been devoted militants before the war, and many were veterans of the International Brigades in the Spanish Civil War. Many were undoubtedly affected by and resentful of Nazi and French anti-Semitism, but they had been politicized long before. During the first two years of the occupation, they often failed to perceive a Nazi menace to *all* Jews in France. They saw a danger that affected immigrant Jewish workers, as opposed to Jewish capitalists, and they equated it with a threat to the working class as a whole. Their presence in specifically Jewish units resulted not from a particularly keen sense of Jewishness but from their commitment to Communism, plus other factors such as lack of fluency in French, the geography of residence or workplace, the influence of family members or predominantly Jewish friends, prewar affiliations that were often traceable back to their countries of origin, or, in some cases, precise party orders or pure chance.[31]

After the July 1942 roundup of foreign Jewish men, women, and children in Paris, FTP-MOI units began to swell with a new type of recruit—what one historian has called "la génération de la rafle."[32] These newcomers were survivors of the roundup—young men and women who had often lost entire families and were determined to seek revenge. Of those later executed with Thomas Elek, for example, seventeen-year-old Wolf Wajsbrot, born in Poland, had watched from hiding while his mother and father were arrested and carted off to Drancy on July 16, 1942. He wandered desolately around Paris for a time before drifting into an FTP-MOI unit. Twenty-year-old Lajb, or Léon, Goldberg, from Lodz, lost his entire family on July 16—his parents and two brothers. Twenty-one-year-old Maurice Fingercwajg, from Warsaw, lost his parents and two brothers. Nineteen-year-old Marcel Rayman lost his father, also from Warsaw.

Of these and countless other young men and women, Adam Rayski later remembered: "At the age of fourteen or fifteen, they became adults in the space of one night. Without being Communists they massively joined our ranks, our youth organization being well established in a majority of the popular quarters of the capital."[33] In order to be trusted and accepted in clandestine units in 1942 and 1943, these young recruits studied Communist doctrine and often found hope and consolation within the fold, but their initial motivation was more personal than political. By the end of 1943, as the Communist party struggled to replace hundreds of losses from FTP-MOI units and became ever more committed to mass insurrection, ideological preparation became still less important, and all volunteers, including non-Communists, were eligible to join more loosely structured *groupes de combat,* the Union de la jeunesse juive, or the Milice patriotique juive.[34]

Abraham Lissner, a foreign Jewish Communist Resistant and a director of FTP-MOI groups, claimed after the war that Jewish fighters were involved in 459 military actions in Paris between March 1942 and November 1943.[35] Only a tiny fraction of those actions can be mentioned. On August 11, 1942, Resistants from the largely Jewish Second Detachment placed a bomb in a German hotel near the Iena métro stop. On December 12, they threw grenades into a German army unit in the Place de la Nation. At the Porte Dauphine on Christmas Day 1942, they attacked a truck full of German soldiers, again with grenades. The following day, they threw a grenade into a German restaurant on avenue Hoche.[36]

Incidents and casualties multiplied in 1943. On March 9, Wolf Wajsbrot threw a grenade into a train full of German soldiers in Versailles, causing, in Lissner's words, "undescribable damage."[37] On March 16, a thirty-three-year-old Bessarabian Jew and veteran of the Spanish Civil War named Paul Silberman threw a bomb into a line of German soldiers outside the Rex movie theater. Although the bomb did its damage, it blew up prematurely, injuring Silberman as well. He died in captivity, without medical care, two days later. His wife, also a partisan, could not attend his burial.[38]

By mid-1943, the largely Jewish First and Second Detachments were decimated. Survivors were scattered among three other units, the Third (Italian) Detachment; the Fourth, now known as the groupe des dérailleurs—literally, the derailment group—under a Romanian Jew named Francisc Boczor; and the équipe spéciale, under Marcel Rayman.[39] A majority of those in the last two groups were Jewish. These units, with no more than sixty-five fighters and support personnel, were virtually the only armed Communist Resistance presence in Paris from June to November 1943.[40]

Despite severe shortages of weapons, ammunition, and men, FTP-MOI actions by mid-1943 were even more daring, spectacular, and frequent, averaging fifteen a month. A group led by Rayman, for example, threw a bomb into the car of General von Schaumburg, the German commander of Greater Paris, on July 28.[41] A mixed team including Rayman, Celestino Alfonso (Spanish), Spartaco Fontanot (Italian), and Arsène Tchakarian (Armenian) shot and killed SS General Julius Ritter, the hated chief of the Nazi forced-labor program in France, on September 28 in front of his residence on the rue Pétrarque. Ritter was the representative in France of Fritz Saukel, the chief of Germany's slave labor recruitment program. He was also a personal friend of Hitler. The FTP-MOI partisans considered his execution a great triumph. It would be among their last. After the mass arrests in November which included Thomas Elek's group, most FTP-MOI survivors were transferred to other cities. The estimated 150 to 200 younger and less political Jews who participated in the final liberation of Paris were members not of FTP-MOI but of newer groups, especially the recently formed Milices patriotiques juives.[42]

Many women, including many Jewish women, contributed to FTP-MOI actions. Women participated in the general Resistance as well, as messengers, liaison agents, propagandists, spies, saboteurs, and, occasionally, armed soldiers. But the particular conditions of the FTP-MOI actions created a special role for women. Small teams of men moving to attack a German post could not easily carry weapons through the city streets. Women, arousing less suspicion, carried guns or bombs in their handbags, shopping baskets, or skirts, handed them to men at the critical moment, and then retrieved the guns as the men fled. After any incident, the Germans surrounded and combed the entire district. The women, now alone, had to slip through the net with their precious bundles. It was not flamboyant work, but it was critical and required nerves of steel. For as Arsène Tchakarian, a survivor of the final Boczor group, later told an interviewer, "The women who carried arms performed a much more dangerous work than those who used them. If [the women] were taken, they could not defend themselves."[43]

Many were taken. Olga Bancic, for example, a Romanian Jewess who carried dynamite and arms in about 100 partisan attacks, was arrested in November 1943 with Thomas Elek's group. Tried and convicted, she was decapitated with an axe, in the Nazi fashion, in Stuttgart on May 10, 1944. She left behind a husband and a two-year-old daughter.[44] The Jewish Communist militants Simone Schloss and France Bloch were also decapitated, in July 1942 and February 1943, respectively. The twenty-nine-year-old liaison agent and arms carrier Hania Mansfeld, better known by her nom de guerre Hélène Kro, was captured by the Gestapo in the act of transporting dynamite. She was a former seamstress with a husband who was a prisoner of war and a four-year-old son in hiding. Fearing to reveal her comrades under torture, she threw herself from a fourth-floor window to her death.[45] And there were many others.

FTP-MOI units of foreign Communist Resistants operated in several cities other than Paris during the war. Partisans in these units were of mixed origins, although foreign Jews seem to have formed a majority in most cases. In Lyon, for example, the Carmagnole unit of about forty partisans in the summer of 1944 seems to have been from 65 to 80 percent Jewish.[46] In Grenoble, the Liberté detachment, with twenty-five to thirty mostly foreign partisans in November 1943, may also have been as much as 80 percent Jewish.[47] Most of its leaders, including Raymond Sacks from Poland, Herbert Hertz from Germany, Étienne Goldberger from Hungary, and Isy Shernetsky from Russia, were foreign Jews.[48]

In Toulouse, the 35th Brigade, described by one historian as "the best example of the participation of the immigrants of Central Europe in a regional resistance," may also have been as much as 60 percent Jewish—volunteers from the Spanish Civil War who settled in southwestern France, refugees from the occupation of Paris in 1940 or from the July 1942 roundup, and escapees from the expulsions of foreign Jews in August 1942.[49] The most famous member of the 35th Brigade was Marcel Langer, a Polish Jew and veteran of Spain caught with a suitcase of explosives in a secondary railroad station in Toulouse on February 6, 1943. Langer was tried by a French court, convicted of transporting explosives, and guillotined on July 23. In reprisal, Langer's comrades killed the French special prosecutor Lespinasse on October 10.[50]

Foreign Jews in Lyon, Grenoble, Toulouse, Marseille, Nice, and elsewhere fought beside Communists from all nations. As in Paris, partisans threw bombs at German vehicles, killed individual German soldiers and French miliciens, sabotaged factories, destroyed bridges, and derailed trains.[51] Also as in Paris, they acted almost alone at times—in Grenoble between September 1943 and March 1944, and in Lyon after May 1944. For several units, the moment of greatest glory came during the Liberation. Carmagnole partisans, for example, found themselves in Villeurbanne, adjacent to Lyon, when workers launched a spontaneous anti-German insurrection on August 24, 1944, a few days before the Allies' arrival. At last, lonely urban partisans received broad popular support. They responded by organizing units of volunteers, building barricades, seizing municipal offices, and holding out against German soldiers for several days.[52] About 1,000 Jews of all political persuasions participated in the liberation of Villeurbanne and other towns in the region.[53]

As in Paris, women served in support roles and sometimes in battle. Some died in combat, like nineteen-year-old Jeanine Sonntag, killed on August 24, 1944, at Saint-Genis-Laval. Others fought and survived. All would have agreed with combatant Dina Krischer, born in France to Polish Jewish immigrants, when she later declared, "I who am not a Communist and never have been . . . I am proud to have belonged to the FTP-MOI, and especially to *Carmagnole*. I have the sense of having defended my dignity as a French Jewish woman, and avenged so many of our people."[54]

Young foreigners, Jews and non-Jews alike, in Communist FTP-MOI units chose a particularly arduous and dangerous form of resistance. Between military actions, they were required for reasons of security to live alone in isolated apartments and renounce all family and social contacts. Forbidden even from going to a café, restaurant, or movie theater with a friend or spouse—rules that were occasionally honored in the breach—and often unaware of the whereabouts and, if Jewish, even of the existence of their families, these high-spirited and courageous young people endured an isolation that was often more daunting than the military actions, which may have provided temporary relief.[55] And for more than 50 percent of them, torture and death awaited—by execution, as a hostage, or in deportation. Their death rate far exceeded that of about 24 percent for the Jewish community in general, and even that of 41 to 45 percent for the foreign Jews in France—figures that include the very young, the old, and the sick. For arrested Jewish Resistants, also, punishment often included the deportation of their families. These able-bodied young people might have chosen to hide and live out the war in relative safety. They chose resistance instead, and they paid a heavy price.

Jews in Communist urban Resistance groups have been criticized both as Communists and as Jews. As Communists, they have been charged with putting the interests of the party and the Soviet Union ahead of all else, and with provoking the Germans into acts of bloody reprisal for no clear military purpose. As Jews, they have been censured for focusing on military objectives rather than on rescue—a charge that, curiously enough, is leveled at them much more often than at Jews who participated in the general Resistance. The purpose here is not to defend or condemn the choices they made, but to point out that they chose to act when they might have remained passive. They played a significant role in the armed French Resistance, in proportions of their overall population that clearly exceeded those of the native French.

Still more specifically Jewish than any immigrant Communist Resistance units were the various Zionist forces that fought the Germans in the *maquis,* wild and isolated rural areas, especially in the department of the Tarn and in the Cévennes in south central France. Many of these partisans were dedicated immigrant Zionists with a broad diversity of political orientations ranging from revisionist Zionism through several shades of socialism. Exceptions included individuals such as the Armée juive military chief Jacques Lazarus, a career officer from an old French family who had been retired by the racial laws; fighters from the EIF, or Jewish Boy Scouts, many of whom were French-born; and, by August 1944, many local non-Jewish peasants who joined the nearest maquis force in their eagerness to escape labor conscription and fight against the Germans. Despite the diversity of backgrounds, however, most Jews in these units were highly motivated by their Jewish heritage and consciously chose involvement with specifically Jewish groups rather than with the general non-Communist Resistance. As Lazarus himself later explained, "Our goal was not to support a kind of separatism, a racism in reverse. But, hunted as Jews, we wanted to show the enemy that it was also as Jews that we fought."[56]

In late June 1940, just days after the armistice, young Zionists began to gather in Toulouse. Special leaders of the group were the Russian-born journalist and demobilized soldier David Knout and his wife Ariane, and the engineer Abraham Polonski and his wife Eugénie.[57] Some of the young people were revisionist Zionists; others supported Socialist Zionist groups such as Poalé-Zion and Hashomer Hatzair. From their cooperative efforts came an urban organization called Main forte, directed toward assistance and rescue of Jewish refugees. By autumn, they began to focus on preparation for armed resistance as well. The Armée juive was born.

For the next three years, military leaders of the Armée juive organized young people in Toulouse, Nice, Lyon, and Grenoble into the commando groups called groupes francs. Although they continued to hide and provision fugitives while escorting others into Spain or Switzerland, an equally important objective became the recruiting of partisans and their training in weaponry, military tactics, and discipline for eventual group combat against the German army in the countryside. Knout and Polonski also expected that a "Jewish army" would be useful after the war in the creation of a Jewish state in Palestine.[58] Besides the French flag, their units trained and fought under a Jewish flag—a blue star of David on a white field. Recruits underwent an elaborate and mysterious secret initiation ceremony in which they faced their special flag and swore an oath on a Hebrew

Bible. Recruits who were Zionists also swore allegiance to a future Jewish state in Palestine.[59]

During the winter of 1943–44, Jacques Lazarus trained one of the first maquis units of the Armée juive at Bic, near Alban, twenty-nine kilometers east of Albi (Tarn). Another unit closely coordinated with the Armée juive, and linked also with the Service André, was established on the Cévennes plateau near Le Chambon-sur-Lignon.[60] In addition, the Armée juive during the same winter established close ties to partisan units with three other affiliations: EIF, MJS, and Poalé-Zion. There were two EIF groups with about thirty Scout-partisans, mostly from the former farm-residences at Lautrec, Frette-serpes, and Charry. They trained and lived in dilapidated abandoned buildings of La Malquière and Lacado, in the vicinity of the Black Mountain near Vabre (Tarn).[61]

Contacts between maquis units of the Armée juive and the EIF grew until cooperation was formalized by written agreement on June 1, 1944. Coordination with the MJS also increased, and an integrated body called the Organisation juive de combat (OJC) resulted. During that same summer, Jewish maquis groups of the OJC also developed effective working relationships with local FFI units of the general non-Communist and Communist Resistance operating in their region under the command of Pierre Dunoyer de Segonzac.

At least 400 partisans are estimated to have fought with the OJC.[62] The period of greatest military activity was the summer of 1944, after the Allies landed in Normandy in June and on beaches in southern France in August. As the Germans retreated through France, groupes francs of the Armée juive fought as part of the FFI in the liberation of Paris, Lyon, Grenoble, Nice, and Toulouse. An EIF maquis unit of about 60 partisans became the Marc Haguenau Company in June and saw combat around Vabre.[63] Its well-disciplined members were assigned the dangerous task of retrieving supplies delivered by parachute to the local FFI. The company's proudest moment was the capture on August 19 outside Mazamet, near Castres (Tarn), of a German train loaded with 60 soldiers and considerable supplies of weapons, ammunition, and food. Two days later, as an integral part of Segonzac's force of about 350 FFI men, the company marched into a liberated Castres to receive the surrender of a German garrison of 4,000 soldiers. Many partisans from the OJC went on to fight, and some to die, with the regular French army in Alsace and in western Germany. But nothing later compared to those first victories in southern France, when Jewish partisans, many of them immigrants and all wearing blue and white armbands, triumphantly informed terrified German prisoners from the captured train, "Ich bin Jude," and were subsequently welcomed as heroes by jubilant crowds in Castres.[64]

Different from Jewish Communist and Zionist groups but still classifiable as specifically Jewish Resistants were the several hundred young people in Algeria who began to gather together as early as October 1940 to coordinate opposition to the Vichy regime. As seen, Algerian Jews had lost their French nationality by the repeal of the Crémieux decree on October 7, 1940. They were also subject to the same racial laws that applied in metropolitan France. As a result, most were ardent anti-Vichyites.

Among the several clandestine Jewish groups to emerge in Algeria in 1940 was the Groupe Géo-Gras, named after the unsuspecting director and coach at a gymnasium in Algiers where some 250 activists met and trained. The young men received help especially from the brothers Raphaël and Stéphane Aboulker. Another group consisted of Jewish students unable to attend the University of Algiers because of Vichy's numerus clausus for Jews. Still another student group existed in Oran. Resistance leaders included, in Algiers, Doctor Henri Aboulker and his twenty-three-year-old son José, a medical student, and in Oran, Roger Carcassonne, a young industrialist. The primary purpose of these groups was to prepare a plan of action, in coordination with non-Jewish Resistants, to help the Allies during Operation Torch, the landings in North Africa. The great moment arrived in the early hours of November 8, 1942. As Allied forces landed on Algerian beaches west of Algiers, about 400 local Resistants, of whom roughly 250 to 300 were Jews, seized buildings of strategic importance throughout the city from startled Vichy forces.[65] Nowhere in mainland France was this proportion of Jews in the armed Resistance equaled, and nowhere were Jewish efforts less rewarded. For despite the Allied presence, the racial laws remained in effect in North Africa under the American and British-supported François Darlan and Henri Giraud administrations. They were abolished only in the spring of 1943; the Crémieux decree granting citizenship to Jews in Algeria was not reinstated until October 20.

Historians studying Jews and the Resistance in France inevitably address three points: the definition and nature of resistance, the existence of a "Jewish" Resistance, and the ultimate usefulness of the armed Resistance to Jews in general. The first two points have been discussed. Certainly resistance took many forms, and the thousands of Jews in France who refused to register for the census, wear the star, use only legal documents, or remain only at legal residences— Jews, in other words, who defied the government and struggled to survive—exhibited admirable courage and imagination. They "resisted." Thousands of others who extended that defiance to benefit others—who hid and looked after children, produced and distributed false papers, and escorted fugitives across frontiers—were even more certainly Resistants and heroes of great stature who risked and often lost their lives to help others. The term "armed Resistance" applies to those who resorted to arms and endorsed violence in the struggle against the oppressor. They were no more and no less courageous than rescuers. They were simply different.

Did the armed Resistance, either the general or the specifically Jewish, help Jews in France? Insofar as it contributed to the German defeat and the liberation of the nation—its primary purpose for existence—it most certainly helped them indirectly. For more direct help, however, the *general* Resistance offered little. The case of the specifically Jewish *armed* Resistance is more complex. Certainly individual armed Resistants, especially in specifically Jewish Communist and Zionist units, contributed to nonmilitary efforts to issue false documents, escort fugitives across frontiers, rescue children, and print news sheets warning of the danger. Indeed, the lines between rescue groups and armed units are often difficult to separate, for personnel overlapped. The Marc Haguenau Company drew many of its fighters from young Scouts in the Sixiéme who were also working to rescue Jews; the urban groupes francs and maquis units of the Armée juive called upon Zionist rescuers; the FTP-MOI recruited among the Jewish Communist Solidarité; a maquis unit in the Cévennes was linked to the Service André rescue group; the groupe franc of the Armée juive in Nice interacted with the Maurice Cachoud rescue group. But even specifically Jewish armed partisan units did not attack deportation trains, prisons, internment camps, hospitals, or UGIF children's homes to save Jews. Partisans rarely assassinated Nazis or French collaborators known to be persecutors of Jews.

There were some exceptions. The groupe franc in Nice, for example, not only targeted White Russian anti-Jewish informers, as seen, but placed bombs in several locales owned or frequented by known persecutors of Jews. Communists in Lyon killed an anti-Jewish informer as well as a Vichy official responsible for the arrests and pillaging of many Jews. Communist groupes de combat attacked UGIF offices in Marseille in December 1943 and in Lyon in January 1944, seizing files and lists with the names and addresses of thousands of Jewish clients.[66] There were other cases, but in the light of what is now known about the Holocaust, they were few. Many individuals, looking back, regret that they did not do more. They agree with Henri Rosencher, whose parents, helpless deaf-mute brother, and brother's family were deported while he was away fighting the Germans. Rosencher later wrote, "I reproach myself for my egocentrism, for my egoism. I chose to be Don Quixote and fight against windmills. I should have been a Sancho Panza with his humble effectiveness."[67]

There are several reasons why armed Jewish Resistants failed to employ their weapons to help their people. First, every armed action brought danger of arrest, torture, and betrayal of the entire group. For security reasons, armed Resistants often made a decision to leave clandestine rescue and welfare work to others and to know as little about it as possible. Since so many had previously been involved in rescue, they knew that others were continuing the work. For themselves, it seemed best to remain apart.

Léon Habif and Georges Goutchtat, members of a Communist groupe de combat in Lyon, broke that policy when they acted on their own initiative to rescue six Jewish children scheduled for immediate deportation from the local Hôpital de l'Antiquaille. Thanks to the help of a nun at the hospital who had originally told them of the danger, the children were saved, but Habif and Goutchtat were severely reprimanded for a breach of discipline. They had endangered their group.[68]

The most fundamental reason for the reluctance to use arms to protect Jews and for the willingness to leave rescue to others, however, was the failure of most Resistants, both Jewish and non-Jewish, to grasp the full consequences of deportation. Despite their greater politicization, most Resistants knew no more about gas chambers and mass murder than average uninvolved civilians. Some, because of their isolation and their clandestine life, knew even less. A partisan attack on an internment camp or a deportation train would involve a high number of civilian casualties, including women and children. Those casualties could only be justified if the victims were known to be destined for death in deportation. No one could believe that that was precisely where they were headed.

CONCLUSION

IN CAMBRIDGE, MASSACHUSETTS, LONG AFTER THE WAR, PROFESSOR Stanley Hoffmann of Harvard University addressed himself to his memories of persecution. Of his own background, he wrote, "I remained in France [as a teenager] throughout the war as a Frenchified Austrian—French by education and feeling, Austrian by passport only, a partly Jewish alien in a xenophobic anti-Semitic police state." To his American readers and, by extension, to citizens of other countries that escaped defeat and occupation by the Germans, he advised:

> For Americans—who have never experienced sudden, total defeat and the almost overnight disappearance of their accustomed political elites; who have never lived under foreign occupation; who do not know what Nazi pressure meant; who have never had an apparently legal government, headed by a national hero and claiming total obedience, sinking deeper and deeper into a morass of impotence, absurdity, and crime; who have never had to worry first and last about food and physical survival—the wise and gentle warning of Anthony Eden must be heeded: do not judge too harshly.[1]

Keeping the warning in mind, with its succinct reminder of the context of the criminal actions against the Jews, how do we finally assess the Holocaust in France?

More than 24 percent of the approximately 330,000 Jews in France at the end of 1940 were deported or died within the country during the Holocaust. They totaled nearly 80,000 men, women, and children. More than 77,000 of them were murdered in deportation, executed in French prisons, or killed from starvation, exhaustion, and disease in French internment camps. The reasons for their deaths have been discussed. Certainly the German occupiers of France bear the primary responsibility. Following the general policy initiated by Adolf Hitler and defined by Heinrich Himmler, Reinhard Heydrich, Adolf Eichmann, and others, German anti-Jewish agents in France rounded up Jews or, much more frequently, demanded that French police perform the dirty work. Nazis then organized the deportations and murdered Jews when they arrived in the east.

The French government at Vichy, however, and many French civilians share the burden of guilt. Vichy politicians began preparing racial laws before any had been decreed by the German occupiers of the northern zone, and quite apart from any German demands. Vichy bureaucrats decreed and performed detailed censuses of Jews in France, and later made the data available to those who would arrest and deport them. Vichy police rounded up and interned foreign Jews in the southern zone at a time when their counterparts in the German-occupied north remained quite free. At first Jews were seized because they were enemy nationals, but long after the armistice they were still being held, often in life-threatening conditions, *explicitly* because they were Jews.

French offenses did not end with racial laws and internment. Vichy officials at the highest levels ordered French police to round up mostly foreign Jewish men in Paris in 1941 and made no protest when they and many French Jewish men were deported in March 1942. In July 1942, those same French authorities ordered the arrests in Paris of more foreign Jews, this time including women and their often French-born children. French police duly complied by seizing 12,884 people. Officials then demonstrated appalling contempt for human life by depositing more than 8,000 prisoners in the Vélodrome d'Hiver, with little preparation for their maintenance. Prior to the arrests, Pierre Laval, the head of government, had urged the Nazis to deport the children, before the Germans had decided what to do with them. They were deported.

Also in July, Vichy authorities agreed to supply the Nazis in the north with foreign Jews from the south, from the so-called free zone where the Germans had as yet no jurisdiction. These Jews too were deported. First to be delivered were recent Jewish immigrants already in Vichy internment camps. Most were refugees from the Third Reich or from German-occupied countries in the east; they included the German Jews expelled from their homes in October 1940 and dumped by the Nazis in France. They were followed by other immigrants especially arrested throughout the unoccupied zone for that purpose. More than 11,000 people were sent north to Drancy before the Germans occupied the southern zone in November. The expulsions occurred in conditions that replicated exactly those of the Nazi deportation trains. French police locked men, women, and children into cattle cars, with little food or water, soiled straw on the floor, and a bucket for their bodily functions. As in the Third Reich, social workers and other civilians of goodwill were not permitted to alleviate their suffering.

Under more or less severe German pressure, Vichy officials then proceeded to order French police to make more and more roundups. Jews from Poland, the Greater Reich, and the Soviet Union were joined by Jews from Romania, Bulgaria, Belgium, the Netherlands, Greece, and, ever more frequently in 1944, French Jews as well. This gradual escalation had a devastating effect, for Jews who perceived that they did not fit into a category eligible for arrest often neglected to hide and were caught when the rules changed. In addition, news of a roundup in one city, if it was known at all, was often perceived as a local aberration rather than a warning. Meanwhile, Vichy officials ordered gendarmes to guard Drancy and other places where Jews were confined and to accompany deportation trains to the French-German frontier. The manpower supplied made arrests and deportations possible. As seen in Nice in September 1943, understaffed Nazis functioned poorly without help.

And French civilians? Journalists fed the vast anti-Semitic propaganda machine, convincing citizens that Jews were their enemy and the cause of all their troubles. Tens of thousands of collaborators joined Fascist leagues or the Milice, in whose ranks they hunted for Resistants, escaped Allied prisoners of war, draft evaders, and Jews.[2] Informers flourished, persuaded that betrayal was their patriotic duty. Gendarmes and municipal police obeyed orders, warning a few friends, perhaps, of a pending arrest, or turning their backs while a few charming little children and their mothers escaped, but knocking down other doors, searching apartments, interrogating neighbors, and catching their prey. And many average citizens, if they did not actually condone what they saw, simply closed their eyes to it, grateful, perhaps, that they could believe themselves morally uninvolved.

The converse of the terrible death rate is the fact that 76 percent of the Jews in France, or some 250,000 people, survived. How did that happen?

Some of the explanation lies with the physical characteristics of the country and in the complex chronology of the persecution itself. Unlike Belgium and the Netherlands, where overall Jewish deportation and death rates were much higher, France is a large country with extensive tracts of remote, often mountainous terrain favorable to hiding.[3] France also borders two countries that were neutral during the Second World War and were able, if not always willing, to receive fugitives. Also in comparison to Belgium and the Netherlands, far fewer German personnel were allocated to France after the armistice in relation to the size and population of the country. Those devoted to hunting Jews were not numerically adequate to perform the task.[4] They could not hope to comb the country thoroughly without French cooperation.

For the leaders of Nazi anti-Jewish units, securing that cooperation became a constant problem, requiring patience, tact, cajoling, prodding, threats, and compromise. Most of all, it required time—valuable time, especially in 1943, that Heinz Röthke and Aloïs Brunner could have used to plan their own anti-Jewish raids. For with regard to the Jews, Laval had his own agenda: that French Jewish adults and their children should not be arrested and deported, and that French police should not be used in major roundups unless they were so ordered by their own superiors, for clearly defined actions.

Laval frequently compromised on these principles. He allowed French police to arrest *individual* Jews, including citizens, for specific or alleged violations, and he tolerated limited daily arrests of Jews without charges by special anti-Jewish units like the Permilleux service in Paris or the Milice elsewhere. Vichy officials protested only slightly when their wishes were ignored, and French gendarmes continued to guard trains that they knew were carrying French Jews. In 1944, Laval even permitted French police to participate in roundups of native Jews on specific lists. But until then, French Jews, with the tragic exception of the children of immigrants, clearly benefited from a limited protection. Without it, more would have been arrested and the overall Jewish death rate would have been higher.

The existence of an Italian occupation zone in southeastern France between November 1942 and September 1943 also affected survival rates by buying time for the Jews. Some 50,000 people lived free from danger there for many months. The menace of deportation returned when the Italians withdrew, and many were caught unprepared, but each day that had passed without arrests meant fewer arrests overall.

The passing of time had other consequences. Jews and non-Jews alike had time to learn about the deportation of women, children, and old people incapable of labor and to ponder its meaning. Jews were able to make plans and secure false papers. Non-Jews could reflect and ask themselves whether the official anti-Semitic and anti-foreign rhetoric that they perhaps applauded in the abstract justified the dreadful suffering of human beings that they heard about and sometimes even observed personally. Churchmen of goodwill had time to exercise a moral leadership, speaking out against deportations and encouraging alternative attitudes and behavior. And perhaps most important of all, the Allies had time to win victories and convince the French that the Germans were not invincible, the Vichy regime might not last forever, and collaboration might not be the most opportune route to follow. Laval himself seems not to have heeded the warning. In early 1944, when he surely knew that Auschwitz meant certain death for most and that the Germans would lose the war, he actually intensified rather than diminished French police pressure on native Jews. Members of the Milice and other fanatic collaborators were delighted. But many municipal police and gendarmes, along with prefects, mayors, and other local Vichyite bureaucrats, certainly read the handwriting on the wall and made some adjustments.

While the technical reality of the persecution helps explain survival rates, so too does the composition of the Jewish community in France. Roughly 59 percent of that community, or about 195,000 people at the end of 1940, were French citizens. The figures include naturalized adults and the French-born children of immigrants. Except for the French children of immigrants, this group benefited from feeble Vichy protective measures, with the effect on survival rates that has been seen.

About 41 percent of the Jewish community, or some 135,000 people, were foreign-born. In addition to the fact that they were prime Vichy targets, foreign Jews, with their revealing characteristics, fewer non-Jewish contacts, limited financial resources, and slight firsthand experience of France outside the old Jewish neighborhoods, had far more difficulty finding hiding places. They suffered much more than French Jews, proportionate to their numbers. From 41 percent to 45 percent of them were murdered during the war, compared with 9 percent to 12.6 percent of French Jews.[5] If their proportion of the Jewish population had been higher, as it was in Belgium, the overall death rate in France would most certainly have been higher.[6] On the other hand, if their proportion had been lower, as it was in Italy, the overall death rate in France would probably have been lower.[7]

In addition to the size and topography of their adopted country, however, foreign Jews in France had certain other slight advantages over their counterparts elsewhere in Western Europe, including Italy. A larger percentage of them had arrived as immigrants looking for work in the 1920s or even earlier, rather than as refugees escaping the Nazis after 1933 or even 1940. They had had more time and opportunity to put down roots, learn the language and customs, and make the local contacts indispensable for survival. Most men knew a few non-Jewish employers, coworkers, or political activists. Women knew shopkeepers, concierges, or their children's teachers. Their children often had the most contacts of all. In many cases, that knowledge saved their lives.

Specifically in Paris, the large size of the foreign Jewish community and the existence of many Jewish social organizations had both advantages and disadvantages, but the long-term balance was probably favorable. At first, their numbers provided immigrant Jews with a dangerous illusion of strength and security. As in Eastern Europe, they could not imagine that the Nazis could harm so many, and they believed that if they could stick together and hold out, they could survive. That illusion was clearly fatal, but often temporary. As foreign Jews perceived the need to hide, they found support within their community. A Jewish friend had a contact or an idea; a Jewish agency could supply false documents, or a free meal; a Jewish rescue network could hide a child or a grandparent.

Some Jewish leaders, from rabbis to social workers, have been criticized for not warning and dispersing their people, for keeping synagogues, schools, orphanages, and soup kitchens open too long, for fostering that illusion of strength in numbers. With the benefit of hindsight, we know that there is some truth in the criticism. Many Jews died from these mistakes. Some were caught in synagogues or social centers when they were raided. Others were lulled into a sense of security and discouraged from hiding by the sight of Jewish institutions still in operation. But many more were quietly encouraged to hide and were then provided with the means to survive clandestinely—the false documents, the free meals, the health care at local dispensaries, the weekly stipend, the moral support. As Doctor Eugène Minkowski of OSE testified after the war:

> More than once we asked ourselves if it would not be better to close the popular canteens where the Gestapo had made several raids. The words of the director of one of those centers come back to me in this regard: "Without doubt," he said, "that would be prudent, but my clients, especially the elderly, without lodging, without defenses, have told me that if we close, they would turn themselves in voluntarily to be sent to Drancy. Under those conditions, I cannot take such a decision."[8]

In addition, many native and foreign Jews in France were directly hidden by Jewish rescue networks. Their exact numbers will never be known, for many reasons. Few networks kept complete records. Many fugitives were helped by overlapping or cooperating organizations, or by different agencies at different times. They were later claimed as clients by several groups. Those directly saved—that is, those for whom a rescue network located a hiding place, escorted them there, and then provisioned them throughout the war—certainly represent a minority of those who survived. They may number several tens of thousands, of the 250,000 survivors. But they also often represent the most helpless—individuals without resources who could not have made it on their own. They owe their lives to the extraordinary courage and commitment of others.

Finally, Jewish survival in France depended upon attitudes within the non-Jewish community. Whether hidden by rescue organizations or making their own arrangements for family members, many Jews had to find willing hosts. Many more who simply moved independently to a new address needed help with documents plus some assurance that they would not be reported as "newcomers." Dependence upon at least a mild tolerance was total. Survival rates in France suggest that large numbers of Jews received it.

In 1977, the researcher and historian Lucien Steinberg came to a similar conclusion:

I would like to emphasize that the majority of the Jews saved in France do not owe their rescue to Jewish organizations. The various Jewish bodies which worked with such great dedication managed to save only a few tens of thousands, while the others were saved mostly thanks to the assistance of the French population. In many cases, groups of Jews lived in small villages. Every one of the Jews was convinced that no one in that area knew their true identity; after the war it turned out that everyone knew that they were Jews.[9]

The young Stanley Hoffmann encountered similar informal assistance during the war and judged it to be representative. Years later, he wrote:

In my memory, the schoolteacher—now seventy-five, and still vibrant—who taught me French history, gave me hope in the worst days, dried my tears when my best friend was deported along with his mother, and gave false papers to my mother and me so that we could flee a Gestapo-infested city in which the complicity of friends and neighbors was no longer a guarantee of safety—this man wipes out all the bad moments, and the humiliations, and the terrors. He and his gentle wife were not Resistance heroes, but if there is an average Frenchman, it was this man who was representative of his nation.[10]

The historian and former Jewish Resistant Léon Poliakov agreed, writing in 1949 of "the good sense . . . the profound humanity of the immense majority of the French people."[11]

In 1940, such attitudes might not have been predictable. The resentment of Jews and foreigners that had permeated the general population throughout the depression years of the 1930s had been exacerbated by the military defeat and by the Vichy regime. Few French men and women protested when foreign Jews, along with many other refugees and immigrants, were interned in the south. Few knew, or cared to know, when they starved or froze to death in French camps, well out of public view. Few protested the racial laws or worried about economic and psychological suffering that they rarely witnessed. Not many were concerned about the arrests in Paris in 1941 of mostly foreign Jewish young men. Nor did they worry when those same usually young men were deported between March and July 1942, allegedly for labor. After all, more than a million and a half young French prisoners of war were already in German prison camps. Why, the argument ran, should the French worry about immigrants, many of them without papers, when they had all they could do taking care of themselves?

Attitudes changed when suffering became unavoidably visible. They changed also when the victims were no longer strong young men, but *families*. When women, children, and old people were packed into sealed freight cars and delivered to the Nazis, many French men and women experienced a sense of shame. That shame was deepened by the public protests of churchmen who finally broke the silence and reminded the French to think for themselves. And so the climate of sullen resentment shifted into one of benign neglect, vague goodwill, and, occasionally, active support.

EIF child rescuers Shatta and Bouli Simon well understood that non-Jewish attitudes changed when persecution acquired a visible and personal dimension. Shatta Simon recalled after the war:

> The Germans [after they occupied the southern zone] must have noticed that very often their arrest plans were thwarted because the French living among Jews whom they knew could hardly keep from warning them of great danger; thus they [the Germans] operated with [French] people brought to town from elsewhere, who had to deal with people whom they did not know and to whom they were indifferent.

Toward the end of 1943, the Simons went to the local prefect, whom they called a Pétainist, and asked quite openly for 150 ration cards for Jewish children hiding in Christian institutions. They explain, "We had the experience that in that region we could talk clearly to the French, even the collaborators, when it was a question of children: they always agreed that they should be saved."[12] The prefect not only agreed to supply the cards regularly but arranged that the Simons should not have to carry them through the streets. He asked the mayor of Moissac to deliver them!

That prefect was replaced in 1944 by one known to be much more fanatically Fascist. Several German divisions were stationed in the area, and two Resistants had just been hung. Shatta Simon went to the new prefect and asked him to continue what his predecessor had done for Jewish children. She relates, "He closed all the windows, and then said to me in a whisper, 'O.K., but don't tell anyone that I have been nice to you.'"[13] The response seems very human, very normal. It is in many ways easier to understand than a refusal.

Those willing to help had an ability to perceive the human dimension that lay beyond the bureaucratic jargon. They were skeptical of political rhetoric and propaganda and able to think independently. They demonstrated, in the last analysis, a respect for human life, a tolerance of diversity, and a willingness to ignore regulations that threatened the survival of others. Some broke important rules, guiding illegal fugitives across frontiers or taking others into their homes or schools and keeping them alive. They were immensely courageous. They were also not numerous. More people acted in less dramatic but equally crucial ways. Police did not try too hard to find individuals on their lists. Others leaked information about pending arrests. Petty bureaucrats overlooked suspicious documents, issued new ones with few questions, or investigated newcomers in their area only superficially.

And then there were those who helped by simply doing nothing. Shopkeepers, teachers, priests and pastors, mailmen, bus drivers, municipal employees—hundreds of thousands of French men and women, scattered throughout the country, could not help but notice that there was a new face in town. They helped by asking no questions, by minding their own business. They created an environment conducive, with a strong dose of good luck, to survival.

Perhaps no case of survival cited in this book is more typical than that of Mr. and Mrs. Caraco, middle-class French Jews of modest means who were able to live independently without organized assistance. Despite warnings from their daughter in the Jewish rescue service, they were slow to perceive their danger. They left Marseille after the indiscriminate roundups there in January 1943, but they insisted on registering as Jews in their new village. For a time, they benefitted from their citizenship and from the few anti-Jewish forces in rural areas. Later they benefitted from luck—when the Nazis came for them, they were out. And finally, they benefitted from a benevolent environment. Their neighbors told the Germans that they had moved away, and then told the Caracos of the visit. There was no outstanding act of courage, no spectacular rescue, but the Caracos did not need that. Children needed that, as did the elderly, the handicapped, the foreign and totally different. In addition to good luck, the Caracos needed only a vague goodwill—a lack of overt hostility—but that was indispensable. And that they found.[14]

It is useful to recall that both Jews and non-Jews who decided to be helpful in France rarely understood that they were directly saving lives. Rumors of gas chambers and deliberate extermination were vague and inconsistent, dismissed as enemy propaganda or as simply unbelievable. Instead, rescuers and more casual helpers often risked their lives to spare Jews the sufferings of deportation to camps known to be harsh and cruel, where families would be dispersed and where children and the elderly, at least, might die. Because of that generosity, tolerance, and fundamental humanity, 250,000 people were able to survive.

NOTES

INTRODUCTION

1. Henri Rosencher, *Le Sel, la cendre et la flamme* (Paris: Henri Rosencher, 1985), 13–14.
2. Ibid., 22.
3. Moschkovitch testimony, in [n.a.], *Jawischowitz, une annexe d'Auschwitz: 45 deportés 8 mineurs témoignent* (Paris: Amicale d'Auschwitz, 1985), 260–83, 260.
4. Ibid., 261, 262.
5. For an explanation of these statistics, see chap. 11.
6. Annette Monod Leiris, interview with the author, Paris, July 15, 1991. All subsequent quotes from Annette Leiris are from this interview.

CHAPTER 1

1. For the general history of Jews in France before the Revolution, see, among others, Bernhard Blumenkranz, ed., *Histoire des Juifs en France* (Toulouse: Édouard Privat, 1972); Philippe Bourdrel, *Histoire des Juifs de France* (Paris: Albin Michel, 1974); Patrick Girard, *Pour le meilleur et pour le pire: Vingt siècles d'histoire juive en France* (Paris: Bibliophane, 1986); René Moulinas, *Les Juifs du pape en France: Les communautés d'Avignon et du Comtat Venaissin aux 17ème et 18ème siècles* (Paris: Édouard Privat, 1981); and Marianne

Calmann, *The Carriere of Carpentras* (New York: Oxford University Press, 1984).

2. Sephardic and Comtadin Jews were emancipated by legislation on January 28, 1790, and Jews in eastern France, on September 27, 1791. For more on Jews during the Revolution, see Bernhard Blumenkranz and Albert Soboul, eds., *Les Juifs et la Révolution Française: Problèmes et aspirations* (Toulouse: Édouard Privat, 1976); Patrick Girard, *La Révolution française et les Juifs* (Paris: Robert Laffont, 1989); and David Feuerwerker, *L'Émancipation des Juifs en France: De l'Ancien Régime à la fin du Second Empire* (Paris: Albin Michel, 1976).

3. Two restrictions lasted until the Orleanist monarchy. Unlike Christian churches, synagogues received no public funding until 1831, when a special vote of the Chamber of Deputies and the Chamber of Peers placed the Jewish religion on the level of others reimbursed by the Ministry of Cults. The despised *more judaïco*, a special oath required of Jews before giving testimony in court, was abolished in 1846.

4. See especially Arthur Hertzberg, *The French Enlightenment and the Jews* (New York: Columbia University Press, 1968).

5. For an excellent study of the process of integration among Parisian Jews, see Christine Piette, *Les Juifs de Paris, 1808–1840: La marche vers l'assimilation* (Quebec: Les Presses de l'Université Laval, 1983).

6. Julien Benda, *La Jeunesse d'un clerc* (Paris: Gallimard, 1936), 36–37, 42.

7. Raymond Aron, *Mémoires: Cinquante ans de réflexion politique* (Paris: Julliard, 1983), 12–13; published in English as *Memoirs: Fifty Years of Political Reflection,* trans. George Holoch (New York: Holmes and Meier, 1990).

8. Phyllis Cohen Albert, *The Modernization of French Jewry: Consistory and Community in the Nineteenth Century* (Hanover, N.H.: University Press of New England, 1977), 37.

9. For details on Jewish participation in economic, political, military, and cultural life during the Second Empire, see David Cohen, *La Promotion des Juifs en France à l'époque du Second Empire, 1852–1870,* 2 vols. (Aix-en-Provence: Université de Provence, 1980), esp. vol. 2.

10. Fould served three times as minister of finance between 1848 and 1852, and then as Napoleon III's minister of state from 1852 to 1860 and minister of finance from 1861 until his death. Goudchaux was minister of finance during the Second Republic. Crémieux served as minister of justice from 1848 to 1849 and again, after the fall of Napoleon III, from 1870 to 1871. He is best known as the author and promoter of the decree of October 24, 1870, which

granted French citizenship to the 34,574 native-born Jews of Algeria. For the text of the decree and the number of Jews affected, see Joëlle Allouche-Benayoun and Doris Bensimon, *Juifs d'Algérie hier et aujourd'hui: Mémoires et identités* (Toulouse: Édouard Privat, 1989), 38–39.

11. Eugen Weber, *France, Fin de Siècle* (Cambridge, Mass.: Belknap Press of Harvard University Press, 1986), 133.

12. Michael R. Marrus, *The Politics of Assimilation: A Study of the French Jewish Community at the Time of the Dreyfus Affair* (London: Oxford University Press, 1971), 41.

13. Like Offenbach, Giacomo Meyerbeer (1791–1864) was a German Jewish composer closely associated with France. He profoundly influenced the development of French grand opera through his four principal operas in French—*Robert le Diable* (1831), *Les Huguenots* (1836), *Le Prophète* (1849), and *L'Africaine* (1865)— and he composed lighter works in the same language.

14. Weber (*France*, 133) cites cases of non-Jews in the theater business who actually changed their names to compete more effectively!

15. H. Stuart Hughes, *Consciousness and Society: The Reorientation of European Social Thought, 1890–1930* (1958; New York: Vintage Books, 1961), 58.

16. Precise population statistics for Jews in France are difficult to obtain because after 1872 religion was officially regarded as a private matter and was not a subject of census inquiry. The *consistoires,* elected Jewish local administrative bodies, continued to collect data, however, and one report in 1897 declared the population to be 71,249 in metropolitan France, of whom about 45,000 lived in the Paris region. An additional 45,000 Jews were claimed for Algeria. Including Jews in transit to other countries and others outside consistorial supervision, Marrus (*Politics of Assimilation,* 31) accepts estimates of a population of 80,000 Jews in France, of whom 50,000 were in Paris. The overall French population was about 38,500,000; the Parisian population, 2,714,000.

17. Robert Debré, *L'Honneur de vivre: Témoignage* ([n.p.]: Hermann et Stock, 1974), 27. Debré's father had moved to Paris from Alsace when that region became German after the Franco-Prussian War. His son, Michel Debré, was the first prime minister of the Fifth Republic.

18. Jules Isaac, *Expériences de ma vie,* part 1, *Péguy* (Paris: Calmann-Lévy, 1959), 24–25, 123–24.

19. Girard, *Pour le meilleur,* 316. The 8,000 consisted of about 4,000 from the Russian Empire, including eastern Poland; 3,000 Romanians; and 1,000 Galicians from Austro-Hungary.

20. Weber, *France,* 105.

21. The French diplomat, author, and would-be ethnologist Count Joseph Arthur Gobineau (1816–82), who from 1853 to 1855 published his four-volume *Essai sur l'inégalité des races humaines* espousing concepts of "Aryan" racial purity and superiority, was clearly a product of the Second Empire. Gobineau's "scientific" racism, however, became more fashionable in Germany and Austria than in France.

22. Adolphe Crémieux, for example, a Freemason, favored lay teaching and the separation of church and state; the nonobservant Jewish deputy Alfred Nacquet, also a Freemason, a member of the Radical party, and an advocate of separation of church and state, strenuously supported a law on divorce that passed in 1884. But most Jewish politicians tried to avoid the clerical issue. Joseph Reinach (1856–1921), *chef du cabinet* to Prime Minister Léon Gambetta in 1881, a deputy after 1889, and an early and dedicated Dreyfusard, was a firm advocate of tolerance and moderation in church-state issues.

23. *L'Action française,* March 28, 1911, quoted in Colette Capitan Peter, *Charles Maurras et l'idéologie d'Action française* (Paris: Éditions du Seuil, 1972), 75.

24. For details, see especially Jeannine Verdès-Leroux, *Scandale financier et antisémitisme catholique: Le krach de l'Union générale* (Paris: Éditions du Centurion, 1969).

25. Jean-Louis Bredin, *The Affair: The Case of Alfred Dreyfus,* trans. Jeffrey Mehlman (New York: George Braziller, 1986), 28.

26. Robert Byrnes, *Antisemitism in Modern France,* vol. 1, *The Prologue to the Dreyfus Affair* (New Brunswick, N.J.: Rutgers University Press, 1950), 152. Drumont's friend Alphonse Daudet (1840–97) led the press campaign, and a series of highly public duels sparked by the book also bolstered sales.

27. Ibid., 196. See also Pierre Sorlin, *"La Croix" et les Juifs* (Paris: Grasset, 1967); and Pierre Pierrard, *Juifs et catholiques français: De Drumond à Jules Isaac 1886–1945* (Paris: Fayard, 1970).

28. Byrnes, *Prologue to Dreyfus Affair,* 240. Drumont himself received barely 600 votes in the district where he had lived all his life.

29. See Marrus, *Politics of Assimilation,* 196–200.

30. Weber, *France,* 135.

31. Cited in Marcel Thomas, *L'Affaire sans Dreyfus* (Paris: Fayard, 1961), 130. The general staff's intelligence bureau was officially called the section of statistics.

32. This point is made by Eugen Weber in his article "Reflection on the Jews in France," in Frances Malino and Bernard Wasserstein, eds., *The Jews in Modern France* (Hanover, N.H.: University Press of New England, 1985), 8–27, 25.

33. For analysis of social and economic conditions within the French officer corps, see William Serman, *Les Officiers dans la nation* (Paris: Aubier-Montaigne, 1982).

34. This view is articulated by Weber: "Antisemitism plays a seminal role in the Affair, but the Affair is not really about Jews" (in Malino and Wasserstein, *Jews in Modern France*, 23–24). It is also professed by Bredin (*The Affair*, esp. 531–45).

35. For details, see Bredin, *The Affair*, 285–86, 346–52.

36. The phrase is a chapter title in Paula Hyman, *From Dreyfus to Vichy: The Remaking of French Jewry, 1906–1939* (New York: Columbia University Press, 1979), 33.

37. Ibid., 48.

38. Michel Roblin, *Les Juifs de Paris: Démographie, économie, culture* (Paris: A. et J. Picard, 1952), 105–9.

39. Pierre Abraham, *Les Trois frères* (Paris: Français Réunis, 1971), 42, 43. Pierre Abraham's mother was deported and gassed at Auschwitz at the age of eighty-four.

40. Charles Lopata, *J'ai survécu* (Paris: Droit et Liberté, 1977), 79.

41. Abraham, *Les Trois frères*, 59, 64.

42. Quoted in Girard, *Pour le meilleur*, 349.

43. Ibid.

44. Ibid., 347, 351. These statistics are rough estimates, for the religion of soldiers was not a matter of public record.

45. The letter is quoted in full in Maurice Barrès, *Les Diverses familles spirituelles de la France* (Paris: Émile-Paul Frères, 1917), 76.

46. Hyman, *From Dreyfus to Vichy*, 51. For examples of mutual help, see Pierrard, *Juifs et catholiques*, 229–31.

47. Maurice Barrès, *Scènes et doctrines du nationalisme*, vol. 1 (1902; Paris: Plon-Nourrit, 1925), 67.

48. Barrès, *Les Diverses familles*, 67.

49. Roblin, *Les Juifs de Paris*, 73–74. See also the first chapter in David H. Weinberg, *A Community on Trial: The Jews of Paris in the 1930s* (1974; Chicago: University of Chicago Press, 1977), 8. Weinberg explains that these figures do not include the large floating population of Jewish refugees who stayed briefly in Paris but did not settle there. That population at any given time in the 1930s may have reached 40,000.

50. The Pletzl remains today a predominantly Jewish neighborhood. For details, see especially Nancy L. Green, *The Pletzl of Paris: Jewish Immigrant Workers in the Belle Epoque* (New York: Holmes and Meier, 1986), 68–78.

51. Ibid., 101–48; Hyman, *From Dreyfus to Vichy*, 73–77; and Weinberg, *Community on Trial*, 11–19. Maurice Rajsfus, the son of a Polish Jewish immigrant to France in 1923, uses the term "Jewish

296 Notes to Pages 21–25

trades" and estimates that only about 12 percent of Jewish immigrants were able to find alternative employment. See his *Mon Père l'Étranger: Un immigré juif polonais à Paris dans les années 1920* (Paris: L'Harmattan, 1989), 99.

52. Bernard Lazare, "La Solidarité juive," *Entretiens politiques et littéraires,* (September 1890): 222–32, 232.
53. Abraham, *Les Trois frères,* 42–43.
54. Weinberg, *Community on Trial,* 50.
55. J. Tchernoff, *Dans le creuset des civilisations: De l'affaire Dreyfus au dimanche rouge à Saint-Petersbourg* (Paris: Rieder, 1937), 14–15.
56. A. Honig, *La Métamorphose du Juif érrant* (Paris: La Pensée Universelle, 1978), 105–6. To compound the shock, this friend was originally from Poland.
57. Philippe Erlanger, *La France sans étoile: Souvenirs de l'avant-guerre et du temps de l'occupation* (Paris: Plon, 1974), 64.
58. This calculation is made by Stephen A. Schuker, "Origins of the 'Jewish Problem' in the Later Third Republic," in Malino and Wasserstein, *Jews in Modern France,* 135–80, 152.
59. Henri Rosencher, *Le Sel, la cendre et la flamme* (Paris: Henri Rosencher, 1985), 19–20. Rosencher's family knew Schwartzbard.
60. Quoted in Pierrard, *Juifs et catholiques,* 273.
61. Ibid.
62. Léon Poliakov, *Histoire de l'antisémitisme,* vol. 2, *L'Âge de la science* (1955; Paris: Calmann-Lévy, 1981), 460, 468.
63. Pierrard, *Juifs et catholiques,* 297–98, 298.
64. Michael R. Marrus and Robert O. Paxton, *Vichy France and the Jews* (New York: Basic Books, 1981), 37.
65. Jean-Charles Bonnet, *Les Pouvoirs publics français et l'immigration dans l'entre-deux-guerres* (Lyon: Centres d'histoire économique et social de la région lyonnaise, 1976), 193. Foreign-born residents in France today, incidentally, number about four million, or roughly 7 percent of the population.
66. Georges Mauco, *Les Étrangers en France et le problème du racisme* (Paris: La Pensée Universelle, 1977), 26. Precise statistics are difficult because Jews were not recorded as such.
67. Right-wing leagues active at the time included retired Colonel Count François de La Rocque's Croix de feu, reconstituted after 1936 as the Parti social français (PSF), with a membership estimated at from 700,000 to 3 million; Pierre Taittinger's Jeunesses patriotes; Action française with some 70,000 activists in 1934; René Coty's Solidarité Française and Marcel Bucard's Francistes, both dating from 1933 to 1936; and, after 1936, Jacques Doriot's

Parti populaire français (PPF) and Eugène Deloncle and Jean Filliol's Comité secret d'action révolutionnaire, or Cagoule. Antiforeign and anti-Semitic authors and journalists included Jean and Jérome Tharaud, Céline, Pierre Drieu la Rochelle, Marcel Jouhandeau, Lucien Rebatet, Pierre Gaxotte, Maurice Bardèche, Pierre-Antoine Cousteau, Georges Blond, Alain Laubreaux, and Robert Brasillach.

68. The statistics are from Roblin, *Les Juifs de Paris,* 73. Many refugees from Germany were not actually German but carried Polish or Russian passports, or were stateless (*apatrides*).

69. On the participation of churchmen, including Jean Cardinal Verdier, archbishop of Paris from 1929 to 1940, in anti-Nazi meetings, see Pierrard, *Juifs et catholiques,* 268–72.

70. *Journal officiel de la république française: Lois et décrets* (November 13, 1938).

71. Eve Dessarre, *Mon enfance d'avant le déluge* (Paris: Fayard, 1976), esp. 172–77. The reference to the bureau des larmes is from Rajsfus, *Mon Père l'étranger,* 46.

72. Honig, *La Métamorphose,* 133, 140.

73. As will be seen, this decree was among the first to be rescinded by the Vichy regime, on August 27, 1940.

74. These cuts were restored under Vichy, and an uncensored version appeared in 1942.

75. At least two critics of racism in 1938, Archbishop Jules-Gérard Saliège of Toulouse and Pierre Cardinal Gerlier, archbishop of Lyon, were critics of the persecution of Jews under Vichy as well.

76. Marc Bloch, *Strange Defeat: A Statement of Evidence Written in 1940,* trans. Gerard Hopkins (New York: Norton, 1968), 177–78. Despite the book's title, the testament itself was written in 1943. For more on Marc Bloch, see chap. 2.

77. Erlanger, *France sans étoile,* 39.

78. Georges Friedmann, *The End of the Jewish People?* trans. Eric Mosbacher (Garden City, N.Y.: Doubleday, 1967), 9.

79. Gaby Cohen, interview with the author, Paris, April 29, 1988.

80. Ginette Hirtz, *Les Hortillonnages sous la grêle: Histoire d'une famille juive en France sous l'occupation* (Paris: Mercure de France, 1982), 25.

81. Lion Feuchtwanger, *The Devil in France: My Encounter with Him in the Summer of 1940,* trans. from German by Elisabeth Abbott (New York: Viking, 1941), 21.

82. From an interview with an Israeli reporter, reprinted in Jean-Marie Lustiger, *Osez croire: Articles, conférences, sermons, interviews, 1981–1984,* vol. 1 (Paris: Le Centurion, 1985), 57.

83. Rosencher, *Le Sel*, 22.
84. Jacqueline Wolf, *"Take Care of Josette"*: *A Memoir in Defense of Occupied France* (London: Franklin Watts, 1981), 5.
85. George Frybergh, interview with the author, East Hampton, N.Y., October 21, 1989.
86. Honig, *La Métamorphose*, 132.
87. Dessarre, *Mon enfance*, 151–60.
88. Lopata, *J'ai survécu*, 36–38.
89. Claudine Vegh, *I Didn't Say Goodbye*, trans. Ros Schwartz (1979; Hampstead, Eng.: Caliban Books, 1984), 27–29.
90. Maurice Rajsfus tells his story in *Mon Père l'étranger*, and also in *Jeudi noir: 16 juillet 1942, l'honneur perdu de la France profonde* (Paris: L'Harmattan: 1988).

CHAPTER 2

1. Doris Bensimon, *Les Grandes rafles: Juifs en France, 1940–1944* (Toulouse: Édouard Privat, 1987), 110; Michael R. Marrus and Robert O. Paxton, *Vichy France and the Jews* (New York: Basic Books, 1981), 68; and Jean-Louis Crémieux-Brilhac, "Engagés volontaires et prestataires," in Karel Bartosek, René Gallissot, and Denis Peschanski, eds., *De l'exil à la résistance: Réfugiés et immigrés d'Europe centrale en France, 1933–1945* (Saint Denis: Presses Universitaires de Vincennes, 1989), 95–100, 99. Foreigners were subject to the wartime draft if they had lived in France for a specific number of years.
2. A. Honig, *La Métamorphose du Juif érrant* (Paris: La Pensée Universelle, 1978), 149.
3. Gustav Regler, *The Owl of Minerva: The Autobiography of Gustav Regler*, trans. from German by Norman Denny (1958; London: Rupert Hart-Davis, 1959), 331.
4. Koestler recorded his experiences at Le Vernet in *Scum of the Earth* (New York: Macmillan, 1941).
5. Gilbert Badia, "Camps répressifs ou camps de concentration?" in his *Les Barbelés de l'exil: Études sur l'émigration allemande et autrichienne, 1938–1940* (Grenoble: Presses Universitaires de Grenoble, 1979), 291–32, 311. Koestler confirms the statistic (95). See also Anne Grynberg, *Les Camps de la honte: Les internés Juifs des camps français, 1939–1944* (Paris: La Découverte, 1991), 19–87.
6. Badia, "Camps Répressifs," 311.
7. Both Frei and Bondy wrote about their experiences at Le Vernet, the former in *Die Männer von Vernet: Ein Tatsachenbericht* (Berlin: Deutscher Militarverlag, 1961), and the latter in *Rapport sur le*

camp du Vernet (Ariège) et sur les conditions de l'arrestation et de l'internement de nombreux étrangers en France (Geneva, 1940). Badia points out that while Friedrich Wolf was interned, the film made from his play *Le Professeur Mamlock* was shown with great success in England during the winter of 1939–40. Badia concludes, ironically, "In England, they were heaping praise upon the anti-Fascist writer, while at Le Vernet, they were treating him as a criminal" ("Camps répressifs," 322).

8. Peter Lipman-Wulf, interview with the author, Sag Harbor, N.Y., August 18, 1988. For accounts of Les Milles by internees, see Lion Feuchtwanger, *The Devil in France: My Encounter with Him in the Summer of 1940,* trans. from German by Elisabeth Abbott (New York: Viking, 1941); and Alfred Kantorowicz, *Exil in Frankreich: Merkwurdigkeiten und Denkwurdigkeiten* (Bremen: Schunemann Universitatsverlag, 1971). For subsequent histories, see André Fontaine, *Le Camp d'étrangers des Milles, 1939–1943 (Aix-en-Provence)* (Aix-en-Provence: Edisud, 1989); and [n.a.], *Les Camps en Provence: Exil, internement, déportation, 1933–1942* (Aix-en-Provence: Alinéa et LLCG, 1984).

9. Marrus and Paxton, *Vichy France,* 65; and Richard I. Cohen, *The Burden of Conscience: French Jewry's Response to the Holocaust* (Bloomington: Indiana University Press, 1987), 16. According to Grynberg, about 5,000 of the 8,000 held in the spring of 1940 were Jewish (*Les Camps de la honte,* 12).

10. Lipman-Wulf interview. Ernst had moved to France in 1923 for artistic rather than political reasons.

11. Koestler, *Scum of the Earth,* 94, 98.

12. Women interned at this time in Gurs included Hannah Arendt (1906–75), subsequently a prominent political scientist, philosopher, educator, and author in the United States; Hedwige Kampfer, a former Social Democratic deputy from Munich; and the German actress Dita Parlo. According to Claude Laharie (*Le Camp de Gurs, 1939–1945: Un aspect méconnu de l'histoire du Béarn* [Biarritz: Société Atlantique d'Impression, 1985], 143), there were 9,283 women and children at Gurs in June 1940. The internee Hanna Schramm later estimated that, in her barracks, about half the women were Jewish, one-quarter were political refugees, and another quarter had come to France for work, some as long as fifteen years before. See her "Souvenirs d'une emigrée allemande dans un camp d'internement français 1940–1941," in Hanna Schramm and Barbara Vormeier, *Vivre à Gurs: Un camp de concentration français, 1940–1941,* trans. from German by Irène Petit (Paris: François Maspero, 1979), 7–176, 21.

13. See descriptions in Fontaine, *Le Camp d'étrangers,* 120–24. French

gendarmes were members of the Gendarmerie nationale, the national police force.

14. Lisa Fittko, *Le Chemin des Pyrénées: Souvenirs, 1940–41,* trans. from German by Lea Marcou (1985; Paris: Maren Sell, 1987), 29–33; published in English as *Escape through the Pyrenees,* trans. from German by David Koblick (Evanston, Ill.: Northwestern University Press, 1991). See other incidents in Badia, "Camps répressifs," 93.

15. See the description by Fittko, *Le Chemin,* 29–33. According to Laharie, 6,600 of the 9,771 women prisoners at Gurs left by the end of July, and another 2,052 departed in August (*Le Camp de Gurs,* 148). Hannah Arendt left at this time and, with help from the American Emergency Rescue Committee and the Hebrew Immigrant Aid and Sheltering Society (HIAS), managed to secure American visas for herself, her husband Heinrich Blücher, and her mother Martha Arendt. The three traveled through Spain and Portugal by train and sailed for New York in May and June 1941. For her story, see especially Elisabeth Young-Bruehl, *Hannah Arendt: For Love of the World* (New Haven: Yale University Press, 1982).

16. For descriptions of the strange train trip, see Feuchtwanger, *Devil in France,* 89–165; and Fontaine, *Le Camp d'étrangers,* 87–99. Ernst remained in France until mid-1941, when he emigrated to New York by way of Spain and Portugal. He returned to France after the war. Feuchtwanger and Mann are discussed later in this chapter.

17. Grynberg finds that 28,000 of 40,000, or 70 percent, were Jewish (*Les Camps de la honte,* 12); Georges Wellers, a physician and an Auschwitz survivor, states in his *L'Étoile jaune à l'heure de Vichy: De Drancy à Auschwitz* (Paris: Fayard, 1973) that there were 53,610 internees in November 1940, of whom two-thirds were Jewish (99).

18. For the number of Jewish refugees, most of whom were from Belgium, see Cohen, *Burden of Conscience,* 16; and François Delpech, *Sur les Juifs: Études d'histoire contemporaine* (Lyon: Presses Universitaires de Lyon, 1983), 298.

19. Statistics are necessarily rough estimates; those cited here are from Cohen, *Burden of Conscience,* 17.

20. Nina Gourfinkel, *L'Autre patrie* (Paris: Éditions du Seuil, 1953), 130.

21. Paul Reichmann, interview with the author, New York City, August 22, 1989.

22. Arno J. Mayer, *Why Did the Heavens Not Darken?: The "Final Solution" in History* (New York: Pantheon, 1988), viii.

23. Gret Arnoldsen, *Silence, on tue* (Paris: La Pensée Universelle, 1981).

24. Claude Vigée, *La Lune d'hiver* (Paris: Flammarion, 1970), 40. See also pp. 34, 36, and 37.

25. Frédéric Chimon Hammel, *Souviens-toi d'Amalek: Témoignage sur la lutte des Juifs en France, 1938–1944* (Paris: CLKH, 1982), 26.

26. Darius Milhaud, *Notes without Music,* trans. Donald Evans (1949; New York: Knopf, 1953), 272–73.

27. Gourfinkel, *L'Autre patrie,* 130.

28. Honig, *La Métamorphose, 153.*

29. Claude Mauriac, *Les Espaces imaginaires* (Paris: Bernard Grasset, 1975), 216–17.

30. Philippe Erlanger, *La France sans étoile: Souvenirs de l'avant-guerre et du temps de l'occupation* (Paris: Plon, 1974), 33. On Erlanger in the prewar period, see chap. 1.

31. Through a separate French-Italian armistice, also signed in June 1940, another small part of France, including some of the Vallée de la Tarentaise and the city of Menton, came under Italian occupation. Also, within the German occupied zone, an area north and east of a line extending roughly from Abbeville to Amiens, Laon, Rethel, Sainte-Menehould, Saint-Dizier, Chamont, and Dole was declared a *zone interdite*—a forbidden zone.

32. A group of German bureaucrats and Gestapo agents known as the Kundt Commission visited internment camps in the unoccupied zone in the summer of 1940 and claimed about 800 prisoners, mostly political opponents and only rarely Jews, for repatriation. Vichy officials duly delivered them. (Marrus and Paxton, *Vichy France,* 70). Among those delivered was the young Herschel Grynszpan, whose killing of a German diplomat in Paris in November 1938 sparked Kristallnacht. Grynszpan disappeared in Nazi Germany.

33. Cohen, *Burden of Conscience,* 18.

34. Erlanger, *La France sans étoile,* 91.

35. Wellers, *L'Étoile jaune,* 109. Like René Blum, Wellers was arrested on December 12, 1941. The two men were together at Compiègne.

36. Erlanger, *La France sans étoile,* 99.

37. René Blum's name appears on the list of deportees in convoy 36, printed in full in Serge Klarsfeld, *Memorial to the Jews Deported from France, 1942–1944* (New York: Beate Klarsfeld Foundation, 1983), 306–11, 306. For more on the December 1941 roundup of Jewish professionals in Paris, see chap. 5.

38. For biographies of Blum, see Joel Colton, *Léon Blum: Humanist in Politics* (New York: Knopf, 1966); and Jean Lacouture, *Léon Blum,* trans. George Holoch (New York: Holmes and Meier, 1982).

39. For more on the racial laws and exemptions, see chap. 3.

40. Raymond-Raoul Lambert, *Carnet d'un témoin, 1940–1943,* ed. Richard Cohen (Paris: Fayard, 1985), 85.

41. The names of the six members of the Lambert family appear on the list of deportees in convoy 64, reprinted in full in Klarsfeld, *Memorial,* 478–83, 480.

42. Robert Debré, *L'Honneur de vivre: Témoignage* ([n.p.]: Hermann et Stock, 1974), 221.

43. Once in hiding, Debré spent the rest of the war aiding Jewish children and Resistants and working on medical projects.

44. Claude Lévi-Strauss, interview with Didier Eribon, reprinted in full in their *De Près et de loin* (Paris: Odile Jacob, 1988), 42. See also Claude Lévi-Strauss, *Tristes tropiques* (Paris: Plon, 1955), 20–36.

45. Quoted in Carole Fink, *Marc Bloch: A Life in History* (Cambridge and New York: Cambridge University Press, 1989), 267.

46. Two of the twenty-eight survived the massacre.

47. Emmanuel Berl, interview with Patrick Modiano, in Emmanuel Berl, *Intérrogatoire par Patrick Modiano suivi de Il fait beau, allons au cimetière* (Paris: Gallimard, 1976), 87.

48. Excerpts from Kessel's letters to his brother are quoted in Yves Courrière, *Joseph Kessel, ou, Sur la piste du lion* (Paris: Plon, 1985), 540–42, 547. In London, Kessel first offered his services to de Gaulle, but in 1944, at the age of forty-six, he joined the British Sussex Squadron and flew reconnaissance missions over occupied France.

49. The American Emergency Rescue Committee was organized in 1940 to aid important Jewish and non-Jewish political and literary figures escape from Europe. Its chief representative in France was Varian Fry (1907–67), a former journalist for *Foreign Affairs* who set up the Centre Americain de Secours in Marseille. For accounts of Fry's activities, see Varian Fry, *Surrender on Demand* (New York: Random House, 1945); and Daniel Bénédite, *La Filière marseillaise: Un chemin vers la liberté sous l'occupation* (Paris: Éditions Clancier Guenaud, 1984). Bénédite was one of Fry's French assistants.

50. Andrew Kagan, *Marc Chagall* (New York: Abbeville Press, 1989), 69–70; and Jean-Paul Crespelle, *Chagall,* trans. Benita Eisler (1969; New York: Coward-McCann, 1970), 213–24. Bella died in the United States in 1944; Chagall returned to France in 1948.

51. Gertrude Stein, *Wars I Have Seen* (New York: Random House, 1945). Culoz was not far from the village of Izieu, where the Gestapo seized forty-four children and seven adults from a Jewish children's home on April 6, 1944. They were deported to Drancy and Auschwitz (for details, see chap. 11). Because they were Ameri-

cans and thus enemy nationals, Stein and Toklas, if caught, would have been interned but probably not deported.

52. The June figure is from Philippe Bourdrel, *Histore des Juifs de France* (Paris: Albin Michel, 1974), 357; that for September, from Cohen, *Burden of Conscience*, 18. Fifty-five-year-old Aristides de Sousa Mendes, who issued thousands of Portuguese entry visas to Jews in Bordeaux and Bayonne in defiance of explicit orders to the contrary from his superiors, was promptly recalled and dismissed. He lost his pension, was barred from practicing law, and died in poverty in 1954. He was honored posthumously as "Righteous among the Nations" at Yad Vashem, Israel, and a tree was planted there in his honor.

53. For the HICEM statistic, see its postwar organizational report in Centre de documentation juive contemporaine (CDJC), *L'Activité des organisations juives en France sous l'occupation* (1947; Paris: CDJC, 1983), 93.

54. All of them also received help from the American Emergency Rescue Committee. For Marta Feuchtwanger's account of her escape from France, see her article, "Transit," in *Women of Exile: German-Jewish Autobiographies since 1933,* ed. Andreas Lixl-Purcell (New York: Greenwood Press, 1988), 63–67.

55. For details, see the account by Fittko, *Le Chemin,* 149–65. Fittko guided Benjamin across the Pyrenees. For more on Spanish policy toward immigrants who arrived without French exit visas, Spanish transit visas, or often even passports, see chap. 14.

56. Milhaud, *Notes,* 273.

57. Raymond Aron, *Mémoires: Cinquante ans de réflexion politique* (Paris: Julliard, 1983), 164–65; published in English as *Memoirs: Fifty Years of Political Reflection,* trans. George Holoch (New York: Holmes and Meier, 1990). For Cassin's account of the trip, see his *Les Hommes partis de rien: Le réveil de la France abattue, 1940–1941* (Paris: Plon, 1975), 66. For more on Cassin and some other Jews with the Free French, see chap. 15.

58. For his own account of events up to his escape from France, see Pierre Mendes France, *Liberté, liberté chérie ... choses vécues* (New York: Didier, 1943). See also Jean Lacouture, *Pierre Mendes France,* trans. George Holoch (1981; New York: Holmes and Meier, 1984), esp. 101–54.

59. John M. Sherwood, *Georges Mandel and the Third Republic* (Stanford, Calif.: Stanford University Press, 1970), 251–94. The Milice was a paramilitary organization created by Pierre Laval on January 30, 1943, from what had been the *Service d'ordre Légionnaire,* a war veterans' group. Its purpose was to defend the National Revolution and to combat the Resistance, and, especially, the Commu-

nists. Under the leadership of Joseph Darnand, it became increasingly collaborationist, autonomous, and powerful. By 1944, its violence toward Jews fully equalled that of any Nazi units in France.

60. Aline Berlin, interview with the author, Oxford, Eng., November 7, 1987.

61. Ibid.

62. Berl, *Intérrogatorie,* 91.

CHAPTER 3

1. Quoted from her own diary by Denise Baumann, "Jeu de cartes" (unpublished memoir, June 1981), 2.

2. Léon Poliakov, *L'Auberge des musiciens: Mémoires* (Paris: Mazarine, 1981), 78 (written in 1946).

3. Lisa Fittko, *Le Chemin des Pyrénées: Souvenirs, 1940–41,* trans. from German by Lea Marcou (1985; Paris: Maren Sell, 1987), 258; published in English as *Escape through the Pyrenees,* trans. from German by David Koblick (Evanston, Ill.: Northwestern University Press, 1991).

4. Henry Bulawko, *Les Jeux de la mort et de l'espoir: Auschwitz-Jaworzno* (Paris: Amicale des Anciens Deportés Juifs de France, 1954), 28–29.

5. Philippe Erlanger, *La France sans étoile: Souvenirs de l'avant-guerre et du temps de l'occupation* (Paris: Plon, 1974), 93.

6. Emmanuel Ewenczyk, interview with the author, Paris, November 16, 1988.

7. The exact number of those expelled is uncertain. Médard Brogly (*La Grande épreuve: l'Alsace sous l'occupation allemande, 1940–44* [Paris: Éditions du Cerf, 1945], 128), estimated that 10,000 Jews were expelled from Alsace alone.

8. See the letter from Irène B. to Claude Vigée, quoted at length in his *La Lune d'hiver* (Paris: Flammarion, 1970), 91. Jews were not the only victims of forcible expulsion, for the Germans drove out thousands of non-Jews as well, especially former French political figures, military officers, civil servants, and known anti-Nazis. Others who had chosen to evacuate earlier were prevented from returning.

9. A. Honig, *La Métamorphose du Juif érrant* (Paris: La Pensée Universelle, 1978), 164–65.

10. *Journal officiel de la république française: Lois et décrets* (July 18, 1940): 4,537. Hereinafter cited as *JO,* it became in 1941 the *Journal officiel de l'état francais.* The law provided for exceptions for those who had served in the French army during World War I or in 1939–40, and for their descendants.

11. *JO* (August 19 and September 11, 1940): 4,735–36 and 4,958.

12. *JO* (July 23, 1940): 4,587.
13. Report of Maurice Gabolde, Keeper of the Seals, to Fernand de Brinon, Vichy representative to the German occupying forces in Paris, and recorded by de Brinon, September 8, 1943, CDJC, XXVII–47. According to the report, the commission retained the citizenship of 1,984 Jews and reserved judgment for about 4,800 Jewish prisoners of war, internees, and North Africans. It also stated that 23,648 Jews had been naturalized between 1927 and 1940, and that 9,801 cases remained to be reviewed.
14. *JO,* (September 4 and October 1, 1940): 4,490 and 5,198.
15. *La Métamorphose,* 167.
16. Prefect of Police to Militärbefehlshaber in Frankreich (MBF) (German Military Administration), October 26, 1940, Centre de documentation juive contemporaine (CDJC), LXXIXa–10. The figure is for the department of the Seine; about 20,000 Jews lived in the rest of the occupied zone in 1940.
17. Lemberger's son Jean told the story to Gerard Israël, who included it in his book *Heureux comme Dieu en France ... 1940–1944* (Paris: Robert Laffont, 1975), 94.
18. Poliakov, *L'Auberge,* 78–79.
19. Maurice Rajsfus, *Jeudi noir: 16 juillet 1942, L'honneur perdu de la France profonde* (Paris: L'Harmattan, 1988), 168, and interview with the author, Paris, July 2, 1990.
20. Denise Baumann tells the tragic story of her family in *Une Famille comme les autres* (1973; Paris: Albin Michel, 1985).
21. Erlanger, *La France,* 126.
22. Poliakov, *L'Auberge,* 79.
23. Ibid.
24. Henri du Moulin de Labarthète, *Le Temps des illusions: Souvenirs (Juillet 1940–Avril 1942)* (Geneva: Les Éditions du Cheval Aile, 1946), 280.
25. Paul Baudouin, *Neuf mois au governement (Avril–Décembre 1940)* (Paris: Éditions de la Table Ronde, 1948), 366. For the best analysis of the reasons for the racial laws, see Michael R. Marrus and Robert O. Paxton, *Vichy France and the Jews* (New York: Basic Books, 1981), 75–119.
26. *JO,* (October 18, 1940): 5,323. Thus it resembled the racial laws in Germany but not those imposed by the Germans in the occupied zone. Also, the German measure in the occupied zone did not use the word "race" but referred rather to religion. The Statut des Juifs was applied in Algeria and, with modifications, in Morocco and Tunisia. It is interesting to note that, unlike racial laws in Germany and Italy, the French decrees never prohibited intermarriage.
27. Archives nationales, AJ 40 555. Two of the ten, Professors Robert

Debré and Marc Bloch, are mentioned in chap. 2. Also in December 1940, two Jewish officers, General Darius-Paul Bloch and Chief of Artillery Squadron Pierre-Solomon-Isaac Brisac, received exemptions, cited with descriptions of their special merit in *JO* (December 13, 1940, and January 1, 1941): 6,097–98 and 10–11.

28. *JO,* (October 18, 1940): 5,324. Special internment camps were to be organized by the Ministry of the Interior for this purpose.

29. Estimates range from 109,000 to 117,600; for sources and explanations, see Joëlle Allouche-Benayoun and Doris Bensimon, *Juifs d'Algérie hier et aujourd'hui: Mémoires et identités* (Toulouse: Édouard Privat, 1989), 44.

30. Raymond-Raoul Lambert, *Carnet d'un témoin, 1940–1943*, ed. Richard Cohen (Paris: Fayard, 1985), 84.

31. Ibid., 85.

32. Vigée, *La Lune,* 105.

33. Georges Friedmann, *The End of the Jewish People?* trans. Eric Mosbacher (Garden City, N.Y.: Doubleday, 1967), 10. Friedmann subsequently became active in the French Resistance.

34. Frédéric Chimon Hammel, *Souviens-toi d'Amalek: Témoignage sur la lutte des Juifs en France, 1938–1944* (Paris: CLKH, 1982), 30.

35. Told by Pierre Weill Raynal to Israël (*Heureux,* 237–39, 242).

36. Lambert, *Carnet,* 86–87.

37. Until April 1942, Pétain was officially both head of state and, as president of the Council of Ministers, head of government. Laval from June to December 1940, Pierre-Étienne Flandin in January and February 1941, and Darlan from February 1941 to April 1942, were only vice-presidents of the council, or vice-prime ministers. Upon his return to power in April 1942, Laval became full prime minister and head of government.

38. For details, see François Delpech, "Les Églises et la persécution raciale," in *Églises et chrétiens dans la IIème guerre mondiale: La France: Actes du Colloque national tenu à Lyon du 27 au 30 janvier 1978,* ed. Xavier de Montclos, Monique Luirard, François Delpech, Pierre Bolle (Lyon: Presses Universitaires de Lyon, 1982), 257–72, 264.

39. Raymond Aron, *Mémoires: Cinquante ans de réflexion politique* (Paris: Juillard, 1983), 162; published in English as *Memoirs: Fifty Years of Political Reflection,* trans. George Holoch (New York: Holmes and Meier, 1990).

40. Told by Pierre Weill Raynal to Israël, *Heureux,* 242.

41. The letter, subsequently reprinted in many works, appeared as early as 1948 in [n.a.], *Hommage à Pierre Masse* (Paris: Calmann-Lévy, 1948), 47–48.

42. Pierre Masse's name appears on the list of deportees in convoy 39,

reprinted in full in Serge Klarsfeld, *Memorial to the Jews Deported from France, 1942–1944* (New York: Beate Klarsfeld Foundation, 1983), 326–27, 326.

43. Roger Masse's name appears on the list of deportees in convoy 2, reprinted in full in Klarsfeld, *Memorial*, 18–24, 21.
44. *JO* (March 31, 1941): 1,386.
45. *JO* (August 26, 1941): 3,594–95.
46. *JO* (June 14, 1941): 2,475–76.
47. Adding to the confusion, the law (*JO* [June 14, 1941]: 2,475) declared that grandparents were to be considered "of the Jewish race" if they had "belonged to the Jewish religion."
48. CGQJ to Controleur général d'armée December 2, 1941, CDJC, CXCIII–86. Lucien Lazare (*La Résistance juive en France* [Paris: Stock, 1987], 49) estimates that about 180,000 Jews were actually present in the unoccupied zone at the time. There had been about 40,000 Jews in the same area before the war.
49. *JO* (June 24, 1941): 2,628. In metropolitan France, students in primary and secondary schools were unaffected. In Algeria, however, with the cooperation of Governor General Maxime Weygand, anti-Semitic educators succeeded in September 1941 in imposing a numerus clausus of 14 percent, and later of 7 percent, on Jewish students in primary and secondary schools, at first by special local decree and subsequently by law. See Michel Ansky, *Les Juifs d'Algérie du décret Crémieux à la libération* (Paris: Éditions du Centre, 1950), 107–37.
50. *JO,* (July 17, 1941): 3,000–3,001.
51. Philippe Bourdrel, *Histoire des Juifs de France* (Paris: Albin Michel, 1974), 373.
52. *JO,* (September 6, 1941): 3,787.
53. Bourdrel, *Histoire,* 374.
54. Theses 7 and 8 are reprinted in Delpech, "Les Églises," 266.
55. Ibid.
56. *JO* (December 2, 1941): 5,181.
57. UGIF's wartime role will be discussed again in subsequent chapters. For more detailed analysis, see Richard I. Cohen, *The Burden of Conscience: French Jewry's Response to the Holocaust* (Bloomington: Indiana University Press, 1987); and Jacques Adler, *The Jews of Paris and the Final Solution: Communal Response and Internal Conflicts, 1940–1944* (1985; New York and Oxford: Oxford University Press, 1987). For the case against UGIF, see two books by Maurice Rajsfus, *Des Juifs dans la collaboration: L'UGIF, 1941–1944* (Paris: Études et documentation internationales, 1980); and *Des Juifs dans la collaboration (II): Une terre promise? (1941–1944)* (Paris: L'Harmattan, 1989).

58. Thus, the organization Entraide française israélite (EFI) became section 1 of UGIF-South's First Department, for the family; Organisation pour la reconstruction et le travail (ORT) became the Second Department, for job training; Oeuvre de secours aux enfants (OSE), the child health organization, became the Third Department, in charge of health; Éclaireurs israélites de France (EIF), the French Jewish Boy Scouts of France, became the Fourth Department, for youth activities; and in the Fifth Department, for assistance, the Comité d'assistance aux refugiés d'Allemagne (CAR) provided German Jews with family allowances and other subsidies as section 1, while the Fédération des sociétés juives de France (FSJF) did much the same, as section 2, for East European Jews.

CHAPTER 4

1. See Claude Laharie, *Le Camp de Gurs, 1939–1945: Un aspect méconnu de l'histoire du Béarn* (Biarritz: Société Atlantique d'Impression, 1985), 173.
2. German Jews were sent west by Nazi fanatics eager to remove all Jews from their districts at a time when policies of deportation and destruction in the east had not yet been defined. Plans to expel more Jews to France were effectively thwarted by vehement protests at the Armistice Commission from French officials anxious not to be burdened by more refugees.
3. The 3,309 consisted of 1,640 Spaniards, 689 Frenchmen, and 980 Jewish women. The remaining French and all but 300 of the Spaniards left after October 24, 1940. See Laharie, *Le Camp de Gurs,* 137–68.
4. Excerpts from a longer letter quoted in Joseph Weill, *Contribution à l'histoire des camps d'internement dans l'Anti-France* (Paris: Éditions du Centre, 1946), 23–24. During the occupation, Dr. Weill was the chief medical adviser of OSE.
5. Donald A. Lowrie, *The Hunted Children* (New York: Norton, 1963), 60.
6. Gret Arnoldsen, *Silence, on tue* (Paris: La Pensée Universelle, 1981), 145, 154.
7. Louis Lecoin, *De Prison en prison* (Antony, Seine: Louis Lecoin, n.d.), 231.
8. Admiral François Darlan, circular to the prefects, July 1941 [no day on document], CDJC, CCXIII-125.
9. The names, birthplaces, and dates of birth and death of about 2,000 Jews who died in specific French internment camps are listed in Serge Klarsfeld, *Memorial to the Jews Deported from France, 1942–1944* (New York: Beate Klarsfeld Foundation, 1983), 612–40. Klarsfeld estimates the total to be about 3,000.

10. *Le Camp de Gurs*, Laharie, 232–33. Of the 1,710, 345 were freed because they volunteered to return to their countries of origin. The others were freed, either before Darlan's decree or in disregard of it, because they were able to prove that they could support themselves or be supported, could obtain a permit from the mayor of their selected commune of residence, and could pass an inquiry into their "morals."

11. Ibid., 223–26, 234–35. It was not impossible to escape from Gurs, but it was extremely difficult for foreigners to live in France without documents and outside help.

12. Ibid.

13. Ibid., 223

14. Ibid., 194–95.

15. Ibid., 166, 195, 228.

16. For more on Barot, see her report "La CIMADE et les camps d'internement de la zone sud, 1940–1944," in *Églises et chrétiens dans la IIème guerre mondiale: La France: Actes du Colloque national tenu à Lyon du 27 au 30 janvier 1978*, ed. de Montclos. et al. (Lyon: Presses Universitaires de Lyon, 1982), 293–303; and André Jacques, *Madeleine Barot* (Paris: Éditions du Cerf, 1989). Madeleine Barot is honored at Yad Vashem, Israel, as "Righteous among the Nations."

17. Nina Gourfinkel, a Russian Jewish social worker, declared that of all the international charities, "the Swiss were the best organized and the best supplied." (*L'Autre patrie* [Paris: Éditions du Seuil, 1953], 206). This was high praise from Gourfinkel, who was a caustic critic with no patience for the self-righteousness and pretense of what she called the *"potentats de la bienfaisance"*—"charity potentates [who] reappeared one after another, in the various [Hotel] Claridges and Reginas of the southern zone"(137).

18. Funding for the Secours Quaker came from American Quakers and from the American Jewish Joint Distribution Committee, or "Joint," a major American Jewish philanthropic organization. See Weill, Contribution, 89–90; and Laharie, *Le Camp de Gurs,* 350–51.

19. Jeanne Merle, d'Aubigné, "Gurs. La faim. L'attente," in Jeanne Merle d'Aubigné, Violette Mouchon, and Émile C. Fabre, eds., *Les Clandestins de Dieu: CIMADE 1939–1945* (Paris: Fayard, 1968), 61–75; published in English as *God's Underground: CIMADE 1939–1945*, trans. William and Patricia Nottingham (St. Louis: Bethany Press, 1970).

20. Rabbi René S. Kapel described his visit in his postwar memoirs, *Un Rabbin dans la tourmente, 1940–1944: Dans les camps d'internement et au sein de l'Organisation juive de combat* (Paris: Éditions du Centre, 1986). He specifically confirmed the disarray of the Jewish welfare agencies in the fall of 1940 (18).

21. The OSE was founded in Russia in 1912 to provide health care to Jewish adults and children. Its offices were moved to Berlin in 1923, and to Paris in 1933. See especially Sabine Zeitoun, *L'Oeuvre de secours aux enfants (OSE) sous l'occupation en France: Du légalisme à la résistance, 1940–1944* (Paris: L'Harmattan, 1990); Hillel J. Kieval, "Legality and Resistance in Vichy France: The Rescue of Jewish Children," *Proceedings of the American Philosophical Society* 124, no. 5 (October 1980): 339–66; and Lucien Lazare, *La Résistance juive en France* (Paris: Stock, 1987).
22. Founded in Russia in 1880, ORT was moved to Berlin in 1921, and to Paris in 1933.
23. For details, see Anne Grynberg, *Les Camps de la honte: Les internés Juifs des camps français, 1939–1944* (Paris: La Découverte, 1991).
24. Kapel, *Un Rabbin,* 20–22.
25. Ibid., 20.
26. Arnoldsen, *Silence,* 21.
27. The statistic is from a report dated September 3, 1941, reprinted in Weill, *Contribution,* 128; the term "family camp" is from Gourfinkel, *L'Autre patrie,* 217.
28. Vivette Hermann Samuel, "Journal d'une internée volontaire," entry of November 7, 1941, *Evidence,* no. 14 (November 1950): 7–12, 9. See also her longer account of her wartime work with Jewish children in "Comme des brebis . . . " (unpublished manuscript, 1947, OSE Archives, Paris, 138 pp.).
29. Report submitted to the Committee of Nîmes in September 1941, reprinted in Lazare, *La Résistance,* 105.
30. Statistics on internees are from Weill, *Contribution,* 112–15. They were compiled in November 1940 by Maurice Dubois of the Secours suisse. In his medical capacity, Dr. Weill also inspected camps in unoccupied France in the autumn of 1940.
31. Arnoldsen, *Silence,* 182.
32. A law of November 17, 1940, awarded administration of the internment camps to the Ministry of the Interior. One result was the change at Noé; another was the replacement on December 1, 1940, of a visibly relieved army officer who had been the director of Gurs.
33. Weill, *Contribution,* 112.
34. Kapel, *Un Rabbin,* 30–32.
35. Madeleine Barot, interview with the author, Paris, November 3, 1987.
36. The report is quoted in Renée Bédarida, *Pierre Chaillet: Témoin de la résistance spirituelle* (Paris: Fayard, 1988), 123–25. More will be said of Abbé Glasberg and Father Chaillet later in this chapter.
37. Kapel, *Un Rabbin,* 20–24.
38. More complete lists of the twenty-five agencies involved are in

Weill, *Contribution*, 110–11. Archbishop Gerlier's delegates to the committee were the Jesuit Fathers Arnou and Pierre Chaillet.

39. Lowrie, *Hunted Children*, 85.

40. Zosa Szajkowski, *Analytical Franco-Jewish Gazetteer* (New York: S. Frydman, 1966), 34. Résumés of the monthly meetings may be found at the Leo Baeck Institute, New York City, AR 3987, f. I and II.

41. Once released to a specific department, children under fifteen, not needing special identification cards, could easily be moved quietly to OSE homes elsewhere. Jewish welfare agencies were beginning their transition into illegality. See Centre de documentation juive contemporaine, *L'Activité des organisations juives en France sous l'occupation* (1947; Paris: CDJC, 1983), 131–32. The book is a collection of reports of the activities of various Jewish social welfare organizations, written by their individual directors immediately after the war.

42. "Compte-rendu de la réunion du Comité de Coordination, Séance du 31 octobre 1941," Leo Baeck Institute, AR 3987, f. I (6 pp.), 5.

43. Leo Baeck Institute, AR 3987, f. IV, additional report for November, 1941.

44. "Compte-rendu de la réunion du Comité de Coordination, Séance du 20 mai 1942," Leo Baeck Institute, AR 3987, f. I (6 pp.), 4.

45. Gourfinkel, *L'Autre patrie,* 240. In agreement is Gilbert Lesage (interview with the author, Paris, April 29, 1988). See also the affectionate description by Frédéric Chimon Hammel in his *Souviens-toi d'Amalek: Témoignage sur la lutte des Juifs en France, 1938–1944* (Paris: CLKH, 1982), 69; and the biography by Lucien Lazare, *L'Abbé Glasberg* (Paris: Éditions du Cerf, 1990).

46. Victor Vermont, also a priest, was deported to Auschwitz on March 7, 1944, and did not return. David Donoff was killed by Milice and Gestapo agents in a street in Lyon on June 27, 1944. Jean-Pierre Soutou, who had worked with Emmanuel Mounier at *Esprit* until that liberal Catholic journal was banned in August 1941 for articles critical of Vichy's policies, survived. For more on Soutou, see chapter 7.

47. See Glasberg, Gourfinkel, and Weill's "Rapport de la Direction des centres d'accueil," addressed to the Committee of Nîmes and reprinted in full in Weill, *Contribution,* 158–63, and Gourfinkel, *L'Autre patrie,* 252.

48. Gourfinkel, *L'Autre patrie,* 246–47.

49. Ibid., 248, 257.

50. Abbé Alexandre Glasberg's report, reprinted in Weill, *Contribution,* 161; and Abbé Glasberg, "Rapport sur l'activité de la Direction des centres d'accueil (DCA), 1941–1944," Lyon, September 15, 1944, CDJC, CCXVII–41a (8 pp.).

51. Gourfinkel, *L'Autre patrie*, 252–55.
52. See Barot, "La CIMADE et les camps," 300; and Madeleine Barot, "La CIMADE: Une présence, une communauté, une action," in d'Aubigné, Mouchon, and Fabre, *Les Clandestins de Dieu*, 29–38, 33.
53. Laharie, *Le Camp de Gurs*, 227.
54. See the report prepared by the Committee of Nîmes for Vichy officials in October 1941, reprinted in Weill, *Contribution*, 167–71.
55. Gourfinkel, *L'Autre patrie*, 210–22.
56. Weill, *Contribution*, 109–10. It might be pointed out that Weill wrote these words before Gourfinkel leveled her charges in 1953.
57. Letter, OSE France to OSE New York, July 15, 1941, YIVO Institute for Jewish Research, New York, records of the American OSE Committee, f. 1.
58. Kapel, *Un Rabbin*, 86.
59. Weill, *Contribution*, 177–78.
60. Ibid., 178.
61. Kapel, *Un Rabbin*, 86.

CHAPTER 5

1. See a reproduction of the green card on the cover of David Diamant, *Le Billet vert: La vie et la résistance à Pithiviers et Beune-la-Rolande, camps pour Juifs, camps pour chrétiens, camps pour patriotes* (Paris: Renouveau, 1977). For the number of those who received the card, see a report from the Paris Prefecture of Police, May 14, 1941, reprinted in full in Serge Klarsfeld, *Vichy-Auschwitz: Le rôle de Vichy dans la solution finale de la question juive en France—1942* (Paris: Fayard, 1983), 15. The Czech and Austrian Jews summoned were between the ages of eighteen and sixty; the Polish Jews were between eighteen and forty.
2. Diamant, *Le Billet vert*, 22.
3. The number of men arrested is from the police report in Klarsfeld, *Vichy-Auschwitz: 1942*, 15. The number who did not report is calculated by the difference between those summoned and those arrested. Of the 3,710 prisoners whose nationality is known, 3,430 were Polish.
4. Quoted in Diamant, *Le Billet vert*, 241.
5. Told to Claudine Vegh, *I Didn't Say Goodbye*, trans. Ros Schwartz (1979; Hampstead, Eng.: Caliban Books, 1984), 35.
6. Quoted in Diamant, *Le Billet vert*, 247.
7. Annette Monod Leiris, interview with the author, Paris, November 16, 1988.
8. Quoted in Diamant, *Le Billet vert*, 244.

9. Quoted in ibid, 258.

10. Quoted in ibid., 249. The clenched-fist salute, of course, was the Communist party symbol of solidarity.

11. Ibid., 175–78, 256.

12. Quoted in ibid., 257.

13. Prefect of Police to Prefect Delegate of the French Ministry of the Interior to the Occupied Zone Ingrand, Paris, August 21, 1941, reprinted in full in Klarsfeld, *Vichy-Auschwitz: 1942*, 26–27.

14. Prefect Ingrand to Minister of the Interior, Paris, August 21, 1941, reprinted in full in Klarsfeld, *Vichy-Auschwitz: 1942*, 25–26.

15. Roger Gompel, *Pour que tu n'oublies pas . . .* (Paris: Mme. S. de Lalène Laprade [private printing], 1980), 89. Mme. de Lalène Laprade, Gompel's daughter, explains in the introduction that he was released from Drancy on September 14, 1942, and wrote of his experiences between December 1942 and April 1943. Gompel himself explains that he was released because a family member was employed by UGIF. Roger Gompel died in 1976.

16. See the description by Étienne Rosenfeld, a twenty-year-old immigrant from Budapest—married for just ten weeks when he was arrested on August 20 and sent to Drancy—in his *De Drancy à ces camps dont on ne parle pas* (Paris: L'Harmattan, 1991), 38; Maurice Rajsfus, *Drancy: Un camp de concentration très ordinaire, 1941–1944* (Levallois-Perret: Manya, 1991); and descriptions, photographs, and photocopies of relevant documents in [n.a.], *Drancy 1941–1944* (Le Bourget: Presses de GM Imprimerie, 1988).

17. Simone de Beauvoir, *La Force de l'âge* (Paris: Gallimard, 1960), 592.

18. Sylvain Kaufmann, *Au-delà de l'enfer* (Paris: Garamont, 1987), 32.

19. The unfinished buildings Gompel described were completed after the war and form a viable housing complex today. Exterior walls, doors, and shutters are now a cheerful blue or peach. The bleak cinder courtyard, which comprised the dining area, latrines, and exercise space, and where thousands of prisoners assembled in the early morning hours for their last trip toward death, is now a parking lot, playground, and tree-adorned grassy space. A brown granite monument to the Jews of Drancy was placed in front of the courtyard in 1976. Just behind it, a small section of railroad track leads to a boxcar dating from the war.

20. Nöel (Nissim) Calef, *Drancy 1941: Camp de représailles: Drancy la faim* (Paris: Fils et filles des deportés Juifs de France [FFDJF], 1991), xix. Calef, an Italian citizen, was arrested on August 20 and confined at Drancy, from where he was released at the end of 1941 upon the intervention of his government.

21. Gompel, *Pour que tu n'oublies pas . . .*, 9, 12.

22. Like Gompel, Bernard and Wellers survived to write of their experiences. See Jean-Jacques Bernard, "Le Camp de la mort lente: Choses vécues," *Les oeuvres libres*, vol. 227 (Paris: Fayard, 1944), 87–127; and George Wellers, *L'Étoile jaune à l'heure de Vichy: De Drancy à Auschwitz* (Paris: Fayard, 1973). Bernard (1888–1972) was the son of the playwright Tristan Bernard (1866–1947). Wellers (1905–91) was a Russian immigrant naturalized in 1938. Maurice Goudeket, freed a few months after his arrest, also survived. Jacques Ancel, born in 1882, died in 1943.

23. Militärbefehlshaber (MBF) to the delegate of the French government, report, December 21, 1941, reprinted as document 34 in Henri Monneray, ed., *La Persécution des Juifs en France et dans les autres pays de l'ouest presentée par la France à Nuremberg* (Paris: Éditions du Centre, 1947), 177–78. An annex to the document provides the names and ages of the 95 executed men (178–81). Calef writes movingly of the hostages removed from Drancy (*Drancy 1941*, 308–22).

24. Wellers, *L'Étoile jaune*, 80–82.

25. For the statistics on professions, see Klarsfeld, *Vichy-Auschwitz: 1942*, 32.

26. Gompel, *Pour que tu n'oublies pas . . .*, 14.

27. Bernard, "Le Camp de la mort lente," 89, 108.

28. The description of camp structure, conditions, and prisoner releases is from Wellers, *L'Étoile jaune*, 106–97.

29. Gompel, *Pour que tu n'oublies pas . . .*, 79, 82.

30. Wellers, *L'Étoile jaune*, 118.

31. Serge Klarsfeld, *Memorial to the Jews Deported from France, 1942–1944* (New York: Beate Klarsfeld Foundation, 1983), 1–9. The book, based on original deportation lists and Gestapo reports, describes seventy-four deportation convoys carrying Jews from France to the east, as well as several mixed convoys, and prints the passenger lists in full. For the first convoy, Klarsfeld mentions 34 Yugoslavian Jews imprisoned at Compiègne in addition to the 1,112 other deportees, but very little is known of them.

32. Information about the convoys is from Klarsfeld, *Memorial*, 1–56. Although convoy 2 on June 5 left from Compiègne, it carried Jews who had been sent there from Drancy, Pithiviers, and Beaune-la-Rolande. Convoy 3 on June 22 left from Drancy; convoys 4 and 6 on June 25 and July 17, however, left directly from Pithiviers, and convoy 5 on June 28 left from Beaune. Departures from camps other than Drancy subsequently became unusual. Of a total of seventy-four all-Jewish convoys, two left from Compiègne, six from Pithiviers, two from Beaune, one from Angers, one from Lyon, and sixty-two from Drancy.

33. Ibid., 42.

34. Foreign Jews exempted from wearing the star included those from enemy countries such as the United States and Britain; from neutral countries such as Spain and Switzerland; and, for a time, from German-allied nations that had not imposed a similar ordinance, such as Italy, Hungary, and Bulgaria. A handful of French Jews were exempted by special decree. They included the wife of Fernand de Brinon, the Vichy representative to the Germans in Paris; the widow of Henri Bergson; Maurice Goudeket, Colette's husband; three women recommended by Pétain; and a few who were working with German agencies at the time. For details, see Léon Poliakov, *L'Étoile jaune* (Paris: Éditions du Centre, 1949), 37–42, 61–66; and Serge Klarsfeld, *L'Étoile des Juifs* (Paris: L'Archipel, 1992).

35. Annette Muller Bessmann, "Manuscrit-témoignage (unpublished document), CDJC, 35; and Annette Muller, *La Petite fille du Vel' d'Hiv': Récit* (Paris: Denöel, 1991), 76 (a published version of much of "Manuscrit-témoignage").

36. Told to Vegh, *I Didn't Say Goodbye,* 143.

37. Maurice Rajsfus, *Jeudi noir: 16 juillet 1942, L'honneur perdu de la France profonde* (Paris: L'Harmattan, 1988), 25; and interview with the author, Paris, July 2, 1990.

38. Told to Claude Bochurberg, *Mémoirs et vigilance* (Paris: Le Lisère Bleu, 1986), 152. Tsevery was mistaken about the month.

39. Wellers, *L'Étoile jaune,* 69 and 349.

40. Ginette Hirtz, *Les Hortillonnages sous la grêle: Histoire d'une famille juive en France sous l'occupation* (Paris: Mercure de France, 1982), 59.

41. Told to Sabine Zeitoun, *Ces enfants qu'il fallait sauver* (Paris: Albin Michel, 1989), 19.

42. Rajsfus, *Jeudi noir,* 23–25.

43. Told to Vegh, *I Didn't Say Goodbye,* 39.

44. Ibid., 109.

45. Ibid., 150.

46. Told to Bochurberg, *Mémoirs,* 188.

47. Told to Vegh, *I Didn't Say Goodbye,* 103.

48. Fania Elbinger Ewenczyk, interview with the author, Paris, November 16, 1988.

49. Rajsfus, *Jeudi noir,* 23.

50. Hirtz, *Les Hortillonnages,* 53, 56.

51. Bessmann, "Manuscrit-témoignage," 36 (Muller, *La Petite,* 76).

52. Poliakov, quoted in Zeitoun, *Ces enfants,* 18.

53. Alice Couroble, *Amie des Juifs* (Paris: Bloud and Gay, 1946), 16.

54. Wellers, *L'Étoile jaune,* 136–37.

55. Leiris interview. Unlike most of the other non-Jews at Drancy, Dr.

Adelaide Hautval was deported to Auschwitz with a group of women political prisoners. She worked as a camp doctor there and was sometimes able to protect the sick and victims of medical experiments. She was honored as "Righteous among the Nations" at Yad Vashem, Israel, in 1965. Her story is told in Eric Silver, *The Book of the Just* (New York: Grove Press, 1992), 66–70.

56. Wellers, *L'Étoile jaune*, 137.

57. Ibid., 68. Poliakov, investigating immediately after the war, reported that he found evidence of only a few public anti-Semitic incidents at the time of the star decree. In these cases, Jews were booed or otherwise harassed, usually by activists from the collaborationist leagues—the Parti populaire français (PPF), the Mouvement social révolutionnaire (MSR), and the Rassemblement national populaire (RNP). See Poliakov, *L'Étoile jaune*, 77.

58. These reports are reprinted in Poliakov, *L'Étoile jaune*, 80–83 (italics in original).

59. The Italians refused to permit enforcement of this Vichy law in the part of France that they occupied between November 1942 and September 1943.

60. Göring probably did not initiate the order; many historians believe that Heydrich actually drafted it for Göring's signature. See Raul Hilberg, *The Destruction of the European Jews*, 3 vols. (New York: Holmes and Meier, 1985), 2:401.

61. The *Reichssicherheitshauptamt* (RSHA) or Reich Central Security Office in Berlin was one of twelve departments of Himmler's SS. It fused the security police of the state (the Secret State Police, or *Geheime Staatspolizei* [Gestapo], and the Criminal Police [Kripo]) and the Nazi party intelligence system (the Security Service, or *Sicherheitsdienst* [SD]). Heydrich headed the agency until his assassination by Czech resistants in May 1942; he was replaced by Ernst Kaltenbrunner. The RSHA had seven divisions, one of which, section IV, was the Gestapo, under Heinrich Muller. Gestapo unit B (there were five others) was concerned with subversive elements affiliated with sects. Section IV (Gestapo)-B (sects)-4 was concerned with Jews. That agency was headed by Adolf Eichmann. In a parallel structure in France, the head of the RSHA was SS Colonel Helmut Knochen, and, until the end of July 1942, the head of section IV-B-4 was Dannecker. Dannecker was replaced by SS First Lieutenant Heinz Röthke. For the most part, Dannecker and Röthke took orders directly from Eichmann.

62. Theodor Dannecker report, June 15, 1942, reprinted in full in Klarsfeld, *Vichy-Auschwitz: 1942*, 202–3. At the same meeting, it was agreed that Belgium would supply 10,000 Jews, and the Netherlands 15,000.

63. Admiral François Darlan to the prefects, July 1941, CDJC, CCXIII–125. The circular is discussed in chap. 4. French Jews often referred to themselves as "*Israélites*," and called foreign Jews "*Juifs*." Darlan was apparently unaware of the distinction.

64. German Consul General Schleier, résumé of meetings on the Jewish question (September 11, 1942), quoted at length in Klarsfeld, *Vichy-Auschwitz: 1942*, 55.

65. Major Herbert Hagen, résumé of July 2 meeting, July 4, 1942, CDJC, XXVI–40 (11 pp.), 8.

66. Ibid., 9.

67. Theodor Dannecker, report to RSHA office IV-B-4 (Eichmann), July 6, 1942, CDJC, XLIX–35.

68. "Réunion du Conseil des ministres en date du vendredi 10 juillet," reprinted in full in Klarsfeld, *Vichy-Auschwitz: 1942*, 244.

69. Pétain and Laval were tried for collaboration after the war, found guilty, and sentenced to death. Their Jewish policies played little role in their trials. Pétain's sentence was commuted to life in prison; he died on the Ile d'Yeu in the Bay of Biscay in 1951. Laval was executed. Bousquet was tried for collaboration in 1949, after three years of detention. He was found guilty, sentenced to five years of "national indignity," meaning loss of the right to vote or hold public office, and given a suspended sentence. He enjoyed a successful postwar banking career, serving as a senior executive at the Banque d'Indochine. Especially for his role in deporting Jews, he was indicted in 1989 for crimes against humanity under a definition of crime established by the French Parliament in 1964 and carrying no statute of limitations. He was then eighty. He has not yet come to trial. Leguay, never tried after the war, also had a successful and quiet career in business. Largely for his role in the July 1942 roundup of Jews in Paris, he became in 1979 the first Frenchman indicted for crimes against humanity. He died in 1989 at the age of eighty-one, before his case was tried.

70. David S. Wyman, *The Abandonment of the Jews: America and the Holocaust, 1941–1945* (New York: Pantheon, 1984), 23. Wyman describes many other types and sources of information.

71. Ibid., 42–58.

72. Protest of the Consistoire central des Israélites de France, August 25, 1942, CDJC, CCXIII–15 (4 pp.), 1–2.

73. Ambassador Henri Haye's telegram, September 16, 1942, is reprinted in full in Klarsfeld, *Vichy-Auschwitz 1942*, 438–39.

74. Denis Peschanski, "Que savait Vichy?" in *Qui savait quoi?: L'extermination des Juifs, 1941–1945*, ed. Stéphane Courtois and Adam Rayski (Paris: La Découverte, 1987), 53–66, 57.

75. Léon Poliakov, interview with the author, Massy, July 16, 1991. By

the end of 1942, Pope Pius XII had almost certainly received the graphic report of SS Colonel Kurt Gerstein, who personally witnessed mass gassings at Belzek in August. Gerstein's report was confirmed for Vatican officials by diplomatic, Jewish, and Catholic sources. See especially Saul Friedländer, *Pius XII and the Third Reich: A Documentation,* trans. Charles Fullman (New York: Knopf, 1966); and Walter Laqueur, *The Terrible Secret: Suppression of the Truth about Hitler's "Final Solution"* (Boston: Little, Brown, 1980). Laqueur points out that "the Vatican . . . had direct or indirect channels of communication with every European country but Russia," and he concludes that "the Vatican was either the first, or among the first, to learn about the fate of the deported Jews" (56).

76. Rajsfus interview.
77. Poliakov interview.
78. Theodor Dannecker report of meeting with Louis Darquier de Pellepoix, Jean Leguay, and other French police officials, July 8, 1942, CDJC, XXVb–55. Darquier (1897–1980) was tried *in absentia* by the French High Court of Justice in December 1947, found guilty, and sentenced to death. The French government made no attempt to obtain his extradition from Spain, where he remained for the rest of his life.

CHAPTER 6

1. Adam Rayski, *Nos illusions perdues* (Paris: Balland, 1985), 94.
2. Annie Kriegel, *Réflexion sur les questions juives* (Paris: Hachette, 1984), 18, 19.
3. For the detailed police instructions on arrests and exemptions, see Paris Prefecture of Police, "Consignes pour les équipes chargées des arrestations," July 12, 1942, and "Secret circulaire no. 173–42," July 13, 1942, both reprinted in full in Serge Klarsfeld, *Vichy-Auschwitz: Le rôle de Vichy dans la solution finale de la question juive en France—1942* (Paris: Fayard, 1983), 248–56. Originally scheduled for July 13–15, the roundup was postponed until July 16 because of fears that French crowds celebrating Bastille Day would interfere with police operations.
4. Ibid.
5. For examples based especially on interviews with survivors, see Claude Lévy and Paul Tillard, *Betrayal at the Vel d'Hiv,* trans. Inéa Bushnaq (1967; New York: Hill and Wang, 1969), 26–27.
6. For examples of the latter, see Annette Zaidman's interview in Claude Bochurberg, *Mémoirs et vigilance* (Paris: Le Lisère Bleu, 1986), 186–87; and Lévy and Tillard, *Betrayal,* 32, 38.

7. Maurice Rajsfus, *Jeudi noir: 16 juillet 1942, l'honneur perdu de la France profonde* (Paris: L'Harmattan, 1988), 28.

8. In their investigations, Lévy and Tillard traced two policemen who resigned after the event and saw a report about two gendarmes at Choisy who publicly refused to make arrests (*Betrayal,* 206).

9. Annette Muller Bessmann, "Manuscrit-témoignage," (unpublished document): CDJC, 38–40; Annette Muller, *La Petite fille du Vel' d'Hiv': Récit* (Paris: Denoël, 1991), 86–87 (a published version of much of "Manuscrit-témoignage"); and interview with the author, Paris, November 13, 1987.

10. Told to Bochurberg, *Mémoirs,* 186–87.

11. Odette Meyers's testimony is printed in Carol Rittner and Sandra Myers, *The Courage to Care: Rescuers of Jews during the Holocaust* (New York: New York University Press, 1986), 18–23. Marie and Henri Chotel are honored as "Righteous among the Nations" at Yad Vashem, Israel.

12. Rayski, *Nos illusions,* 97.

13. These two cases were described in testimony collected by Lévy and Tillard, *Betrayal,* 27, 33. These authors accept estimates of 106 suicides and 24 deaths from illness during the entire July operation, including the days at the Vel' d'Hiv' (33–34).

14. Paris Prefecture of Police report, July 17, 1942, cited in Klarsfeld, *Vichy-Auschwitz: 1942,* 262. These are the statistics generally cited, although apparently more people were arrested on July 18, and the total may have reached 13,152 (126).

15. Heinz Röthke report, "Abtransport staatenloser Juden," July 18, 1942, CDJC, XLIX–67 (5 pp.), 1. Although Dannecker had laid the groundwork for the July roundup, he was on a tour of the unoccupied zone during the actual event. Röthke, then interim chief, replaced Dannecker formally at the end of the month.

16. The testimony of one woman so employed appears in Lévy and Tillard, *Betrayal,* 15. See also Maurice Rajsfus, *Des Juifs dans la collaboration: L'UGIF 1941–1944* (Paris: Études et Documentation Internationales, 1980), 54.

17. Hélène Elek, *La Mémoire d'Hélène* (Paris: Maspero, 1977), 186–87.

18. Rajsfus, *Jeudi noir,* 39, 168.

19. Fania Elbinger Ewenczyk, interview with the author, Paris, November 16, 1988.

20. Annette Muller Bessmann interview. For the story of the children's survival, see chap. 13.

21. Told to Lévy and Tillard, *Betrayal,* 39.

22. Claude Mauriac, *Les Espaces imaginaires* (Paris: Bernard Grasset, 1975), 237.

23. Rajsfus, *Jeudi noir,* 69; and interview with the author, Paris, July 2, 1990.
24. Bessmann, "Manuscrit-témoignage," 41 (*La Petite,* 88); and Annette Muller Bessmann interview.
25. They told their stories to Lévy and Tillard, *Betrayal,* 41–42.
26. Quoted in Serge Klarsfeld, *Memorial to the Jews Deported from France, 1942–1944* (New York: Beate Klarsfeld Foundation, 1983), 87. As the testimony suggests, many arrestees were over the age limit. Mr. and Mrs. Epstein were deported to Auschwitz on July 24, 1942.
27. Ibid., 64. These five convoys bore the numbers 7, 9, 10, 11, and 12.
28. Ibid., 64–109. In addition to the five convoys from Drancy, another train, convoy 8, left Angers for Auschwitz on July 20 with 824 Jews, most of whom had been arrested in or near the Loire Valley (Saint-Nazaire, Nantes, Angers, Saumur, Tours, Rennes, Laval, Le Mans, Cholet, Niort, Poitiers, and as far south as Chalais) in roundups planned to coincide with the Paris raid of July 16. Three hundred thirty-seven of the deportees were Polish. The next largest national group consisted of 201 French men, women, and children, included to fill the quota of 1,000 for a deportation. Twenty-three were apparently refused admission to the camp and gassed. The other 801 deportees were admitted. Nineteen men from this convoy returned after the war (Klarsfeld, *Memorial,* 72–79).
29. Lévy and Tillard estimate that only twenty to thirty people left Vel' d'Hiv' for medical reasons (*Betrayal,* 122).
30. Quoted at greater length in Klarsfeld, *Memorial,* 59–60. As will be seen in chapter 10, André Baur was himself later arrested and deported to Auschwitz, where he was gassed with his entire family.
31. Quoted in ibid., 60.
32. Interview in Bocherburg, *Mémoirs,* 146.
33. These cases, based on interviews with survivors, are all cited in Lévy and Tillard, *Betrayal,* 51–53.
34. The Vélodrome d'Hiver was torn down after the war, but the site on the boulevard de Grenelle, just a few steps from the intersection with the rue Nelaton, is marked by a wall plaque. The plaque is in a small garden with trees and flower beds, in the shadow of an elevated métro line and with a view of the Eiffel Tower. A larger intersection of the boulevard de Grenelle with the quai de Grenelle nearby has been named the Place des Martyrs Juifs du Vélodrome d'Hiver.
35. Bessmann, "Manuscrit-témoignage," 48 (*La Petite,* 101).
36. Klarsfeld, *Memorial,* 110–39. These convoys bore the numbers 13 through 16. As Klarsfeld explains (xvii–xxii), the number of people from each convoy to be refused admission to Auschwitz and gassed

is, in most cases, calculated from the difference between the numbers of people on the trains themselves (known from the surviving lists drawn up by the Gestapo's Jewish Office in France, which provide the names of deportees) and the numbers actually admitted to the camp (known from carefully compiled records at Auschwitz which noted dates of arrival and registration numbers, but not names, of those assigned to work). In some instances, especially in late 1942, trains stopped before arriving at Auschwitz to release some workers at other labor sites. When this occurred, the calculations of those gassed at Auschwitz before admission have been adjusted accordingly.

37. See SS Second Lieutenant Horst Ahnert, Paris, telex to IV-B-4, Berlin, August 11, 1942, and response by SS Major Guenther, Berlin, August 13, 1942, CDJC, XXVb–123, XXVb–126.

38. Quoted at length in Lévy and Tillard, *Betrayal*, 158–60.

39. Georges Wellers, *L'Étoile jaune à l'heure de Vichy: De Drancy à Auschwitz* (Paris: Fayard, 1973), 140–41. Wellers had arrived at Drancy from Compiègne in April.

40. Extracts from a longer testimony reprinted in Klarsfeld, *Memorial*, 166–69.

41. Wellers, *L'Étoile jaune*, 245.

42. Most of the adults deported with the children of the July 16 roundup were foreign Jews who had been expelled from the unoccupied zone in August 1942. Many had been permitted to leave their own children behind. Their story is told in chap. 7.

43. Wellers, *L'Étoile jaune*, 245.

44. From these seven convoys, numbered 20 through 26 and carrying a total of about 7,000 people, 67 adults are known to have returned. See Klarsfeld, *Memorial*, 172–235.

CHAPTER 7

1. The dispatch is cited in full in Serge Klarsfeld, *Vichy-Auschwitz: Le rôle de Vichy dans la solution finale de la question juive en France—1942* (Paris: Fayard, 1983), 318–19.

2. For discussion of Grand Rabbi Hirschler's arrest and deportation, see chap. 10.

3. Quoted in Hanna Schramm, "Souvenirs d'une emigrée allemande dans un camp d'internement français 1940–1941," in Hanna Schramm and Barbara Vormeier, *Vivre à Gurs: Un camp de concentration français, 1940–1941,* trans. from German by Irène Petit (Paris: François Maspero, 1979), 7–175, 165.

4. Ibid.

5. Ibid., 170, 173.

6. Ibid., 170.

7. For details on these convoys from Drancy to Auschwitz, including the names, birth dates, and cities of origin of deportees, as listed by the Nazis, see Serge Klarsfeld, *Memorial to the Jews Deported from France, 1942-1944* (New York: Beate Klarsfeld Foundation, 1983), 140-55. The convoys were numbered 17 and 18.

8. Thérèse Dauty, "Départ des hébergés des camps-hôpitaux de Noé et de Récébédou en date des 8 et 10 août 1942," August 1942, reprinted in full in *Le Monde Juif*, no. 94 (April–June 1979): 52–58, 55. Dauty worked for Monseigneur Louis de Courrèges d'Uston, the director of the Comité catholique d'aide aux étrangers in Toulouse. She sent him her report, and he relayed it to his superior, Archbishop Jules-Gérard Saliège. It prompted the latter's public protest on August 23. For more on the protest and on the two churchmen, see chapters 8 and 12.

9. Klarsfeld, *Vichy-Auschwitz: 1942*, 142.

10. René Nodot, *Les Enfants ne partiront pas! Témoignages sur la déportation des Juifs: Lyon et Région, 1942–1943* (Lyon: Imprimerie Nouvelle Lyonnaise, 1970), 9–10. Nodot, an active Protestant layman, was the delegate of the Vichy government's Service social des étrangers in the Ain and the Jura. For his Jewish rescue activities during the war, he was honored as "Righteous among the Nations" at Yad Vashem, Israel, in 1974. Grand Rabbi Jacob Kaplan also recalls going to the Lyon train station to try to console prisoners passing through and being prevented from speaking to them. He boarded a train waiting on the next track and spoke to them through the window. See his *Justice pour la foi juive: Pierre Pierrard intérroge le Grand Rabbin Kaplan* (Paris: Centurion, 1977), 86–87.

11. Klarsfeld, *Memorial*, 156–62. This convoy, number 19, is thought to have included 1,015 deportees, but the origins of about 25 individuals are unclear.

12. Witnesses are cited in André Fontaine, *Le Camp d'étrangers des Milles, 1939–1943* (Aix-en-Provence: Edisud, 1989), 137.

13. The *gardes mobiles* were highly disciplined motorized troops assigned to the regional prefects. They could be sent anywhere within their respective regions, which included several departments. The office of regional prefect had itself been created in April 1941, especially to address problems of public order and food supply. At the departmental level, regular prefects remained responsible for administration.

14. The information about Miramas is from witnesses Jean Engel and Jules Stern, cited in Fontaine, *Le Camp d'étrangers*, 137–38. That about Saint-Cyr-sur-Mer and La Ciotat is from the report of Hans

Fraenkel, written in August 1942 while he was interned at Les Milles and reprinted in [n.a.], *Les Camps en Provence: Exil, internement, déportation, 1933–1942* (Aix-en-Provence: Alinéa et LLCG, 1984), 220–27, 221. The reference to Salin-de-Giraud is from the journal and report of Pastor Henri Manen, who was present at Les Milles during the deportations and wrote while there or in the days just following his departure. Manen's report was sent to the Conseil oecuménique in Geneva on or about September 20, 1942, and first published in Henri Cadier, *Le Calvaire d'Israël et la solidarité chrétienne* (Geneva: Éditions Labor et Fides, 1945), 93–116. I cite from the version published in *Les Camps en Provence*, 206–19, 207. Manen learned about Salin-de-Giraud from Fraenkel.

15. Fraenkel report, 222.

16. Ibid., 220.

17. For one dramatic case—the parents of a son in the Foreign Legion obtained proof and were actually released from a sealed boxcar at Les Milles just before departure—see Henri Manen's journal entry for August 10, 1942, in *Les Camps en Provence*, 210. Pastor Manen is honored as "Righteous among the Nations" at Yad Vashem, Israel.

18. Fontaine, *Le Camp d'étrangers*, 140. Fraenkel, in his report, also writes of Dr. Raybaud that he "tried to save as many of his patients as possible" (*Les Camps en Provence*, 222).

19. As seen in chap. 3, baptismal certificates dated before June 25, 1940, could only help those with just two Jewish grandparents who were not themselves married to Jews. Conversion was of no help to those with more than two Jewish grandparents. However, false parental and grandparental baptismal certificates could be supplied.

20. *Les Camps en Provence*, 195.

21. Testimony of a social worker, CDJC, CCXIII–60 (5 pp.), 2.

22. Raymond-Raoul Lambert, *Carnet d'un témoin, 1940–1943,* ed. Richard Cohen (Paris: Fayard, 1985), 184–85.

23. *Les Camps en Provence*, 209.

24. Fraenkel estimated that sixteen people attempted suicide, two successfully, and fifty hid; of the fifty, only about four were found. He observed that the police made only a half-hearted attempt to find escapees, adding that "the directors and guards did their best to notice nothing and to provide support" (*Les Camps en Provence*, 225).

25. Testimony of Marcel Neiger, one of the rescued children, cited in Fontaine, *Le Camp d'étrangers*, 145. For his many rescue missions, Auguste César Boyer was honored as "Righteous among the Nations" at Yad Vashem, Israel, in 1981.

26. Pastor Manen wrote in his journal on August 12, 1942, that Maulavé had always been "very humane." Sometime between September 11 and 20, Manen also wrote, "The camp authorities—especially the Commander—always helped us in our work [of assistance] and contributed as best they could to the task of alleviating suffering" (see his journal and subsequent report in *Les Camps en Provence*, 211, 215). Fraenkel also testified to Maulavé's decency and added that the camp administrator, Pierre Baratier-Buisson, and the chief of the screening process, Gausse, were also sympathetic (*Les Camps en Provence*, 222). On September 29, after most activity at Les Milles had ceased, Robert Maulavé was suspended and imprisoned in Aix-en-Provence for his uncooperative attitude. Four camp guards—Auguste César Boyer, Lucien Mercier, Aimé Bondi, and Jean-Louis Kissy—were accused of helping Jews escape and were also arrested. See *Les Camps en Provence*, 198.

27. Of police thievery, Pastor Manen wrote in his journal on August 10 that upon first learning of it from Grand Rabbi Israël Salzer, "I could not believe it and I thought it was a case of objects misplaced by the internees in the confusion. Alas! the thing was confirmed" (*Les Camps en Provence*, 211).

28. Grand Rabbi Israël Salzer report, September 1942, reprinted in *Les Camps en Provence*, 228–32, 230.

29. On Boyer, see testimony of M. Simoni, in Fontaine, *Le Camp d'étrangers*, 146. Fontaine puts the number of deportees at 262 (147).

30. Klarsfeld, *Vichy-Auschwitz: 1942*, 146; Fontaine says the deportees that day numbered 542 (*Le Camp d'étrangers*, 149).

31. CDJC, CCXIII–60, 4. Lambert confirms the police brutality, saying that it was so bad that he and Pastor Manen protested (*Carnet*, 186).

32. CDJC, CCXIII–60, 5.

33. Klarsfeld, *Memorial*, 172–81. The August 17 train was convoy 20.

34. Ibid., 182–90.

35. The words *about, approximately,* and *roughly,* so coldly inappropriate where human lives are concerned, are inevitable in this and many other cases. Slight discrepancies in deportation statistics exist for many reasons. Because of last-minute changes, deaths, and escapes from the trains, bureaucratic reports of departures and arrivals sometimes vary. Also, officials sometimes simply miscounted. In addition, the original lists of individual names are occasionally unclear.

36. For Les Milles, see Fontaine, *Le Camp d'étrangers*, 152; and *Les Camps en Provence*, 196.

37. Fontaine, *Le Camp d'étrangers*, 152. Nina Gourfinkel later remem-

bered that residents in two of Abbé Glasberg's centers, in the Drôme and in the Hautes-Alpes, were seized and expelled to the occupied zone despite personal promises from the local prefects that they would be spared. In the Drôme, the prefect's office advised the director of the center that arrests were imminent, but the director, afraid of compromising himself, did not relay the warning. In the Hautes-Alpes, the prefect tried to keep his promise, but a local collaborator initiated the arrests. See Nina Gourfinkel, *L'Autre patrie* (Paris: Éditions du Seuil, 1953), 263, 267–68; and Abbé Alexandre Glasberg, "Rapport sur l'activité de la Direction des centres d'accueil (DCA), 1941–1944," Lyon, September 15, 1944, CDJC, CCXVII–41a (8 pp.), 4–5.

38. These three trains were convoys 24, 25, and 26. From approximately 3,000 deportees, 49 are known to have survived. See Klarsfeld, *Memorial,* 209–35; and his *Vichy-Auschwitz: 1942,* 158–59. Beginning with convoy 24 and continuing with fourteen other convoys until the end of 1942, more than 3,000 male deportees fit for hard labor were taken off the trains at Kosel, not far from Auschwitz, and sent to local work camps. Survivors of that ordeal did not arrive at Auschwitz until 1944.

39. SS Major Herbert Hagen, report of an August 3 interview with Pierre Laval and René Bousquet, August 4, 1942, CDJC, XXVI–54 (2 pp.)

40. This secret telegram is reprinted in full in Klarsfeld, *Vichy-Auschwitz: 1942,* 339. On the office of regional perfect, see n. 13, above.

41. Police intendant, attachment to instructions of regional prefect, Region of Limoges, August 22, 1942, CDJC, LVII–68 (8 pp.), 7.

42. Nodot, *Les Enfants,* 13.

43. Ibid.

44. The Swiss correspondent's article appeared in the *Berner Tagewacht* (Berne, Switzerland) on September 2, 1942. It is quoted in Barbara Vormeier, *The Deportation of German and Austrian Jews from France* (Paris: La Solidarité, 1980), 58. The entire text is also reprinted in German and French.

45. René Bousquet telegram reprinted in full in Klarsfeld, *Vichy-Auschwitz: 1942,* 348.

46. Regional Prefect, Region of Limoges, August 22, 1942, CDJC, LVII–68, 1.

47. Told by the mother to Rachel Minc, *L'Enfer des innocents: Les enfants Juifs dans la tourmente nazie: Récits* (Paris: Éditions du Centurion, 1966), 140–43.

48. Ibid., 155–57.

49. Reprinted in full in Klarsfeld, *Vichy-Auschwitz: 1942,* 393.

50. Ibid., 158–61.
51. The number 12,686 is from the Ministry of the Interior report, September 1, 1942, reprinted in Klarsfeld, *Vichy-Auschwitz: 1942*, 393.
52. See, for example, documents in ibid., 378, 381.
53. Reprinted in ibid., 395.
54. Post-war report of Georges Garel, "Travail clandestin de l'OSE," CDJC, CCXVIII–104 (9 pp.).
55. For details on Amitiés chrétiennes, see chap. 8.
56. Annie Latour, interview with Georges Garel, [n.d.], CDJC, DLXXII–7.
57. Actual witnesses of these events disagree about the precise number of children involved. According to Gilbert Lesage (interview with the author, Paris, April 29, 1988), 84 children were officially released, and another 36 were hidden. According to the report of Regional Prefect Angeli in Lyon (who would not have known about the hidden children, and who would in any case have wanted to minimize the number) to the national police on September 1, 1942 (reprinted in Klarsfeld, *Vichy-Auschwitz: 1942,* 398–400), only 84 children left. Lucien Lazare, then a teenager and Jewish Boy Scout who helped feed the children when they left Vénissieux for EIF headquarters, puts their number at 108. See his *La Résistance juive en France* (Paris: Stock, 1987), 208. Georges Garel ("Travail") said there were 108 or 110 children and 60 adults released officially, and about 12 children hidden. Other sources put the number of adults much higher. These slight discrepancies in no way affect the general outline of the story, about which all witnesses agree.
58. Jean-Marie Soutou, "Souvenirs des années noires," *Cahiers, Alliance israélite universelle,* no. 201 (October–November 1979): 9–14, 12. Jean-Marie Soutou went on to have a distinguished diplomatic and public service career after the war. He was, among other things, *directeur adjoint* of the cabinet of Prime Minister Pierre Mendes France from June 1954 to February 1955, ambassador to Algeria from 1971 to 1975, secretary-general at the Ministry of Foreign Affairs, and president of the French Red Cross from 1978 to 1983.
59. Lesage interview. Gilbert Lesage (1910–90) was honored as "Righteous among the Nations" at Yad Vashem, Israel, in 1985. The description of Glasberg's car is from Soutou, *Cahiers,* 12.
60. Regional Prefect Angeli, report, 398; and Lazare, *La Résistance,* 208.
61. Quoted from Regional Prefect Angeli, report, September 1, 1942, 398. Angeli went on to describe his efforts to learn from Cardinal Gerlier and Jesuit Father Pierre Chaillet, respectively an honorary

patron and an activist of *Amitiés chrétiennes,* where the children had been hidden. According to Angeli, both churchmen refused to reveal their locations. According to Abbé Glasberg, however, Gerlier (but *not* Chaillet) supplied a list of hiding places which he believed to be accurate, trusting promises that the children would not be harmed. French police tried to arrest them, but the list was false. For Glasberg's testimony, see *Églises et chrétiens dans la IIème guerre mondiale: La Région Rhône-Alpes: Actes du Colloque tenu à Grenoble du 7 au 9 octobre 1976,* ed. de Montclos, et al. (Lyon: Presses Universitaires de Lyon, 1978), 204–5. For his deliberate obstruction of the authorities' pursuit, Chaillet was punished with assignment to a supervised residence for a month.

62. Regional Prefect Angeli, report, September 1, 1942, 398.
63. Lesage interview. Abbé Glasberg's associate Nina Gourfinkel also tells the story (*L'Autre patrie,* 265–66).
64. Told to Nodot, *Les Enfants,* 14–16.
65. Klarsfeld, *Vichy-Auschwitz: 1942,* 159.
66. Annou's report to his regional prefect, quoted in Maurice Vanino (the director of the Center for Political Documentation of the Ministry of Information of the French Provisional Government in Algiers), *Le Temps de la honte: De Rethondes à l'Ile d'Yeu* (Paris: Créator, 1952), 239.
67. Ibid.
68. Klarsfeld, *Memorial,* 236–42. The September 2 train was convoy 27.
69. Ibid., 243–50. The September 4 train was convoy 28.
70. Klarsfeld puts the number expelled from Les Milles on September 2 at 500 and states that 250 were picked up from Rivesaltes on September 3 (*Vichy-Auschwitz: 1942,* 159). *Les Camps en Provence* (197) estimates expellees from Les Milles at 574.
71. *Les Camps en Provence,* 197.
72. Quoted in ibid., 215.
73. Lambert, *Carnet,* 188–89.
74. *Les Camps en Provence,* 216.
75. Klarsfeld, *Vichy-Auschwitz: 1942,* 159.
76. Father Roger Braun, preface to Gret Arnoldsen, *Silence, on tue* (Paris: La Pensée Universelle, 1981), 10. Father Roger Braun is honored as "Righteous among the Nations" at Yad Vashem, Israel.
77. Klarsfeld, *Vichy-Auschwitz: 1942,* 159.
78. Ibid. The September 7 train was convoy 29. Thirty-four men, but no women or children, returned. See Klarsfeld, *Memorial,* 251–58.
79. Klarsfeld, *Vichy-Auschwitz: 1942,* 159. The trains on September 9, 11, 14, and 16 were convoys 30, 31, 32, and 33.
80. Annette Monod Leiris, interview with the author, Paris, July 15, 1991.

CHAPTER 8

1. Jean Pierre-Bloch, *Jusqu'au dernier jour: Mémoires* (Paris: Albin Michel, 1983), 210.
2. Ibid., 184. Henriot joined the Milice in 1943, became a daily contributor to Radio-Vichy advocating collaboration and denouncing Jews, Communists, and Resistants, and joined the government in January 1944 as the secretary of state for information and propaganda. He was assassinated by Resistants in June 1944.
3. For details of those protests, see chap. 3.
4. Two Catholic journals that discreetly advocated opposition to the Vichy regime, Stanislas Fumet's *Temps nouveau* and Emmanuel Mounier's *Esprit,* were banned in August 1941. The two publications did not devote much space to Jewish issues, but in May and June 1941, both attacked a violently anti-Semitic German film entitled *Le Juif Süss,* which was being shown throughout France at the time. During the same period, partly as a result of the attacks, several dozen students demonstrated against a theater in Lyon where the film was showing, until they were dispersed by police. See especially Renée Bédarida, *Les Armes de l'esprit: Témoignage chrétien, 1941–1944* (Paris: Éditions Ouvrières, 1977), 29–30.
5. For examples in southeastern France, see François Delpech, "La Persécution des Juifs et l'Amitié chrétienne," in *Églises et chrétiens dans la IIème guerre mondiale: La Région Rhône-Alpes: Actes du Colloque tenu à Grenoble du 7 au 9 octobre 1976,* ed. de Montclos, et al. (Lyon: Presses Universitaires de Lyon, 1978), 143–79, 158.
6. Jacques Duquesne, *Les Catholiques français sous l'occupation* (Paris: Bernard Grasset, 1966), 245.
7. Monseigneur Émile Guerry, *L'Église catholique en France sous l'occupation* (Paris: Flammarion, 1947), 38–39. Guerry himself delivered the message to the minister's chef du cabinet. See also Duquesne, *Les Catholiques,* 245. Interestingly enough, Abbé Glasberg claimed in October 1976 that when he and Father Pierre Chaillet met with Cardinal Gerlier to ask him to protest against conditions in the internment camps, they learned that Jacques Helbronner, the cardinal's old friend and schoolmate who was then president of the Consistoire central, had asked that he not intervene. Such a protest against the treatment of foreign Jews, Helbronner felt, would only aggravate the situation and endanger French Jews. See Glasberg's testimony in de Montclos, et al., eds., *Églises et chrétiens: Rhône-Alpes,* 203. Jacques Helbronner and his wife Jeanne, both seventy years old, were deported to Auschwitz on November 20, 1943.
8. Delpech, "La Persécution," 162.
9. Annie Kriegel, "Résistants communistes et Juifs persécutés," in her

Réflexion sur les questions juives (Paris: Hachette, 1984), 29–58, 35–36; and Stéphane Courtois, "Que savait la presse communiste clandestine?" in *Qui savait quoi?: L'extermination des Juifs, 1941–1945,* ed. Stéphane Courtois and Adam Rayski (Paris: La Découverte, 1987), 103–12, 104.

10. Quoted in Kriegel, "Résistants," 37.

11. Ibid., 35; and Courtois, "Qui savait quoi?" 104.

12. Kriegel, "Résistants," 35.

13. For example, a two-page Resistance tract intended for doctors in the department of Seine Maritime (reprinted in Claude-Paul Couture, *La Déportation raciale en Seine-Maritime de 1940 à 1944* [Rouen: CRDP, 1981], 43–44) described and denounced the brutal emptying of the Rothschild Hospital in Paris in early July 1942. Jewish camp inmates still recovering from illness or operations were returned to Drancy to make room for those about to be arrested on July 16.

14. Claude Lévy, "Que savait la presse clandestine non communiste?" in Courtois and Rayski, *Qui savait quoi?,* 93–102.

15. Quotation from Delpech, "La Persécution," 162. For a detailed biography of Chaillet, see Renée Bédarida, *Pierre Chaillet: Témoin de la résistance spirituelle* (Paris: Fayard, 1988). For details on *Témoignage chrétien,* see both her *Pierre Chaillet* and her *Les Armes de l'esprit.*

16. "Droits de l'homme et du chrétien," *Cahiers du Témoignage chrétien* (August 1942): 5.

17. According to Delpech, "La Persécution," 164, Beaujolin and de Pierrebourg were "liberal Protestants." According to Abbé Glasberg's testimony in *Églises et chrétiens: Rhône-Alpes,* they were both "rather anti-clerical" (203).

18. Bédarida, *Les Armes de l'esprit,* 132–33.

19. Prefect of the Var to the Ministry of the Interior, October 1, 1941, 8, in Archives nationales, *Rapports des préfets,* F/1C–III, box 1194. Subsequent references to this series will be designated AN, with the box number. The major city of the Var is Toulon.

20. November 3, 1941, chap. B, 2–3, in AN, 1143.

21. August 4, 1941, 9, in AN, 1137.

22. April 3, 1941, 1, in AN, 1183.

23. Prefect delegate of the Rhône, January 5, 1942, chap. B, 2, in AN, 1183.

24. May 5, 1941, 2, in AN, 1194.

25. October 30, 1940, 3, in AN, 1154. The major city of Haute-Garonne is Toulouse.

26. November 3, 1941, chap. B, 2–3, in AN, 1143.

27. Ibid., 1.

28. June 3, 1942, introduction, 1, in AN, 1143.

29. May 5, 1941, 2, in AN, 1194.
30. May 1, 1942, 8, in AN, 1194.
31. Prefect of Belfort, November 4, 1941, chap. B, 1, AN, 1142.
32. Prefect of the Rhône, February 5, 1942, 2, in AN, 1183.
33. "Rapport d'information," October 1, 1941, 1, in AN, 1194.
34. June 1, 1942, 6, in AN, 1194.
35. Prefect of the Var, November 3, 1941, 6, in AN, 1194.
36. Prefect of Bouches-du-Rhône, September 25, 1941, chap. B, 2, in AN, 1143.
37. Police investigation report, quoted in full in Serge Klarsfeld, *Vichy-Auschwitz: Le rôle de Vichy dans la solution finale de la question juive en France—1942* (Paris: Fayard, 1983), 31.
38. Courtois, "Que savait," 109.
39. Lévy, "Que savait," 97.
40. Regional Perfect, Region of Marseille, to Ministry of the Interior, October 7, 1942, chap. B, 4–5, in AN, 1143.
41. "Adresse des cardinaux et archévêques de zone occupée à M. le Maréchal Pétain," July 22, 1942, CDJC, CIX–114.
42. Henri de Lubac, *Résistance chrétienne à l'antisemitisme: Souvenirs 1940–1944* (Paris: Fayard, 1988), 159. Father de Lubac (1896–1991) was a Jesuit priest and an early contributor to *Témoignage chrétien*. He later played a leading role in the Second Vatican Council, which reformed the Catholic church in the 1960s.
43. Gerlier's letter is reprinted in full in Klarsfeld, *Vichy-Auschwitz: 1942*, 342.
44. Ibid., 344–45.
45. CDJC, CIX–115.
46. See the report from the prefecture of the Haute-Garonne to René Bousquet, August 22, 1942, reprinted in Klarsfeld, *Vichy-Auschwitz: 1942*, 353–54.
47. CDJC, CIX–113. It is interesting that Bishop Théas, whose protest against the racial persecutions is considered, with that of Saliège, to be the strongest and most sincere of the bishops' statements, and who later did much to shelter Jews hiding in his diocese, utilized the pseudo-scientific Nazi racial terms "Aryan" and "non-Aryan."
48. *Témoignage chrétien*, testimony of Marie-Rose Gineste (10 pp.), in AN, 72 AJ 73. Marie-Rose Gineste is honored as "Righteous among the Nations" at Yad Vashem, Israel, as are, among those cited in this chapter, Cardinal Gerlier, Archbishop Saliège, Bishop Théas, Father Chaillet, Pastor Boegner, Pastor Roland de Pury and his wife Jacqueline, Olivier de Pierrebourg, and Germaine Ribière.
49. For the full texts of the protests, see CDJC, CCXIV–6 and CIX–113.

50. Regional Prefect, Region of Toulouse, to Ministry of the Interior, October 5, 1942, 2, in AN, 1204.
51. For a reference to Catholic bookstores, see Prefect Delegate of Haute-Garonne to Ministry of the Interior, October 5, 1942, chap. B, 1, in AN, 1154.
52. Testimony of Delpech, *Églises et chrétiens,* 202.
53. Regional Prefect, Region of Marseille, to Ministry of the Interior, October 7, 1942, chap. B, 4–5, in AN, 1143; and Prefect of the Rhône, September 5, 1942, chap. B, 1–2, AN, 1183.
54. Robert Lévy testimony, in [n.a.], *De l'université aux camps de concentration: Témoignages strasbourgeois* (Paris: Société d'Édition "Les Belles Lettres," 1954), 457–66, 457.
55. For more on these sources, and for what Vichy officials knew during the summer of 1942, see chap. 5.
56. Courtois, "Que savait," 109.
57. Adam Rayski, *Nos illusions perdues* (Paris: Balland, 1985), 125.
58. CDJC, CIX–115; CDJC, CIX–113; and CDJC, CCXIV–6.
59. Jacob Kaplan, *Justice pour la foi juive: Pierre Pierrard intérroge le Grand Rabbin Kaplan* (Paris: Centurion, 1977), 87–90; and Jacob Kaplan, *N'oublie pas* (Paris: Stock, 1984), 10.
60. CDJC, CCXIII–15 (4 pp.), 1–2. This letter is discussed in chap. 5.
61. Ibid., 3–4.
62. Georges Wellers, *L'Étoile jaune à l'heure de Vichy: De Drancy à Auschwitz* (Paris: Fayard, 1973), 231.
63. "Compte rendu du Comité de Coordination, Séance du 9 septembre 1942," Leo Baeck Institute, AR 3987, f. I.
64. Vivette Hermann Samuel, interview with the author, Paris, May 10, 1989.
65. Raymond Aron, *Mémoires: Cinquante ans de réflexion politique* (Paris: Julliard, 1983), 176; published in English as *Memoirs: Fifty Years of Political Reflection,* trans. George Holoch (New York: Holmes and Meier, 1990).
66. Wellers, *L'Étoile jaune,* 5, 226.
67. Ibid., 228. For more on Rapoport and the Comité rue Amelot, see chapter 12.
68. Robert Debré, *L'Honneur de vivre: Témoignage* ([n.p.]: Hermann et Stock, 1974), 231–32.
69. Henri Krasucki testimony, in [n.a.], *Jawischowitz, une annexe d'Auschwitz: 45 deportés 8 mineurs témoignent* (Paris: Amicale d'Auschwitz, 1985), 221.
70. Henry Bulawko, *Les Jeux de la mort et de l'espoir: Auschwitz-Jawarzno* (Paris: Amicale des anciens deportés Juifs de France, 1954), 60.

71. Wellers, *L'Étoile jaune,* 7.
72. Marc Klein testimony, in [n.a.], *De l'université aux camps,* 429–55, 432.
73. Samuel interview.
74. Paris Prefecture of Police report, reprinted in Klarsfeld, *Vichy-Auschwitz: 1942,* 263.
75. Heinz Röthke report, "Abtransport staatenloser Juden," CDJC, July 18, 1942, XLIX–67, (5 pp.), 2.
76. SS Captain Comte von Korff to his superiors, Chalons-sur-Marne, July 25, 1942, CDJC, XXVb–90.
77. October 1, 1942, 2, in AN, 1194.
78. Report for August 1942, in "Rapports du Préfet Régional de Limoges de Juin 1942 à Juin 1944," in AN, 1200.
79. Regional Prefect, Region of Marseille, to Ministry of the Interior, October 7, 1942, chap. B, 4–5, in AN, 1143.
80. Prefect of Alpes-Maritimes, report for July-August 1942, 4, in AN, 1137.
81. September 5, 1942, chap. B, 1–2, in AN, 1183.
82. October 5, 1942, chap. B, 1, in AN, 1154.
83. Labor service for non-Jews in Germany was at first either voluntary or connected with a German promise to release one prisoner of war for every three skilled workers to volunteer—a program initiated in June 1942 and known as the *relève.* A Vichy law of September 4, 1942, provided for government mobilization for labor of men between the ages of eighteen and fifty and single women between twenty-one and thirty-five. Another law on February 16, 1943, instituted the *Service de travail obligatoire,* making all non-Jewish young people born in 1920, 1921, and 1922 eligible for forced-labor service in Germany.

    Complaints against the PPF, particularly by late 1943, centered on its actions against Resistants and young men hiding from the labor draft.

CHAPTER 9

1. Paris police report, September 12, 1942, reprinted in full in Serge Klarsfeld, *Vichy-Auschwitz: Le rôle de Vichy dans la solution finale de la question juive en France—1942* (Paris: Fayard, 1983), 429–30.
2. Dr. Carltheo Zeitschel (an expert on Jewish affairs), German Embassy, report, Paris, September 24, 1942, CDJC, XXVa–252.
3. Orders of municipal police chief Emile Hennequin, Paris, September 23, 1942, reprinted in full in Klarsfeld, *Vichy-Auschwitz: 1942,* 447–50.

4. Heinz Röthke report, "Festnahme rumänischer Juden," September 24, 1942, CDJC, XXVI–65.
5. Collected German police reports, October 1942, CDJC, XXVc–253.
6. Heinz Röthke report, "Festnahme von Juden griechischer Staatsangehörigkeit am 5.11.1942 früh," November 5, 1942, CDJC, XXV–51a.
7. Serge Klarsfeld, *Memorial to the Jews Deported from France, 1942–1944* (New York: Beate Klarsfeld Foundation, 1983), 283–91, 312–59. Convoy numbers were 33 (September 16), 37 (September 25), 38 (September 28), 39 (September 30), 40 (November 4), 42 (November 6), 44 (November 9), and 45 (November 11). There were no convoys numbered 41 or 43.
8. Heinz Röthke, report to Helmut Knochen, "Plan für die Verhaftungsaktion am 22.9.1942," September 21, 1942, CDJC, XLIX–43a (3 pp).
9. French police report, September 23, 1942, reprinted in full in Klarsfeld, *Vichy-Auschwitz: 1942,* 447.
10. The Permilleux service, named for its chief, was a specialized anti-Jewish unit of the Paris police prefecture created at the end of 1942 to take over the arrest powers of the CGQJ's defunct Police aux questions juives (PQJ) and to attempt to prevent those powers from being assumed by the PQJ's formal replacement, the Section d'enquête et de contrôle (SEC). It included about twenty policemen. In contrast to other French police units, the Permilleux service often took orders directly from Röthke. It was charged with acting on tips from informers, rounding up families of those charged with infractions, and, increasingly, making arbitrary arrests. It sent some 30 to 60 victims a day to Drancy, thus ensuring that, with the addition of Jews arrested in specialized roundups, the camp would always have a complement of at least 1,000 eligible for a deportation convoy. In the autumn of 1943, the Milice (described in chap. 2) had some 29,000 adherents. See Jacques Delperrie de Bayac, *Histoire de la Milice: 1918–1945,* 2 vols. (Paris: Fayard, 1969), 1: 181.
11. Serge Klarsfeld, *Vichy-Auschwitz: Le rôle de Vichy dans la solution finale de la question juive en France—1943–1944* (Paris: Fayard, 1985), 155; and Klarsfeld, interviews with the author, New York, March 14 and September 28, 1988. Maurice Rajsfus confirmed this phenomenon from his own observation in an interview with the author, Paris, July 2, 1990.
12. Rajsfus interview. SS Captain Aloïs Brunner was Röthke's aide. He became director of Drancy after July 2, 1943.
13. Quoted in Klarsfeld, *Memorial,* 601 (italics added). The July 30 train was convoy 81.

14. Henry Bulawko, *Les Jeux de la mort et de l'espoir: Auschwitz-Jaworzno* (Paris: Amicale des anciens deportés Juifs de France, 1954), 37. Information also from Bulawko's "Témoignage sur la résistance juive en France occupée" (unpublished manuscript, Paris, November 30, 1982); and interview with the author, Paris, November 9, 1987.

15. Gaby Cohen, interview with the author, Paris, April 29, 1988.

16. Ibid.

17. Denise Caraco Siekierski, interview with the author, Paris, November 10, 1987. For more on her Jewish rescue activities, see chap. 12.

18. Léon Poliakov, *L'Auberge des musiciens: Mémoires* (Paris: Mazarine, 1981), 144 (written in 1946).

19. Those eight departments were the Var, Alpes-Maritimes, Basses-Alpes, Hautes-Alpes, Savoie, Haute-Savoie, and parts of the Drôme and Isère. Departments east of the Rhône but occupied by the Germans were Bouches-du-Rhône, with the cities of Aix-en-Provence, Arles, and Marseille; the Vaucluse, which includes Avignon; and parts of the Drôme and Isère.

20. Angelo Donati, from Modena, served as a liaison officer between the French and Italian armies during the First World War. After the war, he helped found and direct a French-Italian bank in Paris. He became involved with German Jewish refugee relief after 1933. He moved to Nice when the Germans occupied Paris in 1940 and continued his assistance to refugees. For details, see especially Jean-Louis Panicacci, "Les Juifs et la question juive dans les Alpes-Maritimes de 1939 à 1945," *Recherches régionales Côte d'Azur et contrées limitrophes: Bulletin trimestriel* (Departmental Archives of the Alpes-Maritimes), no. 3 (1983): 239–330.

21. Heinz Röthke, "Present State of the Jewish Question in France," July 21, 1943, reprinted in full in English translation as document 25 in Léon Poliakov, "The Jews under the Italian Occupation in France," in Léon Poliakov and Jacques Sabille, *Jews under the Italian Occupation* (Paris: Éditions du Centre, 1955), 19–128, 104–6.

22. Adam Munz, interview with the author, New York City, April 15, 1987.

23. Alfred Feldman testimony, September 6, 1976, quoted in Alberto Cavaglion, *Nella notte straniera: Gli ebrei di S. Martin Vésubie e il campo di Borgo S. Dalmazzo, 8 settembre–21 novembre 1943* (Cuneo: L'Arciere, 1981), 44.

24. Report from the Italian Embassy in Paris to its representative in Vichy, January 1943, reprinted in English translation in Poliakov and Sabille, *Italian Occupation,* 25.

25. For details, see especially Poliakov and Sabille, *Italian Occupation, 32–38;* Meir Michaelis, *Mussolini and the Jews: German-Italian Relations and the Jewish Question in Italy, 1922–1945* (Oxford: Clarendon, 1978), 308–10; and Susan Zuccotti, *The Italians and the Holocaust: Persecution, Rescue, and Survival* (New York: Basic Books, 1987), 85–87.

26. Helmut Knochen report, "Abtransport von Juden aus dem Judenlager Drancy bei Paris nach Auschwitz," January 21, 1943, CDJC, XXVc–195.

27. SS Major Guenther, telegram to Helmut Knochen, January 25, 1943, CDJC, XXVI–70.

28. As Röthke explained it, "The French police have, on their own initiative, proposed to arrest these [foreign] Jews in time, because they wished to avoid the deportation of Jews with French citizenship." (Heinz Röthke report, "Abschub von Juden französischer Staatsangehörigkeit aus dem Judenlager Drancy nach Auschwitz/O.S.," February 10, 1943, XXVc–204 [3 pp.], 2).

29. Paris Prefect of Police report, February 13, 1943, reprinted in full in Klarsfeld, *Vichy-Auschwitz: 1943–1944,* 221.

30. Klarsfeld, *Vichy-Auschwitz: 1943–1944,* 24–25.

31. Helmut Knochen to SS Lieutenant General Heinrich Muller (Gestapo chief in Berlin), "Endlösung der Judenfrage in Frankreich," February 12, 1943, CDJC, XXVI–71 (5 pp.), 3.

32. Klarsfeld, *Memorial,* 360–76. The February 11 train was convoy 47. Of its 998 passengers, 802 were refused admission to Auschwitz and gassed; 196 were selected for work; and 14 survived. The train scheduled for February 9, convoy 46, left as planned. It carried 1,000 prisoners: a few escaped; 169 were admitted, of whom 22 survived; and the rest were gassed.

33. Heinz Röthke report, "Abschub von Juden Franzosischer Staatsangehörigkeit aus dem Judenlager Drancy nach Auschwitz/O.S.," February 16, 1943, CDJC, XXVc–207.

34. Klarsfeld, *Memorial,* 377–83. The train of February 13 was convoy 48. Of the 1,000, 681 were selected for immediate gassing; 311 were admitted to the camp.

35. SS Lieutenant Colonel Kurt Lischka, aide to Helmut Knochen, report, "Endlösung der Judenfrage in Frankreich; hier: Stellung der Italiener zur Judenfrage," February 24, 1943, CDJC, XXVa–277.

36. For documents describing the trains from Gurs to Drancy, see Klarsfeld, *Vichy-Auschwitz: 1943–1944,* 34–35.

37. Klarsfeld, *Memorial,* 392–409. The trains of March 4 and 6 were convoys 50 and 51.

CHAPTER 10

1. Claude-Paul Couture, *La Déportation raciale en Seine-Maritime de 1940 à 1944* (Rouen: CRDP, 1981), 18.

2. Raymond-Raoul Lambert, diary entry for February 1, 1943, Marseille, in *Carnet d'un témoin, 1940–1943,* ed. Richard Cohen (Paris: Fayard, 1985), 206–8.

3. Serge Klarsfeld, *Vichy-Auschwitz: Le rôle de Vichy dans la solution finale de la question juive en France—1943–1944* (Paris: Fayard, 1985), 21.

4. Dr. A. Drucker testimony, February 15, 1946, CDJC, CCXVI–66 (12 pp.), 4.

5. Serge Klarsfeld, *Memorial to the Jews Deported from France, 1942–1944* (New York: Beate Klarsfeld Foundation, 1983), 410–25. The trains of March 23 and 25 were convoys 52 and 53.

6. For details, see Serge Klarsfeld, *La Rafle de la rue Sainte-Catherine à Lyon le 9 février 1943 dans les locaux de la Ire section (CAR) et de la 2e section (FSJF) de la 5e Direction "Assistance" de l'UGIF* ([n.p.]: Serge Klarsfeld, [n.d., but after 1986]).

7. Klarsfeld, *Vichy-Auschwitz: 1943–1944,* 40, 61. Desperate to fill two trains to Auschwitz, Röthke ordered furriers and their families arrested on March 15. French police duly arrested 720 people, but 336 were released because of the importance of their work to the German army.

8. Lambert, *Carnet,* 222.

9. Ibid., 223–29.

10. Klarsfeld, *Vichy-Auschwitz: 1943–1944,* 61.

11. Ibid., 61 and 127–28.

12. Lambert, *Carnet,* 232. Such releases, while a blessing for those involved, effectively served to disguise the fact that the Germans intended ultimately to arrest all Jews in France without exception.

13. Rapoport's name appears on the deportation list for convoy 60, October 7, 1943, in Klarsfeld, *Memorial,* 456–61, 460. For more on the Comité rue Amelot, see chap. 12.

14. Their names appear on the list for convoy 63, reprinted in full in ibid., 484–89, 485.

15. Ibid., 477–83 (convoy 64). The numbers of convoys 63 and 64 were reversed because of a German error at the time.

16. Ibid., 426–33. The June 23 train was convoy 55.

17. Brunner introduced many other changes. French police and administrators withdrew from inside the camp but continued to guard the exterior. In an effort to reassure prisoners and deceive them about their fate, Brunner improved food supplies and hygiene and permitted the supervised receipt of packages. He assigned a greater administrative role to certain inmates—usually but not always prisoners

classified as "nondeportable" because they were half-Jewish, married to non-Jews, mothers or wives of Jewish prisoners of war, or ineligible by nationality. Also temporarily nondeportable were many whose families were still free. Brunner set up an infamous system by which some prisoners left Drancy to find and bring in the families of fellow inmates. They and their own families were threatened with immediate deportation if they refused but promised immunity if they cooperated. Their own families, of course, remained at Drancy as hostages for their return. They left each day with special *ordres de mission* and were promptly labeled *missionaires* by other prisoners. For an excellent firsthand account of Brunner's changes, see Georges Wellers, *L'Étoile jaune à l'heure de Vichy: De Drancy à Auschwitz* (Paris: Fayard, 1973), 185–219.

18. For the trains of July 18 and 31, 1943 (convoys 57 and 58), for example, see Klarsfeld, *Memorial,* 434–47. Klarsfeld lists deportees with place of birth in cases where it has been discovered, and quotes one contemporary document stating that there were many French Jews on the July 18 train.

19. A total of 23,648 Jews had been naturalized between 1927 and 1940, but 7,055 of them had already been denaturalized by a special commission of the Ministry of Justice. See the report of Maurice Gabolde, Keeper of the Seals, to Fernand de Brinon, Vichy representative to the German occupying forces in Paris, recorded by de Brinon and forwarded by him to Knochen on September 8, 1943, CDJC, XXVII–47. For more on the denaturalization process, see Chapter 2. The Germans expected that the general denaturalization of recent Jewish citizens in 1943 would affect many more.

20. Heinz Röthke report of meeting, Paris, August 15, 1943, CDJC, XXVII–36.

21. Knochen's veto of the September roundup is discussed in chapter 9.

22. For more on what Laval knew in 1943, see chapter 5.

23. Reprinted in full in Monseigneur Émile Guerry, *L'Église catholique en France sous l'occupation* (Paris: Flammarion, 1947), 44–46, 45.

24. Prefect of the Var to the Ministry of the Interior, April 1, 1943, 8, in Archives Nationales, *Rapports des préfets,* F/1C–III, box 1194. Subsequent AN documents in this chapter are from this series.

25. Léon Poliakov, *L'Auberge des musiciens: Mémoires* (Paris: Mazarine, 1981), 105 (written in 1946). The word *maquis* refers to remote rural areas of low scrub growth. Since many armed Resistants were based in the maquis during the war, the word came to refer directly to their units as well.

26. Prefect of the Rhône, May 5, 1943, chap. B, 1, in AN, 1183.

27. Marshal Philippe Pétain to Fernand de Brinon, August 24, 1943, CDJC, XXVII–33.

28. Heinz Röthke report, August 15, 1943, CDJC, XXVII–36.
29. This rough statistic is from Lucy Dawidowicz, *The War against the Jews, 1933–1945* (1975; New York: Bantam Books, 1976), 516, 544.
30. The police order never specified that Jews should be delivered to the Nazis for deportation, but drafters of the order could have had no illusions about the ability of Italian officials to resist such a demand once Jews were actually interned. For details, see Renzo De Felice, *Storia degli ebrei italiani sotto il fascismo* (1961; Turin: Einaudi, 1988), 446–47; Giuseppe Mayda, *Ebrei sotto Salò: La persecuzione antisemita, 1943–1945* (Milan: Feltrinelli, 1978), 111–13, 126–28; and Susan Zuccotti, *The Italians and the Holocaust: Persecution, Rescue, and Survival* (New York: Basic Books, 1987), 166–67. The Republic of Salò received its informal name from the town on Lake Garda that hosted many of its ministries.
31. Klarsfeld, *Vichy-Auschwitz: 1943–1944,* 341; and his *Memorial,* 448–54. The September 2 train was convoy 59.
32. Report from SS First Lieutenant Schmidt, Paris, August 24, 1943, reprinted in full in Klarsfeld, *Vichy-Auschwitz: 1943–1944,* 331–32. According to Schmidt, Röthke delivered his ultimatum to the CGQJ director, Louis Darquier de Pellepoix, on August 19. Joseph Antignac (who became CGQJ director in May 1944) passed the information along to Fernand de Brinon, and de Brinon informed Laval the same day, asking the latter to tell Pétain.
33. Philippe Erlanger, *La France sans étoile: Souvenirs de l'avant-guerre et du temps de l'occupation* (Paris: Plon, 1974), 278.
34. Donati's account of the arrangements is quoted at length in Léon Poliakov, "The Jews under the Italian Occupation in France," in Léon Poliakov and Jacques Sabille, *Jews under the Italian Occupation* (Paris: Éditions du Centre, 1955), 19–128, 40–42. For personal testimony by Father Benoît on his role, see De Felice, *Storia,* 444–46, 633.
35. On the speed of the German occupation of Nice, see Poliakov, *L'Auberge des musiciens,* 122–23. The Russian-born and French-naturalized Poliakov helped rescue Jews in Nice.
36. Ibid., 124–25, 129.
37. Quoted in Beate Klarsfeld (wife of Serge), *Wherever They May Be!* trans. Monroe Stearns and Natalie Gerardi (1972; New York: Vanguard, 1975), 12. Serge Klarsfeld also describes the incident in his *Vichy-Auschwitz: 1943–1944,* 119–20.
38. Arno Klarsfeld's name appears on the list for convoy 61, in Klarsfeld, *Memorial,* 462–68, 465.
39. Heinz Röthke report, "Vorbereitung zur Durchfuhrung der

Maßnahmen gegen die Juden im italienischbesetzten Gebiet," September 4, 1943, CDJC, XXVa–338 (4 pp.), 3.

40. Jacques Neufeld, *Le Seuil de l'abîme: Jour après jour: La résistance juive dans le sud-est de la France, 1940–1945* (Montreal: Guerin Littérature, 1988), 64–69. Henri Pohorylès, chief of the groupe franc in Nice, also mentioned these actions in his testimony, January 1945, reprinted in David Diamant, *250 Combattants de la résistance témoignent: Témoignages recueillis de septembre 1944 à décembre 1989* (Paris: L'Harmattan, 1991), 258–60. For an explanation of the groupes francs, see chap. 15.

41. Erlanger, *la France,* 290.

42. Poliakov, *L'Auberge des musiciens,* 125. Goukassov apparently escaped deportation, but barely.

43. Erlanger, *La France,* 288.

44. Ibid., 292–96.

45. Testimony of a Jewish rescuer, December 20, 1943, CDJC, CC-CLXVI–64 (4 pp.), 1.

46. Erlanger, *La France,* 290.

47. Drucker testimony, 8, 9, 10. Dr. Drucker, who had seen Jews from Marseille arrive at and leave Compiègne in March, was himself transferred to Drancy in May. He was sent back to Drancy after his service in Nice and was liberated there in August 1944.

48. Klarsfeld, *Vichy-Auschwitz: 1943–1944,* 124.

49. Of the 5,050 Jews in the last five French convoys to Auschwitz in 1943 (number 60, October 7; 61, October 28; 62, November 20; 64, December 7; and 63, December 17), 183 are known to have returned (Klarsfeld, *Memorial,* 455–89).

50. Of public opinion in his department just before the Nice roundup, the recently appointed prefect, Jean Chaigneau, himself far more sympathetic to the Jews than his predecessor Marcel Ribière, wrote frankly: "Despite the hostility of the local people toward the [then Italian] occupiers and their disapproval of the methods of violence employed by the German Authorities against the Israelites, a certain anti-Semitism is beginning to appear, and bitter criticism is frequently heard now of the attitude of certain Jews who live too well and too comfortably thanks to the fortune of which they dispose while many other Frenchmen suffer from particularly difficult measures, such as, for example, the obligatory labor service." Prefect of Alpes-Maritimes, September 8, 1943, 2, in AN, 1137.

51. Erlanger, *La France,* 292.

52. Testimony of an unidentified Jewish Resistant, Nice, December 20, 1943, CDJC, CCCLXVI–64 (4 pp.), 3.

53. See especially Alberto Cavaglion, *Nella notte straniera: Gli ebrei di*

S. *Martin Vésubie e il campo di Borgo S. Dalmazzo, 8 settembre–21
novembre 1943* (Cuneo: L'Arciere, 1981).

54. René S. Kapel, *Un Rabbin dans la tourmente, 1940–1944: Dans les
camps d'internement et au sein de l'Organisation juive de combat*
(Paris: Éditions du Centre, 1986), 109.
55. Quoted in ibid., 104.
56. Regional Prefect, Region of Toulouse, November 5, 1943, 5, in
AN, 1204.
57. Regional Prefect, Region of Rouen, October 1943, 10, in AN, 1204.
58. Klarsfeld, *Vichy-Auschwitz: 1943–1944,* 128.
59. Centre de documentation juive contemporaine, *L'Activité des organisations juives en France sous l'occupation* (1947; Paris: CDJC,
1983), 174.
60. See the Salomon and Helbronner names on the list for convoy 62 in
Klarsfeld, *Memorial,* 469–76, 472, 475.
61. Prefect Delegate of the Gironde, February 2, 1944 (2 pp.) in AN,
1155.
62. "Comment M. René Hirschler, Grand Rabbin de Strasbourg, Au-
monier Général fut arreté par la Gestapo le 22 décembre 1943 à
Marseille," CDJC, CCXVII–45. The document cites no author or
date but was written before May 1945 by someone who knew the
Hirschlers personally.
63. Their names appear on the list for convoy 67 in Klarsfeld, *Memorial,* 498–507, 503.

CHAPTER 11

1. Darnand was tried for war crimes by a special French court after
the war and executed on October 10, 1945.
2. Regional Prefect, Region of Bordeaux, report, January 11, 1944,
reprinted in full in Serge Klarsfeld, *Vichy-Auschwitz: Le rôle de
Vichy dans la solution finale de la question juive en France—
1943–1944* (Paris: Fayard, 1985), 368. For his role in the arrests of
Jews in Bordeaux, Maurice Papon, then secretary-general at the regional prefecture in Bordeaux, has been indicted for crimes against
humanity. His case has been under court investigation since 1982.
Papon served as minister of the budget under President Valéry Giscard d'Estaing in the 1970s.
3. See the full text of the prefect's request and the authorization in
ibid., 372.
4. Ibid., 151.
5. Maurice Rajsfus, *Des Juifs dans la collaboration (II): Une terre
promise? (1941–1944)* (Paris: L'Harmattan, 1989), 250–54. The
January 20 train was convoy 66.

6. Ibid., 260.

7. See Klarsfeld (*Vichy-Auschwitz: 1943–1944,* 370–71) for the national police director's report to his superiors (January 25, 1944) declaring that he had authorized regional prefects in the southern zone to give such lists to German police.

8. Prefect Delegate of the Gironde, February 2, 1944 (2 pp.), in Archives Nationales, *Rapports des préfets,* F/1C–III, box 1155. The official erred in the date of the arrests.

9. Cited in Klarsfeld, *Vichy-Auschwitz: 1943–1944,* 152.

10. Ginette Hirtz, *Les Hortillonnages sous la grêle: Histoire d'une famille juive en France sous l'occupation* (Paris: Mercure de France, 1982), 23, 171.

11. Ibid., 24, 98, 97.

12. Vivette Samuel, interview with the author, Paris, May 10, 1989.

13. Centre de documentation juive contemporaine, *L'Activité des organisations juives en France sous l'occupation* (1947; Paris: CDJC 1983), 175. Alain Mosse was deported to Auschwitz on convoy 69 on March 7, 1944. See the convoy list in Serge Klarsfeld, *Memorial to the Jews Deported from France, 1942–1944* (New York: Beate Klarsfeld Foundation, 1983), 518–26, 523.

14. CDJC, *L'Activité,* 46. The AIP was founded in Paris in 1936 by Grand Rabbi Zalman Chneersohn.

15. Klarsfeld, *Vichy-Auschwitz: 1943–1944,* 153, 155.

16. Michel Sarazin, *Une femme Simone Veil* (Paris: Robert Laffont, 1987). For testimony of survivors of the deportations to Kovno and Reval, see Klarsfeld, *Memorial,* 544–46. For the lists of deportees on the trains of April 13 and May 15, convoys 71 and 73, see *Memorial,* 534–57. The names of the Jacob family appear in *Memorial,* 538, 555.

17. The personal histories of the children and adults at Izieu are told in poignant detail in Serge Klarsfeld, *The Children of Izieu: A Human Tragedy,* trans. Kenneth Jacobson (1984; New York: Harry N. Abrams, 1985).

18. For details on prefect officials, villagers, and informers, see Antoine Spire, *Ces enfants qui nous manquent* (Paris: Maren Sell, 1990).

19. Reprinted in full as document 46 in Henri Monneray, ed., *La Persécution des Juifs en France et dans les autres pays de l'ouest presentée par la France à Nuremberg* (Paris: Éditions du Centre, 1947), 198. Barbie was tried for crimes against humanity in Lyon in 1987 and sentenced to life in prison. He died in 1991.

20. Klarsfeld, *Children of Izieu,* 6; and Klarsfeld, *Memorial,* 534–81. The trains were, respectively, convoys 72 through 76.

21. Helmut Knochen, "Merkblatt: über Steigerung der Festnahmezahl von Juden im Bereich des BdS in Frankreich," Paris, April 14, 1944,

CDJC, CXXXII–56 (6 pp.). According to the Nuremberg Laws of September 15, 1935, Jews in the Third Reich were no longer full citizens but subjects. By subsequent law, those who emigrated lost all rights as German nationals, and were considered stateless.

22. From the introduction to Yitzhak Katznelson, *Vittel Diary*, trans. from Hebrew by Myer Cohen (Tel Aviv: Ghetto Fighters' House, 1964). Although written at Vittel, the diary focuses primarily on Katznelson's experiences in Warsaw. Vittel, not far from Nancy, was a relatively comfortable camp mostly for British and North and South American citizens.

23. Klarsfeld, *Vichy-Auschwitz: 1943–1944*, 162, 167. The May group included about 240 Jewish prisoners still at Le Vernet; that of June included about 100 Jews building fortifications along the Atlantic coast for the Todt Organization. For some Nazis, the Final Solution took precedence over defense.

24. Klarsfeld, *Memorial*, 574–94. These were convoys 76 on June 30 and 77 on July 31. Also from Drancy on May 2 and 3 and July 21 and 23, some 400 wives and children of Jewish prisoners of war, hitherto not deportable, were sent to Bergen-Belsen.

25. This convoy, number 81, also carried Resistance fighters in separate cars. Many of the Jews went to Ravensbruck and Buchenwald. Their exact numbers are not known; Klarsfeld (*Memorial*, xxvii) estimates them at about 360.

26. Ibid., 595–98. This train, which left on August 11, was convoy 78. Of the 308 Jews, 180—an unusually large proportion, due in part to low numbers of children and elderly people—were selected for labor. Thirty-six, also a large proportion, survived.

27. Jeanne Kahn is quoted by her daughter Annette Kahn, who describes her parents' wartime experiences in *Robert et Jeanne: À Lyon sous l'occupation* (Paris: Payot, 1990), 133–34.

28. Ibid., 153–69. See also Annette Kahn, *Why My Father Died: A Daughter Confronts Her Family's Past at the Trial of Klaus Barbie*, trans. Anna Cancogni (New York: Summit, 1991).

29. Klarsfeld, *Vichy-Auschwitz: 1943–1944*, 177; and his *Memorial*, 641–54. One incident of hostage execution, in Lyon, now constitutes the principle case against Paul Touvier, the intelligence chief of the Lyon Milice who was sentenced to death in absentia in 1946 for collaboration but who evaded arrest with the help of right-wing Catholic priests and laymen until the statute of limitations expired in 1967. He was pardoned in 1971 by French President Georges Pompidou. In 1981, his arrest was ordered again, this time for crimes against humanity—and specifically for selecting seven Jews for execution in reprisal for the Resistance slaying of a Vichy official. The eighth hostage, a non-Jew, was not executed. Touvier

evaded authorities until 1989. On April 13, 1992, a three-judge investigative court with the authority to decide to proceed to trial dismissed the charges. It declared that Touvier's acts did not fit an earlier court definition of a crime against humanity as one committed in the name of "a state practicing a policy of ideological hegemony." On November 27, 1992, the French Supreme Court ruled that Touvier *could* stand trial, but did not address the lower court's interpretion of the Vichy regime.

30. Klarsfeld, *Vichy-Auschwitz: 1943–1944*, 153, 162, 167, 389.

31. Prefect of police report, Paris, January 28, 1944, reprinted in full in ibid., 372–73; and Klarsfeld, *Memorial*, 498–507. The February 3 train was convoy 67. Of the 1,214 deportees, 999 were immediately gassed, and 43, including 20 men and 23 women, survived.

32. Prefect of police report, Paris, February 5, 1944, reprinted in full in Klarsfeld, *Vichy-Auschwitz: 1943–1944*, 378; and Klarsfeld, *Memorial*, 508–17. The February 10 train was convoy 68. Of the 1,500 deportees, 1,229 were refused admission to the camp and gassed. Fifty-nine, including 27 men and 32 women, survived.

33. Klarsfeld, *Vichy-Auschwitz: 1943–1944*, 167.

34. Maurice Rajsfus, interview with the author, Paris, July 2, 1990.

35. Special measures to protect children in Jewish institutions in the provinces are discussed in chap. 12.

36. Jacques Adler (*The Jews of Paris and the Final Solution: Communal Response and Internal Conflicts, 1940–1944* [1985; New York and Oxford: Oxford University Press, 1987], 133–61) discusses this difficult issue in detail. In his teens during the war, Adler was a member of a foreign Jewish Communist Resistance unit. Maurice Rajsfus (*Des Juifs dans la collaboration: L'UGIF, 1941–1944* [Paris: Études et documentation internationales, 1980]) strongly condemns UGIF policies.

37. See reports of UGIF-North President Georges Edinger to CGQJ, July 24 and July 27, 1944, at YIVO Institute for Jewish Research, New York, UGIF–111.1.

38. Klarsfeld, *Memorial*, 582–94. The July 31 train was convoy 77. About 214 adults are known to have survived.

39. The statistic is from Maurice Rajsfus, *Drancy: Un camp de concentration très ordinaire, 1941–1944* (Levallois-Perret: Manya, 1991), 356.

40. Annette Monod Leiris, interview with the author, Paris, July 15, 1991.

41. See the deportation list for convoy 79 in Klarsfeld, *Memorial*, 599. Also on the train was the engineer Marcel Bloch (1892–1986). He returned from the camps to become, under the name Marcel Dassault, director of the Société Marcel Dassault, which produced the

Mystère, Mirage III, and Mirage IV jets, among others, after the war.

42. Ernest Appenzeller's story is told in Jean-François Chaigneau's detailed account of convoy 79, *Le Dernier Wagon* (Paris: France Loisirs, 1981), 135–40. Montandon was killed by French Resistants in July 1944.

43. The names of the three Morgensterns appear on the deportation list for convoy 74 in Klarsfeld, *Memorial*, 561–67, 565. The information about their arrest is from the testimony of Jacqueline's aunt, Dorothéa Morgenstern, reprinted in Günther Schwarberg, *The Murders at Bullenhuser Damm: The SS Doctor and the Children*, trans. from German by Erna Baber Rosenfeld and Alvin H. Rosenfeld (1980; Bloomington: Indiana University Press, 1984), 159–63.

44. In his *Swastika over Paris* (New York: Arcade, 1989), Jeremy Josephs tells the story of the Kohn family, based largely on the testimony of Philippe Kohn. See also Schwarberg, *Murders*.

45. The remaining pockets of German occupation along the Alsatian frontier were cleared by March 1945, leaving only a few small isolated German strongholds on the coast that were not freed until the war ended in May.

46. Klarsfeld, *Memorial*, xxvii, 601–3. The August 22 train from Clermont-Ferrand was convoy 82.

47. Henry Bulawko, *Les Jeux de la mort et de l'espoir: Auschwitz-Jaworzno* (Paris: Amicale des anciens déportés Juifs de France, 1954), 185.

48. Klarsfeld, *Children of Izieu*, 88.

49. Denise Baumann, "Jeu de cartes" (unpublished memoir, June 1981), 5. For more on her family, see chap. 12.

50. Roughly 138,806 civilians were deported to Nazi concentration camps during the war, of whom about 75,720, or 54.5 percent, were Jews and 63,085, or 45.5 percent, were Resistants or political offenders. (These figures do not include the more than 1,600,000 prisoners of war or the at least 735,000 non-Jewish forced laborers, deported for different reasons, to different places, and under very different conditions.) Many Jews, of course, were first caught for political acts, but if their Jewishness became known, they were usually separated out and deported as Jews. About 2,800 Jews, or 3 percent of the total number deported, returned from the camps; 37,025 political deportees, or 59 percent of their total, returned. Many returning deportees passed through the Hotel Lutétia, but not all. For the statistics of non-Jewish and Jewish deportees, see Annette Wieviorka, *Déportation et genocide: Entre la mémoire et l'oubli* (Paris: Plon, 1992), 21.

51. Leiris interview. Annette Monod Leiris provided many of the details about the Hotel Lutétia recorded here.

52. Kahn, *Robert et Jeanne,* 152.
53. Klarsfeld, *Memorial,* xxvii. See also the author's explanation of the sources of his statistics (xvii–xxii).
54. Ibid., 612–40. For explanation of this statistic, see chap. 4, n. 9.
55. See Klarsfeld, *Vichy-Auschwitz: 1943–1944,* 179–80, for a careful explanation of overall population statistics.
56. Ibid.
57. Ibid., 180–81.

CHAPTER 12

1. Denise Caraco Siekierski, interviews with the author, Paris, November 10, 1987, and April 26, 1988.
2. An OSE report (Paris, May 17, 1945, CDJC, CCXV–38a) estimated that during the entire war a total of between 300 and 350 Jewish children in OSE, EIF, and other institutions were deported, of whom 134 were from OSE homes. Ernst Papanek, an OSE children's home director who helped move children from northern France to Montintin in 1940, claims that 69 children were seized from OSE homes by French police during the week following August 26 and were ultimately murdered at Auschwitz. Papanek was in the United States at the time, but he cites letters from two OSE activists present at the raids. See his *Out of the Fire,* written with Edward Linn (New York: William Morrow, 1975), 248–50.
3. Official OSE reports record 1,055 children in fourteen homes in September, 955 in October, 1,021 in November, and 1,060 in December. They also record 192 children "placed elsewhere" in October, 165 in November, and 132 in December. See "UGIF, compte rendu de l'activité de la 3° Direction (Santé) pour le mois de Septembre 1942," and "[same title] pour les mois Octobre-Novembre-Décembre 1942," in YIVO Institute for Jewish Research, New York, UGIF–98.1.
4. Siekierski interviews.
5. For much more on Le Chambon, Pastor Trocmé, and Pastor Lemaire, see chap. 13.
6. Siekierski interview.
7. Georges Garel testimony, "Travail clandestin de l'OSE," [n.d.; circa 1945–46] CDJC, CCXVIII–104 (9 pp.), 3.
8. Annie Latour, interview with Georges Garel, [n.d.; prob. late 1960s or early 1970s] CDJC, DLXXII–7, 11.
9. Both Saliège and de Courrèges d'Uston are honored as "Righteous among the Nations" at Yad Vashem, Israel.
10. More specifically, OSE leaders were convinced of the increased dan-

ger by the arrests of twenty-nine children and their director at La Verdière in October. For details, see chap. 10.

11. Garel, "Travail clandestin," 5–8. The "Garel circuit" eventually acquired a formal structure, with four regional subdivision headquarters in Lyon, Valence, Limoges, and Toulouse. Each subdivision office supervised activities within specific departments.

12. Centre de documentation juive contemporaine, *L'Activité des organisations juives en France sous l'occupation* (1947; Paris: CDJC, 1983), 158.

13. Gaby Cohen, interview with the author, Paris, April 29, 1988. She tells her story also in Carol Rittner and Sandra Myers, *The Courage to Care: Rescuers of Jews during the Holocaust* (New York: New York University Press, 1986), 66–73.

14. Garel, "Travail clandestin," 4.

15. Parents were not allowed to know where their children were hidden. Social workers kept scrupulously accurate but coded lists of children's true identities and locations, with duplicates filed at OSE offices in Switzerland.

16. Denise Baumann, interview with the author, Paris, July 7, 1988.

17. Denise Baumann, *Une famille comme les autres* (1973; Paris: Albin Michel, 1985), 184. The book is a collection of family letters written in 1943. Renée and Léon Baumann's names appear on the deportation list for convoy 62, reprinted in full in Serge Klarsfeld, *Memorial to the Jews Deported from France, 1942–1944* (New York: Beate Klarsfeld Foundation, 1983), 469–76, 470; the Weill family appears on the list for convoy 63, 484–89, 489.

18. Denise Baumann, "Jeu de cartes" (unpublished memoir, June 1981), 5.

19. Latour, Garel interview, 26–27; CDJC, *L'Activité,* 170; and Jacques Neufeld, *Le Seuil de l'abîme: Jour après jour: La résistance juive dans le sud-est de la France, 1940–1945* (Montreal: Guérin littérature, 1988). Neufeld was a Jewish Resistant with the Maurice Cachoud Group, affiliated with the Sixième and the MJS, discussed later in this chapter. He also hid children with help from Monseigneur Rémond.

20. Latour, Garel interview, 26–27. According to Garel, one of the officials, a Mr. Brès, was later shot by the Germans for other Resistance activities. For more on the Joint, see CDJC, *L'Activité,* 15–18.

21. CDJC, *L'Activité,* 170. Huguette Wahl was arrested and tortured in September 1943 and then sent to Auschwitz, where she died in November; Dr. Odette Rosenstock was arrested in April 1944 and sent to Auschwitz and then to Bergen-Belsen, where she worked as a medical doctor and survived.

22. Garel, "Travail clandestin," 8; and CDJC, *L'Activité,* 142. Maurice

Rajsfus (*Des Juifs dans la collaboration: L'UGIF, 1941–1944* [Paris: Études et documentation internationales, 1980] 248) refers to Minkowski's efforts as "the fantastic work accomplished by the clandestine teams of OSE." Since Rajsfus is profoundly critical of UGIF, this is high praise indeed.

23. Dorothéa Morgenstern testimony, reprinted in Günther Schwarberg, *The Murders at Bullenhuser Damm: The SS Doctor and the Children,* trans. from German by Erna Baber Rosenfeld and Alvin H. Rosenfeld (1980; Bloomington: Indiana University Press, 1984), 159–63, 161. Dr. Rita Breton, was honored as "Righteous among the Nations" at Yad Vashem, Israel.

24. This incident is discussed in chap. 11.

25. Robert Frank testimony, reprinted in Rajsfus, *Des Juifs,* 261–64. Denise and Fred Milhaud were the initiators of this particular "kidnapping" ring. Dr. Fred Milhaud provided medical services to the youngsters at the École de travail. He later told Robert Frank that he tried to give priority to the youngest residents there. Since 1942, the Milhauds had worked with a clandestine group called *Entraide temporaire* (ET), organized under the cover of a private non-Jewish charity called *Service social d'aide aux émigrants* (SSAE). The fully legal SSAE existed to aid the families of foreign workers in forced-labor companies. Its president, Lucie Chevalley, a Protestant, created the ET secretly, to rescue Jewish children. The ET succeeded in hiding about 500 children.

26. Garel, "Travail clandestin," 8.

27. See chap. 14.

28. For detailed studies of OSE during the war, see Sabine Zeitoun, *L'Oeuvre de secours aux enfants (OSE) sous l'occupation en France: Du légalisme à la résistance, 1940–1944* (Paris: L'Harmattan, 1990); and her *Ces enfants qu'il fallait sauver* (Paris: Albin Michel, 1989).

29. On Moissac, see especially the firsthand accounts of Isaac Pougatch, *À l'écoute de son peuple: Un éducateur raconte* (Neuchatel: À la Baconnière, 1980); and Frédéric Chimon Hammel, *Souviens-toi d'Amalek: Témoignage sur la lutte des Juifs en France, 1938–1944* (Paris: CLKH, 1982). Gérard Israël (*Heureux comme Dieu en France . . . 1940–1944* [Paris: Robert Laffont, 1975] based his book on a series of interviews with individuals aided by EIF. Alain Michel's *Les Éclaireurs israélites de France pendant la seconde guerre mondiale, Septembre 1939–Septembre 1944: Action et évolution* (Paris: Éditions des EIF, 1984) is a detailed history. The statistics of twenty-two and forty children are from Michel, *Les Éclaireurs,* 121–22.

30. On Gamzon, see especially Isaac Pougatch, *Un batisseur Robert*

Gamzon dit "Castor soucieux" 1905–1961 (Paris: Service technique pour l'éducation, 1971); Robert Gamzon, *Les Eaux claires: Journal, 1940–41* (Paris: Éditions des EIF, 1982); and Michel, *Les Éclaireurs.*

31. For descriptions of the farms, see especially Hammel, *Souviens-toi,* on Taluyers; and Isaac Pougatch, *Charry: Vie d'une communauté de jeunesse* (Paris: Chant nouveau, 1946).

32. Shatta and Bouli Simon testimony, [n.d.] CDJC, DLXXII–46 (16 pp.), 1. Lesage's role at Vénissieux three days after the August 26 roundups is discussed in chap. 7.

33. Gérard Israël, interview with Kurt Maïer, in Israël, *Heureux,* 135–58.

34. Hammel, *Souviens-toi,* 76–79.

35. EIF, dissolved by decree in the spring of 1942, was incorporated into UGIF-South as the Fourth *Direction,* in charge of youth. Within that department, five legal subdivisions developed with particular bureaucratic functions. Sometime in the summer of 1942, a sixth division, called the Service social des jeunes (SSJ), appeared within the Fourth Direction, and the Sixième was born. Its role and status remained murky on paper, but it was in fact a cover for a clandestine rescue organization. In January 1943, Vichy officials dissolved the entire Fourth Direction. Some of its functions were transferred to the Second Direction, while the SSJ was moved to the Third Direction-Health, which incorporated the OSE. Thus, ironically, the Vichy measure served to facilitate cooperation between OSE and the Sixième, both increasingly clandestine at that point. See Michel, *Les Éclaireurs,* 123–28.

36. Hammel, *Souviens-toi,* 80–81.

37. Simon testimony, 6.

38. Ibid., 7.

39. Hammel, *Souviens-toi,* 155.

40. Simon testimony, 7. Although the testimony is in both names, Shatta rather than Bouli Simon seems to be the principal speaker. Bishop Théas was arrested by the Germans on June 9, 1944, for protecting Jews and other fugitives. He was imprisoned at Compiègne until the Liberation.

41. Hammel, *Souviens-toi,* 198.

42. CDJC, *L'Activité,* 65, 186.

43. Fania Elbinger Ewenczyk, interview with the author, Paris, November 16, 1988.

44. CDJC, *L'Activité,* 67, 186. Those killed included: forty-year-old Marc Haguenau, a founder of the Sixième, shot trying to escape from the Gestapo in February 1944; Haguenau's secretary, Edith Pulver, deported to Auschwitz; twenty-nine-year-old Léo Cohn,

arrested in the Toulouse train station on May 20, 1944, as he attempted to lead sixty boys across the Pyrenees, and deported; twenty-four-year-old Gilbert Bloch, with Cohn a founder of the EIF farm at Lautrec, killed in a Resistance action against the Germans in August 1944; twenty-four-year-old David Donoff, a Sixième agent shot trying to escape the Gestapo; and Jacques Weintrob of Éducation physique, Fernand Musnik, EIF organizer in the northern zone, and Claude Gutmann of the Sixième, all deported. Mila Racine and Marianne Cohn, two young women of the Sixième who died because of their rescue activities involving escorting children to Switzerland, are discussed in chap. 14.

45. CDJC, *L'Activité,* mentions several such organizations. Lucien Lazare (*La Résistance juive en France* [Paris: Stock, 1987], 408–9) lists and describes all major Jewish rescue organizations.

46. For details, see Jacques Adler, *The Jews of Paris and the Final Solution: Communal Response and Internal Conflicts, 1940–1944* (New York and Oxford: Oxford University Press, 1987), 181–85. As seen, Adler was an active Communist Resistant during the war.

47. Richard I. Cohen, *The Burden of Conscience: French Jewry's Response to the Holocaust* (Bloomington: Indiana University Press, 1987), 102.

48. Rapoport, described by Dr. Eugène Minkowski of OSE as "more than the chief, he was the soul [of the Comité rue Amelot]," was incriminated for illegal activities when a fugitive caught with false papers supplied by the committee revealed his name. He died at Auschwitz. Fifty-seven-year-old Glaeser, born in Riga and an immigrant to Paris for political reasons in 1907, was arrested by the Milice on June 20, 1944, and shot two days later. On Rapoport, see Dr. Eugène Minkowski testimony, (1946), reprinted in David Diamant, *250 Combattants de la Résistance témoignent: Témoignages recueillis de septembre 1944 à décembre 1989* (Paris: L'Harmattan, 1991), 73–78, 76. On Glaeser, see B. Adamitch testimony, in ibid., 84–85. For additional material on the Comité rue Amelot, see especially YIVO, UGIF-41; CDJC, *L'Activité,* 189–95; and Henry Bulawko, "Témoignage sur la résistance juive en France occupée," (unpublished manuscript, Paris, November 30, 1982).

49. For excellent accounts of Solidarité, see Adler, *Jews of Paris,* 196–210; and Jacques Ravine, *La Résistance organisée des Juifs en France, 1940–1944* (Paris: Julliard, 1973), 29–31. Ravine was among the founders of Solidarité.

50. Léon Poliakov, *L'Auberge des musiciens: Mémoires* (Paris: Mazarine, 1981), (written in 1946), 93.

51. Joseph Bass testimony, "Joseph Bass, Service André," [n.d.] CDJC, DLXII-2 (11 pp.).

52. Ibid.
53. Poliakov, *L'Auberge,* 127.
54. Henri Pohorylès testimony, Nice, January 1945, in Diamant, *250 Combattants,* 258–60. Cachoud was arrested by the Gestapo in Paris on July 17, 1944, and died from torture the following day.
55. These questions are raised particularly in Hillel J. Kieval, "Legality and Resistance in Vichy France: The Rescue of Jewish Children," *Proceedings of the American Philosophical Society* 124, no. 5 (October 1980): 339–66. Cohen, *Burden of Conscience,* and Adler, *Jews of Paris,* explore the relationships of OSE and EIF to UGIF.

CHAPTER 13

1. Joseph Bass report, "L'Église protestante," [n.d.] CDJC, CCXVIII–84, 3. Bass's distances were slightly off, for Le Chambon is in fact forty-six kilometers from Puy-en-Velay but sixty-two from Saint-Étienne.
2. Léon Poliakov, *L'Auberge des musiciens: Mémoires* (Paris: Mazarine, 1981), 107, 108 (written in 1946).
3. Magda Trocmé tells of the first German Jewish woman to knock on her door. The woman had heard that it was a pastor's house. See Mrs. Trocmé's interview in Carol Rittner and Sandra Myers, *The Courage to Care: Rescuers of Jews during the Holocaust* (New York: New York University Press, 1986), 101. Philip P. Hallie also relates the story, as told to him by Magda Trocmé, in *Lest Innocent Blood Be Shed: The Story of the Village of Le Chambon and How Goodness Happened There* (1979; New York: Harper Colophon Books, 1980), 120–23.
4. The population figures are from Hallie, who estimates that there were only about 100 Catholics in the area of Le Chambon (*Lest Innocent Blood,* 24).
5. Albert Camus, convalescing from tuberculosis and working on *La Peste,* stayed at a boardinghouse at Le Panelier, a hamlet about two and a half miles from Le Chambon, from August 1942 to November 1943. His arrival coincided with police searches for foreign Jews in the area. Although Camus knew several Resistants, he did not become active himself until he moved to Paris.
6. See accounts by Barot, her assistant Jeanne Merle d'Aubigné, and Pastor Marc Donadille in Jeanne Merle d'Aubigné, Violette Mouchon, and Émile C. Fabre, eds., *Les Clandestins de Dieu: CIMADE 1939–1945* (Paris: Fayard, 1968); published in English as *God's Underground: CIMADE 1939–1945,* trans. William and Patricia Nottingham (St. Louis: Bethany Press, 1970). Like Barot, Pastor and Mrs. Marc Donadille are honored as "Righteous among the Nations" at Yad Vashem, Israel.

7. These and other smaller refugee facilities are described in Pierre Fayol, *Le Chambon-sur-Lignon sous l'occupation: Les résistances locales, l'aide interalliée, l'action de Virginia Hall (OSS)* (Paris: L'Harmattan, 1990), 38–42.

8. See Hallie, *Lest Innocent Blood,* 107–12, for an account of the raid.

9. Bass, "L'Église," 4.

10. Poliakov, *L'Auberge,* 108.

11. This is the figure given by Pierre Sauvage, who was born in 1944 to Jewish parents hidden in Le Chambon, and who conducted extensive research for his film on the subject, *Weapons of the Spirit.* The film opened in the United States in 1989 and in France in 1990. Denise Caraco Siekierski (interview with the author, Paris, November 10, 1987) agreed with the estimate.

12. Poliakov, *L'Auberge,* 109.

13. Mordecai Paldiel (director of the Department for the Righteous among the Nations, Yad Vashem, Israel), interview with the author, New York City, March 8, 1988.

14. Hallie, *Lest Innocent Blood,* 251. André and Magda Trocmé and Édouard and Mildred Theis and their daughter Louise are honored as "Righteous among the Nations" at Yad Vashem, Israel.

15. Bass, "L'Église," 4. Although he wrote Betrix, Bass probably meant Pastor André Bettex.

16. Paldiel believes that many in the area of Le Chambon helped Jews without having any contact with Trocmé. Hallie also writes that about one-third of the Protestants in the area were Darbyists, members of a sect that rejected formal churches and pastors and adhered fervently to the Bible. The Darbyists in Le Chambon regularly sheltered Jews (*Lest Innocent Blood,* 95).

17. Bass, "L'Église," 5.

18. Madeleine Barot, interview with the author, Paris, November 3, 1987.

19. Pastor Evrard of Nice, for example, testifying in 1945 about the help he gave to Jews during the war, declared, "What we did was entirely natural. We other Christians, Protestants, and especially those of the Baptist Church, are nourished by the Bible. The history of the people of Israel is our history; Palestine—our second country. We love the Jews and we venerate them" (Evrard testimony, 1945, CDJC, CCXVIII–87).

20. Daniel Trocmé is honored as "Righteous among the Nations" at Yad Vashem, Israel.

21. Among those articulating this idea is Denise Caraco Siekierski (interview). Some students of the subject also believe that the German army commander in nearby Le Puy, Major Julius Schmehling, discouraged the SS from destroying Le Chambon during the last weeks of the war. According to Hallie, Schmehling himself so informed

Pastor Trocmé during an interview in Munich in the 1960s, and Trocmé believed him (*Lest Innocent Blood,* 244–47). Pierre Sauvage also believes that Schmehling helped, while others, including Barot, are more skeptical.

22. Madeleine Barot, "La CIMADE: Une présence, une communauté, une action," in d'Aubigné, Mouchon, and Fabre, *Les Clandestins,* 29–38, 34.

23. Poliakov, *L'Auberge,* 108.

24. Philippe Joutard, Jacques Poujol, and Patrick Cabanel, *Cévennes: Terre de refuge, 1940–1944* (Montpellier: Presses du Languedoc, 1987), 13. The area, in the southeast corner of Lozère department and the northwest corner of the Gard, lay between the towns and villages of Alès, Le Vigan, Meyrueis, and Florac. It was the subject of a special study, described in the book.

25. Juliette B. testimony, in ibid., 303–25, 308, 319.

26. Simone Serrière testimony, in ibid., 293–97. Simone Serrière is honored as "Righteous among the Nations " at Yad Vashem, Israel.

27. Lucien Simon, *Les Juifs à Nîmes et dans le Gard durant las deuxième guerre mondiale de 1939 à 1944* (Nîmes: Lacour Librairie, 1985).

28. Emmanuel Ewenczyk, interview with the author, Paris, November 16, 1988.

29. Claudine [Rozengard] Vegh, *I Didn't Say Goodbye,* trans. Ros Schwartz (1979; Hampstead, Eng.: Caliban Books, 1984), 23. Claudine's father is mentioned in Chap. 1.

30. For their remarkable story, see Albert Haas, *The Doctor and the Damned* (New York: St. Martin's Press, 1984).

31. Albert Haas, interview with the author, New York City, January 11, 1988.

32. Ibid.

33. Claude Morhange-Bégué, *Chamberet: Recollections from an Ordinary Childhood,* trans. Austryn Wainhouse (Marlboro, Vt.: Marlboro Press, 1987), 51, 73. Claude's mother was deported to Auschwitz but returned, so emaciated that her daughter scarcely recognized her.

34. Ibid., 53.

35. M. Hosiasson, written testimony, Marseille, March 3, 1945, CDJC, CCXVII–52.

36. Saul Friedländer, *When Memory Comes,* trans. Helen R. Lane (1978; New York: Farrar, Straus, and Giroux, 1979), 51.

37. Jan and Elli Friedländer's names appear on the list for convoy 40 reprinted in Serge Klarsfeld, *Memorial to the Jews Deported from France, 1942–1944* (New York: Beate Klarsfeld Foundation, 1983), 328–35, 331.

38. Saul Friedländer's parents in fact tried an organizational option first, placing their son at a Jewish children's home near La Souterraine (Creuse) in August 1942. When, soon after arrival, he barely escaped a French police raid, his parents withdrew him and began a search for an independent placement (Friedländer, *When Memory Comes,* 70–74).

39. Renée [Fersztenfeld] Fersen-Osten, *Don't They Know the World Stopped Breathing?: Reminiscences of a French Child during the Holocaust Years* (New York: Shapolsky, 1991).

40. Ginette Hirtz, *Les Hortillonnages sous la grêle: Histoire d'une famille juive en France sous l'occupation* (Paris: Mercure de France, 1982), 98.

41. Raia Bretnel Jacob testimony, [n.d.], OSE archives, Paris (12 pp.).

42. Faivel Schrager, *Un Militant Juif,* trans. from Yiddish by Henry Bulawko (1976; Paris: Les Éditions polyglottes, 1979), 106–7.

43. Estréa Zaharia Asséo, *Les Souvenirs d'une rescapée* (Paris: La Pensée universelle, 1974), 46–49. She finally placed her children with a couple in the country. She paid room and board and provided ration cards. She told the couple that she wanted to get the children away from air raids, and she did not know if they suspected the truth. She herself was deported to Auschwitz but survived.

44. Father Marie Benoît, interview with the author, Paris, April 25, 1988. Father Marie Benoît is honored as "Righteous among the Nations" at Yad Vashem, Israel.

45. Annette Muller Bessmann, "Manuscrit-témoignage," unpublished document, [n.d.], CDJC; Annette Muller, *La Petite fille du Vel' d'Hiv': Récit* (Paris: Denoël, 1991), 115–16 (a published version of much of "Manuscrit-témoignage"); and interview with the author, Paris, November 13, 1987. See the story of the Muller family in chap. 6.

46. Germaine Ribière, interview with the author, Paris, May 24, 1989.

47. For another personal account of survival in a church institution, see Frida Scheps Weinstein, *A Hidden Childhood, 1942–1945,* trans. Barbara Loeb Kennedy (1983; New York: Hill and Wang, 1985). According to Mordecai Paldiel (interview) the French clergy were the most helpful in Europe.

48. Renée Bédarida, interview with the author, Paris, May 11, 1989. Mrs. Bédarida lived at the student residence of Notre-Dame de Sion in Lyon during the war and helped hide and provision Jewish fugitives.

49. See Rudy Appel's testimony in Rittner and Myers, *Courage to Care,* 119. Some French pastors and laymen, however, seem to have made special efforts to assist Jews who had previously converted, in part from religious preference but also because those same converts

turned to them for help sooner and established personal ties of friendship. For examples of these relationships, see the numerous personal testimonies in [n.a.], *Les Camps en Provence: Exil, internement, déportation, 1933–1942* (Aix-en-Provence: Alinéa et LLCG, 1984).

50. Denise Baumann, *La Mémoire des oubliés: Grandir après Auschwitz* (Paris: Albin Michel, 1988), 95.

51. Liliane Klein-Lieber, "'Assistante sociale' de la Sixième à Grenoble," *Les Nouveaux Cahiers*, no. 76 (Spring 1984): 28–31, 30. Renée Bédarida (interview) points out that, officially, the order decreased its conversion efforts during the war, focusing instead on saving lives. There is no doubt that it saved hundreds. However, some pressure for conversion inevitably occurred.

52. Fersen-Osten, *Don't They Know*, 54. Maurice and Annette Fersztenfeld were arrested by the Gestapo in their village of Grenade-sur-Garonne, twenty kilometers from Toulouse, on July 7, 1943, and deported to Auschwitz on July 18. After the Liberation, relatives requested that Yvonne and Renée be sent to a Jewish orphanage. The nuns did not resist the request but strongly urged the girls, then ages sixteen and eleven, to keep their Catholic faith. Defying all odds, both Maurice and Annette returned, separately, in 1945.

53. Baumann, *La Mémoire*, 96.

54. Ibid.

55. Weinstein, *Hidden Childhood*, 32.

56. Baumann, *La Mémoire*, 96.

57. Ibid., 95.

58. Ibid., 96–97.

59. Bessmann, "Manuscrit-témoignage"; and Bessmann interview. In the interview, Mrs. Bessmann stressed her belief that the nuns were acting out of love and from a desire to save a soul.

60. Friedländer, *When Memory Comes*, 138. Saul Friedländer did not remain a Catholic.

61. Jacques Chegaray, *Un Carme héroïque: La vie du Père Jacques* (Paris: Nouvelle Cité, 1988), 193–94, 326. The boys' names are as given by Chegaray; the deportation lists from Klarsfeld (*Memorial*, 503–6) refer to Jacques Halpern, Maurice Schlosser, and Jean Michel. The boys came to the school under false names: Jacques Dupré, Maurice Sabatier, and Jean Bonnet, respectively. Chegaray himself taught at Father Jacques's school from 1936 to 1946. The story of Father Jacques is told—with some alterations—in the French director Louis Malle's film *Au revoir les enfants* (1987). Malle was an eleven-year-old student at the school in 1944.

62. Maurice B. testimony, reported in *Le Parisien* (November 4, 1987), in the dossier "Aux revoir les enfants," CDJC. Chegaray describes

Maurice but does not mention his brother (*Un carme,* 327). According to Maryvonne Braunschweig and Bernard Gidel (*Les Deportés d'Avon: Enquête autour du film de Louis Malle "Au revoir les enfants"* [Paris: La Découverte, 1989], 27), Mother Louisa placed twenty-three Jewish children in a family boardinghouse in Bourron-Marlotte, eight kilometers from Fontainebleau. When Father Jacques and the three students were arrested in Avon, the sisters of Notre-Dame de Sion, in civilian clothes, went to the boardinghouse and escorted the children in small groups to other hiding places.

63. Chegaray, *Un carme,* 194, 326; and Braunschweig and Gidel, *Les Deportés,* 27. The names of Sozie and Abraham Halpern and Fejga Schlosser are on deportation lists in Klarsfeld, *Memorial,* 128, 382.

64. Maurice B. testimony.

65. Testimony of a priest who saw the former student's declaration at Gestapo headquarters, in Chegaray, *Un carme,* 222–25. Father Jacques had told the older boys at the school of the presence of the Jewish students. Chegaray believes that the informer was not the young kitchen worker, as in the film (324).

66. Ibid., 267.

67. In 1988 at Yad Vashem, Israel, Father Jacques was designated as "Righteous among the Nations," and a tree was planted in his honor. For more on Father Jacques, see also [n.a.] *Livre d'or des congrégations françaises, 1939–1945* (Paris: DRAC, 1948), 181–87; R. P. Philippe de la Trinité (a former assistant director at the school), *Le Père Jacques, martyr de la charité* (Paris: Desclée de Brouwer, 1947); and Michel Carrouges, *Le Père Jacques: "Au revoir les enfants"* (1958; Paris: Les Éditions du Cerf, 1988).

68. "Cérémonie à la mémoire du Pasteur Jean S. Lemaire," testimony of Denise Caraco Siekierski at a commemorative ceremony for Pastor Lemaire at the Israeli Consulate, Marseille, September 18, 1986, in "Dossier des justes," CDJC, 6. See also Bass, "L'Églises," 1–2. Pastor Lemaire was honored as "Righteous among the Nations" at Yad Vashem, Israel, in 1976. He died in 1985. He is also mentioned in Chap. 12.

CHAPTER 14

1. René Nodot, "Résistance non violente, 1940–1944, (unpublished manuscript, 1978), 55. Nodot was discussed in chap. 7.

2. CIMADE report, "Parlons de la CIMADE," February 15, 1950, CDJC, CCI–49.

3. See Geneviève Priacel-Pittet (Tatchou) report, "Passages de frontières" (116–21), and Suzanne Loiseau-Chevalley report, "Sur la

356 Notes to Pages 249-53

356   Notes to Pages 249–53

frontière" (147–53), in Jeanne Merle d'Aubigné, Violette Mouchon, and Émile C. Fabre, eds., *Les Clandestins de Dieu: CIMADE 1939–1945* (Paris: Fayard, 1968); published in English as *God's Underground: CIMADE 1939–1945,* trans. William and Patricia Nottingham (St. Louis: Bethany Press, 1970). See also Nodot, "Résistance non violente," 52.

4. Rolande Birgy testimony, in [n.a.], "Résistance non violente: La filière de Douvaine—l'Abbé Jean Rosay, Joseph Lancon, François Perillat—morts en déportation," Douvaine, Haute-Savoie, (unpublished brochure, May 24, 1987), 31–33, 32. Rolande Birgy is honored as "Righteous among the Nations" at Yad Vashem, Israel.

5. Suzanne Loiseau-Chevalley testimony, in ibid., 34–35, 35.

6. Thérèse Neury testimony, in ibid., 28–30, 28.

7. Abbé Jean Rosay is honored as "Righteous among the Nations" at Yad Vashem, Israel.

8. Priacel-Pittet, "Passages," 116–21.

9. Nodot, "Résistance non violente," 47.

10. Ibid., 45–50. Abbé Marius Jolivet is honored as "Righteous among the Nations" at Yad Vashem, Israel.

11. Emmanuel Haymann, *Le Camp du Bout du Monde: 1942, des enfants Juifs de France à la frontière suisse* (Lausanne: Pierre Marcel Favre, 1984), 129–31. Father Louis Favre is honored as "Righteous among the Nations" at Yad Vashem, Israel.

12. René Nodot, *Les Enfants ne partiront pas! Témoignages sur la déportation des Juifs: Lyon et Région 1942–1943* (Lyon: Imprimerie Nouvelle Lyonnaise, 1970), 19.

13. Haymann, *Le Camp,* 115–16.

14. Jean Lacouture, *Pierre Mendes France,* trans. George Holoch (1981; New York: Holmes and Meier, 1984), 133–34. From Switzerland, but by then with Resistance help, Mendes France traveled back across France to Spain and Portugal, from where he took an RAF plane to London. For more on Pierre Mendes France, see chap. 2.

15. Quoted in Haymann, *Le Camp,* 66.

16. Quoted in ibid., 72.

17. Nodot, "Résistance non violente," 59.

18. Roger Fichtenberg testimony, June 30, 1974, CDJC, DLXI–10.

19. Quoted in Michele Sarfatti, "Dopo l'8 settembre: Gli ebrei e la rete confinaria italo-svizzera," *La Rassegna Mensile di Israel,* nos. 1, 2, and 3 (January–June 1981), 150–73, 171.

20. Haymann declares that police reports mention 9,751 people turned back directly at the frontier between August 1942 and the end of the war (*Le Camp,* 138), but these statistics are surely incomplete. Nor do they include those taken in and later rejected. The individuals involved were neither all Jews nor all from France.

21. Zacouto's testimony is quoted at length in Haymann, *Le Camp,* 143–46.

22. Ibid., 239.

23. For discussion of the conditions in the centers and the testimony of former residents, see ibid., 159–78.

24. For Jean Deffaugt's testimony [n.d.], see CDJC, DLXI–9. For more on Racine and Cohn, see Frédéric Chimon Hammel *Souviens-toi d'Amalek: Témoignage sur la lutte des Juifs en France, 1938–1944* (Paris: CLKH, 1982), 149 and 449–51; Haymann, *Le Camp,* 201–16. According to Hammel, Deffaugt also intervened to save the children caught with Mila Racine (*Souviens-toi,* 449). Jean Deffaugt is honored as "Righteous among the Nations" at Yad Vashem, Israel.

25. Claude Vigée, *La Lune d'hiver* (Paris: Flammarion, 1970), 127–28. Vigée, later a respected poet, reached the United States, where he lived and taught for many years.

26. On passeurs' fees and their equivalents in wages, see Émilienne Eychenne, *Montagnes de la peur et de l'espérance: Le franchissement de la frontière espagnole pendant la seconde guerre mondiale dans le département des Hautes Pyrénées* (Paris: Édouard Privat, 1980), 50. The author has written several other books on refugees in the Pyrenees, including *Les Pyrénées de la liberté* (Paris: France-Empire, 1983); *Montagnards de la liberté* (Toulouse: Éditions Milan, 1984); *Les Portes de la liberté* (Toulouse: Édouard Privat, 1985); and *Les Fougères de la liberté* (Toulouse: Éditions Milan, 1987).

27. Chaim U. Lipschitz, *Franco, Spain, the Jews, and the Holocaust* (New York: KTAV, 1984), 141–43.

28. Maurice Shotland, interview with the author, East Hampton, N.Y., September 18, 1988.

29. Lucien Lazare, *La Résistance juive en France* (Paris: Stock, 1987), 311. For details on the Armée juive, see chap. 15.

30. Ibid. For harrowing accounts by adult survivors of one passage arranged by the Armée juive, see Hammel, *Souviens-toi,* 177–84. Andrée Salomon of OSE arranged the children's passages; for her testimony, see Hammel, *Souviens-toi,* 233. For more on the Dutch group, see Lazare, *La Résistance,* 307–9.

31. Rabbi Yehuda Ansbacher, letter to Chaim U. Lipschitz, February 21, 1971, quoted at length in Lipschitz, *Franco, Spain,* 128–34, 129.

32. Haim Avni, *Spain, the Jews, and Franco,* trans. from Hebrew by Emanuel Shimoni (Philadelphia: Jewish Publication Society of America, 1982), 76–77.

33. Ansbacher to Lipschitz, 129.

34. Thomas Hamilton, *Appeasement's Child: The Franco Regime in Spain* (New York: Knopf, 1943), 222–23.

35. Samuel Hoare, *Complacent Dictator* (New York: Knopf, 1947), 229.

36. Eli Rubin, "Twenty-six Months in Miranda de Ebro," *Catholic Tablet* (London) (May 1943), reprinted in Lipschitz, *Franco, Spain,* 127.

CHAPTER 15

1. For his account of his flight to England and his first two years with de Gaulle, see René Cassin, *Les Hommes partis de rien: Le réveil de la France abattue, 1940–41* (Paris: Plon, 1975). Cassin rarely refers to his Jewishness in his book but suggests delicately that it was an initial encumbrance because anti-Semitism had made inroads among the Free French volunteers (136). After the war, Cassin served, among other positions, as vice-president of the Conseil d'état, from 1944 to 1960, and with the United Nations and UNESCO. He was awarded the Nobel Peace Prize in 1968 for his postwar work in human rights. For biographies, see Marc Agi, *René Cassin: Fantassin des droits de l'homme* (Paris: Plon, 1979); and Gérard Israël, *René Cassin (1887–1976): La guerre hors la loi; Avec de Gaulle; Les droits de l'homme* (Paris: Desclée de Brouwer, 1990).

2. See the monograph by his son Pierre Kahn, *Essai sur les méthodes de pensée et d'action de l'ingénieur général du Génie maritime Louis Kahn* (Paris: Académie de marine, 1973); and Jean-Louis Kohn, "L'Amiral Louis Kahn: Une résistance auprès de de Gaulle," in Association pour la recherche sur l'histoire contemporaine des Juifs (ARHCJ), *Les Juifs dans la résistance et la libération: Histoire, témoignages, débats,* proceedings of an ARHCJ conference, Paris, October 7, 1984 (Paris: Éditions du Scribe, 1985), 62–65. Among other activities after the war, Kahn was president of the Académie de marine from 1959 to 1961. He also served the Jewish community as president of the Alliance israélite universelle, vice-president of ORT, and president of the Consistoire central from 1963 to 1967.

3. For more on Thomas Elek, see especially the memoirs of his mother, Hélène Elek, *La Mémoire d'Hélène* (Paris: Maspero, 1977). Philippe Ganier Raymond devotes a chapter to Elek in his study, *L'Affiche rouge* (Paris: Fayard, 1975), 91–115.

4. This case is often referred to as *l'Affaire Manouchian*—from its highest ranking victim, Missak Manouchian, an Armenian and a chief of the FTP-MOI (Francs-tireurs et partisans–Main-d'oeuvre imigrée)—or as *l'Affiche rouge,* from the red poster that the Nazis circulated after the executions. The poster presented the names and

photographs of ten of the twenty-three victims; all were recognizably foreign, and seven were identified as foreign Jews. Intended to convince the French that armed Resistants were alien criminals rather than respectable patriots, it in fact evoked mixed responses. For accounts by contemporaries, see Melinée Manouchian (the wife of Missak), *Manouchian* (Paris: Éditeurs français réunis, 1974); Arsène Tchakarian, *Les Francs-Tireurs de l'Affiche rouge* (Paris: Messidor, 1986); and Gaston Laroche, *On les nommait des étrangers . . . (Les immigrés dans la résistance)* (Paris: Éditeurs français réunis, 1965), 27–124. Later histories include Philippe Robrieux, *L'Affaire Manouchian: Vie et mort d'un héros communiste* (Paris: Fayard, 1986); and Stéphane Courtois, Denis Peschanski, and Adam Rayski, *Le Sang de l'étranger: Les immigrés de la MOI dans la résistance* (Paris: Fayard, 1989).

5. Léo Hamon testimony, "Le témoignage hexagonal d'un français de l'intérieur," in ARHCJ, *Les Juifs dans la résistance,* 51.
6. Ibid., 50.
7. Ibid., 51.
8. Ibid.
9. Ibid., 50. In agreement with Hamon's claim, the Resistant David Knout (*Contribution à l'histoire de la résistance juive en France, 1940–1944* [Paris: Éditions du Centre, 1947], 85) claimed that Henri Frenay's Combat was at least 20 percent Jewish and estimated that Jews in certain other general non-Communist Resistance units reached levels of 30 percent.
10. Henri Noguères testimony, "Juifs et résistants," in ARHCJ, *Les Juifs dans la résistance,* 47. Noguères is the author of a definitive five-volume study entitled *Histoire de la résistance en France* (Paris: Robert Laffont, 1967–81).
11. The CNR ultimately included eight delegates from Resistance movements, two labor representatives, and six members of political parties and tendencies. For Mayer's analysis of the influence of his socialism and his Judaism on his Resistance activities, see his testimony, "Socialiste, puis français et enfin juif," in ARHCJ, *Les Juifs dans la résistance,* 53–57. For an excellent biography that includes extensive descriptions by Mayer himself, see Claude Juin, *Liberté . . . Justice . . . Le combat de Daniel Mayer* (Paris: Anthropos, 1982). Among other roles after the war, Mayer served as a Socialist deputy for twelve years, the minister of labor in seven successive cabinets from 1946 to 1949, the president of the parliamentary commission for foreign affairs, and the president of the Ligue des droits de l'homme for seventeen years (1958–77).
12. See Hamon's account in his memoirs, *Vivre ses choix* (Paris: Robert Laffont, 1991), 163–65.

13. Ibid., 191.
14. Jacques Chaban-Delmas, preface, in ibid., 8. For more on the FFI, see below. After the war, Hamon served as a senator during the Fourth Republic and a deputy during the Fifth.
15. Told to David Schoenbrun, *Soldiers of the Night: The Story of the French Resistance* (New York: Dutton, 1980), 325–26.
16. Grandval wrote of his wartime activities in *Libération de l'est de la France,* with A. Jean Collin (Paris: Hachette, 1974). After the war, he served as military governor and high commissioner in the Saar and as French resident-general in Morocco. With de Gaulle after 1958, he was secretary-general of the merchant marine, state secretary for foreign commerce, and minister of labor.
17. David Knout in fact claims that Libération-Sud was founded in July 1941 by six men, of whom three, identified as d'Astier, Rochon, and Canguilhem, were non-Jews, and three, Samuel-Aubrac, Kohan, and Zerapha, were Jews (*Contribution,* 84).
18. Quoted by Claude Singer, "Des universitaires Juifs dans la Résistance," in ARHCJ, *Les Juifs dans la résistance,* 71–79, 76.
19. In a letter written to his wife in New York during the war, Guy de Rothschild, in London with the Free French, commented on the "important proportion" of Jews in that group and implied that it was a political embarrassment. See parts of the letter reprinted in *The Whims of Fortune: The Memoirs of Guy de Rothschild* (1983; New York: Random House, 1985), 167. For many more names and brief descriptions of Jewish Resistants, as well as for information on the many Jews who participated in the Resistance in Algeria, see Knout, *Contribution,* 82–90.
20. For his account of his wartime activities, see Pierre Villon, *Résistant de la première heure* (Paris: Éditions Sociales, 1983).
21. See Maurice Vaillant's account of COMAC activities in his *La Libération: Les archives du COMAC, Mai-Août 1944* (Paris: Éditions de Minuit, 1964); and his testimony, "Témoignage d'un antifasciste Juif," in ARHCJ, *Les Juifs dans la résistance,* 58–61.
22. See Ouzoulias's two accounts, *Les Bataillons de la jeunesse* (Paris: Éditions Sociales, 1967); and *Les Fils de la nuit* (Paris: Grasset, 1975).
23. Ouzoulias, *Les Fils de la nuit,* 63–66.
24. Quoted by Singer, "Des universitaires," 75.
25. Ouzoulias, *Les Fils de la nuit,* 348–63.
26. Albert Ouzoulias, preface to David Diamant, *Les Juifs dans la résistance française, 1940–1944 (Avec armes ou sans armes)* (Paris: Le Pavillon, 1971), 14.
27. Before the war, Jewish Communist young people had been incorporated into the Jeunesses communistes by a party unwilling to ac-

knowledge national or cultural differences. Anxious to remain together despite the government's dissolution of the party in September 1939, they began a separate grouping in Paris in the autumn of
1940. They were formally recognized by the party only in 1943
with the establishment of the Union de la jeunesse juive.

28. These units were linked in structure if not in function to a prewar
organization, the Mouvement ouvrier immigré (MOI), later called
the *Main-d'oeuvre immigrée,* organized by the French Communist
party to attract and integrate foreigners. With the prohibition of the
party in 1939, MOI groups went underground. As Communist immigrants became ever more determined Resistants after the German
invasion of the Soviet Union, however, MOI units became a natural
vehicle for their activities. There are many memoirs and histories by
FTP-MOI activists and their chiefs. See, for example, Adam Rayski,
Nos illusions perdues (Paris: Balland, 1985); Louis Gronowski-
Brunot, *Le Dernier grand soir: Un Juif de Pologne* (Paris: Éditions
du Seuil, 1980); Boris Holban, *Testament* (Paris: Calmann-Lévy,
1989); Abraham Lissner, *Un Franc-Tireur Juif raconte . . .* (1969;
Paris: IM.PO., 1977); Ouzoulias, *La Bataillons de la jeunesse,* and
Les Fils de la nuit; Tchakarian, *Les Francs-Tireurs;* and Laroche,
On les nommait. For a general history, see especially Courtois,
Peschanski, and Rayski, *Le Sang de l'étranger.*

29. David Douvette presentation, "Une histoire controversée," in
ARHCJ, *Les Juifs dans la résistance,* 153–64, 155. According to
Rayski, who supervised FTP-MOI units for the Communist party,
the Second Detachment numbered about eighty partisans and support staff at the end of 1942 (*Nos illusions perdues,* 132).

30. The organizational structure of FTP-MOI units, their recruiting systems, and their relationship to the Communist party and to the FTP
are described in Courtois, Peschanski, and Rayski, *Le Sang de
l'étranger,* 143–55.

31. Among about eighty Jewish Communist Resistants whom Annette
Wieviorka interviewed for her book (*Ils étaient Juifs, résistants,
communistes* [Paris: Denoël, 1986], 113–14) several were ordered
to join immigrant units.

32. Annette Wieviorka, "Trois générations de communistes Juifs," in
Karel Bartosek, René Gallissot, and Denis Peschanski, eds., *De
l'exil à la résistance: Refugiés et immigrés d'Europe centrale en
France, 1933–1945* (Saint Denis: Presses Universitaires de Vincennes, 1989), 213–20. See also her *Ils étaient Juifs,* 158; and her
remarks in "La Résistance juive en France," *Combat pour la Dias-
pora,* nos. 23–24 (3d trimester 1988): 57–64.

33. Rayski, *Nos illusions perdues,* 132.

34. By mid-1943, these Communist groups, along with *Solidarité* and

the *Union des femmes juives* (discussed in chap. 12), were coordinated by the Union des Juifs pour la résistance et l'entraide (UJRE). For accounts by two of UJRE's founders, see Jacques Ravine, *La Résistance organisée des Juifs en France, 1940–1944* (Paris: Julliard, 1973), 147–48; and Rayski, *Nos illusions perdues,* 133. According to Ravine, the Union de la jeunesse juive had about 150 active members, and the Milice patriotique juive about 250, at the time of the liberation of Paris (*La Résistance,* 278).

35. Lissner, *Un Franc-Tireur,* 120.
36. "Communiqués du détachement Juif (2ème détachement). Année 1942. Extraits," reprinted in Ganier Raymond, *L'Affiche rouge,* 61–62.
37. Lissner, *Un Franc-Tireur,* 57.
38. Ibid.
39. Both Boczor and Rayman were executed with the Affiche rouge group. Boczor was identified as Boczov on the poster. He is also referred to as Ferenz Wolf. Statistics indicate the devastating effectiveness of the "special brigades" of the French prefecture of Police in combating Communist Resistance forces in Paris. According to Lucien Lazare (*La Résistance juive en France* [Paris: Stock, 1987], 302), about 140 militants were arrested in March 1943, and another 80 in June. The arrest of another 150 militants in November led to the Affiche rouge case and ended FTP-MOI Resistance in the city.
40. The statistic is from Courtois, Peschanski, and Rayski, *Le Sang de l'étranger,* 313. Denis Peschanski, ("La Singularité et l'intégration," in Bartosek, Gallissot, and Peschanski, *De l'exil à la résistance,* 151–62, 154) estimates that participants numbered from fifty to sixty. The observation that the FTP-MOI units were alone in Paris is from Wieviorka, *Ils étaient Juifs,* 264; and Courtois, Peschanski, and Rayski, *Le Sang de l'étranger,* 10. The authors of *Le Sang de l'étranger* conclude that Communist party authorities refused to pull FTP-MOI survivors out of Paris in the summer of 1943, despite knowledge that police were close on their track, because they had no replacements (385–86). They point out that after the resultant arrests in November 1943 and the final destruction of the units, there were almost no armed Resistance actions in Paris for six months.
41. According to Lissner, all Germans in the car were killed (*Un Franc-Tireur,* 71–72). The Resistants believed for years that Schaumburg also had died, but in fact he was not present. For descriptions of other actions, see Lissner, *Un Franc-Tireur,* 42–83; and Diamant, *Les Juifs dans la résistance,* 283.
42. The Jewish Resistance survivor Jacob Tancerman to Wieviorka, *Ils étaient Juifs,* 295.

43. Quoted in Marie-Louise Coudert, *Elles, la résistance* (Poitiers: Messidor Temps Actuels, 1983), 163.

44. Ibid., 163–67; Ganier Raymond, *L'Affiche rouge,* 201–23, 244–50.

45. Coudert, *Elles,* 35; Lissner, *Un Franc-Tireur,* 50; and Diamant, *Les Juifs dans la résistance,* 71, 134, 140, 225.

46. The historian David Douvette says 65 percent ("Une histoire controversée," 155); the former Carmagnole partisan Ezer Najman ("'Capitaine Gilles' du groupe Carmagnole" testimony in ARHCJ, *Les Juifs dans la résistance,* 169–73, 171) says 70 to 80 percent; the FTP-MOI director Jacques Ravine says 80 percent (*La Résistance,* 168). The figure of forty members is from the testimony of the Carmagnole chief Henri Krischer, "Les Barricades de la MOI," in ARHCJ, *Les Juifs dans la résistance,* 174–84, 178.

47. Ravine, *La Résistance,* 168.

48. Wieviorka, *Ils étaient Juifs,* 264–66.

49. The percentage is from Ravine, *La Résistance,* 168; the quotation is from Rolande Trempe, "La Résistance dans le Sud-Ouest," in Bartosek, Gallissot, and Peschanski, *De l'exil à la résistance,* 163–68, 165.

50. The best account is by Claude Lévy, *Les Parias de la résistance* (Paris: Calmann-Lévy, 1970). Lévy, a French Jew, was Langer's close friend and a fellow Communist Resistant in the 35th Brigade. FTP-MOI partisans in Lyon similarly killed the French president of the Special Tribunal, Faure-Pengali, on December 13, 1943, holding him responsible for the guillotining of the nineteen-year-old Carmagnole fighter Simon Fried nine days before. See Ravine, *La Résistance,* 236–37.

51. Ravine gives brief descriptions of hundreds of FTP-MOI actions throughout France.

52. For excellent firsthand accounts of the insurrection at Villeurbanne, see Henri Krischer, "Les Barricades," 174–84; Ravine, *La Résistance,* 291–301; and Laroche, *On les nommait,* 408–14.

53. Ravine, *La Résistance,* 298; and Diamant, *Les Juifs dans la résistance,* 289–91.

54. Dina Krischer testimony, "Combattante à Carmagnole," in ARHCJ, *Les Juifs dans la résistance,* 98–100, 100.

55. Fascinating firsthand accounts of the daily life of Resistants include Rayski, *Nos illusions perdues,* 108–16, for Paris; Henri Krischer, "Les Barricades," 177, for Lyon; and Imre Boc, account written in 1947, edited and printed in Wieviorka, *Ils étaient Juifs,* 270–73.

56. Jacques Lazarus testimony, "Sous le drapeau bleu-blanc," in ARHCJ, *Les Juifs dans la résistance,,* 131–33, 132.

57. Ariane Knout, also called Régine, was later killed in a military action in Toulouse on July 22, 1944.

58. Soon after the war, David Knout described the founding and activities of the Armée juive in his *Contribution,* esp. 141–56.

59. The initiation ceremony is described in some detail by Anny Latour (*The Jewish Resistance in France (1940–1944)*, trans. Irene R. Ilton [1970; New York: Holocaust Library, 1981], 94–103), who personally experienced it. It is mentioned more briefly by Saïa Voldman, who also witnessed it, in "Davké: Nous étions là quand même," testimony in ARHCJ, *Les Juifs dans la résistance,* 137–43, 139.

60. Léon Poliakov, *L'Auberge des musiciens: Mémoires* (Paris: Mazarine, 1981), 146 (written in 1946). For the Service André, see chap. 12.

61. Charles Hartanu (EIF Resistant) testimony in Knout, *Contribution,* 121–24.

62. Alain Michel presentation, "Dans les combats de la libération," in ARHCJ, *Les Juifs dans la résistance, 122–26, 123.*

63. Lazare, *La Résistance,* 320.

64. For accounts by participants, see Charles Hartanu and Hubert Beuve-Mery testimony, in Knout, *Contribution,* 121–25; Robert Gamzon, *Les Eaux claires: Journal, 1940–44* (Paris: Éditions des EIF, 1982), 97–160; Lazare, *La Résistance,* 318–20; and Pierre Dunoyer de Segonzac, *Le Vieux chef: Mémoires et pages choisies* (Paris: Éditions du Seuil, 1971), 141–54. On life in the maquis generally, as well as for more detailed discussion of armed actions, see Lazare, *La Résistance,* 306–27; and the memoirs of the EIF leader Frédéric Chimon Hammel, *Souviens-toi d'Amalek: Témoignage sur la lutte des Juifs en France, 1938–1944* (Paris: CLKH, 1982), 217–37.

65. In his presentation in ARHCJ, *Les Juifs dans la résistance,* ("Des Patriotes oubliés," 29–33, 31), the historian Yves-Claude Aouate estimates the number of Jews at 300 out of a total of about 400; the former Jewish Resistant in Algeria Jacques Zermati ("La Libération commence en Algérie," in ibid., 34–41, 38) estimates them at about 250 out of 300 to 400. For details on Jews in the Resistance in Algeria, see especially Michel Ansky, *Les Juifs d'Algérie du décret Crémieux à la libération* (Paris: Éditions du Centre, 1950), 175–221; Michel Abitbol, *The Jews of North Africa during the Second World War,* trans. Catherine Tihanyi Zentelis (1983; Detroit: Wayne State University Press, 1989); and Gitta Amipaz-Silber, *La Résistance juive en Algérie: 1940–1942* (Jerusalem: Rubin Mass, 1986).

66. For brief descriptions of these raids, see Wieviorka, *Ils étaient Juifs,,* 244–45.

67. Henri Rosencher, *Le Sel, la cendre et la flamme* (Paris: Henri Rosencher, 1985), 378.

68. Georges Goutchtat testimony, in Wieviorka, *Ils étaient Juifs,* 246–47.

CONCLUSION

1. Stanley Hoffmann, "In the Looking Glass: Sorrow and Pity?" in *Decline or Renewal: France since the 1930s* (New York: Viking, 1974), 45–60, 59, 58.

2. Henry Rousso, *La Collaboration: Les noms, les thèmes, les lieux* (Paris: M.A. Éditions, 1987), 131, 138–39, and 156, estimates that of the three major leagues during the war, the *Parti populaire français* had some 20,000 to 30,000 adherents; the *Rassemblement national populaire,* 20,000; and the *Mouvement social révolution-naire,* 15,000. As seen in chap. 2, the *Milice* had some 29,000 adherents in the autumn of 1943. Some of these came from the leagues.

3. In the Netherlands, about 105,000 Jews died, or 75 percent of a community of about 140,000. In Belgium, approximately 24,000 Jews died, or nearly 42 percent of a community in October 1940 of some 57,000. (The prewar Jewish population of Belgium had been about 90,000, but nearly half of these fled into France when the Germans invaded.) These statistics are from Michael R. Marrus and Robert O. Paxton, "The Nazis and the Jews in Occupied Western Europe," in *Unanswered Questions: Nazi Germany and the Genocide of the Jews,* Francois Furet, ed. (New York: Schocken, 1989), 172–98, 190, 195.

4. There were fewer than 3,000 German civilians at work in occupied France in August 1941, compared with just over 3,000 in the Netherlands (ibid., 175). The figures are cited from a contemporary study prepared by Werner Best, then head of the military administration civil staff in France. By mid-1942, according to the same authors, there were just three battalions of German police in France, or 2,500 to 3,000 men. That statistic is from Michael R. Marrus and Robert O. Paxton, *Vichy France and the Jews* (New York: Basic Books), 241.

5. For explanations of these percentages, see chap. 11.

6. According to one study cited in Marrus and Paxton, only 6.5 percent of the Jews registered by the Gestapo in Belgium in the autumn of 1940 were citizens. ("The Nazis and the Jews," 190).

7. Of Italy's approximately 45,100 Jews in September 1943, when the Germans occupied the country, about 37,100, or 82 percent, were natives and 8,000, or 18 percent, were foreigners. About 15 percent of the Jews in Italy died during the war. See Susan Zuccotti, *The Italians and the Holocaust: Persecution, Rescue, and Survival* (New York: Basic Books, 1987).

8. Doctor Eugène Minkowski testimony (1946), in David Diamant, *250 Combattants de la résistance témoignent: Témoignages recueillis de septembre 1944 à décembre 1989* (Paris: L'Harmattan, 1991), 73–78, 75.

9. Lucien Steinberg, "Jewish Rescue Activities in Belgium and France," *Rescue Attempts during the Holocaust: Proceedings of the Second Yad Vashem International Historical Conference, Jerusalem: April 8–11, 1974* (Jerusalem: Yad Vashem, 1977), 603–14, 614.

10. Hoffmann, 60.

11. Léon Poliakov, *L'Étoile jaune* (Paris: Éditions du Centre, 1949), 93.

12. Shatta and Bouli Simon testimony, [n.d.], CDJC, DLXXII–46 (16 pp.)

13. Ibid.

14. The story of the Caracos is told in chap. 9.

INDEX